People and Computers IV

THE BRITISH COMPUTER SOCIETY WORKSHOP SERIES

Editor: P. HAMMERSLEY

The BCS Workshop Series aims to report developments of an advanced technical standard undertaken by members of The British Computer Society through the Society's study groups and conference organizations. The series should be compulsive reading for all whose work or interest involves computing technology and for both undergraduate and post-graduate students. Volumes in this Series will mirror the quality of papers published in the BCS's technical periodical *The Computer Journal* and range widely across topics in computer hardware, software, applications and management.

Some current titles:

Current Perspectives in Health Computing
Ed. B. Kostrewski

Research and Development in Information Retrieval
Ed. C. J. van Rijsbergen

Proceedings of the Third British National Conference on Databases (BNCOD3)
Ed. J. Longstaff

Proceedings of the Fourth British National Conference on Databases (BNCOD4)
Ed. A. F. Grundy

People and Computers: Designing the Interface
Eds. P. Johnson and S. Cook

Text Processing and Information Retrieval
Ed. J. C. van Vliet

Proceedings of the Fifth British National Conference on Databases (BNCOD5)
Ed. E. A. Oxborrow

People and Computers: Designing for Usability
Eds. M. D. Harrison and A. F. Monk

Research and Development in Expert Systems III
Ed. M. A. Bramer

People and Computers III
Ed. D. Diaper and R. Winder

Proceedings of the Sixth British National Conference on Databases (BNCOD6)
Ed. W. A. Gray

People and Computers IV
Ed. D. M. Jones and R. Winder

People and Computers IV

Proceedings of the Fourth Conference of the
British Computer Society
Human–Computer Interaction Specialist Group
University of Manchester, 5–9 September 1988

Edited by

D. M. JONES
School of Psychology, University of Wales, Cardiff

R. WINDER
Department of Computer Science, University College London

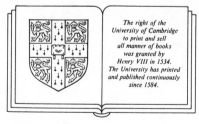

The right of the
University of Cambridge
to print and sell
all manner of books
was granted by
Henry VIII in 1534.
The University has printed
and published continuously
since 1584.

Published by

CAMBRIDGE UNIVERSITY PRESS

on behalf of

THE BRITISH COMPUTER SOCIETY

Cambridge

New York   New Rochelle   Melbourne   Sydney

Published by the Press Syndicate of the University of Cambridge
The Pitt Building, Trumpington Street, Cambridge CB2 1RP
32 East 57th Street, New York, NY 10022, USA
10 Stamford Road, Oakleigh, Melbourne 3166, Australia

© British Informatics Society Ltd 1988

Printed in Great Britain at the University Press, Cambridge

Library of Congress cataloging in publication data: available

British Library cataloguing in publication data: available

ISBN 0 521 36553 8

Contents

Analysis For Early Design

Systems Design: Methods, Tools and Processes

Implementation Tools

Systems Support

Input/Output

Dialogue Design

Artificial Intelligence Issues

Preface

Martin Thomas

Logica

In the UK there is one annual national conference on HCI, organised by the British Computer Society's HCI Specialist Group. This book contains the refereed papers presented at the HCI'88 conference, held in September 1988 at UMIST, Manchester, England. This preface sets out to put the contents into context, both for people reading this book as it stands, and those attending the conference.

What Is The Field Of HCI?

Everyone has their own view of the scope, goals and maturity of Human Computer Interaction. I offer a boiled-down version of its *scope*:

— Research to gain a better understanding of interaction between humans and computers

— Development of design methods, tools and techniques

— Application to the design of real-life computer systems

From my position within the industry, I see just one principle *goal*: to start making computer systems *fit for their purpose*, by making all that wonderful functionality available to the users, without the usual tears or travail. 'Fitness for purpose', of course, is a shorthand definition of 'Quality'.

As to HCI's *maturity*, perhaps the key question for us all to face is: "What does HCI want to be when it grows up?" To some extent, readers can form their own view from the following papers. In addition, I hope that this year's conference will focus on this question with papers from invited speakers, discussion groups and panel sessions.

Conference Goals

The overall goals are constant from year to year:

1. To represent the current state of HCI
2. To increase communication between people working in the different disciplines of HCI
3. To discuss the future of HCI

Within this framework, I have tried to encourage presentations and debates on the worth of HCI to the outside world. Thus:

1. What have we achieved in the key areas of Research, Development and Application?
2. What are we as a community currently contributing to the design of full-scale commercial and government systems?
3. In what ways are we helping with the Assurance of Quality?

What Is This Book For?

To make the refereed papers available in a structured way (see the next section for their organisation into major HCI topics). I hope that this structure will support this book's dual rôles, as an introduction to the field, and as a valuable reference work.

Who Is This Book For?

Well, everyone of course! Researchers, developers and appliers, whether in academia, government or industry, together with anyone else wanting to gain a view of the field through a set of papers representing the current state of HCI.

Acknowledgements

Many people have worked to help make HCI'88 a success. Firstly, I will list the organising committee:

Jane Astley (Aston University) – Deputy Chair
Dan Diaper (Liverpool Polytechnic)
Karmen Guevara (Beta Chi Design Ltd) – Tutorials
Dylan Jones (UWIST) – Papers and Proceedings Editor
Linda Macaulay (UMIST) – Exhibition
Horace Mitchell (Management Technology Associates)
    – Publicity

> Alistair Sutcliffe (City University)
> Martin Thomas (Logica) – Chair
> Russel Winder (University College London)
>   – Proceedings Production Editor
> Louise Worsley (BTEC) – Secretariat

with additional help from Victoria Bellotti, Bill Thompson, Michael Ussher and Paul Walsh.

Next, of course, I must thank BISL for their professional help, especially Julia Allen and Christine Edginton, and the BISL organisation at large. Appreciation also goes to Roger Johnson (BCS Vice President (Specialist Groups)) for his encouragement and support especially on the financial side.

Many have helped specifically with the production of this book, including Jenny and Nigel Chapman, and the Department of Computer Science, University College London who assisted with TEX formatting support.

Lastly, all thanks to Logica for letting me put in time on this conference, though I guess if Laurence Julien or Gordon Kirk had known how much time had been involved, they would never have let me!

Computers for the People: HCI in Prospect. An Introduction to the HCI '88 Conference Proceedings

Dylan Jones

School of Psychology, University of Wales, College of Cardiff, Llwyn-y-Grant, Penylan, Cardiff CF3 7UX, U.K.

1. Conference Aims

As in previous years, the purpose of the conference is to reflect contemporary trends in HCI, drawing in balanced measure from each of the disciplines which comprise its considerable scope. The extent to which this book fulfills these aims is for the reader to judge. Certainly the book will not represent all features of the conference since the papers are intended as the basis on which much of the ensuing discussion will be based.

There is another sense in which these papers cannot be too closely aligned with 'what went on'. This year, hopefully by way of precedent, poster sessions were introduced. Their purpose was to give an airing to work at a less well formalised stage of development, or to expose work which was controversial, as part of the polemic which HCI needs to sustain its growth.

2. The Representativeness of Papers

Concern is expressed every year that the papers should be representative of HCI in general. In last year's proceedings, a valiant attempt was made by Dan Diaper to construct an empirical picture from what data were available on the representativeness of papers which were submitted to the conference. Attempts to establish consensus over the scope of HCI is, of course, frought with difficulty. We may take HCI to be represented by the natural ecology of submitted papers, the areas which draw support from government, from the opinions of the 'good and the great', or from the bias of a particular discipline. But even if we could rid ourselves of the doubt surrounding each of these, we would still have to address the problem of **quality**, that other dimension of representativeness which is important to the outcome of the conference. Hopefully, the attempt to sustain the quality of submissions which had been set in previous years has been successful.

Notwithstanding these difficulties, one must lament the paucity of submissions in certain categories. Work on applications is undersubscribed. More especially, and to the eternal embarrassment of prosletysing researchers, there is very little evidence of good HCI practice associated with a commercial success story. Perhaps the usual paradox applies here, that commercial successes must remain unexposed, lest the commercial opposition catches wind. This may in part explain why so little attention has been given to the use of computer-based domestic products. But also my guess is that HCI researchers regard the perplexity which most people seem to express when attempting to programme a video recorder or microwave oven as a concern to one side of the main thrust of the discipline. Yet, most of these devices owe their complexity to microprocessors, and enshrined within the design problems they pose, are most of the elements of HCI work. Moreover, the need to simplify the interface and extend the constituency of use, creates both challenge and opportunity for HCI. Perhaps more effort and interest is needed in the area where most of the processing power is to be distributed.

In similar vein, individual differences in capacity to use computing devices is also not well represented. Two facets of this issue deserve special concern. First, the work concerning aids for the disabled is almost completely absent. This point has been made before, but the shortfall surely reflects the lack of funding rather than the lack of opportunity or indeed processing power. The second area concerns the effect of age on the use of computing devices. As the average life-span increases, so too will the opportunities for computer use, not simply for physical support but also for intellectual stimulation. At the other end of the age continuum, stimulation and guidance are a priority. That computers in education is barely touched upon in HCI '88 is perhaps the most astonishing feature of the programme.

The foregoing comments seem to point to a rather restricted and conventional view of what constitutes both a **computer** and a **computer user**. Certainly in the future, many people will be using rather complex devices, but very many more will be using relatively less complex devices quite unlike the trinity of processor box, keyboard and screen, but which nevertheless present the user with a very difficult cognitive task. Should our research be directed at CAD for the few or ovens for the many? Surely both but HCI '88 does not reflect this diversity.

As in previous years, the emphasis, at least in submitted papers, on ethical, social and organisational factors is almost non-existent. I am not alone in calling for a remedy, but what shape this should take, and what steps can be taken to encourage submissions (save for exhortations of this sort) is problematical. Certainly these issues should be given greater prominence in subsequent HCI conferences.

3. The Editorial Process

Most of the process of selecting papers was done along the lines discussed by Dan Diaper and used for the HCI '87 conference, but with some changes of detail which must be noted. First, the preliminary round of abstract submissions was subject to review and ranking by a panel. This was an *ad hoc* group comprising six individuals whose work is intimately tied-up with HCI: one was from a major computer manufacturer; two were from different departments of government concerned with the procurement and deployment of computers; two were academic researchers employed on the Alvey programme, and two were academics. Over a hundred abstracts were seen by this group, and the submissions ranked on a five-point scale. The group also agreed comments to be relayed to the author. I am very indebted to this group, who gave their time generously and paid their own, not inconsiderable, expenses. Their duty was a particularly onerous one: as a group, we agreed that a bland or misleading review only served to increase the likelihood that papers written in good faith and confident expectation of acceptance would be rejected at the next round.

A second phase of appraisal began when full versions of the papers were submitted. This involved two referees and in the case of disagreement, a third arbitrating judgement was sought. More full-length papers were submitted than last year (57 as opposed to 48) and rather fewer were sent to arbitration. The referees were given a copy of the panel's comments. It would be nice to present the degree of concurrence between the panel and the referees without qualification, but in this context almost every metric of concordance suffers some confounding factor. I take comfort, probably unreasonably, from the very good degree of agreement between those highly ranked by the panel and by the independent referees.

The selection of referees was similar to that used last year, indeed, we were lucky enough to draw upon a store of those who had acted before. We took the precaution of pairing referees not only on the basis of interest but also on the basis of origin, as much as possible, academics were balanced with those from business and industry.

One man's probity is another man's bias. Alas, I cannot claim that the process of review was free of unintentional bias. But that it was open, and that it was based on high standard of peer review, should not be doubted. Stella Hudson, Jane Matthews and Kevin Hapeshi helped in the enormous burden of administration of this task, and I am in their considerable debt. The considerable personal support and level-headedness of Martin Thomas, whose patience at times I sorely tried, was invaluable.

4. Conclusions

I am conscious that the foregoing has been more in the spirit of a lament and an eulogy. This is apt, if only for the reason that self-critical examination of the current state of play is the most astringent stimulus to progress. But, in doing so I have nearly forgotten to mention the very high quality of submissions which are published in this volume. In terms of excellence, they describe contemporary work of the very highest quality, as judged from every viewpoint. They will, I hope, be an adequate snapshot of the field of play.

The main lesson in the omissions from HCI '88 is that the scope of proceedings must be broadened to embrace the computer as agent within the everyday lives of the mass of people. Such applications are by no means simple, they pose a significant challenge for HCI. As the penetration of devices beyond the domain of the specialist user becomes more evident, so too will ethical and social issues of a scale which make our present preoccupations with these issues appear irresponsible. So much so, that writ large over over the proceedings of 'People and Computers 10' may be the graffito 'Computers **for** the People'.

Analysis For Early Design

Implications of Current Design Practice for the Use of HCI Techniques

Victoria Bellotti

Department of Computer Science, Queen Mary College, Mile End Road, London E1 4NS, U.K.

A study of commercial system-interface design projects was carried out in order to determine the nature of *real world* design practice. Of particular interest were two questions; the first being whether commercial design makes use of *HCI design and evaluative techniques*, and the second being whether commercial design satisfies the *requirements for successful application* of these design aids. The findings suggested that commercial design practice varies both in the constraints under which it operates, and in the approaches adopted. Although many problems relating to interface design appear to be tractable to HCI techniques, these techniques are rarely used. Conditions in commercial design practice sometimes act as unavoidable constraints on what designers can do. These constraints have important implications for the applicability, or inapplicability, of HCI design and evaluative techniques.

Keywords: Design Practice, HCI Task Analysis Techniques.

1. Introduction

1.1. Studies of Interface Design

Recent design studies indicate that usability problems result from poor approaches to user-system interface (USI) design. Although systems designers do practice repeated iteration and evaluation of prototypes, many problems are experienced in attempting to produce satisfactory USI's (Rosson, Maas & Kellogg [1987]). It has been suggested that 'inadequate conceptualisations of users' held by designers are a 'root cause' of users' problems (Dagwell & Weber [1983]). Designers seem to favour logical formalisms which may exclude important user requirements (Hammond et al. [1983]). Evidence from a study by Smith and Mosier (Smith & Mosier [1984]), showed that Human Factors engineers estimated that between only a fifth and a third of system development projects adequately considered USI requirements at various stages of the development process.

Based on their research, Gould and Lewis (Gould & Lewis [1985]) have recommended three principles for better USI design, which they stress are rarely applied in practice. These principles are **early focus on users and tasks**; **empirical measurement**; and **iterative design**. Whilst designers tend to think that these principles are obvious and that they are applying them, Gould and Lewis suggest that they are not. These principles were demonstrated in application by Gould *et al* (Gould et al. [1987]) in a report on the design and development of the 1984 Olympic Messaging System (OMS). The principles were considered to be applicable and useful, and the authors proposed that other design projects would benefit from treating them as essential to the development of a good interface.

In general, the literature on design practice seems to suggest that systems designers' attitudes and approaches to USI design are commonly at fault. Designers are seen as giving inadequate consideration to user issues, and they do not adopt recommended approaches which would increase the likelihood of producing an acceptable interface. It is suggested here that there are further problems for the design of more usable interfaces, even for designers who are supportive of HCI and want to tackle user issues. As Gould and Lewis admit, the process of system development is unpredictable; there are usually unexpected factors involved which may make it difficult to adopt certain approaches or follow any principles, (the principles of Gould and Lewis are specified with this fact in mind).

1.2. HCI Techniques for Design and Evaluation

Recently a number of HCI task analysis techniques, referred to here as design and evaluative techniques (DETs), have been developed. CLG (Moran [1978]; Moran [1981]) and GUEPs (Thimbleby [1984]) are *design approaches* which specify methodologies for the process of USI design itself. *Evaluation techniques* include models of two types: *competence models* such as Reisner's Formal Grammar (Reisner [1981]; Reisner [1982]), ETIT (Moran [1983]), TAG (Payne [1984]; Payne & Green [1986]), and *performance models* such as GOMS (Card, Moran & Newell [1983]), and UDM (Kieras & Polson [1985]). Competence models evaluate the complexity of user-representations of an interface, and performance models predict users' performance of specified tasks using a given interface. For a fuller description of HCI DETs see Mike Wilson et. al. review of task analysis for human-computer systems (Wilson, Barnard & Maclean [1986]).

The research on design practice suggests that systems designers require better techniques for planning, generating and evaluating their systems. HCI DETs should be very helpful, if designers can use them, since they have the following potential benefits which recommend their application wherever possible.

1. A **reduction in the workload** for the HCI specialist, since time need not be spent on development of new techniques if an existing one can be applied.

2. Complete *multi-level* descriptions of the USI (e.g., CLG and GOMS) **help a designer to be more thorough** in dealing with user issues, and spotting inconsistencies and inadequacies in design.

3. Device-dependent and device-independent knowledge required by users (as described by ETIT) should be easier to identify during design enabling a designer to **minimalise negative transfer effects** that users might suffer (Douglas and Moran (Douglas & Moran [1983]) demonstrated that inappropriate transfer of knowledge about typewriters to a text editor caused 59% of the errors experienced by subjects learning to use the text editor).

4. Many DETs **highlight complexity** which is associated with poor performance, particularly in novice users.

5. Performance measures and targets for USI's may be recommended by HCI DETs which can **make evaluation simpler and more directed**.

6. **Early evaluation** of systems should be possible, if HCI Techniques can be applied to specifications before the actual software, which can commit the design to a particular structure, has been written.

These benefits could save time and money on trial-and-error prototyping by providing insight into important user characteristics and likely problem areas in developing USI's. However the most important question to answer regarding the possible success of HCI DETs is whether systems designers in commercial design environments will be able to apply them. Whether they will or not may be determined by the following factors which constitute the *application requirements* of the techniques:

Appropriateness to the design project in question is an important condition; a DET must describe aspects of the interface which are relevant to its success. Not all techniques are appropriate for all design projects; important performance metrics may differ between applications, and design environments may vary with respect to which approaches, if any, are practicable. For example; a GOMS evaluation will not be appropriate to a USI where interaction times are not necessarily important but where errors may be dangerous and expensive.

Designers' Experience with HCI: HCI DETs often require familiarity with principles of psychology and HCI. TAG, for example, expects the evaluator to be able to discern what exactly a 'simple task' might be. A simple task may be difficult to identify, since it depends on both the nature of the task and that of the user. It may also take some experience to interpret what the results of certain models mean, since the complexity of a grammar is not in itself prescriptive as to how to improve the interface.

Existing Specification: TAG; ETIT; GOMS; UDM, and other DETs require an existing specification or USI upon which to base their descriptions. The less detail with which the interface can be specified, the less likely it is that an accurate assessment can be made. This implies that an advanced prototype or detailed specification must be available, and designers may have to be prepared to make radical alterations to their prototype.

Access to Information about Tasks and Users: HCI DETs usually require some sort of specification of how users will accomplish tasks with the system, or what users know. For example, CLG's 'Task-Level System Description' is a general outline of the users' prospective system-tasks, and the concepts involved. ETIT requires a description of users' device-independent knowledge. Designers must research these issues if they are to apply an HCI DET to their design.

Time and Cost: The complexity of a USI affects the complexity of the grammar that describes it. The designer of a complex commercial system must have the available resources to devote to evaluation with such techniques which can turn out to be very time consuming. In the case of GUEPs, the project must have the resources to apply design principles correctly (e.g., expertise in both psychology and formal techniques, in order to produce the necessary specific principles pertaining to the design in question).

2. An Investigation of Current Commercial Design Practice

A study of commercial design practice was undertaken in order to identify the main constraints and problems encountered by designers which might obstruct the application of good design principles and, more specifically, whether USI design meets the application requirements of HCI DETs. If commercial design practice does not fulfill HCI DETs application requirements, the main question is whether there are genuine and unavoidable reasons why it cannot.

2.1. Goals and Targets of the Study

The main **goals** of the study were as follows:

- To determine whether HCI DETs or principles are applied in commercial practice.
- To determine whether commercial design practice satisfies the application requirements of HCI DETs and to examine design environment constraints within which Human Factors approaches will be required to operate.

The **targets** of the investigation were design situations chosen on the basis of their distinctness from each other in terms of the system application domain, the organisation employing the designer, and the size of the design team and project. By selecting projects on this basis, it was hoped that the findings would not be related to a particular kind of design project. The interviews focused specifically on designers attitudes to, and approaches to USI design, also on the problems they face, and the constraints which affect their success in dealing with them.

After casual discussions with commercially experienced systems designers working at Queen Mary College, four formal interviews were conducted. These involved three employees of London University, and one Brighton College of Further Education employee. Three of these designers had been involved in commercial system design projects. The academic based designers' interviews covered the following projects:

(1) A display editor running on a unix system; the designer developed this editor with advice and assistance from other members of the department including computer scientists, and

feedback from potential users with a wide range of computer experience also within the designer's department. This was the only non-commercial project included here.

(2) A network management system, for multiple users employed specifically to monitor and control the information being passed through a network. The designer worked largely alone on this project, receiving relatively formal instructions and information about the nature of the task, which did not yet exist in any form, and user requirements from the management of the client group.

(3) A garment pattern graphical design-aid or CAD system for fashion designers with limited experience of computer technology. This designer devoted a great deal of time to learning about the task of garment design because of its complexity and unfamiliarity.

(4) An educational graphics system for children to design a figure which could dance to music. The designer worked alone using specifications provided by the marketing client. In the event the designer deviated from the specifications to generate more appropriate ones.

To ensure that representative information was collected, four individuals in commercial organisations were also interviewed. Since these people were not easy to contact for further information, a more exhaustive interview procedure was adopted, based on the structure used by Hammond *et al* (Hammond et al. [1983]) in interviews with commercial designers. These interviews were taped for later analysis. They include the following:

(5) A window manager to be used by programmers, produced by a team of a systems architect, a software designer, and a consultant with HCI experience. The window manager was designed for a Unix workstation with a graphics display. The HCI consultant provided a catalogue of interactive techniques recommended for good interfaces. The other two team members did not have a great deal of HCI experience themselves.

(6) A systems designer working for a company which sells products on a wholesale basis. The aim was to computerise the records of orders and sales and provide a word-processor for report and letter writing, all presented as an integrated office system. This designer used an applications generator on a less advanced PC system, but had extremely easy access to the prospective user population.

(7) A simulation training device for process controllers produced

by a large hierarchical organisation. The designer interviewed did not write any software and worked alone on the actual design, with a manager providing requirements specifications. This designer was required to produce many design specification documents which were verified by the manager and by the client for whom the product was being designed, before the programmable-ready material could be written as software.

(8) A distributed building management system sold to monitor and regulate temperature, locks, lifts etc., to be operated by a very wide range of users, from night watchmen to programmers. The design team consisted of the group leader who was interviewed, four software engineers and a hardware engineer, thus comprising the largest design team studied.

2.2. Design Interview Structure

The interview was carried out in the normal work place of the designer, and in all cases the interviewer was able to inspect the result of the commercial design project (i.e., see a demonstration of the USI itself). The interview was conducted in a series of stages which were structured as follows:

Stage 1.

- Designer describes general tasks supported by the system
- Designer describes envisaged user population.
- Designer describes own role in design process with respect to impact on USI.

Interviewer relies on checklist of points and questions to ensure appropriate coverage. Categories dealt with were; *user population, applications, system information presentation, input devices, input methods*, and *user's system model*. The checklist was used to increase detailed information and ensure consistency in the areas covered in interviews.

Stage 2.

General and specific points concerning design decisions discussed. Interviewer includes particular interface characteristics of:

- The primary system
- Sources of information used in design
- Constraints on design activity

Designer determines content. Interviewer uses checklist of general and specific points relating to the USI under discussion. The USI itself is referred to, during the interview, for clarification.

Stage 3.

Designer discusses design philosophy and issues more generally.

**Table 1.   Dimensions Along Which Design
Environments Were Noted to Vary**

Autonomy from client and practice constraints

Autonomy, here, means that the customer, for the project or the designers' own organisation, does not dictate practice (the customer may be the designers' organisation itself).

Size of the design team

From one to six in this study, excluding programmers.

Team structure (rigid vs flexible roles)

Access to information about tasks and users

Affinity to HCI

The fact that the interviews were agreed to, seemed to be related to designers affinity to the interviewer's discipline.

Design method flexibility/formality

Development and testing (top-down vs prototyping)

Design team experience with USI design

Design team familiarity with application domain

In at least five cases designers were not working to design a product for a task with which they were familiar.

System application domain

Sophistication of resources

3. Findings

The designers interviewed provided much qualitative information about the nature of design. Some of the problems and the comments they made were strikingly similar. The academic based designers were however more likely to be working alone as consultants, and generally had greater knowledge about HCI as a discipline. A summary of the findings follows.

3.1. Variations in the Design Environment

The designers interviewed worked in very different conditions. Table 1 lists dimensions along which the design environment was seen to vary.

Each of these dimensions was identified as a factor influencing development of the interface. It seems likely however that some of these will be more strongly associated with a thorough approach to USI design than others. Many of these dimensions reflect external influences on design projects and may represent unavoidable obstacles to incorporation of HCI DETs or recommended design principles. Designers may be constrained to adopt a particular approach which does not satisfy the application requirements of HCI DETs. For example, if no information about users and their tasks is available, or if it is not possible to produce a detailed specification of the interface before generating software, then it may prove impossible for a designer to find an applicable HCI DET.

3.2. Categories of Design and Development Activity

The results of the interviews indicated that there were five categories of development activity. These are the following: *commitment to requirements specification, conceptual specification, generation of a working prototype, testing*, and *finalisation*. These categories of design and development activity are not distinguished by anything other than their goal (they do not occur in any particular order). A brief description of each activity follows.

Commitment to Requirements Specification has contractual importance. It involves agreement on a set of client-requirement specifications and design-team undertakings. The degree of formality of this activity seems to depend largely on organisational policies. Basically, certain responsibilities of both designer (e.g., keeping to time and cost estimates) and client (e.g., providing support or information) are made more or less explicit. For example, the network management system designer received a fairly detailed description, from one of the client's management, of the prospective users' tasks which the system would be expected to support.

Conceptual Specification is the process of deciding what the detailed requirements are, in the light of the client's initial specification. For example, if a client wishes for a highly reliable system, then the design team may translate this into more specific requirements. Some designers interviewed carried out informal task analyses by talking to and watching experts or potential users in the application domain, or by trying out tasks themselves to 'get a feel for the job' and come to a better understanding of what was required. In the case of the simulation training device, which was to have non-computer expert users, it was made impossible for users to enter into a state from which they would have difficulty escaping.

Generation of a Working Prototype seems to take up the most time and effort in development. All of the projects described used prototypes in some way, to determine the reliability and acceptability of the design. In seven of them it appeared that the design process centered on continual adaptation of running software, until it was deemed to meet the requirements specification. The only project using structured, top-down designing with early use of specifications was the development of the simulation training device, which had a highly constrained interface, with a small set of possible states.

Testing determines whether or not the USI meets its specifications. Abstract evaluative descriptions of proposed interface characteristics were not generally used in the projects described. In particular, HCI DETs such as described in the introduction to this paper were lacking altogether. In all cases any prototype testing was conducted by software designers themselves, directly on the prototype. It generally involved unstructured 'try it out' sessions. Some designers simply pretended to be naive users (the window manager designer admitted to doing this). It was clear that many designers did spend considerable time and effort modifying the interface in response to any advice or "wouldn't it be nice if... " suggestions they received. They also tried to find ways of 'crashing' the interface to make sure it was robust. However, evaluation of the developing USI was not rigorous, user performance goals and metrics were not used, and specialists were not consulted.

Finalisation occurs when the benefits of improving the design are outweighed by the costs of putting off implementation or marketing. Designers interviewed were typically critical of the final product, but justified this by explaining that they were unable, for various reasons, to improve it any further. The garment design-aid designer was pressurised by the client into allowing it to be marketed long before that designer felt it was ready. This designer mentioned that there is sometimes a problem of modifications being made to a design after it has been handed it over to a marketing client. The client may wish to make the design fit in with their product-range image, or make it possible to link up with other products. This may occasionally have a detrimental effect on the USI.

Typical development activities do not include abstract specification of a possible form for the USI. The kinds of activities described by interviewees tended to resemble those pinpointed in other design practice studies, being mainly devoted to developing and testing system functionality rather than the interface. Requirements for system functionality were ascertained during commitment to the requirements specification, and conceptual specification. Possible solutions were usually programmed in directly and informally tested, as described above. Consequently, the generation and evaluation of the USI appears to be an informal cycle of an iterative nature. However, in spite of designers' good intentions, repeated user-evaluation during each iteration, as recommended by Gould and Lewis (*ibid*), was not reported. The informality of various approaches to system development may encourage the trivialisation of the requirement for user-evaluation. None of the designers interviewed reported ever having used any HCI DET, some stated that they were unaware of the existence of such techniques. Notably, the finalisation of a system is frequently determined by external market pressures, rather than any design team satisfaction with the state of the USI. As long as the software does not crash and the system has the required functionality, system marketers may be happy to accept interfaces without user-evaluation.

3.3. Commercial Design Problems

The information volunteered by designers about problems they experienced in their projects was of great interest. Table 2 lists problems which appear to be important in USI design, with the projects where they were most apparent. A brief illustration of each problem follows:

Poor Communication seemed to be the first common potential problem. In project 4, poor communication between the designer and the marketing client, meant that designer was unable to make use of the specifications they provided. In project 3 a lack of shared terminology between the designer and potential users made it difficult to communicate task characteristics and possible system functionality.

Uncertainty About Requirements for the design. In project 3, an explicit requirements specification was difficult to provide, so that the designer had to spend a long time finding out exactly what potential users wanted.

Exclusion of Users from the design process led to the designer in project 2 receiving completely misleading information about user-information requirements from a manager who was a system expert, unlike the end-users themselves. This resulted in an interface which was very unsatisfactory for the users who tried it out. Many modifications had to be made, which might have been avoided if users had been involved in the design from the early stages, as was recommended by Gould and Lewis (*ibid*).

Expanding Task Outlines were common. Once users or clients saw a prototype in action, they often got ideas for extra, useful functions they would like, as well as the ones available. At least five of the projects involved in this study had to make significant changes in functionality throughout the design process. Designers from projects 3, 5, 6 and 8 mentioned that this was a problem.

Designers' Unfamiliarity with the Task Domain increased the communication problems. The designer in project 2 reported a shortage of available information about users' tasks. In this project, the system application was a task which did not, as yet, exist so that its nature was difficult to determine. Also prospective users were not involved in the design and development process. The designer in project 3 found it hard to understand what the system requirements were, due to lack of experience with pattern-design tasks, and had problems understanding pattern designers' explanations.

Lack of HCI Guidelines and Standards meant that solution acceptability was left to the designers, or to clients, to evaluate. If they did not have experience with evaluation of usability, then this may not have been adequately considered. In project 5 and 8, design solutions were considered acceptable purely on the basis of their being 'bug' free and running quickly.

Familiar Solution Application was encouraged when there was pressure to complete a design quickly, rather than considering the specific nature of the particular project. In project 6 this problem was made worse by an applications generator running on a non-ideal PC.

Technological Constraints were also a considerable problem for projects 1 and 6. The designers sought compromise solutions in both cases, since these constraints were unavoidable. In project 6, a major problem was caused by the fact that the editor on the PC could not be interrupted if a user wanted to move temporarily to another part of the system; if, for example, the user wanted access to information in the database during a phone-call, and that user was editing at the time, then they would not be able to do so. Compromise solutions would be to re-allocate tasks to different users, or to provide each user with two terminals.

Written Software Constraints could be frustrating later in the design, when seemingly trivial changes turned out to be impossible as a result of the way in which the software had been designed. If the task outline was still expanding later in the design then the system could not always meet it. In project 3 the pattern designers were excited by what the system could do and provided lots of ideas as to how it could be improved. However the designer was unable to implement these ideas.

Table 2.   Problems Experienced in Interface Design and Projects Where They Were More Apparent

Numbered Design Projects

1. Display Editor	6. Office System
2. Network Management System	7. Simulation Training
3. Garment-Pattern Design-Aid	Device
4. Educational Graphics System	8. Distributed Building-
5. Window Manager	Management System

Problems	Design Projects
Poor Communication	2, 4, 8
Uncertainty About Requirements	3, 4, 7
Exclusion of Users	2, 5, 8
Expanding Task Outline	1, 3, 8
Designers' Unfamiliarity with Task Domain	2, 3
Lack of HCI Guidelines & Standards	5, 7, 8
Familiar Solution Application	6
Technological Constraints	1, 6
Written Software Constraints	3
Over-Casual Evaluation	5, 8
Lack of Performance Metrics	2, 5, 8
Market Pressures	3, 5

Problems listed in approximate order of possible occurrence

This designer actually stated that it would have been ideal to have been able to 'go back and start all over again'.

Over-Casual Evaluation was apparent in at least three cases. All of the projects, with the possible exception of 3 and 7, carried out, at best, unstructured user-evaluations. At worst, designers pretended to be naive users themselves when testing the software in action. In project 5 a direct result of over-casual evaluation was an extremely overloaded window control icon which caused several different effects depending on the mouse click combination used to activate it. So a window could close unexpectedly, or disappear behind another one and so on.

Lack of Performance Metrics follows on from casual user evaluation. If users simply try out a system, they are unlikely to be aware of changes in their own performance, becoming engrossed in the novelty and powerful functionality of the 'new toy'. Users' initial opinions are *not* a satisfactory measure of performance.

Market Pressures were a notable excuse for weak USI design. They cannot be trivialised however as their impact on funding and time-scales

Table 3. Summary of Constraints on Good Interface Development Practice

a) **Low autonomy**	l) **Technological constraints**
b) **Small design team**	m) **Market pressures**
c) Uncertainty about requirements	n) Poor communication
d) **Poor access to user/task-info**	o) Exclusion of users
e) Low affinity to HCI	p) **Expanding task outline**
f) Highly inflexible design method	q) Lack of guidelines/standards
g) Highly inflexible design team roles	r) Familiar solution application
h) Non-user oriented prototyping	s) **Written software constraints**
i) **Little USI design/HCI experience**	t) Over-casual evaluation
j) **Unfamiliar application domain**	u) Lack of performance metrics
k) **Unstructured application domain**	v) **Inadequate resources**

(**Unavoidable problems are in bold print**).

is immense and often unavoidable. This encourages cheap solutions to problems or faster system response times, which may have a lot of selling power for a product.

The problems described above appear to be closely related to the nature of the design environment and activities. Pressure imposed by organisational, practical, and technological constraints and the exclusion of HCI oriented development activities in practice were all cited by designers as being responsible for the types of problems listed here. Some problems; namely *exclusion of users, lack of HCI guidelines and standards, familiar solution application, over casual evaluation,* and *lack of performance metrics* appear intuitively to be avoidable, particularly where there is commitment to proper user-oriented design practice. However other problems; namely *poor communication, uncertainty about requirements, expanding task outlines, designers' unfamiliarity with the task domain, technological constraints, written software constraints,* and *market pressure* appear to be relatively unavoidable. If these conditions exist in a commercial design project, it may be impossible to apply current HCI DETs. Although it may be possible for designers to adhere more closely to the kind of principles recommended by Gould and Lewis than they seem to currently, it may not be easy for them to resist external pressure which encourages them to do otherwise. If designers wish to resort to a prescribed HCI DET, they will need one that can be applied in conditions where the above problems exist.

3.4. Summary of Findings

Taken together, design environment variation and problems encountered by designers represent possible constraints on the process of developing a good USI. Table 3 lists constraints indicated by the findings of this study. Some of the constraints listed are probably unavoidable. The other constraints are intuitively not so. If a designer is really committed to producing a good interface, it should be possible to adopt the kind of approach demonstrated by Gould *et al* (*ibid*), in order to overcome some of the avoidable problems, (Gould's principles for better USI design were formulated bearing in mind the existence of unavoidable problems such as expanding and unpredictable task outlines). On the other hand, should a designer wish to apply a more structured HCI DET for the purpose of planning or evaluating an interface, the above, unavoidable constraints will have to be recognised as a basis for choosing a particular DET which will work within them. This state of affairs must be tackled by developing HCI DETs so that at least one technique will be applicable in spite of the constraints existing within in any given design project. The fact that problems which could benefit from HCI DETs appear to emerge early as well as late in design supports the idea that HCI should be introduced as early as possible, in order to avoid problems later on in design, and then applied throughout.

Finally some reasons why HCI techniques are not applied were supplied by the designers themselves and these should be taken as a caveat for Human Factors specialists. They were as follows:

> No confidence in HCI as a discipline, and no perceived need for it.

> Lack of awareness or available information about appropriate techniques.

> HCI is seen to be too time consuming and expensive to be worthwhile.

> Techniques are often intimidating in their complexity.

These comments suggest that there is a certain amount of mistrust or misunderstanding of the discipline of HCI amongst some systems designers. Although such statements have been dismissed as unfounded, or as representing easily solved problems (e.g., by Gould and Lewis, *ibid*), the findings of this investigation suggest that there may also be practical reasons for not applying current HCI DETs.

4. Discussion

4.1. Characteristics of Commercial Interface Design Practice and the Non-Use of HCI DETs

Although considerable time and effort were frequently directed towards planning and evaluating USI designs, this effort seemed to be applied in very haphazard, informal ways. There is some agreement with the findings of the design study by Hammond *et al* (Hammond et al. [1983]) in that, although the designers were not 'computer-centric', their approach often appeared to exclude important user requirements. It should be stressed, however, that user-inclusion or exclusion was sometimes outside the control of the designers, particularly if they were working as consultants and found it hard to gain access to them.

The interviews indicated that the three principles espoused by Gould and his colleagues were not applied, despite positive attitudes held by designers. Some designers spent a great deal of time engaged in user- and task-oriented investigation and development. This kind of activity was only possible when users were accessible. Since users were sometimes hard to approach, it is not surprising that *early focus on users* was sometimes difficult. In some cases users were excluded altogether, or included only at the latest stages in development. Designers' *empirical measurement* was particularly weak; proper performance metrics and goals were not used. It is probable that much better evaluation would be possible if designers were able to characterise interfaces in such a way that testable performance goals could be generated. Finally *iterative prototyping* was most commonly *incremental development* (as described in the design study of Rosson *et al* (Rosson, Maas & Kellogg [1987])) where the prototype is the developing implementation itself. However this prototyping often did not include user-testing in its cycle. This meant that as far as usability was concerned, the value of iteration was often lost. Most notable was the fact that none of the designers interviewed used HCI DETs (they had either not heard of them, or they gave specific reasons for not using them). It therefore appears that this investigation has fulfilled its first aim (see section 2.2) in determining whether or not this was the case.

4.2. Implications of the Findings for the Application Requirements of HCI DETs

Table 3 listed organisational and technological constraints, designers' lack of experience with USI design and with the system application domain plus many other factors which may represent real problems for interface designers. Even if a designer is highly supportive of HCI, these factors may make it impossible to apply DETs successfully to commercial design in general. Hammond *et al* (*ibid*) suggest that, rather than supplying detailed guidelines, Human Factors specialists should perhaps concentrate on more appropriate 'mini-theories' of the user and user-performance for designers to use. What appears to be certain is that the design and development process is unpredictable, with a large number of possible constraints which may emerge. Designers need a wide variety of flexible DETs which can satisfy constraints of the kind identified here. Observations from design studies indicate that HCI DETs must produce useful, comprehensible information and be easy for the non-HCI specialist to apply, since HCI specialists may be a rarity in commercial design projects. The following discussion gives examples of ways in which current HCI DETs application requirements, as described in section 1.2, are not satisfied if certain observed design constraints exist. So, although there are design situations where it may be possible to apply these techniques, they are not adequate as a collective resource for many design projects, and therefore will not be widely applicable.

Appropriateness

It was fairly clear from this study that various HCI evaluative techniques would not have been appropriate to certain design projects observed, purely on the basis of the performance metrics these techniques supply. GOMS, for example, would not have been suited for evaluation of the simulation training device since users would be error prone novices, and the main criterion for user-evaluation was the simplicity and robustness of the interface, (performance times were not of any great interest for this system). However there are other reasons for the inappropriateness of various HCI DETs, which relate to the practical design constraints identified by this study.

Competence and *performance* models could be inappropriate as DETs in design projects where almost any of the constraints shown in Table 3 exist. Some of these are unavoidable problems such as *poor access to information about users/tasks, unfamiliarity of application domain* and *unstructured application domain*. In a design situation including these conditions, Reisner's Formal Grammar ETIT, TAG, GOMS, UDM and other DETs could only be imperfectly applied, if at all. Such models require the evaluator to have a certain degree of knowledge about user performance and/or user task structures, and are therefore inappropriate in design situations where the designer will find it difficult or impossible to acquire the necessary information.

Design models might be inappropriate in design projects with conditions such as *low autonomy* and *expanding task outlines*. If a design team is forced to adopt a particular approach, if, for example, they have to fit in with other projects working on software and hardware design of a system, then certain design methodologies may not be applicable. If the task outline expands, then a structured design approach like CLG may lose its main value, which is to produce a complete structured system description. The task- and semantic-level descriptions of the system would have little value if the functionality planned for the system was completely different by the time the interaction-level was described.

Designers' Experience with HCI

Little USI design/HCI experience and *low affinity to HCI* are conditions which are important to HCI DETs because of the heavy reliance on psychological terminology and user-oriented concepts. TAG and GOMS, for example, both rely on the idea that tasks can be broken down into sub-tasks, sub-sub-tasks, and so on. The level at which tasks stop being decomposed is left to the evaluator's view of what an automatic or skilled action is, in the particular circumstances. If there is to be a wide range of users with different levels of skill, doing different tasks on the system, as was the case in project 8, then deciding what a simple-task is may be extremely difficult even for a psychologist. Since seven of the designers interviewed had little or no experience of HCI or psychology, it is unlikely that they would even attempt to use any of the DETs mentioned in this paper. Dagwell and Weber (*ibid*) suggested that the poor conceptualisations of users held by designers could be improved with better, readily available information rather than education. Perhaps more comprehensible descriptions of psychological theories, as proposed by Hammond *et al* (*ibid*), could be applied to this problem.

Existing Specifications

In cases where the conditions *unfamiliar application domain, unstructured application domain* and *expanding task outlines* exist, it may be difficult to produce a valuable specification of a complex USI to be used for the application of HCI DETs. In seven of the projects examined the USI was developed informally; expanding functionality often occurred as the project progressed making specification difficult. Designers are unlikely to want to spend time and effort specifying systems early on, when they are not sure of what they want the interface to be like. If HCI DETs were to be applied, it would be after the prototype was almost finalised, when all the functionality planned had been added. By this time the benefits of HCI DETs could only be applied to future designs, since it would be impossible to change the current system. ETIT, for example, requires a fairly detailed system specification, so it may not be applicable early enough in design for the analysis to influence the USI design in any significant way, before unmodifiable software is written.

There is a possibility that revised design practice (possibly using incomplete, or partial specifications) and use of certain types of DET could address the existing specification problem, especially where complexity is a major factor. Kieras and Polson (Kieras & Polson [1985]), in their explanation of UDM, which is based in part on GOMS, recommend that the device specification should be modular, to maintain flexibility and simplicity, and that it should not be committed to any particular hardware or software specification. This DET could map directly onto the extension of iterative prototyping suggested by Smith and Mosier (*ibid*), *incremental acquisition*, where separate capabilities are implemented and tested in evolutionary stages, making it possible to specify parts of an interface independently and then add them to the evolving prototype. This may make the whole process of specification and evaluation of a complex commercial USI somewhat more straightforward, and add the benefit of psychologically-based evaluation of each incorporated function as the design progresses. However, whether this will really be feasible in commercial design environments with complex system applications remains to be proved.

Access to Information About Tasks and Users

Information about tasks and users was cited as crucial by several designers. Although there was universal agreement that such information was important, some designers did not involve user and task evaluation in their development. The only project which produced specification documentation did not use it to address user-requirements, as recommended by Smith and Mosier (*ibid*). This documentation was used to verify the design with the client. Lack of time, organisational obstruction and inaccessibility of users all emerged as excuses for not improving user-evaluation. Since all user-oriented development approaches, including the use of HCI DETs, require that designers find out about users and tasks, it seems that whatever the reasons are for excluding user/task investigation, they should be resisted. As it was in this study, the amount of information of this type collected by designers was sometimes certainly inadequate for application of HCI DETs, as well as for any likelihood of a high standard of user interface being developed by any method.

Time and Cost

Small design teams, or lone consultants are unlikely to be able to devote the time and effort required to carry out application of one of the HCI DETs. CLG, for example, was cited by one of the college based designers as being too time consuming to be of any real use. When commercial system interfaces are complex, HCI DETs such as CLG can turn out to be prohibitively time consuming and expensive to apply, which makes the risk of inappropriate application all the more serious for the non HCI expert designer. On the other hand Gould *et al* (*ibid*) claimed that their principled approach saved time and ultimately cost in that the interface of the OMS was highly robust and rarely failed. HCI DETs must also be shown to have these benefits before they are likely to be universally accepted.

Overall it appears that there are many conditions and related problems imposed by the design environment and activities which are incompatible with current HCI DETs application requirements. It is not suggested here that current HCI techniques cannot be applied to commercial design projects. Rather, it is proposed that the current HCI DETs will only be applicable in a proportion of design environments which have compatible conditions with those required by the DETs. In other words more techniques are required to cater for design environments where the existing techniques would be inapplicable. In the meantime, it may be that designers will have to accept the principles recommended by Gould and Lewis (*ibid*) as the most viable approach to interface design and evaluation in many circumstances.

5. Conclusions

This study suggests that HCI DETs, although potentially valuable to commercial design, are not applied in practice. The design environment conditions required for the successful application of current HCI DETs do not appear to be satisfied by commercial design projects. The reason for this is the existence of unavoidable constraints in commercial design which future HCI DETs should try to cater for.

Acknowledgements

The author wishes to thank Dr Peter Johnson for his help, and all of the designers who supplied information for this study, particularly those who agreed to be interviewed.

References

S K Card, T P Moran & A Newell [1983], *The Psychology of Human-Computer Interaction*, Lawrence Erlbaum Associates, Hillsdale, New Jersey.

R Dagwell & R Weber [1983], "System Designer's User-Models: A Comparative Study and Methodological Critique," *Communications of the ACM* 26, 987–997.

S A Douglas & T P Moran [1983], "Learning Text Editor Semantics by Analogy," in *Proceedings of CHI '83 – Human Factors in Computing Systems*, ACM, New York.

J D Gould, S J Boies, S Levy, J T Richards & J Schoonard [1987], "The 1984 Olympic Messaging System: A Test of Behavioral Principles of System Design," *Communications of the ACM* 30, 785–796.

J D Gould & C Lewis [1985], "Designing for Usability – Key Principles and What Designers Think," *Communications of the ACM* 28, 300–311.

N V Hammond, A Jorgensen, A Maclean, P Barnard & J Long [1983], "Design Practice and Interface Usability: evidence from Interviews and Designers," IBM Hursley Research Centre, Report No HF082.

D Kieras & P G Polson [1985], "An Approach to the Formal Analysis of User Complexity," *Int. J. Man-Machine Studies* 22, 365–394.

T P Moran [1978], "Introduction to the Command Language Grammar," Palo Alto CA, Xerox Corporation Report No. SSL-78-3.

T P Moran [1981], "The Command Language Grammar: A Representation for the User Interface of Interactive Computing Systems," *Int. J. Man-Machine Studies* 15, 3–50.

T P Moran [1983], "Getting into a System: External-Internal Task-Mapping Analysis," in *Proceedings of CHI '83 – Human Factors in Computing Systems*, ACM, New York.

S J Payne [1984], "Task-Action Grammars," in *INTERACT '84 – First IFIP Conference on Human-Computer Interaction*, B Shackel, ed., Elsevier-Science, Amsterdam.

S J Payne & T R G Green [1986], "Task-Action Grammars: A Model of the Mental Representation of Task Languages," *Human Computer Interaction* 2, 93–133.

P Reisner [1981], "Formal Grammar and the Design of an Interactive System," *IEEE Trans. on Software Engineering* 7, 229–240.

P Reisner [1982], "Analytical Tools for Human Factors of Software," in *Enduser Systems and Their Human Factors*, A Blaser and M Zoeppritz, ed., Springer-Verlag, Berlin, 94–121.

M B Rosson, S Maas & W A Kellogg [1987], "Designing for Designers: An Analysis of Design Practice in the Real World," in *CHI + GI Conference '87*, ACM, Toronto Canada.

S L Smith & J N Mosier [1984], "Design Guidelines for User-System Interface Software," The Mitre Corporation, Report No. ESD-TR-84-190, Bedford MA.

H W Thimbleby [1984], "Generative User-Engineering Principles for User Interface Design," in *INTERACT '84 – First IFIP Conference on Human-Computer Interaction*, B Shackel, ed., Elsevier-Science, Amsterdam, 102–107.

M D Wilson, P Barnard & A Maclean [1986], "Task Analysis in Human Computer Interaction," IBM Hursley Research Centre, Report No HF122.

Task-Related Knowledge Structures: Analysis, Modelling and Application

Peter Johnson, Hilary Johnson, Ray Waddington & Alan Shouls

Department of Computer Science, Queen Mary College, University of London, Mile End Road, London E1 4NS, U.K.

A theoretical and methodological approach to task modelling is described, with a worked example of the resultant model. The theory holds that task knowledge is represented in a person's memory and that this knowledge can be described by a Task Knowledge Structure (TKS). The method of analysis has been developed for carrying out analyses of real world tasks. The method uses a variety of techniques for collecting information about task knowledge. A second perspective of the paper shows how a developed TKS model can be decomposed into a design for a software system to support the identified tasks within the domain of the analysis. This decompositional method uses the structure of frames to provide consistency between different levels of design decomposition.

Keywords: Task modelling, knowledge representation, frames, design decomposition

1. Introduction

Traditionally, task analysis (TA) has investigated what people do when they carry out one or more tasks and involves collecting information about how people perform those tasks. Various approaches to TA have been developed particularly in the context of human computer interaction (HCI). Probably the most often cited approach to TA in HCI is the GOMS approach of (Card, Moran & Newell [1983]). One central tennet of GOMS is that tasks can be thought of in terms of goal structures, operations, methods and selection rules. By extending the original ideas of (Card, Moran & Newell [1983]) these four elements might be considered to be the basic structural components of any task knowledge that a person might recruit to perform a task. In other words, we might suppose that people not only performed tasks, but developed knowledge structures that reflected the way they recruited particular sources of knowledge to a given task. A strong argument to make would be that people had something akin to goals, operations, methods and selection rules represented in long-term memory and processed in working memory. While not making this strong claim (Card, Moran & Newell [1983]), did identify an approximation of the psychological processors (in the form of the human information processor model) that might operate on some or all of these four elements. The work of (Kieras & Polson [1985]) extends GOMS by arguing that production rules can be used to model goals, operations, methods and selection rules and that these production rules bear a close relationship to the way a person does (or would) structure their knowledge of the task (Kieras & Polson [1985]). They use these production rules to assess the complexity of a user interface by merely counting the number of production rules assumed to be required to perform the task; and assess the degree of learning required by counting the number of new production rules required in the new, as opposed to the old technological domain, in which the task is to be performed.

Neither (Card, Moran & Newell [1983]) nor (Kieras & Polson [1985]) explicitly claim that people actually possess these task-knowledge structures. In task-action grammars (TAG), (Payne & Green [1986]) are explicit in their assumption that people do possess task-knowledge structures. However, they give little detail of what these structures might contain or how they might function. For (Payne & Green [1986]), task knowledge appears to be decomposed into a dictionary of 'simple tasks' and rule schema, which through the use of rewrite rules specify what knowledge is recruited for a given task. TAG also includes the notion of 'family resemblances' for relating together similar task knowledge, and the notion of common knowledge which is task-independent knowledge that a person is assumed to already possess, (for example, pointing, typing, or the meaning of the word 'up').

Both GOMS (including its extension by (Kieras & Polson [1985])) and TAG have assumed that people possess knowledge that is recruited and used in task performance. TAG further assumes that people possess task related knowledge structures. However, the detail of these knowledge structures and the theoretical or empirical evidence for their existence is weak. In the rest of this paper we will argue that task knowledge structures are functionally equivalent to the knowledge structures that people possess and use when performing a task. We then go on to describe a method for identifying, analysing and modelling task knowledge structures (TKS). The contents of these TKS models can be usefully applied to the generation of design solutions. A method for applying these models to design is described. In describing TKS models and their application to design we will use examples taken from real tasks that have been analysed and real designs that have been proposed. However, because these examples are taken from complex domains we have selected them so that they will exemplify our approach rather than as complete models of the tasks within the domains.

2. Theoretical Basis for TKS

We will first outline a number of theoretical assumptions which we have made on the basis of existing theoretical and empirical work in cognitive psychology.

2.1. Task Knowledge as Conceptual Knowledge

Task knowledge is represented in conceptual or general knowledge structures in long term memory. This is akin to the theoretical position taken by (Schank [1982]) in assuming that knowledge of frequently occurring events is structured into meaningful units in memory. Empirical support for our assumption that people possess something akin to TKSs can be found in the work of (Galambos [1986]) who conducted a series of experiments which show that people recognise and use structures of events, such as the order, the sequence and the importance of activities within the event sequence to understand, explain and make predictions about those events. Further support for our view that task knowledge is represented in long term memory comes from the work on text and story comprehension by (Graesser & Clark [1985]) in which general knowledge structures relating goals to causal and enabling states, plans for achieving goals, intermediate states and alternative solutions or paths are all represented in a conceptual knowledge structure for the events of the story.

We assume that all the knowledge a person possesses about a task is contained within the task knowledge structure and that the TKS is activated in association with task performance.

2.2. Structure in Tasks

Task knowledge and therefore TKSs would be 'unstructured' if the knowledge people had about the task world (or domain) was such that all possible elements of the knowledge used in those tasks could be associated, and was associated with equal probability to other knowledge elements. This structure is not just an imposed structure but is a reflection of the structure found in tasks in the real world. All possible elements and attributes of a task do not co-occur with equal probability. Our view here is similar to that of (Garner [1974]) in describing how people represent physical objects based on the structure of those objects in the real world.

We argue that task behaviours do not occur independently of one another. Some pairs and n-tuples of task behaviours are quite probable while others which might be logically or physically possible, never occur together in reality. Within tasks, some behaviours are carried out together, precede or follow other behaviours, and in some cases prime, or are primed by other behaviours. One form of this structuring is in a **PLAN** which provides a feasible and acceptable structuring on the task behaviours. Empirical evidence for the representation of PLANS in long term memory can be found in the work on programming tasks (Green, Bellamy & Parker [1987]). Further evidence for structuring in tasks comes from the work of (Byrne [1977]) on tasks in domains such as cookery and meal planning.

2.3. Representativeness of Task Elements

A TKS is composed of a number of task elements which differ in representativeness. This is similar to the notion of representativeness used by (Rosch [1985]) and (Rosch et al. [1976]) to describe the relations between objects and their categorical representation in memory.

We assume that a TKS includes knowledge about objects (both physical and informational) and their associated actions. This is based on earlier work by (Johnson, Diaper & Long [1984]). These objects and their associated actions differ in how representative they are of the TKS of which they are a part. One implication of this is that the procedures containing these representative objects and actions are more *central* to the TKS than other procedures. Empirical evidence for the notions of procedural centrality and action/object representativeness in task behaviour can be found in (Leddo & Abelson [1986]) who found that for tasks such as borrowing a book from a library there were particular segments which were more central to the particular instantiation of going to the library and more representative of the class of similar tasks. It is interesting to note that frequency of occurrence alone was not a reliable indicator of object and associated action representativeness nor procedural centrality.

3. A theory of TKS

A TKS is a summary representation of the different types of knowledge that are recruited and used in task behaviour. A TKS is related to other TKSs by a number of possible relations.

3.1. Within Role Relations

One form of relation between TKSs is in terms of their association with a given role. A person may take on a number of roles, for example 'author', 'referee', 'teacher' etc. There are tasks associated with each of these roles. For each task that a role may be required to perform there will be a TKS. Those tasks that are related because they are performed by the same role will have the role relation property associating their respective TKSs.

3.2. Between Role Relations

A second form of relation between TKSs is in terms of the similarity between tasks across roles. This occurs when a person is performing a similar task under different roles. For example, a person may carry out the task of 'arranging meeting(s)' while assuming the role of 'chairman', 'client', 'husband'. Each task may be performed differently in one or other respect. However, a single person assuming all these roles would have a knowledge structure for each task and also knowledge (not necessarily explicit) of the relations between these tasks. Thus the TKSs for each of the 'meeting arranging' tasks would have relational links to other 'meeting arranging' tasks performed by that person when assuming a different role.

Within each TKS there are other knowledge representations. The **goal substructure** represents the goals and subgoals identified within the TKS. The goal substructure also includes the enabling and conditional states that must prevail if a goal or subgoal is to be achieved. In this way the goal structure represents the **plan** for carrying out the complete task. The plan defined in the goal substructure is carried out through a **procedural structure** which contains alternative procedures for achieving a particular subgoal. As there may be alternative sets of procedures for achieving a particular subgoal there are also conditional and contextual groupings of these procedures. In this way **strategies** are represented. Strategies are particular sequences of procedures. The procedures rely on other knowledge of the **objects** and **actions** which when combined constitute a given procedure statement. This action and object knowledge is represented in a taxonomic substructure. Within the **taxonomic substructure** information about the properties of the action(s) and object(s) are represented. This includes, the **representativeness** of the object or action, the **class membership** and other attributes such as the procedures in which it is commonly used, its relation to other objects and actions and its features (such as what the object can do or possess). These are described in more detail in (Johnson, Johnson & Russell [1988]).

4. Identifying Knowledge for a TKS

A method of identifying the knowledge for a TKS has been developed (Johnson, Johnson & Russell [1988]) known as Knowledge Analysis of Tasks (KAT). The theory of TKS outlined above requires information about the following knowledge components for a given task; roles, goals, subgoals, subtasks, plans, procedures, strategies, actions and objects. In addition the analysis should identify the representativeness, class membership, and other features represented within the taxonomic substructure. We have chosen to define the more ambiguous task components in the following way:

A role is assumed to be defined by the particular set of tasks that an individual is responsible for performing as part of their duty in a particular social context (a 'job' is one form of social context). A person can and will take on more than one role and more than one person can and will take on a given role.

A goal is assumed to be the state of affairs that a particular task can produce and forms part of a person's conceptualisation of their task world while carrying out a given role.

A plan is the particular formulation and possible ordering of subtasks that are undertaken to achieve a particular goal.

A procedure is a particular element of behaviour that forms part of a subtask. One feature of procedures is that there can be alternative groupings and ordering of procedures for the same subtask, these alternatives are thought to reflect different strategies and as such contain conditional selection rules that enable the correct grouping of procedures to be selected under the appropriate conditions.

Actions and objects are the lowest level of elements of tasks and are the constituents of procedures.

A number of techniques for identifying the components of a TKS have been considered in (Johnson, Johnson & Russell [1988]). For the sake of brevity, we will simply summarise the techniques in terms of their application to particular components of a TKS, in table 1. Most of the techniques need little in the way of explanation as they are standard techniques used in social surveys, however some guidelines are provided as to when to use the various techniques, since more than one technique can be used to identify the same TKS element. The techniques listed in table 1 vary in terms of their appropriateness and in terms of their ease of use, resource and time requirements. As a rule of thumb we recommend that the analyst should apply more than one technique to identify a given TKS component. This enables the information obtained under one technique to be confirmed, rejected or supplemented by the use of a further technique. In terms of effort, the analyst must consider the time requirements of the task performer as well as their own. With this in mind we recommend that where it is possible and appropriate for a particular TKS element, techniques which involve minimal or no direct time costs on the part of the task performer should be applied first (e.g., accessing manuals, texts or other documentation). The next techniques to be used where it is appropriate, should be questionnaires and interviews, since these are also least time consuming for the task performer. However, for some task elements it is necessary to have a more considerable time commitment from the task performer. Direct observation, concurrent and retrospective protocols are all expensive with respect to the task performer's time and they should be carried out in the order mentioned here. Finally techniques such as sorting, constructing tree diagrams and so on, should be carried out once the analyst has a relatively detailed understanding of the person's tasks.

In producing a TKS the analyst is required to identify the above knowledge elements. If the intention is to produce a composite model that is representative of a number of persons' knowledge of a given task then it is necessary to sample from the population of people who carry out the identified tasks. The extent of the sampling is again determined by the access and the time available to the analyst. However, it is rarely the case that only one person performing a given task will be analysed.

5. Identifying the Generic Properties of a TKS

Having collected adequate information about the individual TKS elements, the next step is to identify the generic elements of a TKS. Generic elements are included in a composite task model of the individual task

Table 1.   Summary of techniques for identifying elements of a TKS

TKS element	Identification technique
actions & objects	selecting from texts or manuals; tutorial sessions; pilot study; analyst performing task; structured interview with task performer; questionnaire; direct observation of task performer; concurrent or retrospective protocol.
object representativeness	frequency counting; rating scales; sorting tasks (e.g., card sorting); list ordering.
procedures	direct observation; concurrent protocols.
plans	structured interview; retrospective protocols; direct observation.
goals and subtasks	questionnaires; structured interviews; constructing tree diagrams; retrospective protocols.

performers and instances of the tasks which the TKS is meant to represent. This reduces the effect of variation in the TKS, for instance from non-relevant contextual effects on task behaviour (such as the equipment on which the task is performed). Clearly what is or is not relevant will be dependent upon the purpose of the analysis itself. However, the *method* of generification we have developed is independent of the purpose. The process of generification is summarised in table 2. and is reported in full in (Johnson, Johnson & Russell [1988]). Each element of a TKS and its process of generification is shown. The process should be applied in an iterative manner such that if the generic properties identified on the first attempt are not validated by the task performers then the process should be reiterated with different threshold values (in the case of plans and procedures) and/or different groupings and labels (in the case of actions and objects).

Table 2.   Generification of TKS elements

TKS element	Generification process
Actions & objects	1. Construct lists of actions and objects for a task across all task performers and instances of the same task. 2. Note the frequency of each action and object in the list and remove all repetitions from the list. 3. Using judges from task performers, group all like actions and objects. 4. Identify appropriate labels for the identified groupings of actions and objects. 5. Produce lists of the identified generic actions and generic objects. 6. Validate the list with a different group of task performers.
Plans & procedures	1. List all the procedures and the plans in which they are used, for each task performer and each task instance. 2. Record the frequency of each procedure in a plan and across plans. 3. Record the frequency of each plan across task instances and task performers. 4. Select a frequency threshold level for procedures and for plans (the two need not be the same). 5. Identify all procedures and plans which are above the previously specified threshold. 6. Validate the identified generic procedures and plans with the task performers.

6. Constructing a Complete TKS Model

The resultant task model, produced from the analysis comprises a number of summary representations and substructures which together provide a detailed model of the knowledge associated with a collection of tasks related together by roles.

The highest level of representation of the model is provided by the role/task relations. There are two types of role/task relations:

a) The different roles that are required to perform a given task would be assumed to have a similar TKS for that task.

b) The different TKSs that a person fulfilling a particular role may be expected to access and use.

The next level of representation of the model is the content of the TKS for a given task. This representation includes relations to lower level representations of the model containing the plan, procedures and taxonomic substructure (i.e., action and object property/feature lists). It details the knowledge associated with the specific task from the family of tasks performed by a given role or roles.

At a lower level of representation in the model is the plan and procedural knowledge associated with the specific task. This representation is referred to as a goal-oriented substructure. The plan represents the structure of the subgoals and the states which those subgoals satisfy. Each subgoal is related to one or more sets of procedures for carrying out that subgoal. Where there is more than one alternative set of procedures these constitute different strategies. Within a procedure the specific activity procedures are represented by production rules of the form 'IF ... THEN'. The procedures also have links to the taxonomic substructure which is the lowest level of representation in the model.

The taxonomic substructure contains the category structure for the object and its associated action. The category structure is divided into superordinate, basic and subordinate category levels. The basic level category contains the following information:

> is a member of . . . .
> is used in procedure(s) . . . .
> is related to . . . . . by . . . .
> is associated with actions . . . . .
> has features . . . .
> typical instance . . . .

This concludes our description of the TKS model and its contents.

To help clarify and concretize the detail of a TKS we provide an example of a complete TKS for a task in the domain of office work, namely 'arranging a meeting'. We have shown this task model from the perspective of the role of an office secretary, however we also show relations between the secretary and manager role, and how both might possess corresponding TKSs. Also we show other TKSs which a person in the secretary role might possess. These are shown in figure 1 and figure 2 respectively. The summary contents of the TKS for 'arrange a meeting' are shown in figure 3. Figure 4 shows the goal-oriented substructure which comprises the plan for the task and the procedures which are used to execute one of the subgoals (namely, 'plan the meeting PPM'). This figure also shows the production rules that are used to execute one procedure in that procedure set, namely 'consult a location for an information token of a project meeting' (Consult(LOC, ITs,

Projectmeeting)). Figure 5 shows the taxonomic substructure for the object MESSAGE as it is used in the TKS for the 'arrange meeting' task.

In the basic level category it is revealed that the MESSAGE object has the following properties:

is a member of.	'arrange a project meeting'
is used in procedures	'decide message:to'
	'decide message:body'
is related to objects	reply . . . . . . by . . . . precedes
is associated with actions	decide, consult, storein, select etc.
has features	text, date, address, paper.
typical instance	message suggesting suitable dates
	for a meeting.

This simple example shows how the complete TKS model represents the different attributes of knowledge associated with the task of 'arranging a meeting'.

7. Making Design Recommendations from the TKS Model

The TKS model for 'arranging a meeting' contains useful information that can be used to influence the design of a computer application program to support messaging by electronic mail. The way in which the TKS model can influence design relies upon the overriding assumption that a computer program which is designed to be used by a given user population to carry out an expected range of tasks, will be easier to use if the users are able to transfer some of their existing knowledge about those tasks to the new environment created by the computer program. This assumption underpins the use of 'metaphors' such as 'desk-tops' or 'forms', in which the computer program attempts to retain some identifiable links with a user's assumed extant knowledge about real desk-tops and paper based forms. However, it is clear that a metaphor is only one mechanism by which transfer of extant knowledge might be facilitated; furthermore, the way that a metaphor might function is itself the subject of some debate. It should also be noted that not all aspects of a person's extant knowledge will be relevant or transferable to the new environment. For example, the knowledge of how to dial and use a telephone may have little relevance to support communication by a textual computer-based messaging system. Keeping with the same example, the knowledge a person has about asking questions, making

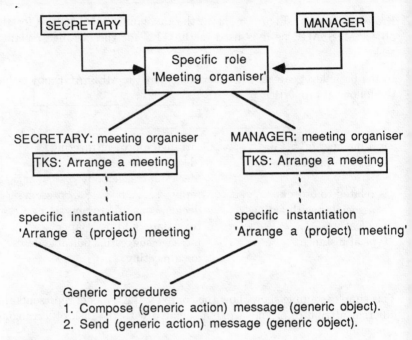

Figure 1. A subpart of a messaging task world

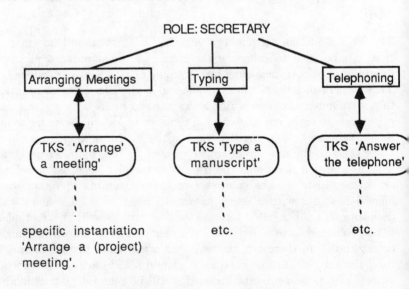

Figure 2. Some of the possible TKSs associated with a single ROLE

requests, or providing answers would be applicable to both the old and new environments for communication and could (should) be supported in the new environment.

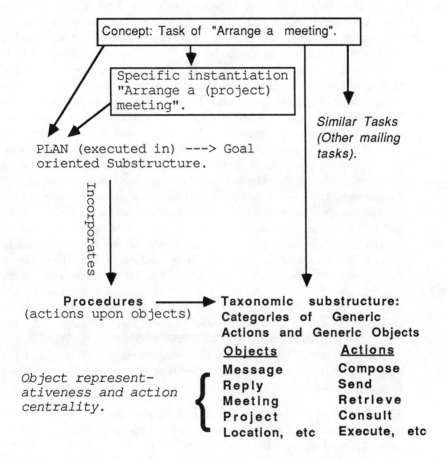

Figure 3. TASK KNOWLEDGE STRUCTURE

The TKS model identifies the knowledge structures that a person is assumed to access when carrying out any task. The method of analysis allows the analyst to identify the contents of those knowledge structures for particular tasks within a given domain. The selection of the domain and the focus of the tasks within the domain is outside the methodology. Having constructed a TKS model the analyst has identified a number of important properties of the users' knowledge about those tasks. At the object level the taxonomic substructure identifies the typical instances of objects within the domain and the features of those objects. The work on concept and object knowledge of (Rosch et al. [1976]) leads us to suggest that if the designer chooses to support this task and provide a visible representation of the objects, then the taxonomic substructure provides an informative and detailed description of the features a person will expect to associate with those objects. At the next level of representation the TKS model identifies the knowledge a person has about how to achieve their subgoals and the plans they construct and use in achieving the identified goal of the task. The procedures represented at this level of the TKS provide a description of the rules that people performing the task would expect to follow and the alternative procedures they would follow under particular conditions. This information can be used by the system designer to decide how the user will expect to make use of the objects and actions (functions). The TKS at this level also identifies what the most frequent or preferred procedure for achieving a subgoal is. This information can be used to set up default modes of operation in the program design. The next level of the TKS represents an overall summary of the plan, procedures and the objects and actions people associate with a particular task. This information may be of interest to the designer in so much as it provides an overview of particular contexts in which specific procedures might be used. It could also be used to provide the user with a summary representation of how the designer expects a task to be carried out. At the highest level the TKS shows the relations between tasks and roles. This information provides the designer with a view as to how different roles might expect to have access to the same task functions and to those task functions which are specific to particular roles. This task/role information is also of use to designers who may be concerned with configuring a system to suit the needs of a particular organisation, since it shows the task/role match of the organisation.

The information contained within a TKS is very rich and can be used as an information source for the design of computer programs to support those tasks. However, the TKS is not itself a design model. It is not decomposable into a design specification. It is simply a user knowledge model. However, it can be transformed into a design model and decomposed into a design. From initial ideas about the use of frame representations to describe analysis for design (Keane & Johnson [1987]), we have developed a method of decomposing a task model into a design for a software system. This method of decomposition is described in the next section.

8. Decomposing a Task Model into a Design Model

In decomposing a design the approach we have developed has three main objectives; first to maintain *consistency* between levels of decomposition, second to *add detail* at each level of decomposition, and third to take as

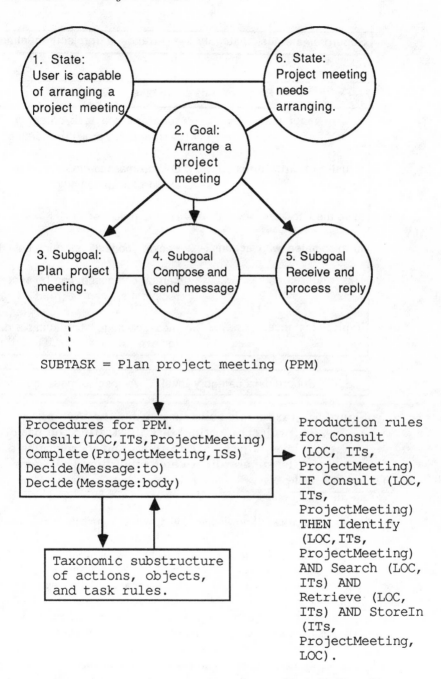

Figure 4. Goal-oriented substructure of the 'Arrange a (project) meeting' task

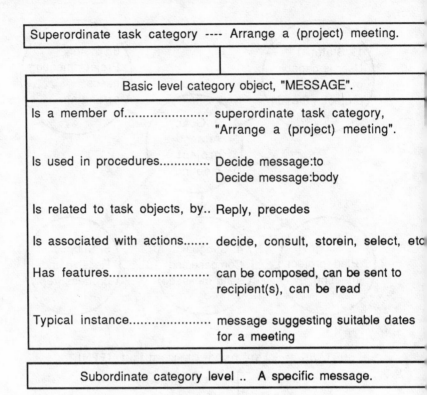

Figure 5. **Taxonomic substructure for the 'Arrange a (project) meeting' task illustrating the basic level object, 'MESSAGE', and its relations to the superordinate and subordinate category levels**

its starting point a task knowledge model, whose structure is consistent with the outcome of the TKS model. The decompositional model we have developed uses the properties of frames to maintain consistency between the different levels of decomposition. Each frame *inherits* the properties of the previous level of design detail. In this way we are able to meet our first objective of consistency. At each level of the decompositional model further design detail is added until, at the lowest level, the visible features of the represented user interface are being designed. This meets our second objective of adding design detail at each level of decomposition. The decompositional model takes as its starting point a task knowledge model consistent with the TKS model, and transforms this into a frame representation, where the decomposition process may begin. This meets our third objective of starting with a structure consistent with the TKS model.

The method has three stages of decomposition. At the first stage the TKS model is transformed into a General Task Model (GTM). The GTM represents the ROLES, GOALS, ACTIONS, STRATEGIES and OBJECT DEFINITIONS of the TKS as a series of frames. At the second stage the GTM is transformed into a Specific Task Model (STM). The STM is different from the GTM in that it contains the additional information of program/user allocation by identifying what features of a task the computer program will support and how these fit into the broader description of the complete user/program definition of the system. Like the GTM the STM is represented in the form of frames and inherits the structure of the task from the GTM. The third stage is to transform the STM into a Specific Interface Model (SIM). The SIM describes the structure and the content of the user interface at a conceptual or semantic level. That is to say, the SIM describes what should be represented at the user interface and how it should support interaction, without describing the particular form of representation that the user interface might have. By defining the interface at this level of abstraction we are able to design independent of the particular machine on which the application might run. Thus, it is possible to implement the design on a standard VT100 type terminal or on a high-resolution, colour workstation with mouse and keyboard input. We propose also that the SIM could be further decomposed into machine-dependent designs. In fact, using this approach we have been able to describe the design of an extant user interface (to electronic mail software) as part of a research project concerned with early evaluation techniques. Thus the decompositional model meets each of our three objectives of consistency, adding design detail and taking input from a model consistent with TKS.

Each of the stages of the decompositional model are exemplified below. We have used the same example of the 'arrange a meeting' task that was used to exemplify the TKS model above. Note that the models presented here show only the generic role of 'meeting arranger' (which might be undertaken by a secretary). We acknowledge that such a task will have a *between role relation* with the generic role of 'meeting participant' (which might be undertaken by a manager – see figure 1). The complete model would show *all* interacting roles in a task, but for the sake of simplicity we show only the former role here.

The first stage is the construction of the GTM. The full GTM for the 'arrange a meeting' task is shown in Appendix A. An example of each of the components of the GTM is shown in figure 6 for convenience. The GTM contains General Goal Frames (GGFs), Instrumental Goal Frames (IGFs), Macro-Actions, Micro-Actions, Strategy Lists and Object Definitions.

The GGF represents the goal and subgoal structure of the TKS and shows the defined plan for the task. The form of the GGF is *General Goal (<Object> (<Specific Object Type>))*. In the example used, this would be *Arrange (Meeting (Managerial))*, assuming that the specific instance of the task concerns arranging this type of meeting. The GGF consists of IGFs – that is those goals which are instrumental to the achievement of the general goal – which are related to each other in that one may be sufficient for carrying out the next (enables), or indeed necessary and sufficient (causes).

IGFs show those elements of the task that are identified by the TKS procedures, and are decomposed into Macro-Actions. Macro-Actions are also related according to sufficient and necessary conditions. For example (see figure 6) PLAN consists of: Consulting a LOCation for Information Tokens associated with an Object; this enables one to Complete the details of that Object using any necessary Information Sources; this enables one to Decide on the precise nature of those Information Tokens.

The Macro- and Micro-Actions, and Strategy Lists represent production rules and strategies of the TKS. Micro-Actions are the decomposed form of Macro-Actions, and are the lowest-level of decomposition in the model. Again they bear the relations showing sufficient and necessary conditions. Figure 6 shows the decomposition of the Consult Macro-Action. (See Appendix A for the interpretation of individual Micro-Actions.) Some Macro-Actions do not get decomposed into Micro-Actions. Typically, these are ones for which analysis is unable to render compartmentalised sequences of behaviour, for example Decide. In these cases the decompositional approach models task behaviour using collections of production rules, called a Strategy List.

The Object definitions represent the objects of the TKS taxonomic sub-structure. Figure 6 shows the example of a Message Object. Objects are represented as frames, in which their structure is defined as Information Tokens that assume particular parameters (values). Thus a Message has a location, envelope, computer etc., and various information sources, Long Term Memory, Contact List etc., that may be used to obtain values for its other information tokens. One of the merits of adopting a frame representation lies in the notion of 'default values.' Many of the information tokens that define an Object may assume meaningful defaults. For example, a person normally (by default) sends a message from themselves; hence Message:header:from will have 'Self' as a default value. The default values are identified in the TKS. This notion of default values is important when considering design. We shall return to it later.

The next stage requires the designer to define the user/program allocation of the system. This is modelled by the Specific Task Model (STM) in the decomposition method. The STM is shown in figure 7, it

General Goal Frame, Arrange

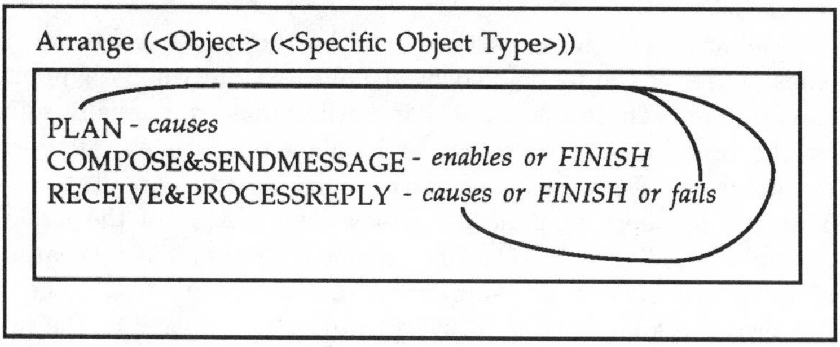

Arrange (<Object> (<Specific Object Type>))

PLAN - *causes*
COMPOSE&SENDMESSAGE - *enables or FINISH*
RECEIVE&PROCESSREPLY - *causes or FINISH or fails*

Instrumental Goal Frame, PLAN

PLAN (<Object> (<Specific Object Type>))

Consult (LOC, ITs, <Object>)- *enables*
Complete (<Object>, ISs)- *enables*
Decide (ITs)

Macro-Action, Consult, decomposed into Micro-Actions

Consult (LOC, ITs, <Object>)
  identify (LOC, ITs, <Object>)- *enables*
  search (LOC, ITs) - *causes*
  retrieve (LOC, ITs)- *enables*
  storeIn (ITs, <Object>, LOC)

Object, Message

Message
location: envelope|computer|person|otherPeople
     |notePaper
informationSource: LongTermMemory, ContactList,
                Diary, Reply,
                PreviousCorrespondence
header: <from: <Self> address: <SelfAddress>
     to: date: <Today> re: >
body: <dictated by current goal>
footer : <signature>

Figure 6. The GTM for the 'arrange a meeting' task

maintains the structure of the GTM but adds detail about the allocation of user/program functions.

This allocation is shown in the model by the use of different typeface. Those parts of the model shown in bold text are wholly supported by the program. Those that appear in outline text are partially supported by the program and those shown in plain text are not supported by the program. The concept of partial support comes about it two ways. The first is inherent in the decompositional nature of the model. For example (see figure 7) 'Consult' is partially supported because some of its Micro-Actions are supported and others are not. The second concerns the kind of support given in terms of objects at the interface and actions performed upon them. For example (see figure 7) 'search' is partially supported because it may occur in different contexts: in the context of Consult (ContactList, Message:to, Message) it is recommended in the STM that the interface support the user in performing search (ContactList, Message:to, Message), since the system has been designed to contain a representation of Message Objects, which includes a ContactList. However, in the context of Consult (LongTermMemory, Message:header:re, Message) a design decision has been made not to provide support for the user to perform search (LongTermMemory, Message:header:re, Message). Thus actions may be partially supported in that the support depends on the kind of objects that are supported at the interface.

The final stage is to model the interface and how it supports interaction. This is achieved by the Specific Interface Model (SIM) which is shown in figure 8. The same conventions of typeface are adopted here as in the STM. The SIM maintains the structure of the GTM and STM but adds the definition of interface objects, and shows how task performance proceeds at the interface by showing the actions of both user and program on these objects.

Figure 8a. is a summary representation of the STM, without the relations between components, and without the decomposition of Macro-Actions. The decomposition of Macro-Actions is shown in figures 8b. and 8c. Figure 8b. shows the decomposition of the Macro-Actions from the IGF, COMPOSE&SENDMESSAGE. Note that the SIM does not show any decomposition for those Macro-Actions which the STM has shown as unsupported at the interface, in this case the Macro-Action, Select. The decomposition of each Macro-Action is enclosed in a dashed-line box. Any necessary steps in the interaction that do not map directly onto a Micro-Action are shown in a solid-line box. The interpretation of figure 8b. is as follows. The user first accesses the application, which is part of the Macro-Action, Execute then displays the appropriate Message Object (e.g., memo, telephone message, reply etc.), which is part of

PLAN (<Object> (<Specific Object Type>)) - *causes*
COMPOSE&SENDMESSAGE (<Object> (<Specific Object
                           Type>)) - *enables or FINISH*
  Consult (ISs, ITs, Message) - *enables*
    identify (ISs, ITs, Message) - *enables*
    search (ISs, ITs, Message) - *causes*
    retrieve (ISs, ITs, Message) - *enables*
    storeIn (ITs, Message, computer)
  Select (Medium, Message) - *enables*
    identify (LOC, Constraints, Message) - *enables*
    choose (Medium, Constraints)
  Complete (Message, ISs) - *enables*
    fillIn (ITs, Message, ISs)
  Execute (TransactionRequirements, Message,
    Medium)
RECEIVE&PROCESSREPLY (<Object> (<Specific Object
                        Type>)) - *causes or FINISH or fails*
  Notice (Reply, Medium) - *enables*
  Execute (TransactionRequirements, Reply,
    Medium) - *enables*
  Consult (Reply, ITs, <Object>) - *enables*
    search (Reply, ITs, <Object>) - *causes*
    retrieve (Reply, ITs, <Object>) - *enables*
    storeIn (ITs, <Object>, LOC)
  Complete (<Object>, Reply) - *causes*
    fillIn (ITs, <Object>, Reply)
  Notice (NewInformation, Reply) - *causes*
  Record (ITs, NewInformation, Reply)
    establish (ITs, NewInformation, Reply) - *enables*
    fillIn (ITs, <Object>, NewInformation)

Figure 7. The STM for the 'arrange a meeting' task

---

the Macro-Action, Complete. At this stage the program responds by filling all defaultable information tokens of the Message Object with their default value. This corresponds to the notion of defaulting referred to above, and, if performed in line with a user's conceptual model, will presumably save effort by performing part of the task automatically. In line with this reasoning the program next automatically displays all information sources for which there is an interface representation and which are pertinent to the particular type of Message Object that the user has chosen to interact with. This is part of the Macro-Action,

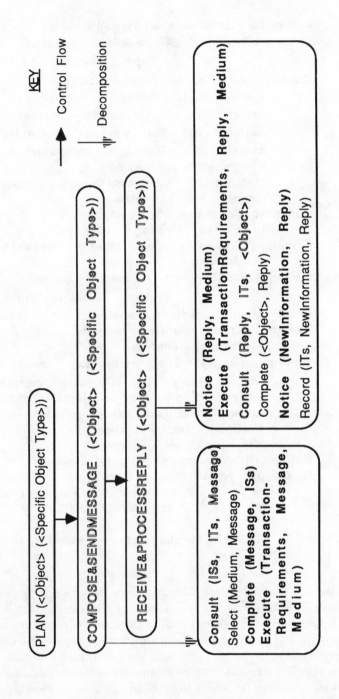

KEY

→ Control Flow

⫫ Decomposition

PLAN (<Object> (<Specific Object Type>))

COMPOSE&SENDMESSAGE (<Object> (<Specific Object Type>))

RECEIVE&PROCESSREPLY (<Object> (<Specific Object Type>))

Notice (Reply, Medium)
Execute (TransactionRequirements, Reply, Medium)
Consult (Reply, ITs, <Object>)
Complete (<Object>, Reply)
Notice (NewInformation, Reply)
Record (ITs, NewInformation, Reply)

Consult (ISs, ITs, Message)
Select (Medium, Message)
Complete (Message, ISs)
Execute (Transaction-Requirements, Message, Medium)

Figure 8a. The SIM for the 'arrange a meeting' task

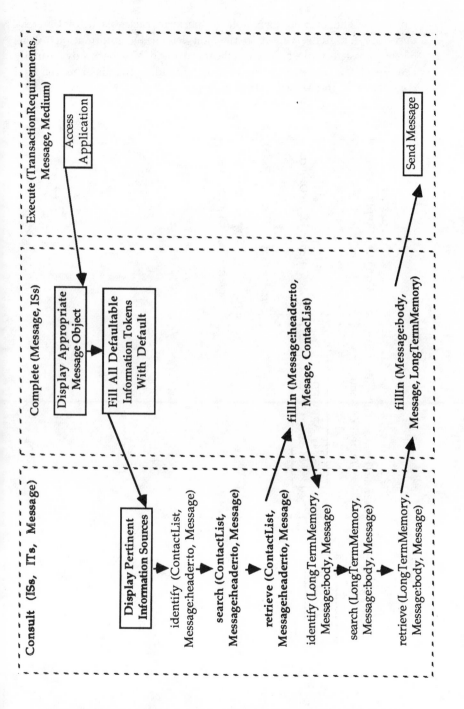

Figure 8b. The SIM for the 'arrange a meeting' task

Consult. The user is then able to perform those parts of the task necessary for giving values to the non-defaultable information tokens of the Message Object, Message:header:to and Message:body. Finally the user must complete the interaction by sending the message, the final component of the Macro-Action, Execute.

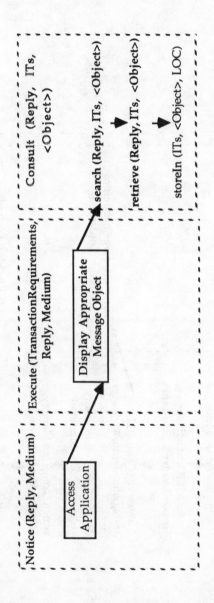

Figure 8c. The SIM for the 'arrange a meeting' task

Figure 8c. shows the decomposition of the Macro-Actions from the IGF, RECEIVE&PROCESSREPLY. Again the decomposition is only shown for those Macro-Actions which are wholly or partially supported in the STM. The interpretation is as follows. The user accesses the application in order to perform the Macro-Action, Notice. In order to perform the Macro-Action, Execute, the user must display the appropriate Message Object (i.e., the reply). Finally, to perform the Macro-Action, Consult, the user performs the associated Micro-Actions. Note that there is no representation in this example of the Macro-Action Notice (NewInformation, Reply). This is because that part of the decomposition of the IGF comes from an analysis of tasks more complex than the meeting arranging example, in which potentially many messages are exchanged between roles before the general goal is likely to be completed. The Macro-Action, Notice (NewInformation, Reply), reflects situations where a reply contains information pertinent to the current state of the recipient, for example comparing a reply that contains an alteration to information sent previously. Since a simple meeting arrangement is not likely to include such sequences of behaviour it has been omitted from the SIM in this example.

9. Summary

In this paper we have described a theory and method of modelling the knowledge people have of tasks and roles in a given domain. We then demonstrated how that model can be used as input to a design decomposition method which has its own form of modelling. The TKS model is rich in its representation of task knowledge but weak with respect to its design decomposition. It provides an information source to which designers can be given access. It prevents the designer having to rely on their own intuitions about people and their tasks and provides a methodological approach to identifying and modelling task knowledge. The decompositional approach provides a method of applying the results of a TKS model to the design of a computer system by allowing the designer to consistently decompose the design adding detail at each stage of decomposition. Neither the TKS nor the decompositional model prevents the use of conventional software development methods, and the TKS can be used independently of the decompositional method.

Acknowledgements

The work reported here has resulted from research supported, in the case of the TKS by ICL URC funding and in the case of the decompositional method, by SERC/Alvey grant no. GR/D/75779MMI-122.

References

R Byrne [1977], "Planning Meals: Problem Solving on a Real Database," *Cognition* 5, 287–332.

S K Card, T P Moran & A Newell [1983], *The Psychology of Human-Computer Interaction*, Lawrence Erlbaum Associates, Hillsdale, New Jersey.

J A Galambos [1986], "Knowledge Structures for Common Activities," in *Knowledge Structures*, J A Galambos R P Abelson and J B Black, ed., Lawrence Erlbaum Associates, Hillsdale, New Jersey.

W R Garner [1974], *The Processing of Information and Structure*, Wiley, New York.

A C Graesser & L F Clark [1985], *Structures and Procedures of Implicit Knowledge*, Ablex, New Jersey.

T R G Green, R K E Bellamy & J M Parker [1987], "Parsing and Gnisrap: A Model of Device Use," in *INTERACT '87 – The Second IFIP Conference on Human-Computer Interaction*, H J Bullinger and B Shackel, ed., Elsevier Science Publishers B.V., North Holland.

P Johnson, D Diaper & J Long [1984], "Tasks, Skills and Knowledge: Task Analysis for Knowledge Based Descriptions," in *INTERACT '84 – First IFIP Conference on Human-Computer Interaction*, B Shackel, ed., Elsevier-Science, Amsterdam.

P Johnson, H Johnson & A Russell [1988], "Collecting and Generalising Knowledge Descriptions from Task Analysis Data," *ICL Technical Journal*, In press.

M Keane & P Johnson [1987], "Preliminary Analysis for Design," in *People and Computers III*, D Diaper and R Winder, ed., Cambridge University Press, Cambridge.

D Kieras & P G Polson [1985], "An Approach to the Formal Analysis of User Complexity," *Int. J. Man-Machine Studies* 22, 365–394.

J Leddo & R P Abelson [1986], "The Nature of Explanations," in *Knowledge Structures*, J A Galambos R P Abelson and J B Black, ed., Lawrence Erlbaum Associates, Hillsdale, New Jersey.

S J Payne & T R G Green [1986], "Task-Action Grammars: A Model of the Mental Representation of Task Languages," *Human Computer Interaction* 2, 93–133.

E Rosch [1985], "Prototype Classification and Logical Classification: The Two Systems," in *New Trends in Conceptual Representation: Challenges to Piaget's Theory?*, E K Scholnick, ed., Lawrence Erlbaum Associates, Hillsdale, New Jersey.

E Rosch, C Mervis, W Gray, D Johnson & P Boyes-Braem [1976], "Basic Objects in Natural Categories," *Cognitive Psychology* 8, 382–439.

R C Schank [1982], *Dynamic Memory: A Theory of Reminding and Learning in Computers and People*, Cambridge University Press, New York.

Appendix A. The Full GTM for the 'arrange a meeting' Task

General Goal Frame

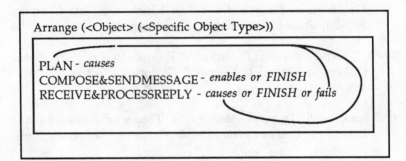

Instrumental Goal Frames

PLAN (<Object> (<Specific Object Type>))

Consult (LOC, ITs, <Object>)- *enables*
Complete (<Object>, ISs)- *enables*
Decide (ITs)

COMPOSE&SENDMESSAGE (<Object> (<Specific Object Type>))

Consult (ISs, ITs, Message)- *enables*
Select (Medium, Message)- *enables*
Complete (Message, ISs)- *enables*
Execute (TransactionRequirements, Message, Medium)

RECEIVE&PROCESSREPLY (<Object> (<Specific Object Type>))

Notice (Reply, Medium)- *enables*
Execute (TransactionRequirements, Reply, Medium)- *enables*
Consult (Reply, ITs, <Object>)- *enables*
Complete (<Object>, Reply)- *causes*
Notice (NewInformation, Reply)- *causes*
Record (ITs, NewInformation, Reply)

Abstract, Generic Models of Interactive Systems

Alan Dix

Human-Computer Interaction Group and Department of Computer Science, University of York, York YO1 5DD, U.K.

For several years at York, we have been investigating the use of abstract models in the design of interactive systems. I will describe why we originally pursued this line and the benefits that have ensued. I will only briefly describe specific models as examples where appropriate. There is an underlying assumption that formal methods are being used during the software design process, but the analysis proves useful even when this is not the case.

Keywords: formal methods, design principles, requirements capture

1. Introduction

Since 1984, the HCI group at York have been investigating the role of formal methods in interactive systems design. This paper reviews a significant strand of this research, the use of abstract models in the design process. These are formal models which are both generic (they describe a whole class of systems) and abstract (they only describe what is necessary), and have been used extensively to define principles of usability. Specific abstract models have been described at previous HCI conferences (Dix [1987a]; Dix & Harrison [1986]; Dix & Runciman [1985]) and elsewhere (Dix & Harrison [1987]; Dix, Harrison & Miranda [1986]; Dix et al. [1987]).

This paper will not describe any particular model but instead it will give some of the rationale behind the use of abstract models, give an overview of different models developed and describe some of the benefits of this approach in the design of a specific application.

1.1. Formal methods

There has been a mounting interest in the use of formal methods in software design; that is in the precise mathematical description of the intended functionality of computer systems. This has been mainly in response to the *software crisis*, the demand for increasingly large and complex systems together with high costs for failure. Software designers may use formal methods directly when they produce a formal specification of a specific program. In addition they may make indirect use of formal methods, for instance when the features in the programming language used have been influenced by the formal study of language design.

The term formal methods is also applied within both software design and HCI to formal methodologies, where fixed steps and guidelines are given for achieving some part of design. However it is the former use of the term which is used in this paper.

1.2. Formal methods + interactive systems

There is a certain amount of culture shock when first bringing together the concepts of formal methods and interactive systems design. The former is largely perceived as dry and uninspiring in line with the popular image of mathematics. Interface design is on the other hand a more colourful and exciting affair. Smalltalk for instance is not so much a programming environment, as a popular culture. Also it is hard to reconcile the multi-facetedness of the user with the rigours of formal notations. Some of these problems are to do with misunderstandings of the nature of formalisms (although even I, a mathematician, find a lot of computer science formalism very dry). Also, arguably, the shock really occurred when living users met dry unemotional computers and has therefore been dealt with already. However, the gut reaction still exists and must be taken account of.

No matter how strong the reaction against it, there is clearly a necessity for a blending of formal specification and human factors of interactive systems. If systems are increasingly designed using formal methods, then the interface will *de facto* be also, and if the issue isn't addressed explicitly the methods used will not be to the advantage of the interface designer. Further, the sort of large critical system where the software crisis is most in evidence clearly need an effective interface to their complexity. The penalty for not including this interface in the formal standards will be increased accidents due to human error such as at Chernobyl and Three Mile Island, and the more powerful the magnifying effect of the control system the more damaging the possible effects.

The need for more formal design is seen also in more mundane software. Many of the problems in interactive systems are with awkward boundary cases and inconsistent behaviour. These are obvious targets for a formal approach.

2. The need for abstract models

2.1. Principled design

There are many principles for the design of interactive systems, some are very specific (e.g., 'error messages should be in red') and others cover more general properties (e.g., 'what you see is what you get'). Hansen (Hansen [1984]) talks about using user engineering principles in the design of a syntax directed editor, 'Emily', and Thimbleby and Bornat describe the use of principles in the design of the display editor 'ded' (Bornat & Thimbleby [1986]).

Thimbleby (Thimbleby [1984]) introduced the concept of *generative user engineering principles* (GUEPS). These principles have several properties:

- They apply to a large class of different systems. That is they are *generic.*
- They can be given both an informal *colloquial* statement and also a *formal* statement.
- They can be used to constrain the design of a given system. That is they *generate* the design.

The last requirement can be met at an informal level using the colloquial statement – as was the case with the development of ded. While not superceding this, it seems that at least some of the generative effect should be obtained using the formal statements. Other workers who have specified particular interactive systems have proved certain properties of their systems, by stating the properties they require in terms of the particular specification and then proving these as theorems (Sufrin [1982]). The same approach could be taken for GUEPS, however there are some problems.

- *Commitment* – The statement of the principles cannot be made until sufficient of the design has been completed to give an infrastructure over which they can be framed. This means that the principles cannot be used to drive this early part of the design process, which lays out the fundamental architecture, and hence may be crucial for the usability of the system.

- *Consistency* – Because the principles are framed in the context of a particular design, there is no guarantee that a given informal principle has been given equivalent formal statements in the different domains.

- *Conflict* – Expanding on the last point there is a conflict between the desire for *generic* principles and the requirement for *formal generative* principles.

Formal *abstract models* (also called *interaction models*) have been used to resolve this conflict. These do not represent a particular interactive systems, but instead model a whole class of systems. The principles required are given a formal statement using this abstract model. When a particular system is being designed, the abstract model can be mapped at a very early stage onto the design – or even refined into the first design. The principles defined over the abstract model can then be applied to the particular system.

We see that this tackles the problem of commitment because the principles are stated before the particular system is even conceived, and the problem of consistency because the principles are only stated once and then the same statement is applied to many systems.

2.2. Abstract models and requirements capture

Designing a system involves a translation from someone's (the client's) informal requirements to an implemented system. Once we are within the formal domain we can *in principle* verify the correctness of the system. For example, the compiler can be proved a correct transformer of source code to object and we can prove the correctness of the program with respect to the specification. Of course, what can not be proved correct is the relation between the informal requirements and the requirements as captured in the specification. This gulf between the informal requirements and their first formal statement is the *formality gap* (fig. 1).

For a DP application like a payroll, this may not be too much of a problem. The requirements are already in a semi-formal form (e.g., pay scales, tax laws) and they are inherently formalisable. The capture of HCI requirements is far more complex. Not only are they less formally

Requirements Capture

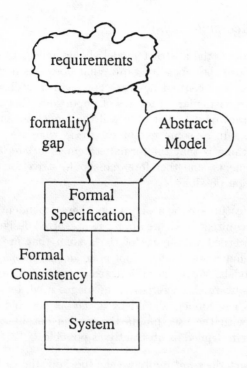

Figure 1. Abstract model bridges the formality gap.

understood to start with, but it is likely that they are fundamentally unformalisable. We are thus aiming to only formalise some aspect of a particular requirement and it is difficult to know if we have what we really want.

If the abstract model is designed well for a particular class of principles, it can bridge the formality gap. It is designed to described the user interface requirements, rather than a particular system. Thus although there is still a gap between it and the requirements, it is smaller. Yet it is a formal model, and thus the relationship between it and the specification of the full system can be verified formally. To achieve this aim, there must be a close correspondence of structure between the abstract model and the informal concepts. This principle of *structural correlation* is a recurrant theme both at this level and throughout the design process.

3. Form and use of abstract models

3.1. Surface philosophy

As we've noted, the abstract model should reflect the requirements in order to bridge the formality gap. What does this mean for interactive systems and user centred design? For particular classes of properties there will be particular structures of importance that must be reflected in the abstract model. Not only will the model depend on the domain of interest, but to some extent on those who use the model. The important thing is that the formal statement *obviously* corresponds to the requirements, and therefore one should strive for the most natural representation possible.

Not all the features of the abstract model are dependent on the particular principles required. If we are after a user centred design, then we should not be concerned with parts of the system that are not apparent to the user. That is we should adopt a *surface philosophy* when designing abstract models. We are not interested in the internal details of systems, such as hardware characteristics, languages used, or even specification notations! The models should be as far as possible *black box models* concerned with the user inputs the system outputs, and the relation between them defined as abstractly as possible.

This approach does *not* imply we can 'peel off' the surface and consider it as the interface, that is study the interface and the underlying func-tionality separately, quite the reverse. It is the whole functionality *as viewed* from the surface that is of interest. Consider a radio, the surface view of it is a set of knobs and a grill (with the speaker behind it). We might be tempted to just take the case, without the internal circuitry, and call this the interface. This does not do as a surface approach as the original radio and the stripped down version would have radically different behaviours when considered as black boxes: the former would work, the latter wouldn't!

Sometimes it may be necessary to break this black box slightly. Often the user may perceive some of the internal structure, and where this is relevant the model should reflect this user model. This may arise because the system is badly designed and you can 'see the bits between the pixels'. For instance, one may be aware of implementation details, such as recirculating buffers or event polling, by the way the system behaves, or even worse be presented with error messages such as 'stack overflow'! It may also occur in a more acceptable fashion. For instance, it is reasonable for the user to be aware of the filing system as a separate layer of abstraction within an operating system. Similarly, when moving the radio about to improve reception, it's useful to know there is a coil inside it that is being aligned.

All this corresponds to drawing the interface line slightly within the machine, looking through the glass of the VDU to the structures within. Sometimes it is appropriate to move the line in the opposite direction and consider the effective interface *within* the user. For instance, where the user has learnt some key-stroke sequence and the user's conceptual commands may correspond to several physical interactions. Similarly, a learner driver may consider operating the clutch and gear lever as separate actions whereas when experienced 'changing gear' is a single conceptual action. Ideally the system will be designed around the user's expected conceptual model, in addition the documentation will reveal the system model to the user. In this case the two directions of movement may be equivalent, the internal details and the user's conceptual model agreeing. This corresponds to one of the facets of direct manipulation described by Hutchins *et al* (Hutchins, Hollan & Norman [1986]). There is thus a strong dualism between models of systems, and models of users.

3.2. Applicability of formal methods to design

Thinking of formalism as the precisely written rules and formulae, what is its range of applicability for interface design? If we asked instead more definitely – "Will we be able to generate a precise definition of usability?" we could answer "NO" with little fear of contradiction. However, just where between being useless and essential formal methods lie is not obvious.

The use that is most obvious and most 'formal' for the abstract models and principles is as a *safety net*. We can see this if we look at the role of formalism in the design of a building. We have two putative designs, one a thatched cottage, and one a concrete block of flats:

Formal properties of building materials can tell us things like the thermal conductivity of thatch, whether a concrete lintel can bear the required weight, whether the structures are water-tight. This may be codified into formal requirements, either explicit like building regulations on insulation and drainage, or implicit – it mustn't fall down. The formal analysis doesn't tell us which is the best design. Even if we formalise more of the requirements for a particular context – How many people will live there? Are they scared of heights? We will still have an incomplete picture. It will not of course tell us that uPVC windows on the cottage would be barbaric and leaded pains on the flats plain silly. So the formalism of building design can tell us whether the building will fall down or leak, but not whether it will be beautiful or pleasant to live in.

Going back to interface design, by defining suitable principles we will be able to stop interfaces being fundamentally unusable, but not ensure that they *are* usable. So we can't make a bad interface good, but we can stop it being abysmal. The challenge of course is can we do this and also allow the good interface designer to be creative? In fact I have found that the uses of abstract models for principled design go way beyond being just a safety net. However even in that capacity only, the experience of other disciplines shows that they would still be worthwhile.

4. Examples of abstract models

We have developed various abstract models dealing with different aspects of interactive systems, these include:

- *General models* – (in particular the PiE model (Dix & Runciman [1985])) looking simply at the commands entered (e.g., keystrokes, mouse clicks) and the effects that arise. The effects can be left undifferentiated or divided into permanent *results* (e.g., print-out) and ephemeral *displays* (the actual screen image) (fig. 2). Principles of interaction include:

  Predictability – 'the gone away for a cup of tea' problem.

  Observability – Can I view the entire result via the display?

  Reachability – Can I do anything I want to?

  More recently these general models have been extended to allow expression of various *direct manipulation* properties (Dix & Harrison [1987]).

- *Windowed systems* – Here we have been interested in the problem of interference between windows (Dix & Harrison [1986]). Where different windows represent different tasks, the user wants to treat these as independent. That is, while there is only one user there are effectively several different personnae, one for each task (fig. 3). Hence a multi-windowed system is rather like a multi-user system, except without most of the protection mechanisms that operate between users. Interference between windows can therefore be very damaging and understanding and defining forms of sharing between windows is crucial.

- *Temporal models* (Dix [1987a]) – Real time interface issues, such as keyboard buffering and display strategies have been

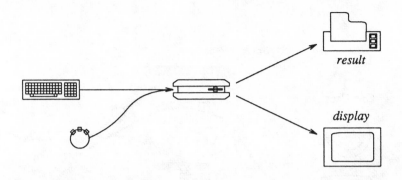

Figure 2. Simple red-PiE model.

considered. Mechanisms to ensure predictability even when the system response time is slow have been specified.

- *Pointers* (Dix [1987b]) – Both older cursor based systems and mouse based systems make use of the concept of pointers as the locus of interaction. These pointers have important properties: For example, we are using a text editor and mark a block starting in the 100th line. We then insert several lines before its start. Of course, we no longer expect the block to begin at the 100th line, but to have moved with the text. That is we are interested in *dynamic* or *semantic* pointers. These occur widely in interactive systems and often have strange idiosyncratic behaviour, frequently inconsistent within the same application. Models to express these which do 'open up' the black box slightly have been formulated, in particular to emphasise consistency and simplicity of different pointers.

- *Editing the view* (Dix [1987b]) – Often interaction is modelled linearly, the user's commands affect the system state, from which display feedback is generated. We have also considered models where the focus of attention is on the display, and the user's commands are seen as affecting the display directly, the internal state being changed in accordance. This leads to a different way of understanding the interface, in particular it focuses the designers attention on what should remain

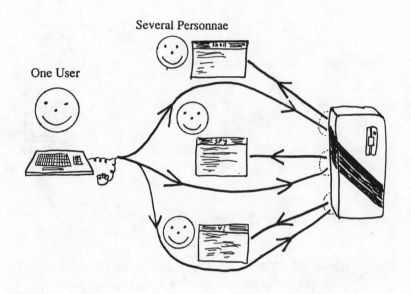

Figure 3.   Multiple windows – multiple personnae.

constant. For instance, if designing a new component on a CAD system, and the system runs out of room, it would be perfectly consistent with our view (the new component) to delete existing components in order to make room. This is clearly not acceptable, and no one would be likely to design such a system. However as the data base and the views of it become more complex it is not so easy to know what is or is not acceptable. Hence, for any view the user has of the system we must specify a complementary view that remains unchanged.

- *Non-determinism* (Dix [1987b]) – When considering various formal properties of the models above there arose the need to use non-deterministic models. For instance, in describing the interaction with one window ignoring the interleaved actions in other windows, the perceived effects will be non-deterministic if there is any interference. Considering this *for-*

mal non-determinism lead to an *informal* recognition of non-determinism as a real interface phenomenon, and prompted the analysis of many common interface problems in terms of the paradigm.

The different models cover different facets of interactive behaviour, so the principles formulated differ. There are some informal concepts that arise with slightly different formal statements in several models.

Predictability is one such concept. This was originally prompted by the desire to formalise the modiness of systems, but is far more wide ranging than that. Early statments over the general models were of the form: "if I've forgotten what I've already typed, can I work out what will happen next by looking at the screen alone". A frequent reason for forgetting exactly what has already been typed is going away for a cup of tea, and then returning some minutes (or hours!) later. Similarly when considering temporal models we wanted to express principles which allow the user to predict whether the system is in steady state, or is still responding to outstanding buffered keystrokes. Clearly only a small amount of information can be on the screen at once, and thus we also studied principles focused on the information, not currently displayed, but easily accessible.

Another related issue that arose repeatedly was *aliasing*. That is the *content* of an object does not unambiguously define its *identity*. For example, if I copy one file into another intending to edit the new file, I may accidentally edit the original file. Once in the editor the mistake will not be apparent unless the file name is displayed. Similar problems arise within a single file when two portions are similar. After encountering these problems within the general models, it was not surprising to meet them again when considering windowed systems. One finds that in order to maintain predictability each window must be distinguishable, and in general this means unique banners as the window contents may be similar. For instance, I frequently confuse windows communicating with two different computers.

5. Benefits of abstract models

When starting this work there were several expected benefits to using abstract models for principled design.

- Bridging the formality gap
- Generic statement of principles
- Constraining design
- Evaluation of systems

The first two of these refer more to the generation of models and principles and the later to the formal use of these. The first two have certainly been fulfilled by the models and principles we have used. We noted earlier that any principles produced would be necessary but not sufficient for good design, and hence the *formal* use in generation (and evaluation) would be limited to that of a safety net. The principles have been applied in that fashion to the design of small multi-window hypertext system, this consists of about 50 pages of formal specification and about 10,000 lines of code and is thus a reasonable test of the methods. A particular issue that arises when applying the abstract models is what level to apply them at. We discussed earlier that different users may perceive different conceptual interfaces, so task oriented knowledge about the users' models must be used when applying principles. Frequently the user group is heterogeneous and thus the same principle may be applied at several levels, e.g., keystroke level, command level, conceptual chunks of commands . . .

There have also been specific developments of the concept of abstract models by various researchers: Anderson (Anderson [1985]; Anderson [1986]) has developed the general models with the intention of easing the proof of properties, Sufrin (Sufrin [1987]) has expressed a variant of the models in 'Z', a widely used specification language, and Runciman and Toyn (Runciman & Toyn [1987]) have represented the PiE model in a functional programming framework to aid its use in rapid prototyping.

The abstract models and principles are also used in order to evaluate existing systems. For instance, not only do most systems fail the predictivity conditions for fully temporal systems, but many window managers and operating systems make it impossible to write conformant systems (Dix [1987a]). Further, Monk (Monk & Dix [1987]) has produced a notation based on the ideas of PiEs, which can be used by non-mathematical interface designers as an early paper and pencil method for evaluating and improving interface decisions.

There are additional uses of the principles beyond the formal ones.

- General understanding
  The models have lead to a general understanding of the concepts and principles involved. This clarification of concepts is an often stated advantage of formal methods which I thoroughly endorse. Often this general understanding has resulted not so much in the solving of problems, but in the better understanding of them, or in the discovery of problems otherwise unnoticed. This leads on to:
- Derivation of concepts
  Various concepts resulted from the formal analysis. For in-

stance, the recognition of interface non-determinism. All of these could be noted without formal analysis, but it is the formal analysis that forces them to attention. In addition diffuse vague notions became solidified, and this was the origin of concepts such as predictability, observability and reachability. The realisation of generality and far reachingness of these concepts was the direct result of formalising them. Further, they become well understood, not just as formal properties but at a much deeper intuitive level also.

- Informal application
  This semi-formal and informal understanding meant that the use of the models and principles went far beyond their strict domains and influenced other parts of the design at a semi-formal or informal level. The formalism of the method lead to advantages well beyond the limits of strict notational and mathematical formalism.

6. The limits of formalism?

So we have seen that the formalism has far exceeded the goals we set for it. We expected it to be convergent, defining precisely existing ideas and principles. In practice it has been more divergent than this suggesting new principles, opening up avenues and ideas. This is not as surprising as it seems. By its nature formalising one aspect leaves others ambiguous. This ambiguity being of course the generality. Mathematics is all about relationships, abstracting out the critical part of things, taking ideas from one domain and seeing similarities elsewhere. This is far from the dry view of formalism. From this perspective mathematics and poetry look like two sides of the same coin, and taking this analogy further, we could liken the complete system specification to an epic saga. The abstract model is of course a Haiku.

Acknowledgements

The work described in this paper was carried out under SERC/Alvey grant GR/D/02317, "Mechanisms for Specification, Implementation and Evaluation of Interactive Systems", by Michael Harrison, Colin Runciman, Harold Thimbleby, Andrew Monk, Nick Hammond, Paul Walsh, Eliot Miranda, Ian Toyn and myself. This paper was written whilst supported by a SERC Post-Doctoral Fellowship.

References

S O Anderson [1985], "Specification and Implementation of User Interfaces. Example: A File Browser," Heriot Watt University, Internal Report, Edinburgh.

S O Anderson [1986], "Proving Properties of Interactive Systems," in *People and Computers: Designing for Usability*, M D Harrison and A F Monk, ed., Cambridge University Press, Cambridge, 402–416.

R Bornat & H W Thimbleby [1986], "The Life and Times of DED, Display Editor," Department of Computer Science, University of York.

A J Dix [1987a], "The Myth of the Infinitely Fast Machine," in *People and Computers III*, D Diaper and R Winder, ed., Cambridge University Press, Cambridge, 215–228.

A J Dix [1987b], "Formal Methods and Interactive Systems: Principles and Practice," Department of Computer Science, University of York, DPhil Thesis.

A J Dix & M D Harrison [1986], "Principles and Interaction Models for Window Managers," in *People and Computers: Designing for Usability*, M D Harrison and A F Monk, ed., Cambridge University Press, Cambridge, 352–366.

A J Dix & M D Harrison [1987], "Formalising Models of Interaction in the Design of a Display Editor," in *INTERACT '87 – The Second IFIP Conference on Human-Computer Interaction*, H J Bullinger and B Shackel, ed., Elsevier Science Publishers B.V., North Holland, 409–414.

A J Dix, M D Harrison & E E Miranda [1986], "Using Principles to Design Features of a Small Programming Environment," in *Software Engineering Environments*, I Sommerville, ed., Peter Peregrinus, 135–150.

A J Dix, M D Harrison, C Runciman & H W Thimbleby [1987], "Interaction Models and the Principled Design of Interactive Systems," in *Proceedings of the European Software Engineering Conference*, 127–135.

A J Dix & C Runciman [1985], "Abstract Models of Interactive Systems," in *People and Computers: Designing the Interface*, P Johnson and S Cook, ed., Cambridge University Press, Cambridge, 13–22.

W J Hansen [1984], "User Engineering Principles for Interactive Design," in *Interactive Programming Environments*, D R Barstow H E Shrobe and E Sandewall, ed., McGraw-Hill, 217–231.

E L Hutchins, J D Hollan & D A Norman [1986], "Direct Manipulation Interfaces," in *User Centered System Design*, D A Norman and S W Draper, ed., Lawrence Erlbaum Associates, Hillsdale, New Jersey, 87–124.

A Monk & A J Dix [1987], "Refining Early Design Decisions with a Black-Box Model," in *People and Computers III*, D Diaper and R Winder, ed., Cambridge University Press, Cambridge, 147–158.

C Runciman & I Toyn [1987], "Transformational Development of Purely Functional Prototypes from PiE Interaction Models," Department of Computer Science, University of York.

B Sufrin [1982], "Formal Specification of a Display-Oriented Text Editor," *Science of Computer Programming* 1, 157–202.

B Sufrin [1987], "A Formal Framework for Classifying Interactive Information Systems," in *IEE Colloquium – Formal Methods and Human-Computer Interaction*, IEE, Savoy Place, London.

H W Thimbleby [1984], "Generative User-Engineering Principles for User Interface Design," in *INTERACT '84 – First IFIP Conference on Human-Computer Interaction*, B Shackel, ed., Elsevier-Science, Amsterdam, 102–107.

Analysing the Scope of Cognitive Models in Human-Computer Interaction: A Trade-Off Approach

Tony Simon

MRC Applied Psychology Unit, 15 Chaucer Road., Cambridge CB2 2EF, U.K.

One of the main contributions of Cognitive Science to HCI has been the development of predictive models of user behaviour. However, such models are necessarily limited in the scope of predictions they can make; their strengths usually being determined on the basis of pragmatic trade-offs. At present, no rational taxonomy of the different types of model exists. Thus, would be user-modellers find little guidance about which model is most likely to deliver the kind of predictions in which they are interested. Even less available is information about what will not be delivered when employing any given model. This paper presents a representation of the space of some user-models in HCI which reveals their scope by making explicit such trade-offs.

Keywords: User-Modelling, Cognitive Science

1. Introduction

There now exists, within the Cognitive Sciences, a group of workers who describe the activities they engage in as the study of Human Computer Interaction (HCI). This comprises research into many aspects of the design and evaluation, as well as the actual building, of interfaces. These interfaces are developed for the purpose of facilitating communication between human users and a vast range of computational devices that those users will wish to put to an equally vast range of uses.

The main goal within this field is to understand how to design interfaces so that they are maximally efficient at facilitating the tasks that the users want done, whilst being minimally demanding on the user's cognitive resources. There are, of course, many ways in which the attainment of these goals is sought. One way, most common in the Computer Science and Software Engineering worlds, is to opt for iterative design where one tries to prove the system by building and testing a series of prototypes.

A second and less established approach, originating from the Cognitive Sciences, is to attempt to develop 'User Models'. Here, given some level of specification of design and task(s), the model will produce predictions about some aspects of behaviour that the user will exhibit when engaged in the envisaged interaction. This, not surprisingly, is where the problems begin. Once one introduces the complexity of the human cognitive and physical systems and then tries to estimate the effect of their interaction with some (more or less) pragmatically designed device, the resulting predictions will necessarily be of limited breadth and depth in coverage. These shortcomings stem largely from the confines of current formal understanding of the human machine. More tangibly though, since any model can only ever hope to account for a part of the massive complexity of human behaviour in any context, the diverse approaches that exist are the result of pragmatic decisions about what function any model that is to be developed will serve (e.g., to provide a mechanism for predicting execution time). The resulting state is that any would-be user of cognitive models faces a confusing array of partial tools when considering which approach to adopt.

An important set of assumptions underlying cognitive HCI models holds that a) there is some representation by the user of the device and task space, that b) some kinds of actions are carried out on this representation to transform it, and that c) there is some method of control within this system (Barnard, personal communication). From such a system as this, one can assume, flows the actual observable behaviour exhibited by the user in the interactive exchange. The actual choices about what aspects of the representation, actions and control scheme are included in any model are critical in determining the scope and focus of the resulting instrument.

It is my contention that, for the purpose of identifying a suitable user-model for HCI analysis it is these decisions that should be focussed upon. Other existing distinctions operate at too coarse a grain, only really sorting models into one class or another rather than identifying their strengths and weaknesses. One such common distinction (e.g., Green, Schiele and Payne (Green, Schiele & Payne [1987])) separates models on the basis of whether they are of the competence or performance type. Competence models tend to be ones that can predict legal behaviour sequences but generally do this without reference to whether they could actually be executed by users. In contrast, performance models not only describe what the necessary behaviour sequences are but usually describe both what the user needs to know and how this is employed in actual task execution.

Alternatively, models have been separated on the basis of whether they best represent routine, skilled behaviour based on large amounts of knowledge or practice, or whether they focus on deliberative, problem solving more typical of the novice user. Clearly, these distinctions have been found to be effective and useful in many ways. What they appear not to be able to do is to inform the potential user-modeller about which kinds of behaviour any one model will be best at predicting and which it cannot. This paper seeks to find a way to make that choice more informed by adopting a different analysis of the space of cognitive HCI models than is usually to be found.

2. The Trade-Off Approach

The proposal here is to try to make explicit precisely those trade-offs that appear to have been used by the originators of each model when deciding which aspects of the user (and, to some extent, the task) to focus on and to try to predict. By doing so, the space of models can be laid out in a way that allows the prospective modeller to see what the primary function is that any model claims to have by looking at the kind of predictions it can deliver. Equally important, it also makes clear what kinds of behavioural analysis one is sacrificing when choosing to employ any one particular approach. In this way it should be possible not only to identify a desirable modelling approach for a given problem, but also to be able to give some idea as to the scope of that approach.

Figure 1 is a first attempt to describe the space of models in this way. The models depicted in the figure do not represent an exhaustive survey of all models that have been developed to predict the behaviour of users when interacting with computers or other complex machines. Rather, the attempt has been to place at least one model that exemplifies each of the main *styles* of cognitive HCI models that have been developed. This paper is an attempt at presenting a methodology for analysing models and not a commitment to any one form of analysis.

When interpreting the diagram the first thing to understand is that the shading of the different models represents the functions for which they were developed, or the outputs they can produce, and these can be seen on the key. In other words these most probably reflect the explicit decisions that were made (such as to develop a calculational model to predict execution time) while the required trade-offs remained implicit. The horizontal and vertical axes refer to the **representation** that is employed within the model. In other words, the axes reflect the commitments to the kind of processing that a model carries out and the nature of the 'data' it manipulates. Each pair of axes in the horizontal and vertical planes illustrates a **trade-off** where, strengthening any one aspect of a representation within a model will necessarily weaken the degree of representation of its complementary characteristic.

So, taking the vertical axis first, this illustrates, for the models included, that representing behaviour in some kind of idealised way is done at the cost of saying very little qualitative about the mental operations involved in the generation of the behaviour that would be predicted. The *Degree of Idealisation* refers to whether the representation of behaviour is fixed and inflexible or whether it has some degree of variability or adaptability built into it. Models higher up have less to say about variability (which may include errorfulness) of behaviour than models lower down. The *Qualitative Representation of Processing* dimension tells us how able any model is to specify what actual mental operations the user will engage in when processing mental data. Models placed nearer the top of the diagram have weaker representations than models nearer the bottom so the lower models are more likely to tell us about which mental operations the user is carrying out whilst the higher ones, if representing cognitive processes at all, are more likely to tell us how many operations are carried out or required.

In a similar fashion, the horizontal axis highlights a trade-off. In this case the more models concentrate on enumerating the data that are mentally manipulated, the less able they are to show what knowledge the user brings into play in the generation of the actual resulting behaviour. The first of the properties addressed concerns how *Parameterised* the mental representation is. Generally, this refers to the extent to which a model represents the user's mental representation in terms of some numerical value. These can be seen as parameters since they set constraints on obeserved behaviour by setting values such as the capacity and decay rate of memories or the latencies of effector actions. The more strongly

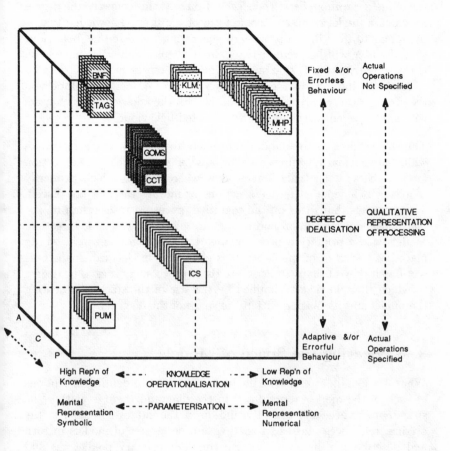

Figure 1. A trade-off space of user-models

parameterised models are further to the right of the diagram. Moving in the opposite direction illustrates an increase in the degree to which the model *Operationalises Knowledge*. Roughly, this concerns the degree to which a model represents some form of the user's knowledge that is brought into play in the process of generating the resultant behaviour that the user will be predicted to exhibit. This means that models on the weaker (rightward) side on this dimension represent mental data by re-casting it into an abstract form such as items in memory. Models on the stronger (leftward) side, however, lay out the knowledge which users will employ when carrying out task-oriented behaviour.

The third dimension of the diagram refers to the *Processing Resources* which are primarily represented by any of the models. The section farthest back along that dimension is where models which primarily represent behaviour in terms of actions or motor processes are placed. Those models that focus on the cognitive processes, rather than on the mechanisms of perception and action, are placed in the middle section. Models whose primary concern relates to perception and sensation are placed at the front of the cube. It is clear that models can span these sections if they attempt to integrate these processing types. The degree to which they do that is signified by the size of the stack representing the model and its placing within the space of the diagram.

3. Navigating the Space of Models

What I will not attempt to do here is to give in-depth descriptions of each of the models represented in the diagram; there is neither the space nor the necessity since I would direct the interested reader to the original references. Instead I shall take each cluster of models in turn and describe the members in terms of their primary predictions and representational trade-offs.

The first group of models, placed in the top right of the diagram, function by producing some kind of predictions about how long it will take the user to carry out a given task or tasks.

The **Model Human Processor** (MHP) approach of Card, Moran and Newell (Card, Moran & Newell [1983]) allows the modeller to make general predictions mainly about the time it will take to carry out tasks. The primary means by which it is able to do this is by adopting a strongly parameterised representation. As well as a set of 'operating principles' for the human cognitive system, the MHP gives parameters for the capacity and speed of its constituent cognitive, perceptual and motor processors and their associated stores. The analyst generates time predictions by analyzing a task into the constituent operations executed by the three subsystems and, from there, calculates how long the task will take and how much processing is involved. Furthermore, this can be done within three bands of performance, called *fastman*, *slowman* and *middleman*, thus allowing predictions at least at the central and extreme points along the behavioural continuum.

The strength of such an approach is that it provides a common processing 'architecture' within which a whole class of psychological phenomena can be expressed. One clear advantage of this is that one acquires a common language for characterising a wide range of behavioural data that were previously hard to relate to one another. More importantly, this practice of casting a range of phenomena into a single architecture provides a set of constraints that set theoretically motivated limits on how such behaviours can be described. This stands in contrast to the familiar proliferation of descriptions developed to account for different psychological observations.

One limitation of the MHP is that, in order to achieve its degree of parameterisation, the behaviour that is dealt with must be highly idealised in nature. This is largely due to the fact that since practically no knowledge can be operationalised at this level of parameterisation there is no capacity to deal with flexibility of behaviour or errors. This is clearly a drawback, especially in the light of Landauer's (Landauer [1987]) calculation that, in a recently published experiment on expert text-editing, 35% of the expert's time and 80% of the variability in time was accounted for by errors.

The MHP also sacrifices representing the nature of processing by its adoption of such a strongly parameterised stance. So, while it can claim some contact with all three areas on the resource dimension by merit of containing perceptual, cognitive and motor subsystems, their representation is extremely weak and so therefore the contact with actual behaviour along that dimension is little more than tenuous. The MHP is is a strong candidate for 'count' predictions but potential users must be clear that it is limited to that kind of prediction alone.

If one is less interested in a general calculation system and has a clear aim to obtain a time prediction for a known decomposition of mental, motor, perceptual and system steps then one can employ the **Keystroke Level Model** (KLM) of Card, Moran and Newell (Card, Moran & Newell [1983]). The KLM is really a special case of the GOMS family of models, to be discussed later. By inputting a known sequence of operators, estimates of execution time can be produced. This is achieved in the same way as the MHP and, while this brings all the attendant limitations, it must be remembered that the primary functions of the model are the prediction of execution time and of which of a set of alternative methods is optimal.

The KLM representation does have some representation of cognition but this is only in the form of a generic mental operator whose content remains minimal. It primarily represents action, with a small set of physical-motor operators such as 'keystroking' or 'pointing' for text editing. The model need not operationalise knowledge since it concentrates on predicting execution time from a sequence of supplied operations. In fact it turns out that the KLM, initially developed as a 'control' case for the more fine grained GOMS models, seems equally effective at doing the same job but without the extra knowledge involved (Card, Moran & Newell [1983]). Nevertheless, the KLM does offer some range of prediction by supplying a choice of keystroking parameters for novices through experts.

Of course, we may have decided that predictions in terms of time are not our primary interest. The following cluster of models concentrate on producing predictions about some aspect of the complexity of user-system interaction. There are two types that I shall call Grammar models and Expert models. They both afford the generation of complexity metrics by operationalising knowledge to create a primary output, usually a sequence of operations. From there, complexity measures can be calculated from the results of the original transformational process.

Grammar models concentrate on the operationalising of knowledge since they are competence models and this is their primary representational device. They are based on the notion of generative grammars, well known in linguistics, whereby it is possible to generate all and only the legal sentences of a given language. In an HCI application these 'sentences' would correspond to sequences of actions, and the language would be the command language of the interface or some interpretation of it.

The device by which the analyst arrives at predictions of actions executed by the user is a set of rules, given in the grammar, that rewrite commands or 'tasks' (c.f., TAG) into user-executable actions. In other words, given a particular 'task' such as **delete a word** the rewrite rule(s) will translate this into a sequence of actions. Thus, although there is an implied reference to performance, nothing is made explicit about the nature of the processing that allows the user to arrive at these actions. As such these models can only represent highly idealised behaviour because the mappings between commands or tasks and the required actions are fixed and so are not only always correct but also never vary and so cannot deal with flexibility of behaviour.

Two such models are represented within the space here. **Reisner's BNF Grammar** (Reisner [1981]) was the earliest and adapted the Backus-Naur notation in order to obtain measures of complexity of an interface, mainly by counting the number of rules required to produce the necessary actions. The enterprise was quite successful in as far as it went but as Green, Schiele and Payne (Green, Schiele & Payne [1987]) point out, Reisner's grammar was both limited in its power and doubtful in its psychological validity.

The most sophisticated example of this type of model is Payne's **Task-Action Grammar** (TAG) (Payne & Green [1986]) which exhibits two main advances over other grammar models. The first is that the representation of what gets rewritten into actions is shifted from actual machine commands to simple 'Tasks' that the analyst assumes to be perceived by the user. This gives the model a little contact with a cognitive representation affording greater ability to translate real meaningful subtasks into actions. The second, which is to some extent afforded by this representational shift, is the alignment between semantic and syntactic aspects of the interface language. This derives from analysing the user's assumed understanding of the relationship between the tasks to be carried out and the commands required to effect these. What results is that predictions about ease of use and learnability based on measures of *consistency* within the interface language can be made. As with the Reisner model, simple complexity measures can be derived by counting the number of rules required to rewrite tasks into actions.

We have seen that the grammar models predict complexity and consistency mainly of machine, as opposed to user, functions. This is because they focus on the action end of the resource dimension and also because they cannot reflect upon the nature of processing. The expert models operate in a similar way but they operationalise knowledge based on a representation of cognitive functions. This is because the nature of processing aspect is strengthened and, while idealisation is still high in that errors cannot be handled, there is at least some element of flexibility in the user's responses to task demands. These models aim to tell us what is going on 'inside the head' of experts on say, text editing, but by restricting their focus cannot tell us where performance might fail due, for example, to memory overload.

The **GOMS** family of models (Card, Moran & Newell [1983]) are probably the best known and most used of current cognitive HCI models. GOMS stands for Goals, Operators, Methods and Selection rules and it is sequences of these four things that are produced to represent the user's behaviour when analysing a given task within this model. As already mentioned, GOMS models deal with error-free behaviour and so what one is basically able to achieve is a prediction about which Methods (compiled sequences of Goals and Operators) any individual user will select for any given task. This can be done at many levels of 'grain size', from the 'unit task' (separate sub-tasks of the job) to the 'keystroke' level. In any event, by inputting any given task, a GOMS model will enable a full decomposition into a sequence of operations. This, of course, does allow the calculation of execution time given that mental operations can be given a parameter of execution and varying keystroking rates can be used for physical operations. Primarily though, measures of complexity are derived from the number of operations that are used, or methods that are available and must be selected from during task performance.

Cognitive Complexity Theory (CCT) (Kieras & Polson [1985]) inherits a great many of the characteristics of GOMS (it is in fact an attempt to implement a sort of dynamic 'GOMS interpreter') but adds some elaborations. Here, the user's 'how to do it' knowledge is cast as a set of productions. Furthermore, there is a representation of the device in the form of a Generalised Transition Network (GTN). In most other respects CCT is like a GOMS model. Complexity metrics exist here in the form of the depth of the goal stack or the number of rules used during a run. In this way measures relating to learnability and transfer to other systems can be calculated in a similar way to that of the grammar models but, since GOMS and CCT are focussed on cognitive resources their delivered predictions are different in content.

The final group is very different from the above models which try to deliver approximations of the interactions they wish to predict. The following models instead attempt to build models of the user's cognitive system by adopting strong representations of the nature of processing coupled with relatively high levels of knowledge operationalisation. These are seen as integrated models, either by nature of an in-depth representation of a large part of user-cognition for example, or by an approximate description of a comprehensive coverage of the processing resources of the user. The first type contrast with more usual cognitive models that only focus on a limited range of cognitive phenomena. The second type contrast by virtue of concentrating on an increased range of behaviour from that which cognitive models usually exhibit whilst attempting to account for more qualitative aspects of the processing than models such as the MHP, for example. The aim of both types of model is to deliver predictions of how the constraints of users' processing systems will affect their ability to carry out given tasks. Examples given below involve models that are under development and, as a result, the capabilities and characteristics discussed are not firmly 'in place' as is the case with features of those models covered above.

An example of the broader, more approximate model is the **Interacting Cognitive Subsystems** (ICS) model (Barnard [1987]). This is being developed to elaborate on the job that the MHP model does; that is to produce substantive qualitative behavioural predictions on the basis of a similarly quantitative analysis. This is difficult for MHP to do because, although it can claim to have some contact with all three resources, its representation of the nature of the processing carried out by those subsystems is minimal. In contrast, ICS represents the nature of processing more strongly and in a less parameterised fashion. It is able, therefore, to capture wider variations in behaviour due to performative factors, including some classes of errors. As a result, the interaction between cognitive resources available to the user and those required by the task should be more adequately covered by ICS than MHP, for example.

The **Programmable User Model** (PUM) approach (Young & Green []) is the least developed of all .those to be discussed here. This approach aims to provide the interface designer with a programmable or instructable 'cognitive architecture' which represents the invariants of the cognitive system of a certain class of computer users. The designer's job is to instruct the PUM about the how to use the embryonic interface design by providing a knowledge analysis which will include the methods required and the particular forms of knowledge (or pointers to general knowledge) that are necessary. The PUM would then simulate a user attempting to carry out tasks with the proposed interface. Its prediction will be the behaviour itself and, since its representation is not parameterised or idealised, it is not intended to directly deliver 'counts' of time or effort or estimates of complexity. It will be up to the designer to attempt to correct any aspects of the interface that are seen to cause problems in the predicted interaction.

As such, a PUM requires the strongest representation of the nature of processing, in its area of application, of all of the models discussed so far. Equally important is the necessity for a strong operationalisation of knowledge since this is how the model (in the form of a production system) will be able to simulate the predicted user behaviour on a given task specification. PUM primarily represents the cognitive system of the user and as such is located in the cognitive area of the resource dimension.

These last two models are the least idealised, least parameterised and most explicitly behavioural of all those seen to date. They attempt to get their predictive power from being explicit about the representation of the user's cognitive system so that task behaviour can be predicted as fully as possible. They are also motivated, like the MHP, by the notion of providing a unified architecture to provide a constrained framework for the expression of a wide range of behavioural phenomena. It may, therefore seem that these two last models are the ideal ones to use for predicting user behaviour. While, it is true that much of the current research effort is heading in the direction of constructing this style of

model, I do not wish to give the impression that these are the only
types of models that analysts should consider using. There are two
main reasons for this.

The first is that not all analysts will always (or ever) be interested in
predictions of user behaviour in its entirety. There may well be occasions
when predictions of execution time are totally sufficient, or when the
consistency of a command set is to be investigated. As such there
is no way that anything can be objectively said about which models
represented here are *better* than any other; they are all designed to do
different jobs. The aim of the present exercise is to try to make clear
what job it is that they claim to be able to do and which jobs, as a
consequence, they will *not* be able to do. The second point involves a
further trade-off, not represented on the diagram, which I shall call the
input/output trade-off.

4. The Input/Output Trade-off

This final trade-off is of a rather different nature to those already
mentioned since it is really only able to tell us something about the
amount of information that it is possible to glean from employing any
one model in relation to how much effort must be put into its use.

The use of any of these models requires the analyst to engage in some
amount of **task analysis**. In other words, the user of the model will
have to have a clear understanding of such things as what tasks any user
of an interface might attempt and how these will be carried out (maybe
both at the interface and in the user's mind); in some cases analysts may
have to put in a lot more work than is justified by what the model can
deliver. Task analysis can be carried in two ways, *Task space analysis*
and *Task instance analysis* (Card & Young [1984]). Task space analysis
requires the analyst to understand the whole range of tasks that the a
user might attempt to carry out on the given interface. Task instance
analysis requires such understanding of only one task. Clearly task space
analysis is going to require considerably more work yet once it is fed into
a model that model can be used again and again to predict behaviour
on a whole range of tasks or even users. If task instance analysis itself
requires a significant amount of work then it may turn out that, for
repeated use on different tasks, models requiring this kind of analysis
turn out to be sub-optimal.

The Model Human Processor is meant to be the most instantly usable
and least effortful cognitive HCI model, requiring only simple task
instance analyses. In practice the MHP proves harder to use than that
description implies and as stated before, delivers relatively little in the

way of predictions of actual user behaviour. The Keystroke Level Model requires the analyst to carry out a considerable amount of task instance analysis such that every single operation by user and machine is specified. The result is mainly just a prediction of execution time and as such the KLM seems to be require a considerable amount of effort in relation to what it can deliver.

Taking Task Action Grammars as a representative of the grammar models, we come into a new kind of situation. Here, the analyst is required to carry out a task space analysis in order to develop a TAG for a given interface by writing rules to generate the action sequences. Once this job is done one can 'run' the model with any given goal and be able to produce the required actions. Having built the grammar, it can be used for the computation of complexity and consistency measures and so little further effort is involved in eliciting these results. Thus, for its target area, TAG seems to deliver considerable predictive power in relation to expended effort.

Most of the other models follow this more balanced pattern; task space analysis while building the model and different task instances as inputs for prediction. One really then has to decide exactly what or how much is being delivered by any given model in order to make a final choice.

The GOMS and CCT models seem to come out quite close together on this trade-off. The GOMS models require successively more analysis with finer grain size but then they also deliver more as a result. The CCT model requires more actual building, including the device representation, but then it results in a more flexible prediction device. As already mentioned, these may be some of the reasons that this type of model, especially GOMS, has been the most popular to date. It is worth remembering, though, the qualification of Landauer's regarding the predictive power of any model not dealing with errors.

The ICS model arguably requires the least input effort of all, since a version that has been implemented into an expert system shell actually guides the task analysis in a kind of knowledge elicitation process from the analyst. While it is likely that the analyst in this case needs psychological training and so may not be the interface designer directly, the resulting ICS model can deliver broad behavioural predictions about users at more than one level of expertise. However, these are only of a descriptive nature rather than any specific account of predicted user behaviour. Nevertheless, taking this limitation into account, ICS does appear to be weighted in favour of outputs in this trade-off.

The Programmable User Model approach is somewhat different to the others due to its attempt to package the kind of psychological information that designers could only otherwise get by testing prototypes against real users. As such PUMs will require considerable task space analysis, but since they are mainly intended for use by the interface designer who, as part of the design process, has presumably already carried out a deep analysis of the system. It may only prove necessary to change the style of that analysis to provide input to the PUM rather than carry out large amounts of extra work by starting a task analysis from scratch. Feedback should be significant, both in terms of considerably deeper analysis of the design as a result of 'instructing' the PUM in how to use the proposed interface, and also in terms of the resultant simulation of the actual processing the the user would be predicted to manifest.

5. Conclusions

This paper has neither attempted an exhaustive, nor an evaluative review of the space of existing or developing models of human behaviour in HCI situations. It has argued that the most common ways of distinguishing between such models are not well suited to the job of providing guidance to potential modellers as to which models are best suited to which jobs.

Instead, it has attempted to provide some kind of rational taxonomy of cognitive models in HCI. It has done this by focussing explicitly on the trade-offs that are made when deciding the focus of a model's development. As such it has laid out the space in such a way as to point out which are the primary deliverables of any one model and what predictive power that model is forced to concede in order to achieve them. It is hoped that in this way, would-be users of cognitive HCI models can choose the best model for the job they have in mind, both by understanding what any one candidate claims it can deliver, and also by being able to see what it can not.

Acknowledgements

I would like to thank Phil Barnard, Richard Young, Stu Card and Pat Wright for their enormous contributions to this paper. However, they cannot be held responsible for any of the misconceptions. This work was funded by the Alvey Project MMI/112 *Towards Programmable User Models*.

References

P Barnard [1987], "Cognitive Resources and the Learning of Human-Computer Dialogues," in *Interfacing Thought: Cognitive Aspects of Human-Computer Interaction*, J M Carroll, ed., MIT Press, Cambridge MA.

S K Card, T P Moran & A Newell [1983], *The Psychology of Human-Computer Interaction*, Lawrence Erlbaum Associates, Hillsdale, New Jersey.

S K Card & R M Young [1984], "Predictive Models of the User: A Selective Review," *NATO Advanced Workshop on User-Computer Interaction*, Loughborough, England.

T R G Green, F Schiele & S J Payne [1987], "Formalisable Models of User Knowledge in Human-Computer Interaction," in *Working with Computers: Theory versus Outcome*, T R G Green G C Van der Veer J-M Hoc and D Murray, ed., Academic Press, London.

D Kieras & P G Polson [1985], "An Approach to the Formal Analysis of User Complexity," *Int. J. Man-Machine Studies* 22, 365–394.

T K Landauer [1987], "Relations between Cognitive Psychology and Computer System Design," in *Interfacing Thought: Cognitive Aspects of Human-Computer Interaction*, J M Carroll, ed., MIT Press, Cambridge MA.

S J Payne & T R G Green [1986], "Task-Action Grammars: A Model of the Mental Representation of Task Languages," *Human Computer Interaction* 2, 93–133.

P Reisner [1981], "Formal Grammar and the Design of an Interactive System," *IEEE Trans. on Software Engineering* 7, 229–240.

R M Young & T R G Green, "Programmable User Models as Aids to the Interface Designer," In preparation.

Systems Design: Methods, Tools and Processes

The Design and Evaluation of an Animated Programming Environment

Kaizad B. Heerjee,
Michael T. Swanston, Colin J. Miller &
William B. Samson

Dundee College of Technology, Bell Street, Dundee, U.K.

APE, an Animated Programming Environment, is an interactive, graphical, program design and development system, that embodies structured programming and top-down design. The system supports the development of programs for a variety of block structured languages whilst working conceptually at the level of Jackson diagrams. Evaluation of APE has been carried out during the design and implementation stages of the development life-cycle. The evaluation was based on responses to a questionnaire and a comparison with conventional means of generating code. The questionnaire evaluation elicited users' general impressions about the system and its interface, and their detailed views on more specific aspects of the system. The comparative evaluation showed no difference in the mean quality of the solution to a programming problem, but a significantly reduced variance in quality compared to conventional methods.

Keywords: Human-Computer Interface, Software Evaluation, Programming Environments

1. Introduction

Researchers in the field of human-computer interaction have long held
the view that well designed interactive systems increase performance
levels over conventional techniques, and intuitively this seems logical.
Increasing effort is being devoted to the development of interactive
systems, but their positive impact is seldom evaluated. Although lists of
goals have been proposed (Hansen [1971]; Lund [1985]; Norman [1983];
Shneiderman [1987]) to assist the design of interactive systems, they can
often be criticised for being contradictory or too imprecisely stated to
be defined and measured.

The interactive system evaluated in this study was the Animated Programming Environment, APE. The characteristics of the system are
described, followed by a description of the method used for evaluation
and its results.

2. Overview of the APE System

APE is an interactive, graphical, program and text design and development system which enables users to develop programs whilst working
conceptually at the level of Jackson diagrams (Jackson [1975]). The APE
system uses a hierarchical structure (Figure 1) to represent a program.

Algorithms are generated by refining a problem into simpler components.
At higher levels, problems can be partitioned into logically disjoint sub-
problems, that can be tackled independently. Each level of refinement
simplifies the sub-problem further until it can be solved directly. This
method of hierarchical program development embodies the approach of
structured programming and top-down design.

APE has been designed to be a diagram driven system with a user
interface that models the development process. The system has been
written in C using the UNIX built-in Curses library functions (Arnold
[1983]), and has been implemented on a VAX-11/750 under ULTRIX
Version 1.2. For a detailed description of the complete system, see
Heerjee (Heerjee [1988a]; Heerjee [1988b]; Heerjee [1988c]; Heerjee et
al. [1988]; Heerjee, Miller & Swanston [1988]).

The system generates nodes for the tree diagram which are based on
Jackson structured diagrams. The system provides facilities for traversing and editing the design diagram. The user may input commands
either by using the pull down menus or by typing them directly at
the keyboard. The system also has a history mechanism that is useful
for storing, retrieving and traversing between tree diagram structures.

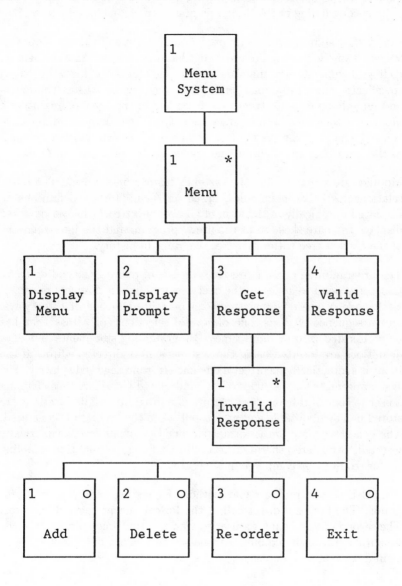

Figure 1. A Jackson Structured Tree Diagram in APE

Furthermore, the interactive learn package gives Computer Aided Instruction courses and practice to help the novice user operate the system.

Several views of the design diagram are possible for the user. The en-

larged diagram is the default and the system also provides a perspective
view of the design diagram, displaying more levels/nodes on the screen.
A hard copy listing of the design diagram can also be obtained.

The APE system provides support for the various software development
stages, namely system design, programming, testing and debugging,
coding, documentation, maintenance and modification. First the design
specification of a program is entered in a system tree using comments
and underlying control structures. Each leaf of this tree, representing a
module, is then refined to produce code. Thus the complete source code
is a refinement of the system tree and contains design information such
as the functional specification and the designer's original comments.

Modules are written using the system's history mechanism. The inter-
relationships between modules, based on their interface definitions, is
displayed graphically in the form of an overview tree. The overview tree
displays the bare skeleton of the users' program and the inter-relations
of the current tree with other tree diagrams in history.

The programming phase in essence consists of refining the coding trees,
that correspond to nodes on the overview tree, into a complete program.
Each node of these coding trees can be refined in one of three ways;
into a sequence of tasks, one of several selections, or a task that has
to be iterated zero or more times. Programming statements and data
definitions are inserted using the systems syntax directed editor. If the
input is syntactically incorrect a one line error message is displayed. The
system prompts for the types of any undeclared identifiers thus enabling
a user to concentrate on the structure of a program. All declarations are
stored in a symbol table and are output when the program is generated.
The generated program is formatted, and comments are automatically
inserted. Stubs are generated for each undefined module, thus enabling
the program to be compiled and executed.

The APE system provides two methods for testing and debugging programs. The first is a direct call to the Pascal interpreter and executor.
The second option enables a user to view the run-time animation of the
design diagram. Breakpoints can be set and values of variables traced
as in a conventional debugger.

3. User Interface

The characteristics of the user interface, as described below, were based
as far as possible on available human factors information. In addition a
number of users provided reports, new suggestions and ideas during the
implementation stage of the system.

3.1. Screen Layout

For most interactive systems, the layout of information on a screen is important, since densely packed or cluttered screens can often overwhelm and distract users. Smith and Mosier (Smith & Mosier [1984]) highlight the complexity of this issue by suggesting 162 guidelines for displaying data on screens.

The display was organised in pages and made use of windows. Sequences of screens were similar throughout the system for similar tasks. Within a sequence, the information on the screen gave an indication to the user of the current position. The option of going backwards in a sequence was also provided. System messages provided guidance which employed a user-centered phrasing (Shneiderman [1987]). Furthermore, all system messages were displayed in a consistent format at a fixed location on the screen. In addition, the use of multiple overlapped windows was limited because of the size of the screen and the time taken to update it.

The APE system created three windows when invoked; the menu, text and node windows. A diagrammatic view of the overall terminal screen is shown in Figure 2.

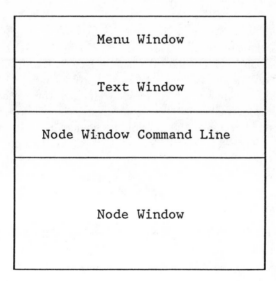

Figure 2. Diagrammatic View of the Screen Layout

The menu window was a single line window at the top of the screen, and highlighted the menu bar options, in inverse video. The coding tree (the default), was displayed in the node window. The number and size of the nodes on this tree could all be varied to a certain degree by the user when invoking the system. The first row of this window was the command line, as all interaction with the system, except with the menu window, occurred there. All system prompts and messages were generated on the command line as well.

The text window was made up of the remaining portion of the screen which consisted of the menu window at the top, and the node window. The text window was the only window in the system in which scrolling was allowed. All input into a node took place here as the system did not provide any direct access to a node except through this window.

3.2. Command Input

Command language and direct manipulation were the two interaction styles initially used in implementing the APE system. The primary input device for manipulating the interface was the alphanumeric keyboard; occasionally the cursor control keys could be used. The commands were usually a single keystroke. For example, the 'S' key was used for generating nodes, while the cursor keys were used for traversing the tree diagram.

As the system was developed the command set became more extensive and complex. This resulted in a strategy employing single letters, shifted single letters, and 'CTRL' key plus single letters. Additionally, some commands stood alone, whereas others had to be combined in different patterns. This profusion of commands enabled the expert users to achieve a complex task with very few keystrokes. However the large command repertoire made the task of the novice and intermittent user more difficult. Therefore, it was decided to incorporate a menu interface into the system. The commands in the menu system were designed in a manner where there was a one-to-one correspondence with the options present in the menus to those that a user would normally type directly at the keyboard.

The APE system makes use of single and tree structured menu systems. In the former case, a combination of pull down, or pop-up, and extended menus is used. The style is similar to that of an Apple Macintosh. The tree structured menus enabled a large collection of data to be made available to a novice or intermittent user. An index was displayed on the screen to enable the user to maintain a sense of position.

4. Empirical Evaluation the APE System

The APE system was evaluated in order to investigate the claim that properly designed interactive tools can increase productivity and have advantages over conventional methods of generating code. The empirical evaluation was also intended to provide feedback on possible modifications to be made to the system. The evaluation was carried out once a major section of the APE system was implemented, and consisted of a questionnaire and an experimental comparison with conventional methods of programming.

4.1. Questionnaire Evaluation

The questionnaire evaluation was designed to solicit users' general impression about the system and its interface, and their detailed views on more specific aspects of the system.

The points addressed in the questionnaire ranged from ease of use, through to the perceived utility of the system and its visual appearance. Some points that were less central to the interface design itself, but which might affect the users' perception of its quality, were also included.

4.1.1. Apparatus

Trials were conducted on CIT-101e (VT100 compatible) monitors, linked to a VAX-11/750, or Micro VAX work-stations. UNIX/ULTRIX was the operating system used in these trials, and was the system on which APE was developed and now runs.

4.1.2. Subjects

The questionnaires were given to forty-one students (mean age 30.5 years, range between nineteen and forty-two years) at Dundee College of Technology. These students were enrolled in one of four courses; postgraduate diploma in Software Engineering, third year undergraduate science degree, fifth year Applicable Mathematics degree, or a Higher National Diploma in Computing.

All candidates had some previous knowledge of computing. Some possessed a knowledge of the UNIX/ULTRIX operating system, although this was not necessary.

4.1.3. Method

The evaluation procedure consisted of three stages. Initially, a brief explanation of the design technique used by the APE system was given. This was found to be necessary because the APE system is conceptually based on Jackson diagrams, and few subjects had experience of this. Subsequently a demonstration was provided to familiarise the users with the basic facilities and tools that were essential for driving the system. The experimenter was always present to answer any queries. The example consisted of using the system to generate a program in Pascal that found the maximum of a set of numbers. This example demonstrated essential features of the system such as the menu interface, on-line help facilities and ways of directly manipulating the design diagram using the command language. First-time users were then allowed to practice and familiarise themselves with the system, following which they were given instructions for the task that they were required to perform.

The subjects then completed one of three programming tasks in order to familiarise themselves with the system. The tasks were chosen to cover a range of applications in Pascal programming. One task was to write a program that played a simple game of noughts and crosses, while the second task was to write a scanner that produced a list of identifiers in a Pascal program. The final task was to generate a stack implementation that would also handle the two cases of stack overflow and underflow. At the end of the familiarisation, subjects were handed the questionnaire which they completed in their own time.

There were three types of question in the questionnaire. The first set (seven questions) concerned commands offered by the system to the user. Another set (ten questions) dealt with specific questions on existing features, while the third set (six questions) consisted of general open-ended questions that concerned users' opinion on some broader aspects of the system. At the end of the questionnaire, users were encouraged to state their complaints and desired modifications to the system. A conventional five point rating scale was used in the questionnaire (Oppenheim [1986]), and the users indicated their degree of agreement/disagreement with the statements given in the questionnaire. A copy of the questionnaire and detailed results are available elsewhere (Heerjee [1988a]).

4.1.4. Results

A total of forty-one questionnaires were administered of which thirty-nine were completed and returned. The results presented in this section are based on the median ratings given to the questions and are shown in parenthesis.

With respect to their general impression, the subjects found the interface good (5) and easy to use (4). Subjects found that the response time of the graphical interface was fast (5), but said that a high level of concentration was required in using the system (4).

Subjects had little or no previous experience of using Jackson diagrams (1). During the learning process, the subjects had some practice sessions with a learning package that was incorporated into the APE system. This was found to be useful (4).

Several questions were asked in order to evaluate the screen design. These ranged from general questions such as the overall graphical interface of the system, to more specific ones, such as the quality of the menu interface.

Subjects agreed that the overall graphical interface was good (5), and were satisfied with the amount of information that was displayed on the screen (4). The help facilities, such as the instructions, on-line help and other accompanied documentation, provided by the system were also found to be good (4). In addition, subjects expressed their satisfaction with the pull down menu selection system (4).

Subjects agreed that the different types of tree diagrams provided by the APE system were useful (5), and that sufficient information was displayed in a node of the tree (4).

Subjects were satisfied (4) with the history mechanism of the APE system. The run-time animation of the design diagram was also found to be useful (4).

Two questions also dealt with the windows in the systems. Subjects felt that the number of windows should not be reduced (4). However, they were undecided (3) on whether the size of the text window needed enlargement.

Subjects found that the system did not allow for reasonably quick error correction (3). Answers to this question may have been influenced by the fact that the system being evaluated was a prototype and could sometimes allow illegal commands that took longer to correct.

In summary, the questionnaire revealed a favourable or encouraging response for most aspects of the user interface. This presumably reflects the use of human-factors design principles throughout the development of the system.

4.2. Comparative Evaluation

The second evaluation procedure involved a comparison between the APE system and conventional means of generating code. This was designed to provide an objective test of the value of the system in program development.

4.2.1. Apparatus

The apparatus used in this experiment was the same as described in the questionnaire evaluation.

4.2.2. Subject Categories

Nineteen post-graduate students (one female and eighteen males), from a diploma course in Software Engineering at Dundee College of Technology took part in this experiment. These subjects had an undergraduate college/university degree or diploma and were studying program design techniques, as part of their curriculum.

Subjects in this experiment had previous experience of using the APE system, as all had taken part in the questionnaire evaluation of the system. The subjects were divided into two groups equated for age and performance in class. The latter characteristic was assessed by a mark based on course-work assignments over the term. The first group (nine males, mean age 24.1 years, mean class performance 61.1%, SD 6.5), used the APE system, while the second group (one female and nine males, mean age 25.7 years, mean class performance 64.0%, SD 9.07), used the screen editor on their machines to produce the pseudocode.

4.2.3. Method

The task was to design a detailed pseudocode algorithm that implemented a restricted form of a decision table. The pseudocode algorithm to be produced had to go through the stages of reading the data into an array from a file. It would ask questions from the user and from the corresponding responses determine which outcome to print. Four pseudocode algorithms were required to be formulated using the conventional pseudocode structuring constructs (e.g., IF ... THEN ... ELSE, etc.), and a given set of primitives (such as READ, PRINT, Rules and Flags). The decomposition process had to be achieved in a top-down manner and each section was required to be refined until details could be input at the primitive level alone. The complete task is presented elsewhere (Heerjee [1988a]).

Both groups undertook their tasks in the same room, but no consultation between subjects was allowed and no help was given during the experiment.

4.2.4. Results

The answer sheets were returned by all nineteen subjects, and were marked by three independent lecturers with experience of teaching program design techniques. They were not involved with the design, implementation or the evaluation of the APE system. Marks were given on a ten point scale, where ten was the maximum.

The three markers were significantly consistent (Kendall's coefficient of concordance (18) = 0.71, $p < 0.01$) (Siegel [1956]). Therefore each subject was assigned the mean of the three lecturers' marks. These scores gave a mean APE score of 6.0 (S.D. = 1.12), and a mean screen editor score of 6.3 (S.D. 2.08), which were not significantly different.

While this result did not demonstrate a practical superiority in the quality of the solution produced on the APE system, it was at least no worse than a conventional code-generating procedure. However the two methods did differ in respect of the uniformity of the code produced by the two groups. Even though there was a wide range of ability in each group, the output from the APE group was of a more consistent standard, compared to the quality of the code produced using conventional methods. This result was predicted for Jackson diagrams (Jackson [1975]), and was demonstrated by a significant difference in the variance of the scores obtained by each group ($F(9,8)$ 3.42, $p < 0.05$) (Groebner & Shannon [1985]).

5. Conclusions

The results presented in this paper concern two issues, namely, obtaining user responses to the interface of the APE system, and the empirical evaluation of its usefulness as a tool.

The questionnaire resulted in a generally positive response to the system, with a majority of answers indicating approval of its characteristics. This showed both that the principle of an animated programming environment was acceptable to users, and that design decisions regarding the user interface were well-founded. After the questionnaire was analysed, changes were made to the system. These included improved error recovery routines, modifications to the on-line help facilities, and extensions to the skeleton tree diagram.

There were some advantages and disadvantages in using the questionnaire as an evaluation tool. Specific questions were found to be the most useful as they resulted in a list of areas that needed attention. However, such questions cannot hope to evaluate the entire interface, because this would result in an over-lengthy questionnaire. On the other hand, users with little or no computer experience may be unable to give a critical response, particularly if these responses must be based either on comparison with other systems or on the user's own conception of what the interface should look like. For this reason, it was also found inadvisable to ask users to pass judgement on questions that proposed new features to a system, without giving them experience with it. This view suggests that users might not be aware of what constitutes a good system, but might only be aware of what they did not like when they had to use it.

During the course of the evaluation it was noted that users tended to switch from the menu selection system to the command language. In part this may have been due to the time penalty involved in requesting a display, waiting for it to be displayed, and then searching for the desired item. Also, the large number of commands required the use of multiple menus, which was designed to give help whether or not it was requested. As expertise was developed, the command language was preferred, although it was relatively difficult to learn, and there were no on-line reminders. This supports the contention that a system should have two or more levels of dialogue, appropriate to the user's level of competence.

In the comparative evaluation, two groups of users generated code to solve a problem, using either the APE system or a screen editor. Although the mean quality of the solutions was the same for both groups, there was significantly more variability in those produced with the screen editor. This demonstrated one of the potential benefits of a structured programming environment. These results also suggest that using such systems helps to produce standard quality products, and reduces the dependence on the experience and ability of the practitioner. It is intended to extend this type of comparative evaluation to larger and more diverse groups of users, where it is possible that differences in performance may be demonstrated. The present study was concerned with the quality of the solution to a problem; it would be of interest to obtain measures of speed as well in future trials.

Future testing of the APE system will employ controlled evaluation, with industrial user groups and in respect of its application to document preparation and as a program design aid. In general, it is hoped to establish a methodology for design and evaluation which will have an application to a range of future projects.

References

K C R Arnold [August 1983], "Screen Updating and Cursor Movement Optimization: A Library Package," in *The UNIX Programmer's Manual 2C*, Computer Science Division, Department of Electrical Engineering and Computer Studies, University of California, Berkeley, CA 94720.

D F Groebner & P W Shannon [1985], *Business Statistics: A Decision-Making Approach*, Charles E Merrill Pub. Co., USA.

W J Hansen [1971], "User Engineering Principles for Interactive Systems," in *Proceedings of the 4th FIPS Fall Joint Conference* #39, 523–532.

K B Heerjee [1988a], "An Interactive Graphical, Program Design and Development Environment," Dundee College of Technology, UK, PhD Thesis.

K B Heerjee [1988b], "APE – An Animated Programming Environment," Dundee College of Technology, UK, Technical Bulletin No. 13.

K B Heerjee [1988c], "APE Programmer's Manual," Dundee College of Technology, UK, Technical Bulletin No. 12.

K B Heerjee, C J Miller, W B Samson & M T Swanston [1988], "The Design, Validation and Evaluation of a Software Development Environment," Submitted for Publication to Software Engineering Journal.

K B Heerjee, C J Miller & M T Swanston [July 1988], "Experiences in Applying Formal Methods to Existing Software," in *Proceedings of a Formal Methods Workshop, Teeside Polytechnic, UK*.

M A Jackson [1975], *Principles of Program Design*, Academic Press.

M A Lund [1985], "Evaluating the User Interface: The Candid Camera Approach," in *Proceedings of CHI '85 – Human Factors in Computing Systems*, ACM, New York, 107–113.

D A Norman [1983], "Design Principles for Human Computer-Interfaces," in *Proceedings of CHI '83 – Human Factors in Computing Systems*, ACM, New York, 1–10.

A N Oppenheim [1986], *Questionnaire Design and Attitude Measurement*, Gower Publications, Aldershot.

B Shneiderman [1987], *Designing the User Interface: Strategies for Effective Human-Computer Interaction*, Addison-Wesley, Reading MA.

S Siegel [1956], *Nonparametric Statistics for the Behavioural Sciences*, McGraw-Hill, Tokyo.

S L Smith & J N Mosier [1984], "Design Guidelines for User-System Interface Software," The Mitre Corporation, Report No. ESD-TR-84-190, Bedford MA.

Overcoming Obstacles to the Validation of User Requirements Specifications

M.A.R. Kirby, C.J.H. Fowler & L.A. Macaulay*

Department of Computer Studies and Mathematics, Huddersfield Polytechnic, Queensgate, Huddersfield HD1 3DH, U.K.

*Department of Computation, University of Manchester Institute of Science and Technology (UMIST), Manchester, U.K.

Poor specification of user requirements is a major reason why computer systems fail or dysfunction. One way of addressing this problem is to validate User Requirements Specifications before proceeding with system development. To date, it has only been possible to validate specifications against checklists of what they should contain. This type of validation indicates gaps but does not check the reliability of a specification; nor does it explain the implications of specification deficiencies for performance of the finished product.

This paper identifies obstacles to the development of validation techniques that do check reliability and do explain the implications of specification deficiencies. An approach to overcoming these obstacles is discussed, particularly a method for ensuring that a specification is verified with the right set of users, and a method of manipulating and analysing the information in a specification to predict dysfunction. This approach has been used to develop the Specified User Requirements Validation and Explication (SURVE) technique.

Keywords: Requirements Specification, User Requirements, System Validation

1. Identifying obstacles to the validation of User Requirements Specifications

The first step towards validating a Requirements Specification is to have a clear idea of what a Requirements Specification should contain. In recent years, increasing recognition of the importance of HCI has led to changes in the way system requirements are specified. These changes are reflected in the guidelines provided to industry by professional institutions. In 1979 the National Computing Centre (Lee [1979]) defined 'User System Specification' primarily in terms of technical functionality with supporting information about user responsibilities. In 1982 the Department of Trade and Industry's STARTS Guide (DTI [1982]) placed greater emphasis on defining the human environment that the system must operate within. In 1985 IEE 'Guidelines for the documentation of software in industrial computer systems' (IEE [1985]) had advanced from general consideration of the environment to more specific definition of system interfaces with the environment and usability attributes. Interfaces and usability are emphasised further still in the second edition of the STARTS guide, published in 1987 (DTI & NCC [1987]). The trend is towards requirements specifications that address human factors issues as well as technical functionality. Industry is now provided with more comprehensive checklists of what should be contained in a requirements specification than were provided ten years ago.

With more comprehensive checklists, the completeness of a requirements specification can be checked more effectively. However, thorough validation involves more than just identifying what has not been specified. It is also desirable to check the validity of what has been specified. There are techniques available for checking the internal logic of those parts of a specification that can be represented formally and this paper does not challenge the validity of using established mathematical techniques for validating mathematical representations. But, the proportion of a requirements specification that can be represented formally has decreased as more emphasis is placed on human factors. Formal methods practitioners have themselves recognised the limitations of mathematical techniques for user requirements specifications: see Efstathiou (Efstathiou, Hawgood & Rajkovic [1979]) and Buckle (Buckle et al. [1979]).

Informal subjective parts of a specification can be validated by verification with users. This method is valuable but limited. Users have difficulties in expressing requirements and understanding system specifications. Nosek and Sherr (Nosek & Sherr [1984]) provide a catalogue of these difficulties in getting requirements right before design and implementation. Harker and Eason (Harker & Eason [1985]) have pointed out that users lack techniques for systematically reviewing their information needs and are unaware of what could be provided.

Even if users are able to understand the specification and express their requirements, it is necessary to check that the specification is being verified by the right set of users. Lucas (Lucas [1976]) has shown that organisational behaviour problems are a major cause of failure of information systems. Thus an information system that a particular user in carrying out a particular task might also affect his power in the organisation and his relationships with others. The others also have a stake in and can contribute to success or failure of the system and their requirements also need to be checked. A method is required for identifying the right set of stakeholders rather than just direct users of the system. Lundeberg (Lundeberg [1982]) gives examples of different interest groups whose needs should be investigated. These interest groups include persons who are indirectly affected by system changes as well as end users.

Another subjective form of validation is review by experts. In industry, it is common for a senior designer or analyst to check a specification produced by a less experienced colleague. Consultants may also be brought in to check requirements. This approach can improve a specification but is limited by the degree of expertise available. To be able to carry out a thorough validation, an expert needs wide and recent experience of the stakeholders' environment, and understanding of the stakeholders' characteristics, and the ability to interpret the implications of the specification, and an understanding of the organisation's objectives, structure and processes. This combination of knowledge and skills is rare indeed.

Imagine a situation in which there is a true expert, the stakeholders can understand the specification and express their requirements, and a comprehensive checklist of specification contents does exist. In this situation, it is possible to identify omissions and errors, and to subjectively state that the system might fail or dysfunction[1] if it is built to meet this

---

[1] In this paper, dysfunction means a mis-match between system attributes and

specification of requirements. Available validation methods still do not have the power to predict with any objective precision how the system will dysfunction. The more precise the prediction is, the more effective is the validation. This is because attention is focussed on those parts of the specification that are critical to the future success of the system and because the predictions help to establish appropriate measures of performance and measures of usability for the system.

The preceding discussion indicates a number of obstacles to effective validation:

— incomplete definition of what a Requirements Specification should contain.

— the lack of appropriate rigorous techniques.

— difficulties in ensuring that a specification is verified by the right set of stakeholders.

— difficulties of verifying a specification with stakeholders.

— the rarity of experts who have the necessary knowledge and skills.

— the lack of techniques for precisely predicting the type and nature of dysfunction.

2. An approach to overcoming the validation obstacles

The following discussion concerns the approach taken in the research and development of the Specified User Requirements Validation and Explication (SURVE) technique.

2.1. Incomplete definition of what a Requirements Specification should contain

It was felt that this obstacle is being overcome by the trend towards definitions of User Requirements Specifications that integrate technical functionality and human factors. The SURVE project did not develop such a definition, but selected one as a start point for developing a validation technique. The selection was the definition of a 'Product Requirements' document that forms part of the User Skills and Task Match (USTM) methodology. This methodology was developed jointly by International Computers Ltd. and Huddersfield Polytechnic on an

---

user requirements, manifest in actual usage not reaching potential usage.

Alvey Project, see Fowler *et al* (Fowler et al. [1988]). The USTM definition provides a sound basis for what a requirement specification should contain because it covers the integration of technical functionality and human factors, and the contents are defined in a detailed, structured way.

2.2. The lack of appropriate rigorous techniques

Despite the inappropriateness of entirely formal techniques, it is possible to overcome this obstacle. The rigour in the SURVE technique has been achieved partially by imposition of a common structure on whatever specification is being validated, and partially by formalisation.

The common structure derives from a concept of roles which integrates human and functional factors. Roles are about the way that responsibility for achieving organisational goals is allocated, about the tasks necessary to achieve those goals and about the people who have responsibility or who carry out the tasks. An organisation can be modelled in terms of a set of roles which is organised to achieve overall goals. Each role is the responsibility of one person and has a primary task to achieve a sub-goal of the overall goals. The subgoals do not necessarily combine in the most effective way for achieving overall goals, and may instead provide what Bjorn Andersen (Bjorn-Andersen [1984]) has described as a "battlefield where the technology is used to further interests of the most powerful groups at the expense of weaker groups". At the organisational level, a requirements specification can be regarded as a definition of the impact of the system on the set of roles. Any person whose role(s) are affected is a stakeholder. Within each role, a requirements specification describes a set of characteristics which defines the relationship between that role and the computer system, and defines the acceptability of a proposed system to the stakeholders. Identifying these characteristics leads to an understanding of why subgoals provide a battlefield rather than common norms.

Unfortunately, requirements specifications are not usually written in a way which reflects the systemic structure of a set of roles. So a pre-validation process had to be developed to elicit information about roles from the diverse formats in which requirements are presented. In effect, a specification is restructured at the organisational level in terms of a set of roles via analysis of the specified tasks, goals and responsibilities. Within each role, structure is provided by a set of characteristics which are essentially common to all roles. With respect to the relationship between a role and a computer system, the Essential characteristics concern Measures of performance, Control, Support and Training, Quantity of data, Usability, Affect on other dependent roles, Relationship with non-dependent roles, Environmental constraints and Dependencies on other roles (the initials spell out the acronym mnemonic $E = MC^2$). The acceptability of the role/system relationship is determined by compatibility with an essential set of stakeholder characteristics, including each stakeholders' skills, knowledge, view of the world and group membership. Structuring in terms of roles and characteristics provides a basis for the predictive part of the validation technique.

Rigour is achieved by formalisation in the predictive part of the validation technique via a simple application of set theory. This is discussed in the section on the lack of techniques for precisely predicting the type and nature of dysfunction.

2.3. Difficulties in ensuring that a specification is verified by the right set of stakeholders

The removal of this obstacle was facilitated by the elicitation of stakeholder roles, particularly the characteristics concerning dependencies and relationships between roles. This information enables the identification of all the people who have a stake in the success or failure of the system. The set of stakeholders is the right set of people to verify a specification. Stakeholders include direct and indirect users: i.e., people who directly use the computer system to carry out their tasks; people whose responsibilities are affected by the system; and people affected by dependencies and relationships with the roles that are supported, changed or replaced by the system.

2.4. Difficulties of verifying a specification with stakeholders

Development of rigorous validation techniques partially removes this obstacle. It is still important to verify the base data with stakeholders, but the rigour of the role elicitation technique and the predictive technique enables validation to proceed without further verification. The SURVE project has not yet addressed the difficulties of user verification, but it is thought that it should be easier to present the base data about the stakeholder's environment in a way stakeholders can understand than it is to present an intricate requirements analysis. It will also be necessary to address the issue of how best to communicate the results and implications of the validation with stakeholders.

2.5. Rarity of experts who have the necessary knowledge and skills

The techniques discussed in this paper allow non-experts to carry out validation, thus removing the obstacle. This does not imply that the validation would not be further enhanced by the subjective evaluation of a true expert, if one can be found.

2.6. The lack of techniques for precisely predicting the type and nature of dysfunction

It is an understanding of the causes of dysfunction that enables this obstacle to be overcome. To reiterate, in this paper dysfunction means a mis-match between system attributes and user requirements, manifest in actual usage not reaching potential usage. The premise is that dysfunction occurs because a computer system is incompatible with the set of stakeholder roles and the characteristics of those roles. For example, at the organisational level, incompatibility is likely to arise if a stakeholder is neglected, i.e., that person's requirements are under-specified. Overspecification is likely to be a problem if the specification meets the requirements of a person who is not a stakeholder. It was hypothesised that such relationships are also true at the lower level of role characteristics. Take a simple example, in which a particular usability characteristic is relevant to the requirements of two stakeholders, but the specification has only addressed the requirements of one of them. In this case, underspecification is likely to result in actual usage being lower than potential usage because a stakeholder is unable to use the system effectively. If the usability characteristic is relevant to only one stakeholder, but the requirements of two stakeholders were represented in the specification, a different problem occurs. In this case, it is complexity resulting from overspecification that keeps actual usage below potential (and the developer has wasted resources to include redundant functionality in the system).

The complex relations between sets of stakeholder characteristics are depicted in figure 1. The SURVE technique allows for any number of stakeholders to be considered, but only three have been shown because the representation would be unclear if more stakeholders were depicted. Each circle represents all the role characteristics of a particular stakeholder. The two hatched regions represent the sub-sets of characteristics that appear in the requirements specification. A characteristic is 'well defined' if it is derived from base data that has been verified with stakeholders. A characteristic is 'assigned' if it is specified in terms of a requirement that must be met by the system.

The 'ideal position' on the Venn Diagram of a particular characteristic is determined by the definition of 'the right set of stakeholders' for that characteristic. This definition was established during the elicitation process. The ideal position is always within the region that is both well defined and assigned, i.e., positions with 4 as the first digit. For example, if the right set of stakeholders includes both stakeholder 2 and stakeholder 3 but not stakeholder 1, the 'ideal position' is position 45.

As well as an ideal position, a 'specified position' can be plotted for each characteristic. This is determined by how the characteristic was treated in the requirements specification For example, if only stakeholder 2's requirements were addressed with respect to the characteristic, and the characteristic was assigned but ill-defined, the 'specified position' is position 32.

For each characteristic, dysfunction can be predicted from discrepancies between the ideal and actual positions. For example, if the specified position is 32 and the ideal position is 45, it is clear that dysfunction is likely to arise from underspecification because a stakeholder's requirements have been neglected. If there is no discrepancy, e.g., both the ideal and specified positions are 44, then system attributes are likely to match user requirements with respect to this characteristic, and actual usage is expected to reach potential usage. Thus general types of dysfunction or match can be predicted from a simple comparison of ideal and actual positions.The technique becomes more powerful when discrepancies between ideal and actual positions are mapped onto the structure of inter-role dependencies and inter-characteristic relationships. It is then possible to predict the nature of dysfunction , for example whether the dysfunction will take the form of communication, control, performance or political problems, depending on the type of characteristic being analysed.

3. The SURVE technique

The above discussion introduced methods of overcoming the obstacles to validation of user requirements specifications. These methods have been combined to form the SURVE technique. Firstly, a specification is restructured in terms of a set of stakeholder roles. The new structure reveals gaps and inconsistencies in the specification. Secondly, the restructured specification is compared against the sets of essential role characteristics. This comparison provides evaluation of errors and omissions. Thirdly, the application of set theory enables predictions to be made about the success or failure of the system, if it is built to specification. The first two steps indicate which parts of an specification are incomplete or inconsistent, and hence which parts need to be reworked and verified with users. The third step indicates how critical it is to get those parts right by explaining the implications of proceeding with the existing specification. A fuller description of the mechanics of the SURVE technique will be available after testing has been completed.

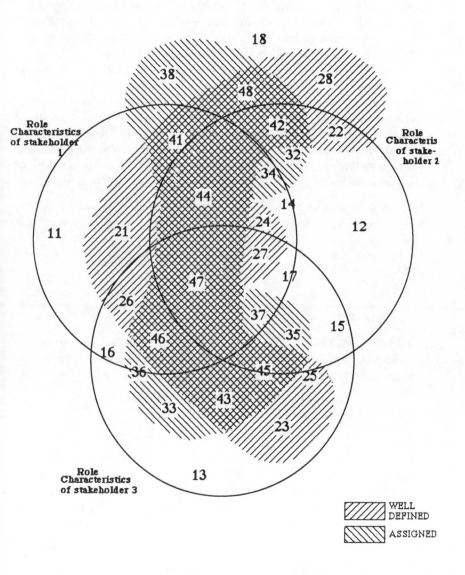

Figure 1. Dysfunction Positions

4. Testing the SURVE technique

The technique is currently being tested on requirements specifications for industrial computer systems. Predictions of dysfunction for each requirements specification are compared with the actual dysfunction that occurs when the subsequent computer system has been developed and implemented. The actual dysfunction is measured by surveying usage of the implemented system and interviewing stakeholders. These surveys are carried out independently of the validation, so that the surveyor has no knowledge of the validation results and the validator has no knowledge of the survey results until both have been completed. The requirements specification are analysed historically, i.e., after the system has been developed, to ensure that the developers do not act upon the validation results in an attempt to reduce dysfunction. This also reduces the time required to carry out the test in cases where there is a long lead time between the specification of requirements and established use of the finished product.

The first results indicate a high positive correlation between predicted and actual dysfunction, to which the validator's expert knowledge may have contributed. Forthcoming results will concern cases in which the validator is non-expert, ensuring that the results are a reliable indicator of the power of the validation technique.

5. Summary

The difficulties of validating requirements specification were discussed, identifying six obstacles in the way of effective validation of user requirements specifications:

— incomplete definition of what a Requirements Specification should contain.

— the lack of appropriate rigorous techniques.

— difficulties in ensuring that a specification is verified by the right set of stakeholders.

— difficulties of verifying a specification with stakeholders.

— the rarity of experts who have the necessary knowledge and skills.

— the lack of techniques for precisely predicting the type and nature of dysfunction.

The paper then described an approach which largely overcomes these obstacles. The approach involves elicitation, restructuring and a formal method of predicting dysfunction. Information about roles is elicited from the specification. The specification is, in effect, restructured in terms of a set of stakeholder roles and sets of role characteristics. Then predictions are made via the logic of relations between the sets of role characteristics.

References

N Bjorn-Andersen [1984], "Challenge to Certainty," in *Beyond Productivity: Information Systems Development for Organisational Effectiveness*, Th M A Bemelmans, ed., North-Holland.

J Buckle, B Langefors, H Mayr & A Solvberg [1979], "What is a Formal Specification, What Does it Contain, How is it Structured and For What is it Useful?," in *Formal Methods and Practical Tools for Information Systems*, H J Schneider, ed., North-Holland.

DTI [1982], *The STARTS Guide*, NCC Publications.

DTI & NCC [1987], *The STARTS Guide:*, NCC Publications, 2nd Edition.

J Efstathiou, J Hawgood & V Rajkovic [1979], "Verbal Measures and Inseparable Multidimensional Utility in System Evaluation," in *Formal Methods and Practical Tools for Information Systems*, H J Schneider, ed., North-Holland.

C Fowler, M Kirby, L Macauley & A Hutt [1988], "User Skills and Task Match (USTM): A Human Factors Based Methodology for Determining Product Requirements," University of Wales, Swansea, Paper Presented at Alvey Conference.

S Harker & K Eason [1985], "Task Analysis and the Definition of User Needs," in *Analysis, Design and Evaluation of Man-Machine Systems*, G Mancini et al, ed., Pergamon.

IEE [1985], *Guidelines for the Documentation of Software for Industrial Computer Systems*, IEE, London.

B Lee [1979], *Introducing System Analysis and Design*, NCC Publications, 2nd Edition.

H Lucas [1976], *Why Information Systems Fail*, Columbia University Press.

M Lundeberg [1982], "The ISAC Approach to Specification of Computer Systems and its Application to the Organisation of an IFIP Working Conference," in *Information System Design Methodologies: A Comparative Review*, T W Olle H G Sol and A A Verrijn-Stuart, ed., North-Holland.

J T Nosek & D M Sherr [1984], "'Getting the Requirements Right' versus 'Getting the System Working' – Evolutionary Development," in *Beyond Productivity: Information Systems Development for Organisational Effectiveness*, Th M A Bemelmans, ed., North-Holland.

The Representation of User Interface Style

William M. Newman

Rank Xerox Cambridge EuroPARC, 61 Regent Street, Cambridge CB2 1AB, U.K.

This paper identifies the need for representations of styles of user interface, particularly as a basis for choosing an application style or porting an application to a new environment. It identifies the requirements that a style representation should meet, and then proceeds to develop a representation based on the use of *points of style*. It shows how this representation is capable of relating style to user requirements, how it helps construct the style's underlying argument, and how it exposes stylistic weaknesses. Several worked examples are included.

Keywords: Human computer interaction, User interface design, Design style, Design rationale, Requirements, Applications design, Software environments, User interface toolkits, Apple Macintosh

1. Introduction

Style has become an increasingly important issue in user interface design since the mid-1970s. There have been dramatic increases since then in the range of applications of computers, in the diversity of users, and in the interaction technologies available. All of these changes have tended to encourage the development of different styles of user interface suited to particular applications, users and technologies.

As interest in 'user interface style' has grown, the term has begun to be applied to user interface designs in different ways. The most common use of the term is to distinguish between *styles of interaction*: basic styles that apply across a range of applications and products. For example, Baecker and Buxton (Baecker & Buxton [1987]) distinguish between nine different interaction styles: command line dialogues, programming language dialogues, natural language interfaces, menu systems, form filling dialogues, iconic interfaces, window systems, direct manipulation and graphical interaction. This type of categorisation has also been used in textbooks such as (Newman & Sproull [1979]; Shneiderman [1987]). It is useful as a basis for establishing the general properties of interfaces: much HCI research is directed at specific interaction styles, such as programming language dialogues, natural language interfaces, window systems and direct manipulation.

A second use of the term 'style' is in describing *styles of user interface*, as presented by a specific product or a specific way of designing an application. In this context, 'style' refers to recognisable features of the user interface design, features that set the design apart from other solutions to the same problem. For example, there are definite styles of text editor, such as the increasingly popular screen word processor employing a bitmap display and mouse, and the VDU-based variety in vogue during the 1970s. The features of a user interface style are often quite explicit, and are easily copied by other designers. For this reason they exert a very strong influence on user interface design practice.

This paper is concerned with user interface style, and how to represent it. Very little work has been done in this area, and the focus of the few available publications has been on proprietary environments. These accounts concentrate on providing design rules and guidelines: for example the Apple Human Interface Guidelines give informal but quite detailed directions for developers of Macintosh applications ([1987]). Such rules and guidelines are useful as long as the designer can adhere to them. The need for a more powerful representation arises when it is no longer possible to comply with the rules: the designer must then modify the defined style, preferably with an understanding of the implications. There are no representations of user interface style that support such modification and extension.

This research began as a result of discussions at a workshop on user interface design, organised by the Alvey Directorate and held at Abingdon, Berkshire, in September 1985. Some of the ideas emerging from this workshop were used in attempts to capture the essence of 'desktop' styles, e.g., Apple Macintosh and Lisa; they have also led into parallel work on design rationale now ongoing at EuroPARC (Maclean et al. []). The paper summarises some ideas on style that have developed since the 1985 workshop. These do not constitute a rigorous analysis of user interface style, but rather the preliminary design for a representational tool that can be used to pass on to designers the implications of previous design work. Emphasis has been placed on making such a tool useful to those trying to understand existing styles and work within them.

2. What do we mean by Style in Design?

User interface design, being one of the youngest design disciplines, can benefit from experience gained in other fields. By studying the role of style in design, for example, we can draw several conclusions.

First, when we discuss style we imply that there are *two or more* different strategies for designing the object or system in question, each strategy leading to a separate style. For example, there are different strategies for designing passenger planes: jet engines on the wings, jet engines near the tail, propjets on high wings, etc. These lead to different styles of plane. Note, however, that there is only one form of supersonic airliner in use, as exemplified by Concorde (and copied unsuccessfully by Tupolev), so we cannot really discuss 'styles of supersonic airliner' – unless we can find other design strategies besides Concorde's. The link between styles and multiple design strategies is important because it implies that designers make *choices* between styles, and need to understand the implications of their choices.

Second, style implies a *cohesion* in the design: a "unity of principle" in the words of Le Corbusier (Corbusier [1937]). This cohesion needs to be visible if the style itself is to be apparent. We can regard this cohesion as a form of logic or argument that binds together the ideas embodied in the design. A useful definition of style is then the visible result of following a line of argument in developing a design. It is this argument underlying styles that the designer must appreciate in order to make stylistic choices successfully.

Finally, style is a subjective matter – different people see style differently. There is often talk of the 'signature' or 'trade mark' left by the designer, but there is rarely consensus about which feature is most central to the particular style in question. This is one of the main sources of difficulty in trying to represent style: one must try to identify all of the features that make a particular style recognisable and copyable. The identification of features, or points of style, has in fact been found useful as a basis for style representation.

3. Implications for the user interface designer

We have seen that designers need to understand how to choose between styles. There are several kinds of 'choice' that the designer may need to make, each involving a particular kind of understanding. Some common examples include:

1. *Choosing an application style*, such as a graphics editor, for use in a new application domain, e.g., for maintaining electricity supply network documentation. Here the designer needs to understand the original requirements for which the style was developed, and how they influenced the design, because the new requirements may be quite different.

2. *Porting an existing application* to a proprietary software environment, and modifying it to comply with the environment's style. Here the designer needs to understand the argument for the environment's style, and how it differs from the argument for the application, in order to determine whether the two styles can be reconciled.

3. *Designing a new application or environment* for which there is no obvious precedent in terms of style. This involves deriving the argument for the design from scratch, making choices that will affect designers who subsequently port or re-use the design.

These examples suggest that there are two categories of design choice concerning style: style setting and style adoption. Clearly the majority of user interface design work involves style adoption, for the invention of a totally new application style is a rare event. The main requirement, therefore, is for a representation of style that will help the designer to adopt an existing style successfully.

4. What should a style representation offer?

In developing a representation for user interface styles, several requirements need to be met:

(a) *Specifying the rules of style.* The representation should provide a clear description of the main concepts, rules or guidelines embodied in the style, so that the designer can easily perceive what is involved in complying with the style.

(b) *Linking to user requirements.* The representation should include a summary of the user requirements that the style was developed to meet, so that the designer can compare these with the current requirements.

(c) *Exposing the argument.* The representation should show the style's underlying argument, i.e., how the concepts, rules, etc., relate to the user requirements and to each other, in such a way that the designer can easily see the implications of modifying the style.

(d) *Simplifying capture.* The representation should be easy to generate, i.e., its use should not involve disproportionate amounts of time, effort, equipment and skill.

Past attempts to describe styles have, almost without exception, failed to tackle anything but requirement (a). This paper attempts to address all four requirements, and thus provide a useful method of style representation.

5. Representation in terms of Points of Style

In order to develop a representation for style, we need to find a suitable structure. It is tempting to start with design decisions and to build up the argument from a decision 'audit trail'. However this approach is unsatisfactory on two counts: the audit trail is difficult to reconstruct after the fact, and there is an implied assumption that designers make decisions, which appears to be partly untrue (Hammond et al. [1983]).

The phrase 'point of style' is commonly used in this context, and is more useful than 'design decision' as a basis for representation. It makes no assumption about the origins of style, but simply implies that a style, once created, can be described in terms of its salient 'points'. For example, screen text editors usually embody the following points of style:

1. *What-you-see-is-what-you-get*: the text appears on the screen exactly as it will be printed, to the limits imposed by the display and printer.

2. *Hierarchic document representation*: documents are divided into paragraphs, words and characters; attributes may be assigned to each level of text object.

3. *Graphical text selection*: the user identifies sequences of text for manipulation by pointing to them with the mouse.

4. *Noun-verb command language*: the user first selects the text, and then gives the editing command.

5. *Direct text entry*: the user can select an insertion point and then enter or erase text.

6. *On-the-fly reformatting*: after each editing operation, or each

character entered or deleted, the displayed text is automatically reformatted.

These points may be considered fundamental to the text editor's design: they are the basic ideas from which the design originates. As we shall see, other points contribute to the style's definition, but they arise more as explanations for the design than as its origins.

6. Relating Points of Style to User Requirements

Points of style need to be related to user requirements. For example, the design of the text editor would normally have developed in response to a set of requirements such as:

R1   Essential editing operations can be performed quickly.
R2   Users can see what they're doing.
R3   Most actions reversible.
R4   User is made aware of irreversible operations.
R5   Permit fast alternative paths to common actions.
R6   User has control over printer output.
R7   Provide a concrete metaphor and use supportive effects.
   . . .

Now it is not possible to test whether a point of style satisfies a particular design requirement: to do this we need a specification or implementation of the user interface itself. In effect, the user interface specification forms a bridge between style and requirements. For example, the third point above, *graphical text selection*, can be related directly to certain properties of the user interface, and of the intended user's conceptual model (UCM):

- The UCM is extended with the addition of the concept of:
  - — a *current selection* object;
  - — an *insertion point* that takes the place of a zero-length selection;
  - — an action to *select* a text object;
  - — action to *extend the selection* to include adjacent objects in the document;
  - — *deselecting* the current objects when a fresh selection is made.
- The selection is displayed to the user by highlighting it: typically the text and its background are inverted from white to black and vice versa.
- Commands are provided for:

— selecting a character, by pointing and 'clicking' a mouse button;

— selecting a word, e.g., by pointing and double-clicking;

— selecting a paragraph, by pointing and clicking in the margin:

— selection extension, by clicking with a different mouse button

This fragment of the user interface can be seen to meet two of the requirements above: it enables users to see what they are doing, and it makes user actions reversible. Thus a connection has been made between the point of style and the user requirements. If we examine the design implications of further points of style, we build up a more complete description of the user interface, and can see how each point in turn contributes to meeting user requirements. Figure 1 shows diagrammatically how, for the text editor example, points of style link to components of the user interface, which in turn meet requirements.

7. Constructing the Argument

Basic stylistic ideas, such as the six shown above, will lead to satisfying only some of the user requirements, leaving others unsatisfied. This is not surprising, because basic ideas provide only part of the user interface. When the rest of the interface is added, the requirements will normally be met more adequately.

The additional components of the user interface are not without their stylistic influence. Consider, for example, the introduction of control-key commands in addition to menu selection, thus meeting the requirement for fast alternative paths:

— ctrl-D to delete the selection

— ctrl-C to copy the selection into a buffer

— ctrl-I to insert the buffer contents before the insertion point

— etc.

This extension has a definite effect on the style of the user interface. The final form of the design thus resembles Figure 2, with the 'infill' components of the user interface design contributing further points of style.

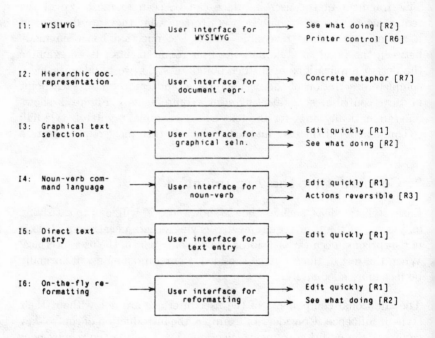

Figure 1.   Linking stylistic ideas to requirements via the user interface

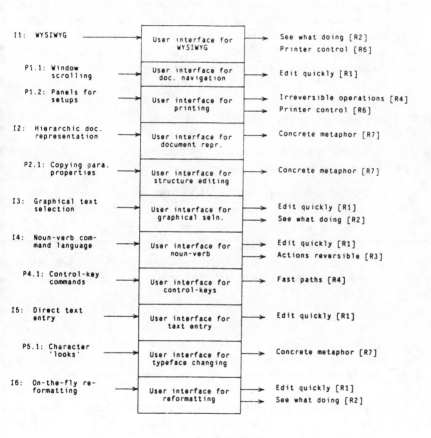

I1: WYSIWYG → User interface for WYSIWYG → See what doing [R2] / Printer control [R6]

P1.1: Window scrolling → User interface for doc. navigation → Edit quickly [R1]

P1.2: Panels for setups → User interface for printing → Irreversible operations [R4] / Printer control [R6]

I2: Hierarchic doc. representation → User interface for document repr. → Concrete metaphor [R7]

P2.1: Copying para. properties → User interface for structure editing → Concrete metaphor [R7]

I3: Graphical text selection → User interface for graphical seln. → Edit quickly [R1] / See what doing [R2]

I4: Noun-verb command language → User interface for noun-verb → Edit quickly [R1] / Actions reversible [R3]

P4.1: Control-key commands → User interface for control-keys → Fast paths [R4]

I5: Direct text entry → User interface for text entry → Edit quickly [R1]

P5.1: Character 'looks' → User interface for typeface changing → Concrete metaphor [R7]

I6: On-the-fly re-formatting → User interface for reformatting → Edit quickly [R1] / See what doing [R2]

Figure 2. The effect of adding user-interface 'infill'

The additional interface components also help us to construct the argument underlying the choice of style. Whereas the initial ideas may have been developed independently, the 'infill' pieces of the interface are strongly linked to the initial design and to each other. The control-key commands, for example, may be chosen to correspond to the menu commands that require a fast alternative path; they may also follow a consistent pattern, e.g., through use of the initial letter of the menu command.

Initial ideas thus play a similar role to requirements in determining how the design subsequently develops. Figure 3 shows diagrammatically how some points of style relate directly to requirements and some indirectly via initial ideas. As the design progresses, and is adopted as a style by others, points of style thus exert an increasing influence.

8. Representing Stylistic Weakness

Many user interface designs suffer from weaknesses in the user interface style. These arise from two main sources:

(a) *Stylistic flaws*: properties of the user interface may conflict with requirements or with other parts of the user interface, and thus cause inconsistencies of style;

(b) *Undefined style*: there may be areas where no single form of user interface satisfies all requirements; therefore the design is left vague, and this is reflected in a lack of definition in the style.

For example, most screen-based text editors have difficulty dealing with the design of the 'Move' command. A mode may be introduced between giving the *Move* command and selecting the destination for the selected text; or an additional concept (a secondary selection) may be introduced solely to support the *Move* command. These represent failure to comply with all requirements or to construct a sound argument for the design. They are reflected back as stylistic flaws.

A common example of lack of stylistic definition is in text editors' interface to the filing system. Naming conventions are usually left vague, with certain 'preferred' styles of naming (e.g., use of specific file-name extensions), and the editor often has the capability to read files in an arbitrary range of foriegn formats. There are usually strong practical arguments for this lack of definition, but the end-result is to leave the designer without clear direction.

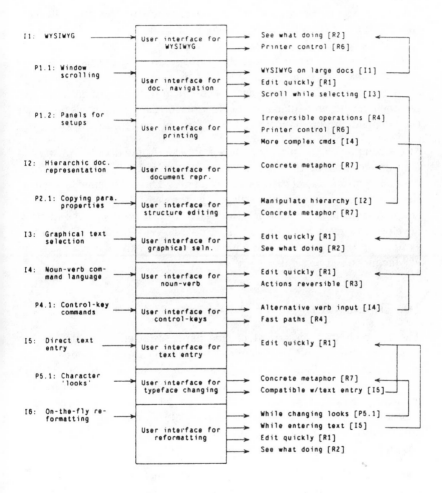

Figure 3. Linking points of style together to show argument

9. Simplifying the Representation

In extending the representation to deal with requirements and arguments, we have added to its complexity. To represent in this manner the style of a complete application, such as a 'desktop' environment, requires an extensive user interface specification with a large number of interconnections. It is unrealistic to expect designers to work with such a representation.

The main source of complexity is the presence of the user interface specification: it contains a large amount of detail that contributes a lot to defining the style but less to understanding it. Therefore one approach to simplifying the representation is to dispense with the user interface specification once it has done its duty as a bridge between points of style, requirements and arguments. The links in the representation can be labelled with an explanation of the user interface properties on which they depend. Figure 4 shows the final form of the representation.

More complete examples are shown in the Appendix. The first is a representation of the user interface style of Apple's Lisa, and has been chosen for its relative purity of style. The requirements used in this example are somewhat artificial, in the sense that they have been adapted from requirements for the Macintosh, a product subsequently developed to meet a similar range of user needs ([1987]). The second example in the Appendix is Macintosh itself; this example exposes some of Macintosh's stylistic flaws.

10. Discussion

The representation described in this paper is in experimental use at EuroPARC as an aid to designing user interfaces and understanding past designs. It is being used particularly in the analysis of the stylistic influence of environments such as Xerox Interlisp: by representing this influence (or lack of it) more formally, user interface designers can gain a better understanding of the need to conform with the style, of the options available to them within the style, and of the places in their design where they are running counter to style.

The representation of style hinges on construction of the underlying argument to the design. This is one of many areas where additional work is needed. The previously mentioned research under way in parallel at EuroPARC promises to provide a stronger basis for representing the underlying rationale to designs.

Even at this early stage, it is possible to discern benefits of trying to represent user interface style. It is useful, for example, to distinguish

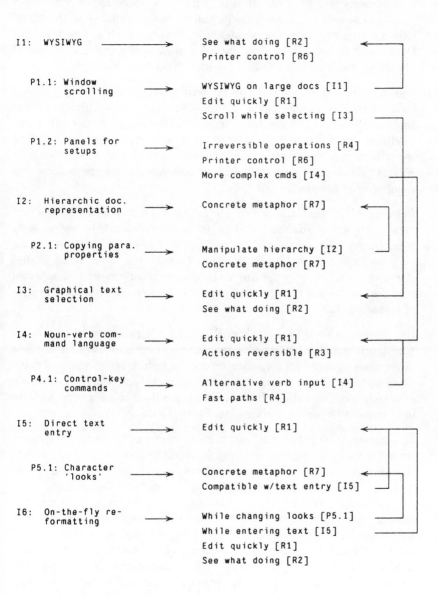

I1: WYSIWYG ⟶ See what doing [R2]
Printer control [R6]

P1.1: Window
scrolling ⟶ WYSIWYG on large docs [I1]
Edit quickly [R1]
Scroll while selecting [I3]

P1.2: Panels for
setups ⟶ Irreversible operations [R4]
Printer control [R6]
More complex cmds [I4]

I2: Hierarchic doc.
representation ⟶ Concrete metaphor [R7]

P2.1: Copying para.
properties ⟶ Manipulate hierarchy [I2]
Concrete metaphor [R7]

I3: Graphical text
selection ⟶ Edit quickly [R1]
See what doing [R2]

I4: Noun-verb com-
mand language ⟶ Edit quickly [R1]
Actions reversible [R3]

P4.1: Control-key
commands ⟶ Alternative verb input [I4]
Fast paths [R4]

I5: Direct text
entry ⟶ Edit quickly [R1]

P5.1: Character
'looks' ⟶ Concrete metaphor [R7]
Compatible w/text entry [I5]

I6: On-the-fly re-
formatting ⟶ While changing looks [P5.1]
While entering text [I5]
Edit quickly [R1]
See what doing [R2]

**Figure 4. Style representation with user interface
definition omitted**

design ideas from the user interface itself, and to remind designers that ideas do not, in the absence of a specific interface, ensure that requirements will be met. It is also useful to show the designer how much influence some ideas have on the design in comparison to others. Designers are prone to pick up highly visible ideas such as 'windows and icons', and to ignore more central ideas such as the use in desktops of capability models rather than file-system models of storage.

One of the weakest areas of user interface design methodology is the incorporation of requirements and design criteria. It is widely accepted that requirements are not fully defined before design begins: they are modified and added to as the design work proceeds (Balzer [1980]). The use of style representations could help designers to deal more effectively with requirements, because the linkage between the designer's ideas and requirements are made clear.

It seems likely that the use of a stronger representation of style will permit objective analysis of style to be performed. It has already been suggested here that stylistic flaws and areas of indefinition can be brought out more clearly; it is also possible that designers will find it easier to select appropriate styles for applications and thus avoid mistakes of the past, such as designing word processors around the style of spreadsheets.

User interface style is a particularly important property of user interface toolkits and interactive programming environments. All of these environments exert an influence on user interface style, some of them more strongly than others. It is interesting that Interlisp, which has a relatively loose stylistic influence, has shown itself to be a very effective environment for user interface experimentation.

In summary, this paper has tried to show how user interface style exerts its influence on all aspects of human-computer interaction. Style affects the user, whose interaction with the computer system is affected by the style of interface. It affects HCI research, where the different basic styles of interaction provide manageable domains within which to conduct experiments or between which to make comparison. It is particularly influential in design, which often uses an existing style as a starting point. It is now beginning to influence the development of user interface toolkits, each of which tends to promote a particular style of interaction. Issues of style thus are present in most situations where interaction with computers is at stake; we need to understand these issues better.

Acknowledgements

I wish to thank Allan MacLean and Richard Young for the contributions to this paper stemming from their work on design rationale. I am also grateful to Thomas Green, Karmen Guevara and Tom Moran for their helpful comments.

Lisa and Macintosh are trademarks of Apple Computer Inc.

References

[1987], in *Apple Human Interface Guidelines*, Addison–Wesley.

R M Baecker & W A S Buxton [1987], "Human-Computer Interaction: A Multi-Disciplinary Approach.

R M Balzer [July 1980], "Note on the Relation of Specification to Design," *Communications of the ACM*.

Le Corbusier [1937], "Toward a New Architecture," London.

N V Hammond, A Jorgensen, A Maclean, P Barnard & J Long [1983], "Design Practice and Interface Usability: evidence from Interviews and Designers," IBM Hursley Research Centre, Report No HF082.

A Maclean, R M Young, T P Moran & W M Newman, "Understanding Design Rationale," In Preparation.

W M Newman & R F Sproull [1979], *Principles of Interactive Computer Graphics*, McGraw-Hill, 2nd Edition.

B Shneiderman [1987], *Designing the User Interface: Strategies for Effective Human-Computer Interaction*, Addison-Wesley, Reading MA.

Appendix I: Partial Style Representation of Apple Lisa User Interface

1. User Requirements

The requirements on which Lisa was based have never been documented. For the purposes of this example, we have adapted the requirements of Macintosh, a system designed to meet a very similar purpose to Lisa's. The Macintosh requirements have been documented, albeit informally, in (Hammond et al. [1983]); the adapted requirements are shown here.

R01:   Users need a consistent and familiar computer environment.

R02:   Users need an environment in which they can perform their many tasks.

R03:   Encourage active, self-directed exploration.

R04:   Provide users with a sense of being in control.

R05:   Exploit skills in symbolic manipulation - verbal, visual, gestural.

R06:   Provide a comfortable, enjoyable, challenging context.

R07:   Provide a concrete metaphor, and use effects that support it.

R08:   Keep users informed about options, status, dangers.

R09:   Protect against serious error from random input.

R10:   Exploit the user's recognition not recall.

R11:   Allow the user to exploit the full power of the computer.

R12:   Allow users to see what they're doing.

R13:   Allow users to point at what they see.

R14:   Permit fast alternative paths to achieving desired actions.

R15:   Maintain consistency across applications, even if there is a loss in efficiency.

R16:   Avoid abstract commands that require mental calculations of future outcomes.

R17:   Ensure printer output corresponds to screen display.

R18:   Allow control over both content and formatting of documents.

R19:   Warn of dangers and permit confirmation of dangerous commands

R20:   Ensure feedback is in the user's vocabulary.

R21:   User actions should be reversible, with warnings if they aren't.

R22:   Provide a feeling of stability of data over time.

R23:   Provide an attractive display.

R24:   Ensure different things look different on the screen.

R25:   Permit users to control superficial appearance of the user interface

R26:   Applications shouldn't leave messes for the user to clean up.

R27:   Provide access to multiple applications.

R28:   Avoid frightening associations.

2. Basic stylistic ideas

Eight major ideas guided the Lisa design. As the following list shows, they were largely independent:

I1. Desktop metaphor: folders, documents, etc., chosen to resemble concrete office objects.

I2. Multiple document types, each with its application: text documents with word processor, line drawings with graphics editor, etc.

I3. Capability model: each document exists in only one place at one time.

I4. WYSIWYG.

I5. Multiple overlapping windows.

I6. Command menu with pull-down submenus.

I7. Transfer data between applications via copy-and-paste.

I8. System state saved on power-down, restored on power-up.

3. Style Representation

No.	Point	Link/requirement
I1	Desktop metaphor	Familiar [R01]
		Concrete metaphor [R07]
		See and point [R12, R13]
		Attractive display [R23]
P1.1	Desktop integrated with applics	Support task performance [R02]
I2	Multiple tools (applications)	Multiple applications [R27]
P2.1	Unique doc type for each tool	Start tool by opening doc [P2.3]
P2.2	Combined repr for doc+tool	Protect against error [R09]
		Support task performance [R02]
		Reinf'ce unique type/tool [P2.1]
		Consistent across applics [R15]
P2.3	Start tool by opening document	Consistent across applics [R15]
		Unique doc type per tool [P2.1]
I3	Capability model: document in one place at one time	Reinf'ces desktop metaphor [I1]
		Support task performance [R02]
		Recognition not recall [R10]
		No messes [R26]
P3.1	Refer to document by pointing	Extends capability model [I3]
P3.2	Non-unique document names	Reinf'ces ref-by-pointing [P3.1]
		Recognition not recall [R10]

P3.3	Set aside documents as icons	Concrete metaphor [R07] Reinforces desktop metaphor Exploit symbolic skills [R05]
I4	WYSIWYG	Concrete metaphor [R07] User in control [R04] Printer/display correspond [R
I5	Multiple overlapping windows	Support task performance [R(Recognition not recall [R10] See and point [R12, R13] Stability of data over time [R Control superf. appearance [F
P5.1	Window/icon represents doc+tool	Reinforces combined repr [P2 Different things look dif't [R2 Supports capability model [I3
P5.2	Single selected window	Extend windows [I5] Protect against error [R09]
P5.3	Selected window on top	Extends One sel'd window [P See and point [R12, R13]
I6	Command menu with pull-down submenus	Support task performance [R(Protect against error [R09] See and point [R12, R13] Consistent across applics [R1 No messes [R26]
P6.1	Menus tool-dependent	Reinforces combined repr [P2
P6.2	Show selected window's menu	Extends One sel'd window [P
I7	Transfer data via copy-and-paste	Support task performance [R(Consistent with Single selecte window [P5.2]
I8	System state saved on power- down	Stability of data over time [R
P8.1	Icons/windows return to previous positions	Consistent with saved state [I Recognition not recall [R10]

Appendix II: Partial Style Representation of Apple Macintosh User Interface

1. User Requirements

The requirements for the Apple Macintosh include the user requirements listed in Section 1 of Appendix I, together with the following technical requirements imposed to keep product costs down:

R29: Permit use of inexpensive memory management technology.
R30: Use micro floppy disks for permanent storage.

2. Basic stylistic ideas.

The basic ideas behind Macintosh are very similar to those of Lisa:

I1. Desktop metaphor: folders, documents, etc., resembling concrete office objects.
I2. Multiple applications, running one at a time.
I3. Capability model within desktop: each document exists in only one place at one time.
I4. WYSIWYG.
I5. Multiple overlapping windows.
I6. Command menu with pull-down submenus.
I7. Transfer data between applications via copy-and-paste.

3. Style Representation

No.	Point	Link/requirement
I1	Desktop metaphor	Familiar [R01]
		Concrete metaphor [R07]
		See and point [R12, R13]
		Attractive display [R23]
P1.1	Desktop runs as separate applic	Memory management [R29]
		Desktop metaphor [I2]
		does not support Task performance [R02]
I2	Multiple applications, one at a time	Multiple applications [R27]
		Memory management [R29]
		does not support Task performance [R02]
P2.1	Docs typed according to tool	Different things look diff't [R24]
P2.2	Tools exist separately from docs	Micro floppy storage [R30]

P2.3	Open document to run tool	Consistent with Documents typed by tool [P2.1] Protect against error [R09] Support task performance [R0
P2.4	Open tool to run tool	Implied by Separate tools and documents [P2.2] *conflicts with* Open document run tool [P2.3]
U2.5	Some tools can read other tools' docs	Implied by Separate tools and documents [P2.2] *fails* Consistency across applications [R15]
I3	Capability model within desktop	Reinforces desktop metaphor Support task performance [R(Recognition not recall [R10]
P3.1	Show tools and docs as icons	Recognition not recall [I3] Attractive display [R23] Reinforces desktop metaphor
F3.2	File-system model within tools	Required by One-at-a-time applications [I2] Simplifies Micro-flop storage [*conflicts with* Capability mod within desktop [I3]
F3.3	Unique document names	Requr'd by File sys model [F: *conflicts with* Recognition not recall [R10]
I4	WYSIWYG	Concrete metaphor [R07] Reinforce desktop metaphor [Printer/display corres [R17]
I5	Multiple overlapping windows	Support task performance [R(Recognition not recall [R10] See and point [R12, R13] Control superf. appearance [F
P5.1	Single selected window	Extend idea of Windows [I5] Protect against error [R09]
P5.3	Selected window on top	Extends idea of Single selecte window [P5.1] See and point [R12, R13]
I6	Command menu with pull-down submenus	Support task performance [R(Protect against error [R09]

		See and point [R12, R13] Consistent across applics [R15] No messes [R26]
P6.1	Menus tool-dependent	Consistent with document typing [P2.2]
P6.2	Show selected window's menu	Extends One sel'd window [P5.1]
I7	Transfer data via copy-and-paste	Support task performance [R02] Consistent with single selected window [P5.1]

Some Experiences in Integrating Specification of Human Computer Interaction within a Structured System Development Method

Alistair Sutcliffe

Dept of Business Systems Analysis, City University,
Northampton Square, London EC1V 0HB, U.K.

Procedures for integrating task analysis and design of human computer interfaces into a structured system design method, Jackson system development (JSD) are described. JSD process structure diagrams are used to describe tasks which are then evaluated for cognitive complexity. Task allocation and complexity analysis produced specification of human tasks, highlighted the need for task support actions, especially information display support for working memory, and produced computer process specifications for human task support. Dialogue specification for a direct manipulation interface design was taken from the JSD object/event model from which permissible manipulations were derived. Further PSD diagrams were constructed to specify interface object management processes. Preliminary evaluation of the method showed that the method was easy to learn even for non HCI specialists.

Keywords: interface design, systems design, task analysis, direct manipulation

1. Introduction

Many specification and design methods for human computer interaction have been proposed which take little or no account of system development methods (see Wilson *et al* (Wilson, Barnard & Maclean [1986])). Likewise authors of system development methods pay no attention to design of the human computer interface (Olle, Sol & Verrijn-Stuart [1986]). It is the contention of this paper that practice of good human computer interface design will only result from integration of HCI principles and procedures within existing system design methods, rather than by creation of stand-alone HCI methods. By using the notational tools with which analysts are already familiar, the HCI community may influence the creators of human computer interface software by supplementing their methods with good HCI practices.

It is beyond the scope of this paper to review a complete methodology of HCI design; consequently, only two topics will be considered: task analysis and dialogue specification. Experiences in adapting and using a commonly practised structured system development method, Jackson System Development (Jackson [1983]; Sutcliffe [1988]), for task analysis and dialogue design are described. This work forms part of a larger study of integrating HCI practices within system development methods (Sutcliffe & McDermott [1988]). Brief details of JSD will be presented and the basic requirements for specification of human computer interaction outlined before extensions to the method are proposed. Use of the method is illustrated by reference to a case study of the UMIST Library system which was used to evaluate the practicalities of HCI specification using JSD.

2. Jackson System Development and HCI requirements

JSD is an object-event oriented development method which makes it appealing for HCI specification. The aim of this study was to use JSD, or more specifically its notation tools, for the purposes of HCI specification whenever possible. JSD makes extensive use of structure diagrams for process specification. These diagrams describe event sequences in terms of three control primitives: sequences, selection and iteration, as well as expressing a process structure which becomes the template for a program design. Figure 1 shows a process structure diagram for the book object/process in a library system. This describes an entity life history composed of events which happen to a book ordered from left to right across the diagram, e.g., the book is acquired, classified, loaned and finally sold or archived. For further details of the method the reader is referred to Jackson (Jackson [1983]) or Sutcliffe (Sutcliffe [1988]). This study investigated how process structure diagrams (PSDs) could be used for task and dialogue specification.

The objectives of task analysis are open to many interpretations (see Wilson *et al* (Wilson, Barnard & Maclean [1986]) for a review). However, two common themes are specification of functionality and cognitive complexity. The former describes activity while the latter evaluates the cognitive demands of tasks on human information processing. Accordingly the requirements of the JSD specification were set as a functional task description in terms of objects and actions, as found in many HCI methods (e.g. (Johnson [1985]; Moran [1981]),); and an estimate of cognitive complexity for information processing, in the spirit of Kieras and Polson (Kieras & Polson [1985]), but with the objective of enabling the designer to trouble-shoot the design for human limitations of working memory. It was not the intention to create a sophisticated, theoretical cognitive task model (e.g. (Barnard [1986]),), rather the aim was to create a simple, easy to use method with immediate practical benefits for systems analysts.

The second objective was to design dialogue structures to support tasks, with the added constraint of specification for direct manipulation interfaces. This constraint was added because, although direct manipulation interfaces are popular, there are few prescriptive methods on how the design them. The design exercise was based on a case study for a library system.

3. Task analysis

The first extension to the method was that all tasks should be described without prejudice as to their eventual automation. Task activities were modelled as processes which interact with objects in the JSD model. JSD makes extensive reference to modelling 'real world' objects yet it does not advise explicit modelling of user tasks. The method is easily extended to explicit modelling of user tasks as a sequence of actions. These tasks, more properly termed 'interactive functions' in JSD, describe functionality in sequential terms, as can be seen in fig 2 which shows a PSD for the 'check reader' task in the library system. This shows the procedural sequence of task actions for checking a reader's identification:

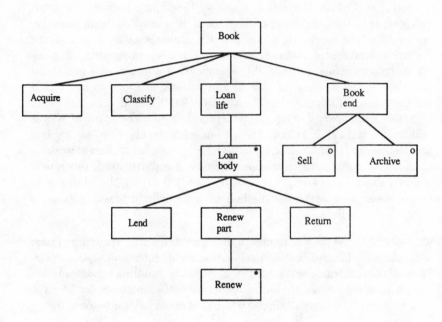

PSD diagrams have three components: sequences (a box); selections (a box marked with an o) and iterations (a box marked with *). The tree diagram expresses hierarchy in the process structure and the sequential ordering of events which may happen to the object. Thus the book will be acquired then classified after which it may be borrowed, possibly have its loan renewed, before being returned, After many loans the book will eventually be sold or archived.

Figure 1. Process Structure diagram showing book object model process

first library membership is checked with possible actions if the reader is banned, then any overdue books and reservations are dealt with before the librarian requests which service the reader requires.

After initial description, tasks were allocated to either users or the computer system according to well established critieria (Bailey [1982]). As many tasks involved both human and computer actions, allocation was performed at the task-action level. Each PSD component was assigned as a system or user action, or a joint cooperating action which required further elaboration to design computer support for the human task step. The output from this step was two sets of PSD diagrams, one set describing user tasks which were not to be computerised, and the other set describing tasks either fully computerised with no interaction (automated tasks) or interactive tasks, eventually becoming part of the interface software. An example of a human interactive task is shown in fig 3. Checking the reader's ID, overdue books and reservations were obvious task steps for automated support; but deciding what action to take with readers was a complex action involving human judgement and was left a human only action. Note that the structure is based on the initial task description, although some actions suitable for complete automation have been omitted, e.g., calculate fines. The corresponding computer task support PSD has display actions for each user decision step, e.g., display reader status for check membership.

The second addition to JSD was a set of simple metrics for estimating probable cognitive loads on working memory from analysis of PSD diagrams. Following production rule approaches to complexity, task actions were counted and conditional statements scored for the complexity of their logic (compound conditions and negatives were assigned higher complexity values). This gave overall complexity measures for each diagram in terms of the range and expected average number of actions per task and the production systems necessary for decision making within a task. A sample complexity measure for the check-reader task is illustrated in figure 4(a); this had a considerable range in actions and two compound decisions which were consequently weighted for complexity.

These measures were used for several purposes: to indicate the need to decompose large complex tasks; to allocate tasks to people matching user skills to task complexity, and providing variety in task complexity within an indiviudal user's work. The task-action sequences, shown in PSD diagrams, were also analysed for length of task. The action sequence was examined to see if it was continuous or not. Closure events were planned for long, continuous tasks either by segmenting large tasks into sub tasks or by inserting breakpoints into long sequences. Breakpoints were placed at the logical end of groups of related actions; and in many PSDs these points were indicated by selections, that is action groups

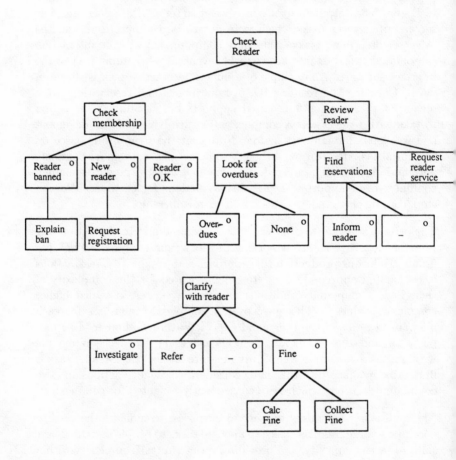

Figure 2. Process structure diagram: Check Reader-ID
initial task description

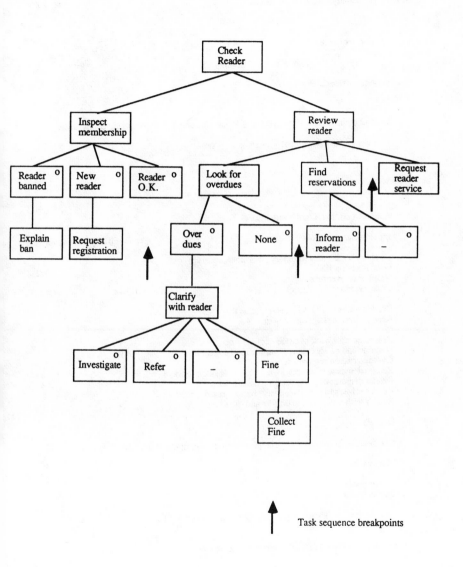

**Figure 3.   Process structure diagram: Check Reader-ID
human task specification after analysis for
complexity and break-points**

(a) Break-point analysis: Check reader task

	Average	Range
Action sequences	5	4 - 8
	Simple	Compound
Conditions/decisions	2	2

Overall complexity = N(av actions) + M(simple conds) + (P(compound conds) x 2)

Task complexity (weighted) = 11 steps

(b) Memory loading analysis

Action/Condition: Clarify with reader

Inputs (Data and Policy rules)	exp familiarity	memory units
Overdue book status (ordinary, short loan, reserve)	-	1
Overdue book ID	-	1/2
Number of overdues	-	1
Time overdue, loan dates	-	2-6
Reader status (staff, PG, student, other)	-	1
Reader fines outstanding -amout	-	1
Reader accepts book overdue - collect fine	Y	1
Overdue and on short loan - warn reader, collect fine	Y	1
Overdue and on reserve - refer	N	2
Reader denies loan - check loan date, check stock for book, refer	N	4
Reader disputes date - check loan date, refer	N	3
Reader refuses to pay fine - insist, request reason, refer	Y	1
Reader with previous unpaid fine and overdues -refer	N	3

Outputs

Decision : refer to senior librarian, investigate, fine, ignore if in error.

Memory loading

4 units per book
2 units for the reader

15 units for 7 policy rules, possibly more for procedure rules

Display support - Details of books overdue, reader details, policy summary

Figure 4.   Complexity analysis: Task step – Clarify with Reader

controlled by a decision. Hence in the check-reader task, break points were placed after checking reader membership, dealing with overdue books and informing readers about books they had reserved (see fig 3). The practical implications of closure event planning lay in specification of response times and design of dialogues.

To evaluate working memory loading, tasks were examined to describe the input to each action in terms of data necessary for human information processing. Specification of the data necessary to complete actions is part of the original JSD method in which input messages are described as 'action attributes' while data, belonging to a process, which are necessary for completion of an action are referred to as 'entity attributes'. These concepts can be generalised in the context of user task actions to input data and information held in long term and working memory. Approximate quantification of memory loading was carried out by recording data items by size, complexity of data structure, and probable familiarity of the item to the user.

As chunking is known to effect working memory capacity, user familiarity with the data was considered important. Simple numbers (up to 100) and text strings (e.g., a short name up to 10 characters) were scored as single chunk units and compounded as complexity increased. Rules were assigned at least two units one for the condition part and another for the action part. If the user was expected to be familiar with the data, and the rules in particular, the chunking was reduced. For instance, familiar rules appeared to be stored as single entities and consequently they were assigned one memory unit. Using the well known working memory limit of 7 plus or minus 2 (Miller [1956]), an approximate calculation of memory loading was carried out as a screening technique. Because calculations based on Miller's statement of memory limitations represents an unjustifiable oversimplification in view of more recent work (Hitch [1987]), the next step was to take a practical approach by consulting users to determine whether they felt they could hold the necessary facts in memory or not.

If either the quantity of data was likely to exceed working memory in the user's opinion or most of the data were expected to be unfamiliar to the user then this suggested that working memory should be supported with computerised information displays. While it is impossible to give accurate quantification of memory loading based on simple counts of data items, this approach does allow quick and simple estimates of possible memory loads which, combined with user testing, are of practical help for the designer when specifying task support displays.

A case in point is data necessary to check the reader's identification in the library system and then to decide what action to take. Here the librarian has to evaluate a considerable quantity of data containing the reader's name, category (staff, student, post graduate, research personnel) as well as reader history relating to fines and bans; also more data has to be remembered about the library's policy in dealing with difficult readers. Analysis of memory loading for one task step, 'clarify with reader' is shown in fig 4(b). Holding the data on overdue books, reader status and all the policy rules in working memory at once was likely to exceed human capacity. Subsequent interviews with the librarians confirmed this and indeed the rules were consulted in a written document. Consequently the design was elaborated to include information displays by the computer system of overdue book details, reader status and policy options to support human decision making.

4. Dialogue design for Direct Manipulation Interfaces

This part of the method takes the computer task description and creates a specification of the human computer interface dialogue. Input to dialogue design came from task specification of the functionality for user support and from the JSD object model for the user -system object interactions. The virtue of JSD for direct manipulation interface design is that it creates an explicit object model of the system which can be used to plan the system representation. For instance in the library system, JSD models objects such as books and readers in terms of events which may happen to those objects in a life history (see fig 1 which describes the book life history from acquisition to removal from the library). Life history events translate directly into permissible manipulations of the object on the interface display.

Discussion of the intricacies of designing the appearance of the whole interface in this paper has to be curtailed because of space constraints. Instead, attention will be focused on the use of JSD to design the software processes which control the object-user interaction via its iconic representation. Design is based on the JSD object life history specifications which define permissable manipulations on the icons in a display. Unfortunately direct manipulation interfaces are often highly moded, i.e., the actions on an object depend on its state and context. This means that permissible manipulations are constrained by an object's status and where it is within the display area. The former constraint is a common system design problem, already addressed by JSD in the form of a state vector. This maintains a life history status record so the system can decide whether a particular object, for instance a book, is on loan, in the library (and may therefore be borrowed), or reserved. These constraints create interface design problems which particularly afflict direct manipulation interfaces as the screen manifestations of objects (e.g., icons) have to react in accordance with their state. The problem for the interface management system is ascertain the user's intentions with an object and an object's history so it can react appropriately.

The interface screen design for the library loans sub-system is illustrated fig 5. The metaphor of interaction, which was derived from analysis of the users' conceptual model, has the library divided into three areas: the stock area which contains the issue desk, short loan collection, ordinary book stock, reserved books, and the re-shelving stack; the reader area within the library; and the out-of-library area. Manipulations are performed on book icons by dragging them between different areas. Hence dragging the book icon from the issue desk to the reserve stack models the action of marking a book as reserved. Book icons can be picked from any part of the stock area, so the object management software has to decide in what context a book has been picked (e.g., from stock, from short loans, on the re-shelving stack, issue desk, etc.) and what are the appropriate actions for that role. Thus book icons picked on the issue desk may be loaned, reserved, or returned by moving them to the out-of-library, reservations or re-shelving stack respectively. The specification for this dialogue control by the book icon object manager is shown in fig 6. Any manipulation of the book object not resulting in it being placed on the reserve list, in the out-of-library area, or reshelving area, etc, had no effect at the interface. The PSD gives an explicit model of all the possible manipulations for each book role, selection of the role being triggered by the location of the first pick.

Control of the display context required a further state vector to be created which tracks where the icon is on the screen and thereby controls the permissible manipulations. To illustrate the point, the book icon has to know where it is on the screen as well as where it is in its life history. The book object in the 'issues desk' area can be moved into the reservation area, to the user area for loans, or the reshelving area if it is a return. This choice will be further constrained by the state vector recording the status of the particular book in question (e.g., if on loan and already renewed 3 times it can not be loaned again). Interaction is controlled by the object role specification within the object management process, in consultation with the state vector containing the life history of a particular book.

5. Evaluation

The method was informally evaluated by giving 10 subjects, UMIST M.Sc. students, a task analysis problem based on the case study of designing an interface for a hotel booking system. Half the students were familiar with JSD but had no HCI training, half had both HCI and

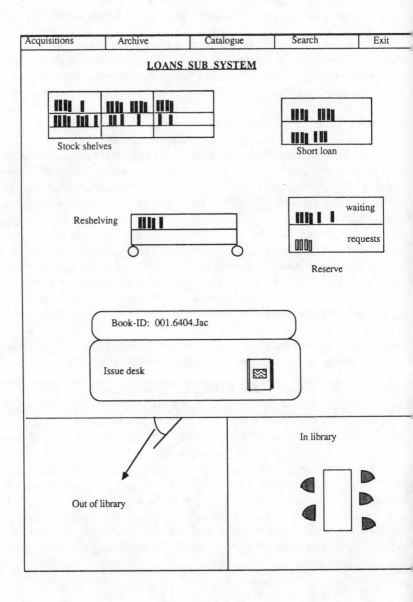

Figure 5.   Screen design for library loans system interface

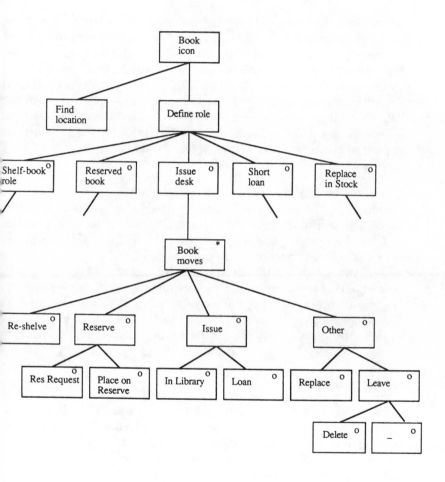

The sub-trees for other roles (reserved book, short loan, replace in stock) have not been illustrated.

Figure 6. Specification of object management process for the book icon

JSD knowledge. Evaluation was carried out by questionnaire requesting the students' assessment of their JSD and HCI knowledge and opinions about the ease of use, problems ecountered, and potential benefit of the method on improving interface design. This analysis was followed up by interviews to establish points of difficulty with the method and by expert judgement on the qualities of the HCI specifications produced for the case study.

All students sucessfully completed the problem; 4 out of 5 without HCI knowledge found the memory complexity metrics hard to interpret (scores of -3, -2 on a seven point -3 to $+3$ questionnaire scale) but found the rest of the method (task analysis, dialogue and DM specification) easy to use. Three out of the same five students considered that the interface design would be improved by the method (scores of $+2$, $+3$). All five students who had JSD and HCI knowledge rated all aspects as easy to use and reported that the method had had a beneficial impact on the HCI aspect of the system design (scores of $+2$, $+3$ on a seven point scale).

Evaluation by expert judgement of the resultant specifications was less encouraging. Three specifications were judged to be good ($+2$, $+3$) all of which belonged to the JSD and HCI expertise group, four were average (-1, 0, $+1$ scores) of which two were from the HCI and JSD group, and the remaining specifications were rated as poor. In follow up interviews all students reported that they found the transfer of PSD notation to the context of HCI specification easy to learn and the use of a single notation for several purposes did not cause confusion. The main criticism was the lack of precision of the memory load metrics, although all subjects did consider it to be a useful indicator for further analysis with the user.

6. Conclusions

The case study demonstrated the practicality of integrating HCI specification within JSD and the experience proved illuminating in influencing the design in directions not originally anticipated, such as highlighting the need for information displays to support working memory. While simple psychological metrics are not statisfactory if used as design parameters, they can be used for filtering analysis and identifying follow up action on design in conjunction with user testing. Perhaps their most important role is in drawing attention to the problem in the first place. Overall application of the method can not be said to have improved the HCI design products of subjects without HCI expertise which underlines the point that methods in combination with human factors knowledge is required. Further evaluation of the JSD-HCI method is required in commercial environments with in-depth study of more complex problems; however this study indicates that use of a specification formalism familiar to systems analysts should encourage adoption of HCI practices within the system development life cycle. This approach capitalises on the analyst's existing knowledge and makes assimilation of HCI models easier, as well as minimising the effort necessary to acquire methods and techniques for human-computer interface design.

While resolution of complex human factors issues requires extensive skill training and automated support of HCI for non experts would require knowledge based systems (Barnard [1986]); modest improvements in HCI practice could be delivered by HCI-system design method integration. It is notable that movements are being made in this direction both by HCI researchers who are making methods more relevant to system development practices (Johnson & Johnson [1987]; Wasserman [1984]) and authors of commercial structured system development methods (Burchett [1986]) who have incorporated steps for simple dialogue design.

It is contended that the approach of integrating HCI procedures and practice with structured system development methods is essential, given the low acceptance of specification and design methods created by the HCI community. Even experience of their use within the HCI community has found such methods to be cumbersome and unworkable without modification (Sharratt [1987]).

Acknowledgments

The author is indebted to Lesley Cowey, whose M.Sc. thesis formed the basis for this work.

References

R W Bailey [1982], *Human Performance Engineering*, Prentice-Hall.

P Barnard [1986], "Cognitive Resources and the Learning of Human Computer Dialogues," IBM Hursley Research Centre, Report No HF118.

Learmont and Burchett [1986], *LBMS Structured Systems Development Methodology*, NCC Publications.

G J Hitch [1987], "Working Memory," in *Applying Cognitive Psychology to User Interface Design*, M M Gardiner and B Christie, ed., Wiley, Chichester.

M A Jackson [1983], *System Development*, Prentice-Hall.

H Johnson & P Johnson [1987], "The Development of Task Analysis as a Design Tool: A Method For Carrying Out Task Analysis," Internal Report, Queen Mary College, Department of Computer Science.

P Johnson [1985], "Towards a Task Model of Messaging: An Example of the Application of TAKD to User Interface Design," in *People and Computers: Designing the Interface*, P Johnson and S Cook, ed., Cambridge University Press, Cambridge.

D Kieras & P G Polson [1985], "An Approach to the Formal Analysis of User Complexity," *Int. J. Man-Machine Studies* 22, 365–394.

G A Miller [1956], "The Magical Number Seven, Plus or Minus Two: Some Limits on our Capacity for Information Processing," *Psychological Review* 63, 81–97.

T P Moran [1981], "The Command Language Grammar: A Representation for the User Interface of Interactive Computing Systems," *Int. J. Man-Machine Studies* 15, 3–50.

T W Olle, H G Sol & A A Verrijn-Stuart [1986], *Information System Design Methodologies: Improving the Practice*, North-Holland.

B Sharratt [1987], "Top-Down Interactive Systems Design: Some Lessons Learnt from Using Command Language Grammar," in *INTER-ACT '87 – The Second IFIP Conference on Human-Computer Interaction*, H J Bullinger and B Shackel, ed., Elsevier Science Publishers B.V., North Holland.

A G Sutcliffe [1988], *Jackson System Development*, Prentice-Hall.

A G Sutcliffe & M McDermott [1988], "Integrating Human-Computer Interface Design with Structured System Development Methods," UMIST, Department of Computation, Internal Report (In preparation).

A I Wasserman [1984], "Developing Interactive Systems with the User Software Engineering Methodology," in *INTERACT '84 – First IFIP Conference on Human-Computer Interaction*, B Shackel, ed., Elsevier-Science, Amsterdam.

M D Wilson, P Barnard & A Maclean [1986], "Task Analysis in Human Computer Interaction," IBM Hursley Research Centre, Report No HF122.

Humans, Computers, and Contracts

A.J. Gundry

Electronic Facilities Design Limited, Channing House, Wargrave, Berkshire RG10 8HD, U.K.

Large interactive systems are increasingly purchased by means of competitive, fixed-price contracts. Under a common form of this arrangement, a purchasing authority sponsors a requirement study and places a contract for a design study with two or more contractors. During the design study, the contractors are in a cost-effectiveness competition, and the one who wins will be held to his bid price for the implementation that follows. This paper looks at both sides of the contractual divide to see how HCI practice fares under these conditions. On the purchasing authority's side, the consequences of expressing HCI requirements in contractually-robust language are examined, with illustrative examples. On the contractor's side, typical constraints on his HCI design team are restricted access to users and the pressure to show that solutions are cost-effective. The paper reviews some other procedures in this context: user demonstrations, technical adjudication and acceptance tests, and outlines their implications. The paper concludes with a discussion of the challenges for HCI knowledge and practice of a contractual environment, and the comparisons to be made with other disciplines.

Keywords: HCI, Procurement, Contracts

1. Introduction

Increasingly, large interactive systems are purchased by means of competitive, fixed-price contracts. In fact, the larger the system the more likely it is to exceed the price threshold above which competitive purchasing is mandatory. The type of systems concerned are diverse, but are particularly those purchased by Government departments. Both the MOD, as a purchaser, and HM Treasury's Central Computers and Telecommunications Agency, which advises Government departments on system acquisition, now require competitive purchasing of large systems.

This paper is however, not concerned with any particular purchasing body or system, and addresses the generic tasks and roles that competitive purchasing imposes. An individual competitive purchase may fit what is said here to greater or lesser extent, depending upon the nature of the system and the agility of the parties involved.

2. A Simplified Description Of Competitive Purchasing

Competitive purchasing will be described here in relation to a simplified system acquisition programme, comprising the five broadly-serial phases listed below and shown with more detail in Figure 1.

- (a) Requirements Definition
- (b) Design
- (c) Development and Production
- (d) Acceptance
- (e) Installation and In-service use

Often, the Development and Production Phase, the Acceptance Phase and Installation are collectively called 'Implementation'.

2.1. Requirements Definition

A single Purchasing Authority (hereafter 'the Authority') is in charge of the Requirements Definition Phase. It is responsible for capturing and specifying the requirements for the System. That System is to be purchased to provide a service to a set of Users, who have been involved during Requirements Definition. The Authority receives advice from Technical Advisors. Whilst the Users' input will centre upon the functionality required of the System, the Technical Advisors will typically define requirements for the '-ilities': availability, maintainability, installability etc. Another distinction is that Users will tend to

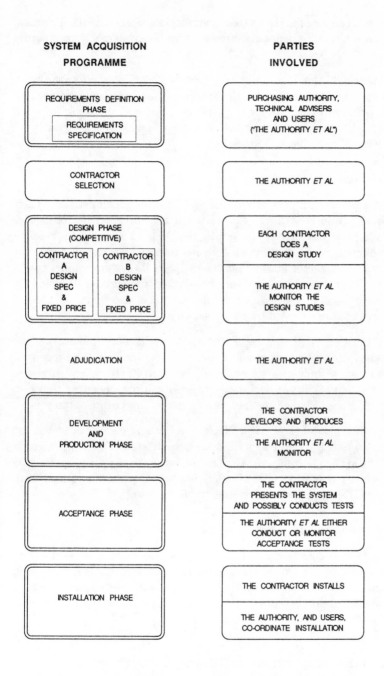

Figure 1.   A model competitive purchase system
acquisition programme and the parties
involved

define requirements for the System's applications, whereas the Technical Advisors will tend to define requirements for the System's infrastructure (see (Gundry [1987])).

The Authority, the Users and the Technical Advisors put together a Requirements Specification for the System. That Specification is accompanied by a draft contract for the Design Phase, and the whole is issued to vendor Companies. A number of them respond with Proposals for the Design Phase, and two are selected.

2.2. Design

The Contractors undertaking the Design Phase are in competition. Their goal is to produce a Design Specification accompanied by fixed-price bids to implement the System. Whilst the Design Phase itself is rarely a source of great profit, the Implementation is more lucrative. To win that work, each Contractor knows that it must price its system competitively. Neither Contractor will, however, be allowed to increase its price for Implementation, if it wins, beyond its bid price, except in the case of contract variations agreed by the Authority.

During the Design Phase, the Authority stays in place, monitoring the work schedule, controlling any newly-arising requirements, and receiving advice about technical progress made visible to its Technical Advisors. Demands for visibility of technical progress will have been written into the draft Design Phase Contract, now accepted by both Contractors.

At the conclusion of the Design Phase, the Design Specifications and the fixed-price bids for Implementation are adjudicated. One Contractor is chosen, who then becomes the Contractor (or perhaps prime Contractor) for the Implementation. The Implementation Contract is formed from the earlier Design Specification and the fixed-price bid.

2.3. Implementation

During Development and Production, the Contractor is working to realise the Design Specification in a concrete, working System. Successful acceptance of that System by the Authority will typically release payment of a large proportion of the Contract value. Following Acceptance, installation at the User site(s) commences.

3. HCI Representation During Competitive Purchasing

In order to illustrate the roles and practice of HCI during competitive purchasing, it is assumed that the Authority's Technical Advisors include

Human-Computer Interaction (HCI) Advisors. Their role is to advise concerning the 'human interface', as defined in the context of IT'86 as concerning "the user, and built in 'usability', at every phase of the system life cycle" (IT '86 [1986]). In that role, the HCI Advisors are concerned with more than just 'usability'. Their responsibility ranges from ergonomics and Users' working environment to System functionality and organisational aspects. Thus as Technical Advisors, the HCI Advisors are somewhat of a special case, having an interest in both the functionality and '-ilities' of the System. It is finally assumed that there is an equivalent HCI Design Team in each of the competing Contractors' Design Teams.

4. HCI Practice In Competitive Purchases

4.1. Overview

The competitive purchasing policy can be contrasted with another policy: that of co-operative system acquisition between the Users and the Suppliers, in which both parties work together, drawing upon the same pool of HCI Advisors. Under this policy, contracts for acquisition phases are flexible, spending is difficult to control, timescales expand, but HCI interests are probably best served. They are best served because communication between parties is not limited by contracts and contractual relationships, and because design and development have less pre-set cost and time constraints.

Principally because money and time are difficult to control, co-operative system acquisition is on the way out. So HCI practitioners either have to operate within a competitive purchasing policy or decide not to apply their expertise to an increasing number of system acquisitions.

For those HCI practitioners who wish to apply their expertise to large interactive systems, the remainder of this paper examines the implications of competitive purchasing. This author does not seek to defend competitive purchasing, but rather to explain the practices that it institutes, and offer practical advice as to how to work, where possible, within those practices.

4.2. The Role Of Contracts

The most important contract is that let by the Authority to govern the Design Phase, in that it should encapsulate the requirements for the System. It is principally this Contract, and its role in the Design Phase, that is the subject of this paper. That Contract has good and bad features for the HCI Advisors who are seeking to get HCI provisions placed on the Design Phase.

On the debit side, these HCI provisions need to be contractually robust. Thus, a contractual language is employed, using the verb 'shall', as in "The System shall provide feedback to every user input". The verb 'shall' is used to distinguish requirements from context, which is expressed using other tenses such as 'is', or 'will'. Also, it is necessary for most provisions to be of the type which the Contractor can show, and the Authority can confirm, have been met when the System undergoes Acceptance. That is they must be testable statements. And further on the debit side, there is typically just one chance to state HCI provisions, at a time before the design of the System has been decided. The Contract is, then, a rather bandwidth-limited, and brief, channel of communication for the HCI Advisors.

On the credit side, the Contract offers assurance. An HCI provision stated there will influence the end-System, and so can be a powerful agent for ensuring that the System will be fit for human use. As an example, Ostberg et al (Ostberg, Moller & Ahlstrom [1986]) report how 'stretching' Contractors' capabilities in terms of workstation design not only led to the Swedish Telecommunications Administration purchasing what they required, but accelerated HCI work by Contractors leading to spontaneously-better-designed workstations being developed. Secondly, stating an HCI provision will draw attention to a topic. Even if the provision turns out to be not applicable to the eventual design, the fact that this has been discovered means that attention will have been paid to the issue addressed by the provision. Thirdly, as we shall see, the right Contract can offer protection to the Contractors' HCI practitioners.

4.3. Contractually-Stated HCI Provisions

One challenge for HCI practice is to use the Contract, accepting its limitations, to convey HCI provisions for the design of the System. The difficulty is, however, well recognised. It is that HCI provisions do not very neatly fall into the unequivocal, testable statements that the Contract requires. Smith (Smith [1984]) distinguishes between hardware and software provisions. Whereas hardware characteristics are susceptible to unequivocal, testable specification, the capabilities of HCI software are less precisely specifiable, and less directly observable, leading to often extensive and time-consuming tests.

To develop Smith's argument, one issue for the HCI practitioner who is writing HCI provisions is that he or she is concerned with the System's Users, and not the System itself. Long and Dowell (Long & Dowell [1988]), in a slightly different context, identify an HCI 'broad view' as concerning not the behaviour of the System alone, nor its User, but the behaviour of the User interacting with the System. The HCI practitioner, in this sense, is seeking to influence the design (and subsequently at run-time, the behaviour) of the System, in order to cause an effect upon the User of that System. Or, perhaps more normally, not cause an effect.

At this point another problem with HCI provisions becomes clear. That is the link between the design of the System and the interactive behaviour the practitioner is trying to affect. So even if clear, testable provisions can be formulated, there can be doubt that they will lead to the interactive behaviours desired. Smith (Smith [1984]) discusses the 'knowledge base' for HCI provisions. In his words, "they are largely based upon expert judgement and accumulated practical experience, rather than on experimental data and quantitative performance measures". Nonetheless, Smith, and this author, believe that we cannot wait for hard data and must be prepared to do the best we can based on accumulated judgement and experience.

Given, then, that it is interactive behaviour that the HCI practitioner is trying to affect by means of contractually-stated provisions, it will improve the clarity of those provisions if there is a conceptual scheme in which to place them. In this scheme, it is the interactive behaviour in every instance of every User's interaction with the System that the HCI practitioner wishes to affect. The achievement of a particular interactive behaviour can be regarded as a **policy** for the System and its subject should be the User and not the System, as in "Users' actions shall not lead to data corruption". However, the policy itself cannot be represented in an implementable program. What achieves the policy are features of the System. If the practitioner can identify a particular System feature that would achieve the policy, he or she can state it as a **requirement**. A requirement is a statement of a feature that 'shall be provided' in the System. Alternatively, the practitioner may not know of any facility that 'shall be provided', but may know some action which would lead to the policy being achieved. The practitioner can then state a **rule**. A rule is a statement of an action that a Design Team 'shall undertake'.

Ideally, it would be possible to state requirements and rules which completely and reliably achieve all the interactive behaviour policies. In most cases, however, it will not be possible to do this. When requirements and rules do not cover all the policies, recourse must be made to **guidelines**. Guidelines are used when the practitioner cannot make precise, testable statements but still wishes to direct the Design Team. A guideline is a statement such as "the Contractor shall make every reasonable effort to ... "

A final set of provisions which the HCI Advisors can pass over the Contractual interface is HCI **data**. These are typically application or context-specific data which are unlikely otherwise to be available to the Design Teams. There is a current purchase for which the HCI Advisors have researched and compiled an albeit-caveated compendium of data concerning the interactive behaviour which Contractors are to assume for the purposes of, particularly, performance budgeting. So this compendium states the times that a User will need to undertake certain operations, and the error rates that are typical.

Unfortunately, a mix of requirements, rules, guidelines and data may be insufficient to lead to the desired interactive behaviour. In this case, the practitioner may simply state the interactive behaviour that is required. The Design Team must, in response, design a feature that they can convince the Authority will meet that policy.

Figure 2 provides some examples of HCI policies, requirements, rules, guidelines and data. They are not all from the same system. The policy statement shown ('the System shall be easy to operate efficiently') is an example of the only HCI provision that was expressed in an early requirement document for a large interactive System. The testability of policies, requirements, rules, guidelines and data is discussed later in Section 4.8.

Before quitting HCI design provisions, there is one more topic: their applicability. It is clearly dangerous for the Authority to parcel off-the-shelf provisions unthinkingly into a Contract. The role of the HCI Advisors is to be informed about the System and its Users. They must then filter and adapt textbook and handbook provisions, as appropriate, to the particular characteristics of the System. Indeed, handbooks of HCI provisions (e.g., (Smith & Mosier [1984])) advise against their portmanteau application to a System. They are directed to HCI practitioners and informed system designers as advice to be selected from. Should HCI Advisors find that they cannot predict the eventual design of the System sufficiently to select only the relevant provisions, there is a contractual device that can assist. This is to be over-inclusive in the provisions stated, but to allow the Contractor to respond with submissions making the case for each provision which is considered inappropriate. Contract amendments can then be made to excise the provisions which are agreed to be irrelevant.

4.4. Restricted Access to Users

Restricted access to Users is a symptom of competitive purchasing which impacts upon the HCI practitioners in the competing Contractors' Design Teams. Although User participation in design discussions,

HCI POLICY

- The System shall be easy to operate efficiently.
- Users shall not be required to memorize instructions in order to operate the System.
- Users shall be able to operate the System without error after one week's training.

HCI REQUIREMENTS

- Inputs initiating an irreversible change to System data shall require a confirmatory input in addition to an initiating input.
- It shall be possible for the User to confirm a default input by entry of a terminator, and to amend or re-write the default value prior to termination.
- A selectable touch-screen box shall be at least 2 cm x 2 cm.

HCI RULES

- The Authority shall be provided with evidence that the advice of training specialists has been taken in the design of the Base Trainer.
- The Contractor shall propose and agree with the Authority the menu hierarchies to be employed.
- The Contractor shall use the Command Language Grammar method in the design of the interface.

HCI DATA

- The Contractor shall assume that Users will complete operation A in 5 (+ or − 15%) seconds.
- The Contractor shall assume that Users will fail to complete operation A correctly, on first attempt, on 10% of occasions.
- The Contractor shall assume that basic operators will not have received any computer literacy training before the first training course.

HCI GUIDELINES

("The System should" = "The Contractor shall make every reasonable effort to design a System which"

- The System should alert users to System failure rapidly but without using auditory warnings.
- The System should employ a visual metaphor which is consistent with manual practices.
- The System should allow Users to re-distribute tasks between themselves to the maximum possible extent.

Figure 2. Examples of HCI policies, requirements, rules, guidelines and data.

and iterative prototyping involving Users, are by-words of 'user-centred systems design', this is often not possible. Restricted access comes about because of the Authority's concern to be even-handed with both Contractors. The Authority is legitimately anxious that something said to one Contractor by one of its User representatives could give an unfair (and later-discovered) advantage or disadvantage to that Contractor. Discussions with Users thus tend to be carefully controlled by the Authority. Users do not join Contractors' Design Teams, and remain remote but available for rather guarded questioning.

Why do HCI practitioners wish to talk to Users? It is principally to fill gaps in their understanding of the Requirements Specification and of the context and use of the System. If the Specification were so complete an account of the System required as to obviate any further questions, contact with Users would not be important. It must be concluded, therefore, that restricted access to Users places a considerable onus on the quality and completeness of the material produced during Requirements Definition.

That being so, what can be done in that earlier Phase to compensate, however partially, for the later restricted access to Users? First and foremost is the need to produce a complete Requirements Specification which answers all foreseeable questions. Unfortunately, that is unlikely to be possible. What is also needed, therefore, is a document which contains sufficient contextual information to allow the HCI Design Team to derive the information they find they need. Such a document is proposed here to supplement the Requirements Specification. It is called the 'Concept of Use'. The Concept of Use is an informal (i.e., not Contractual) document prepared principally by the HCI Advisors on the basis of discussion with its User representatives. It is a description of the 'natural history' of the Users and their work prior to the introduction of the System being acquired. It describes the Users themselves, their work practices, their organisation, and their working environment. It contains their comment on the favourable and unfavourable aspects of their work and working environment. It also describes the changes they would and would not like to see brought about by the System.

The Concept of Use document would, it is proposed, be made available to the competing Contractors. Whilst it would contain only advisory information, it would help to ameliorate the information shortfall caused by restricted access to Users.

4.5. Cost-Effective HCI Design

Cost-effectiveness here concerns the impact on HCI practice of producing a competitive bid price. The aspirations of the HCI Design Team will be to design a more usable and more suitable System. That System is likely to cost more than the 'basic' System that might otherwise be proposed. Can HCI practitioners justify that no savings could be made in their areas of concern? For example, consider the following questions.

(a) "The colour VDU you want is twice the price of monochrome, and we have thirty of them. Do you think the competition are bidding colour? Is it really necessary?"

(b) "The User interface software is 30% of the total. Couldn't we lose those expensive windowing facilities?"

(c) "The Authority won't go ahead with this System if it costs more than the current manual implementation. Given the cost of our System, we need to lose twelve users. Have another look at your workload figures and see if you can't get rid of them."

(d) "Surely they can train on the System itself with those User Manuals you're writing."

Of course, HCI practitioners are not the only members of a Design Team to be asked difficult cost questions. But software and hardware questions can be answered by reference to accepted engineering practice. What HCI practitioners face is being representatives of the less-well-understood: the equivocal functionality and usability of the System, without anything categorical or quantititative to fall back on. For example, the communications engineer will not be questioned when he says that the computers 'won't' talk to one another across an interface. But Users will rarely categorically 'do' or 'not do' things: it is a matter of judgement as to how far their difficulty in struggling with an interface means that they 'can't' use it.

On the other hand, if HCI provisions are stated in the Contract, they can serve to protect the practitioners in the Design Team. If there are requirements for colour, windowing, 32 users and a training system, the HCI practitioner is applauded for meeting the Contract rather than being suspected of jeopardising the bid.

4.6. User Demonstrations

Competitive contracts often call for User demonstrations. These are prototype interfaces, supported by prototype applications code, which are demonstrated to User representatives, and may be an item for adjudication. Whilst prototyping is a recognised technique in interface design, it requires close User involvement. When competitive purchasing precludes this, User demonstrations can have the unfortunate effect of alerting Users, at a rather late stage, to what they really want the screens to look like.

4.7. Technical Adjudication

Adjudication of Proposals brings the Authority's HCI Advisors face to face with the cost-effectiveness issues that their colleagues faced during the Design Phase. If the Proposals have come in above the budgetary estimate, the practitioners will be asked what features could be omitted to save money. And even if Proposals are within budget, there is need for an assessment of the 'weight' of HCI features as a contribution to a marking scheme. HCI practitioners are not necessarily at any disadvantage, however, in comparison to the Users and the other Technical Advisors. They can take a prominent role in the adjudication by introducing a qualitative assessment scheme such as that proposed by the Naval Engineering Standard on Human Factors (Navy [1986])

4.8. Acceptance Testing

Acceptance testing is called for in most contractually-governed system acquisitions, competitive or not. Acceptance occurs at a phase when competition has died out, and its purpose is to prove that the System meets its requirements, or more typically an identified sub-set of requirements.

Looking back to the scheme proposed earlier for HCI design provisions, we find that they have different implications for acceptance testing. A policy for interactive behaviour that "the System shall present information succinctly" (a real example) is practically untestable. A more realistic policy, such as 'The User shall be able to read all textual displays' would require a considerable test programme, even if it used a sample of the User population, rather than all Users. In general, policies for interactive behaviour are very difficult to test economically, because they test Users rather than the System.

Requirements, on the other hand, are testable. "Character height shall be 4.5mm" is testable in a simple manner. "The System shall present alarm messages in red" likewise. More complex requirements require more extensive tests. "The System shall allow the User to recover from any action that he takes" requires a comprehensive test of the System's undo facilities, but not a comprehensive test of Users. Notwithstanding that to test some requirements can be time-consuming, it is their susceptibility to test that should have determined their status as requirements in the first place. Likewise, adherence or adoption of HCI data can be directly tested.

Rules and guidelines are themselves not appropriate for acceptance testing. Their observance will have been monitored by the HCI Advisors during the Design and the Development and Production Phases. What is tested is the requirements that have been agreed as arising from those rules and guidelines.

5. The Challenges To HCI Practice

Competitive purchasing, as described here, presents some challenges to the HCI community. The first and major challenge is the commitment to operate in this environment. To retreat from the challenge would, it is proposed, be to turn one's back on the people who are actual or potential users of those Systems.

If HCI is to meet the challenge of competitive purchasing, what are the 'knowledge base' advances to be made?

(a) A better understanding of advantageous and disadvantageous interactive behaviours.

(b) An extended and more reliable knowledge-base linking computer System facilities to interactive behaviours, for particular User/task/context combinations.

These advances in knowledge are not very novel. What competitive purchasing tends to do is to make them rather keenly felt by HCI practitioners. It is interesting to consider what would happen if these advances were realised. In the fullness of time, one could imagine HCI design being undertaken by reference to a compendium of standards. Entering the compendium knowing that you have a degree-educated Englishman working in an office on a financial forecasting task, the relevant entry would show the workstation standard, the UIMS, the dialogue, and the vocabulary and screen format standards to be employed. As Cockton (Cockton [1987]) amongst others has proposed, formal methods would underlie the expression of the UIMS and the dialogue. Even, however, if this recourse to standards were possible, it would still be necessary to answer design questions when integrating the HCI design with the rest of the System design. It is not obvious that all standards will be compatible.

In respect of competitive purchasing policies, what do we need to lobby Purchasing Authorities about? This paper has revealed some topics.

(a) It is not sensible to take handbooks of HCI provisions and give them status as Contractual requirements. The generality of those provisions will mean they are either platitudes or are misleading or are not precise enough for contractual purposes. They must be interpreted in the context of the System's functionality, environment and Users.

(b) HCI Advisors have a profound role in determining the quality of human-computer interaction in the eventual System, in the following ways.

    i. The HCI provisions they adapt and develop can have a real influence on the eventual System.

    ii. HCI provisions within the Contract will tend to protect HCI design work done on that Contract.

    iii. A topic not hitherto discussed in this paper, but fairly obvious: a team of HCI Advisors monitoring the design and implementation will serve to increase the quality of the HCI work undertaken by Contractors.

(c) The restricted access to Users that accompanies competitive purchasing is a pernicious problem for HCI Design Teams. Its partial amelioration is to spend more money 'up front' during Requirements Definition.

In respect of practitioneering, this paper has offered practical recommendations which if accepted would lead to the following.

(a) Use of a scheme of policies, requirements, rules, data and guidelines to impose clarity and rigour on the formulation of HCI provisions, and their subsequent testing.

(b) Use of the 'Concept of Use' document to record, during the Requirements Definition Phase, at least some of the information that HCI practitioners will need during Design.

Finally, where is HCI practitioneering placed in respect of other disciplines? Mechanical and electrical engineering seem to have the knowledge base reliable enough to provide a compendium of designs which meet requirements. Communications engineering has the OSI model, of sufficient power to be adopted as a standard for a variety of requirements. Software engineering has identified the policies that it wishes to achieve, for example availability, security and maintainability, but those are less context-dependent than those of HCI. Thus, if software engineering has rather greater success than HCI in developing ways to achieve those policies, that success must be qualified. Certainly HCI practitioners should not feel embarrassed about what they have to offer by way of knowledge and techniques, and should comfort themselves by recognising that if the answers to questions about interactive behaviour were obvious there would be no HCI profession.

References

G Cockton [1987], "Some Critical Remarks on Abstractions for Adaptable Dialogue Managers," in *People and Computers III*, D Diaper and R Winder, ed., Cambridge University Press, Cambridge, 215–228.

A J Gundry [1987], "Some Topics Concerning Naval Command System Acquisition," *International CIS Journal* 1, 35–60.

IT '86 [1986], "Report of IT '86 Committee," Working Paper: Report on the Human Interfaces Working Party.

J Long & J Dowell [1988], "Formal Methods, the Broad and Narrow View," in *IEE Colloquium – Formal Methods and Human-Computer Interaction*, IEE, Savoy Place, London.

MOD Controllerate of the Navy [1986], "Human Factors in the Design of Military Computer-Based Systems," Draft Naval Engineering Standard Part 1.

O Ostberg, L Moller & G Ahlstrom [1986], "Ergonomic Procurement Guidelines for Visual Display Units as a Tool for Progressive Change," *Behaviour and Information Technology* 5, 71–80.

S L Smith [1984], "Standards Versus Guidelines for Designing User Interface Software," *Behaviour and Information Technology* 5, 47–61.

S L Smith & J N Mosier [1984], "Design Guidelines for User-System Interface Software," The Mitre Corporation, Report No. ESD-TR-84-190, Bedford MA.

Implementation Tools

A User Oriented Design Process for User Recovery and Command Reuse Support

Yiya Yang

Scottish HCI Centre, Heriot-Watt University, Chambers Street, Edinburgh EH1 1HX, U.K.

This report discusses the typical working environment of user recovery and command reuse support and defines the range of services provided by it. A user-oriented design process for user recovery and command reuse support is described that ascribes a central role to empirical and analytical evaluation. The results of a survey of users' views upon existing and idealised user recovery and command reuse support is reported and discussed. In addition, literature informed analysis is used to explore the issues of support representation and command history organisation. Both are used to illustrate how design considerations enter into design process stages for user recovery and command reuse support. A four component architecture for such support is proposed to underpin these considerations comprising a context information base, a recovery knowledge base, an application model and a recovery manager.

Keywords: undo, redo, reuse, user requirements

1. Introduction

One of the important services provided by a user interface management system is effective error avoidance and recovery. Three groups of error avoidance and recovery features, **escape**, **stop** and **undo**, help a user recover from errors and undesirable situations. The undo group is used to reverse the effects of a command that has been executed. It is the most difficult to provide although it can enhance the usability and learnability of an interactive system in a major way. A user interface reference model has been developed in (Lantz [1986]). According to that reference model, an ideal user interface should provide the following services:

1. multiple communication media.
2. multiple levels of I/O, including:

   a. media-independent I/O
   b. media-dependent I/O
   c. device-dependent I/O
   d. workstation management

3. multiple 'views' of the same input or output stream
4. user-visible multi-tasking, including support for:

   a. multiple simultaneous applications
   b. multiple simultaneous input and output devices
   c. multiple simultaneous contexts

5. global data interchange
6. support for multi-user dialogues (conferences)
7. history facilities, including redo
8. help facilities
9. effective error recovery, including undo
10. user monitoring and modeling
11. choice of control strategies:

    a. internal
    b. external
    c. mixed

These services are provided by many components of a user interface management system. One component can provide several services and one service can be supported by several components. The undo/redo facility in service 7 and service 9 is mainly provided by the user recovery and command reuse support component. This report attempts to address the importance of user recovery and command reuse support by describing a user-centred design process for user recovery and command reuse support. Critical issues in the design process are explained and their potential trade-offs are discussed. An abstract framework is also proposed for user recovery and command reuse support.

2. Design Process Of User Recovery And Command Reuse Support

A user-oriented iterative design process should include requirement analysis, conceptual design, function specification, detailed design, prototyping and evaluation. Furthermore evaluation can and should happen throughout the design process. Part of this evaluation will involve the designer more than the user while other parts of this evaluation will involve the user more. However whatever their respective contributions, the results of later stages of evaluation will and should be used to refine early stages. These stages and evaluations will form a complex feedback controlled evolutionary process concerned with trade-offs between various technical, logistical, and functional objectives. Thus the design process presents itself as an optimisation problem as well as a process of results controlled development. As one interactive system component in this design process, a user recovery and command reuse support facility can only go through the first three stages of this design process relatively independently because it cannot exist itself and it relies for its functionality and presentation on the rest of the system. The later stages of its detailed design and prototyping depend upon the design and prototyping of its host environment and cannot be significantly abstracted from that environment's later design stages.

User recovery and command reuse support is an interface feature which does not change the functionality of a system but enhances its usability and learnability. It has three components – undo support, redo support and reuse support. Undo support consists of undo commands whose execution will reverse the effects of task-oriented commands. Redo support consists of redo commands whose execution will reverse the effects of undo commands. Reuse support consists of reuse commands whose execution will re-use words of task-oriented commands. The definitions of undo and redo commands depend upon the functionality of the system, because they reverse the effects of task-oriented commands which support the system's function. These special characteristics make the design of user recovery and command reuse support different from other functions of an interactive system. According to Lantz's interface reference model, the most complicated working environment of user recovery and command reuse support is a concurrent multi-user dialogue environment in which there are multiple simultaneous activities. Each application can employ multiple communication media simultaneously to interact with the user. This environment allows the user to interact with multiple applications at the same time and with any single application in multiple ways at the same time. In addition, the environment provides support for multiple users engaged in the same dialogue. Within this environment, the basic services provided by user recovery and command reuse support would still be undo support, redo support and reuse support even though the commands were issued through multiple media by various users to various applications at the same time. A user recovery and command reuse support facility for such a complicated environment would have to manage simultaneous demands concurrently for these services but the basic jobs it would do would still be the same as for less complex working environments. In what follows one design process for user recovery and command reuse support is discussed.

3. Requirement Analysis Of User Recovery And Command Reuse Support

According to Smith and Mosier's design guidelines (Smith & Mosier [1984]) for interactive systems, the requirements for user recovery and command reuse support are to undo any (sets of) commands, to redo any (sets of) commands which have been undone, and to reuse any (parts of) commands which have been issued. Whether these requirements are general enough or not and how a user uses existing user recovery and command reuse support are not explained in the guidelines. Since a primary purpose of providing user recovery and command reuse support is to make the system better to use, knowing whether users use this support or not is important for deciding whether a new system should have this support feature or not. A user can use a computer system which does not have user recovery and command reuse support to assist his job although his job may be made more arduous by the support's absence. In order to find out about users' general attitudes to user recovery and command reuse support, an informal survey of users' views was conducted. Five questions were asked of subscribers to JANET's news network.

1. Are there any undo/redo commands in the system you use?
2. What forms do they have?
3. How often do you use undo/redo commands and in what circumstances?
4. Is it easy to use the existing undo/redo commands and how do they meet your needs?
5. What are your ideal undo/redo commands?

25 responses were received to the inquiry. The longest response was 61 lines and the shortest was 2 lines. All responders were experienced computer users. Responses were condensed and the major points can be reported as follows.

3.1. Popular User Recovery And Command Reuse Support Facilities

The following six systems with undo, redo and/or reuse commands were popular with responders and they described the forms of undo/redo commands in the following terms.

1. Unix:
   There is no undo command in any Unix Shell. Most Unix shells have a history substitution command beginning with ! which allows a user to use words from previous commands. In spite of the complexity involved in using this reuse facility, most people expressed their approval for this reuse function since any part of any command within the history (whose length can be set easily) can be re-used.

2. Vi text editor:
   It has two undo commands and one reuse command. The global undo command (u) undoes the last change. The line undo command (U) undoes all changes to the current line. The reuse command (.) reuses the last command. Not every command can be undone or reused. For example, scrolling commands such as Ctrl-f and Ctrl-d can be neither undone by undo commands nor reused by the reuse command.

3. Macintosh Tools:
   They do not have a reuse function. They have an undo command in a pop up menu which undoes the last text-editing function.

4. SunView Texteditor:
   It has an undo function and a reuse function. The undo function key Undo (usually L4 on the keyboard) undoes all edits since the last time a user selected, typed Get, Put, or Delete, or performed any operation except Again that uses Get, Put, or Delete. This Undo behaviour continues back in time by changed insertion point intervals up to the limit specified when the user created the text subwindow (the default value is 50 intervals). Each window keeps its own Undo information. Currently, there is no way to undo an Undo command. The reuse function key Again (usually L2) re-executes all edits performed since the last time the user moved the cursor.

5. Smalltalk-80:
   It has an undo command in a pop up menu to reverse the effects
   of all the user's typing and backspacing since the selection
   made last with the pointing device. The *again* command is
   a reuse command which works for selection, replacement and
   cutting on a literal basis.

6. Emacs:
   Emacs allows all changes made in the text of a buffer to be undone, up to a certain limit to changes (8000 characters). Each
   buffer records changes individually, and the undo command is
   always applied to the current buffer. It has an n-step linear
   undo command (M-number Ctrl-x u or Ctrl-_). When the user
   issues the undo command first time, it undoes the last change
   or the last n changes (n is specified as a numeric parameter)
   and the user can see what was undone. Consecutive repetitions
   of the undo command undo earlier and earlier changes, back
   to the limit of what has been recorded. Any command other
   than an undo command breaks the sequence of undo commands. From this moment, the previous undo commands are
   considered ordinary changes that can themselves be undone.
   There is no simple reuse command.

From the above observations it would seem that the popular application
environments of user recovery and command reuse support are text
writing and programming environments. Furthermore it can be seen
that half of the above six systems fail to provide complete user recovery
and command reuse support. Some only provide undo/redo support.
Others only provide reuse support. Even those systems that provide
undo, redo and reuse support only provide some of it in a limited form.

3.2. Usage Frequency And Circumstances Of Use Among Responders

Responders to the inquiry who had used at least one of the above six
systems used the following phrases to qualify how often they use user
recovery and command reuse support facilities:

1. constantly

2. all the time

3. a lot

4. reasonably often

5. fairly often

6. fairly frequently

7. very often

8. couldn't live without it

9. feel crippled without them

10. undo in the Mac or vi for about 5 to 10% of all commands, reuse in Unix Shell for 40-50% of all commands (starting edits or compiling) and reuse of vi about 5% of all command use

11. 1-10 times a day

12. quite often, about once an hour

13. in every possible circumstances

14. every editing time

15. regularly

Responders to the inquiry used a user recovery and command reuse support facility in different circumstances. They described these circumstances in the following terms.

1. correcting wrong commands:
   This support facility is used for a deletion or insertion that is incorrect. For example, in Emacs, a user may issue a kill-region command in a wrong region or modify accidently a file which he merely wants to look at. In both situations, the user can use the user recovery and command reuse support facility to return the system to a state before the changes.

2. typing mistakes:
   This support is used when some key strokes are unintentionally hit. For example, in Emacs, a user may type g before Ctrl when he wants to issue the command Ctrl-g.

3. dissatisfied with outcomes:
   A user recovery and command reuse facility is employed when a user starts to make a change, then realises his fix won't work and the original situation needs to be reverted to. For example, a user issues a global replace-string command and find the result is not what he wants. At this time he can issue an undo command to revert the document to what it was before the global replace-string command.

4. exploring unfamiliar functions:
   When a user knows some command but is not quite sure how it works, he can try it out with the assistance of undo/redo commands.

5. helping program development:
   In programming environments, a user can change the code of a program and run it. If he does not want the running results,

he can use a user recovery and command reuse support facility to revert the code to what it was before.

6. changing one's mind:

   A user recovery and command reuse facility allows a user to change his mind. When a user uses a computer, he employs some strategy to reach his goal. During the process to reach his goal, he may think out some better strategy to reach the same goal. Although both strategies can make him reach the same goal, the second strategy may be more efficient in time or space. He can use this support facility to return the system to the state before he used the first strategy and start using the second strategy instead.

7. means of fallback:

   A user recovery and command reuse facility can provide a means of fallback. The user can just hack along and later revert the system to a previous state.

From the above descriptions, one can generalise that user recovery and command reuse support is useful for text writing and programming. It has at least five advantages: saving keystrokes, correcting syntax errors, correcting semantic errors, allowing the user to change his mind and allowing the user to explore new or unfamiliar functions freely.

3.3. Preferred Undo, Redo And Reuse Commands For Responders

Responders described their preferred undo, redo and reuse commands in the following terms.

1. It should provide an easy way to tell what commands have been issued, what commands have been executed and what commands have been undone. For example, a window may be brought to the screen which contains numbered lines of key sequence or command/function name. Some method must be used to distinguish three different kinds of lines:

   > command lines which are in effect

   > command lines which are to be undone

   > command lines which have been already undone

2. The command to undo function-oriented commands should be different from that to undo recovery-oriented commands. It should provide a sort of undo checkpoint (or implicit one) at the last undo that was not preceded by an undo so that a whole sequence of undos could be undone at once.

3. A user recovery and command reuse support facility should be context-based and able to undo almost all aspects of the *system state* as perceived by the user, not just the file contents, but also the cursor (or focus) position, meta-information like the printer setup (for a Mac) and actions among files. It should be able to undo any command. If it is impossible, it should tell the user about undoability of some command before executing it.

4. A user recovery and command reuse support facility should be multiple-level and provide a variable undo size which either undoes a single command at once or multiple commands at once. It should provide a query-undo by which a user can have more control over things.

5. A user recovery and command reuse support facility should have an option to specify how much undo should remember and to have some coarser granularity optionally available to mark and undo commands. It should wipe out a sequence of commands followed by a sequence of undos so that a user can skip over the whole undone sequence when using undo again later.

From the responders' preferences, it would seem that experienced computer users want an interactive system to provide different options which can be used in different situations. They are more concerned with how to reach a goal with fewer commands than with the complexity of commands. They prefer an environment where they have more control.

3.4. Discussion Of Responders General Comments

The above six software systems are used for textual writing and programming. One responder to the inquiry argued that a user recovery and command reuse support facility is heavily application-dependent. He claimed that there are not many applications in which such a support facility is very useful. He maintained that the main task domain for a user recovery and command reuse support facility is where things have to be configured (text in editors and pictures in graphics editors) or have to be analysed (situations achieved in a chess game). It is true that not every application needs a user recovery and command reuse support facility. Black board style applications such as batching software do not need this support facility. However in interactive applications, if a task-related goal is achieved by several intermediate steps, user recovery and command reuse support facilities are needed because a user can get into some unintended state at any step to the goal.

A user recovery and command reuse support facility can be used as a

means to enhance the learnability and usability of an interactive system
but one responder to the inquiry disagreed with this literature-justified
conclusion. He only considered a user recovery and command reuse
support facility as a powerful general tool for an experienced user. He
argued that although a simple user recovery and command reuse support
facility can help in learning how to use a system, a general form of this
support facility is neither very simple nor easy to learn. This is true to
certain extent. However, the forms of a user recovery and command
reuse support facility depend upon other functions of a system. If
other functions are complicated, a general form of user recovery and
command reuse support does not put much extra burden on the user in
learning system functionality. Since a user recovery and command reuse
support facility is an *extra* feature augmenting the whole functionality
of a system, it cannot reduce the complexity of functions of the system.
The key point is the trade-off between the *extra* load of a user recovery
and command reuse support facility on the user's conceptual model of
the system and the gains for the user brought about by having it. A user
recovery and command reuse support facility can speed up the process
of getting out of some unintended situations by providing short cuts. It
can release the work stress on a user by reducing the user's anxiety. It
supports one of a user's learning habits which is learning by trying it out
because it makes exploration possible by making it safe. It even provides
an active rest manner by allowing people to hack along and later revert
to a previous state. The above usage frequencies of a user recovery and
command reuse facility and its circumstances of use in real life strongly
indicate that a user recovery and command reuse support facility can
enhance the learnability and usability of an interactive system.

3.5. Conclusions Of Requirements Analysis Survey

There are many ways to conduct requirement analysis such as by inquiry,
interview and observation on existing systems. Among these methods,
none is complete. Every method has its own limitations. They are
complementary to each other and only combined use of them can result
in a satisfactory conclusion. Besides this, requirement analysis for an
interactive system is slightly different from that for a particular software
feature of an interactive system such as user recovery and command
reuse support. For an interactive system, since its user population
and its task environment are roughly known in advance, interviewing
users and observing a task environment can be directly used to conduct
requirement analysis. However, for user recovery and command reuse
support, direct use of interview and observation is not feasible because
the user population and application environment are not clearly known.
Informal inquiry and questionnaire techniques have to be used to find
out who is interested in user recovery and command reuse support, who

is using this support and which system provides this support. After knowing who the designer should interview and which system can be used as the environment of observation, the designer is able to conduct further interviews and make detailed observations. Therefore, informal inquiry and questionnaire methods are a prerequisite for other requirement analysis methods with user recovery and command reuse support.

Although this network inquiry is not a complete evaluation method and has serious limitations, it provides some helpful information about user recovery and command reuse support and about the limitations of users themselves. Firstly, the results indicate that user recovery and command reuse support is useful and used and that its current application environment is text writing and programming. Secondly, they indicate that user recovery and command reuse support is an error avoidance and recovery feature which is complementary to other error avoidance and recovery facilities. Thirdly, the results indicate that users themselves have limitations as analysts of requirements. Different people have different preferences and many users are unable to consider design issues analytically. They can only provide pieces of information. The requirements elicited from one user may be contradictory to those from another user. Sometimes, the requirements from a single user are contradictory in themselves. For example, some people prefer chunky undoing rather than character undoing. Others prefer the opposite. Some people prefer undoing within one editing session than across editing sessions. Others prefer the opposite. Therefore, using a user-oriented design process where problems are considered from the perspective of an end-user and where end-users may be asked to become members of the design team does not mean that design decisions have to be made by a user. It is the designer or analyst who analyses what a user wants and makes an appropriate design decision. Generally speaking, it is better to have the most popular basic preferences as the default form and to have other preferences as an option. For a user recovery and command reuse support facility, for example, the more popular choice of working on the current buffer can be chosen as the default form and working on all buffers can be chosen as an option form.

Since this inquiry was made through the news network and generally speaking only *computer professionals* have access to it, the responders were restricted to *computer professionals*. This does not mean that the results cannot be extrapolated to non-computer professionals. If computer professionals need user recovery and command reuse support in using software systems, it is reasonable to infer that non-computer professionals may also need it. A possible difference may be the context when and how user recovery and command reuse support is used. In order to find out about these differences, a further mail questionnaire about user recovery and command reuse support is being conducted among non-computer professionals. Its results will be available soon.

4. Function Specification Of User Recovery And Command Reuse Support

After getting requirements for user recovery and command reuse support
from the user, a designer has to analyse these requirements and build up
a conceptual model which describes the behavior of user recovery and
command reuse support from the user's point of view and an internal
function model which supports the conceptual model on the required
computer system.

4.1. Conceptual Functionality Of User Recovery And Command Reuse Support

A conceptual model can be seen as having two parts: functionality and
input/output representation. The functionality of a conceptual model
answers what a system can do in terms of functional abstractions. It
can be described by objects, states and functions. The input/output
representation answers how a user can make use of the system in terms
of concrete commands. It can be described by commands and interaction
techniques, especially the syntax of commands. The map between
functions and commands is not necessarily one-to-one. A formal model
for conceptual functionality of user recovery and command reuse support
has been discussed in (Yang [1988]) which is described by objects, states
and functions. It subsumes the functionality of prior models.

4.2. Representation Issues Of User Recovery And Command Reuse Support

Representation issues are largely application-dependent. Without choosing a particular environment, a designer cannot build a complete representation model for user recovery and command reuse support.

An important issue about input/output representations of user recovery
and command reuse support is how to tell the user about the existence
of user recovery and command reuse support in a system. There are
two main methods to deal with this issue. The direct method employs a
visible undo button on the screen such as in Vitter's interactive graphics
layout system (Vitter [1984]), an undo key on the keyboard such as in
the Xerox Star, or less directly as an undo item in a pop-up screen menu
such as in the Apple Macintosh. The indirect method is to have a user-
issued undo command whose syntax can be found in on-line and off-line
manuals.

The indirect method works well if a user is prepared to read a manual to find out what facilities a system provides. Unfortunately, human learning habits do not support this method. Learners at every level of experience avoid reading. They prefer exploratory learning strategies rather than following the step-by-step rote structure of a manual or on-line tutorial. As Carroll and Rosson (Carroll & Rosson [1987]) point out, "what we see in the learning-to-use-a-computer situation is that people are so busy trying things out, thinking things through, and trying to relate what they already know (or believe they know) to what is going on that they often do not notice the small voice of structured instruction crying out to them from behind the manuals." The indirect method is passively available. Its existence makes no claim on the user's attention and its mode of invocation is not manifest.

By contrast, the direct method and its mode of invocation is manifest. It has an undo key on the keyboard or an undo screen button to tell a user about the existence of user recovery and command reuse support. However, it has its own problem. The choice of using an undo key on a keyboard does not provide a flexible way to switch it off when a user does not need it because the undo key is there permanently. On sophisticated keyboard interfaces it can be reprogrammed to have a different function but it still wears its physical label and this limits the usefulness of reprogramming. An undo screen button can overcome this problem, but it faces other problems. Usually, a system offers a large number of functions. It is impossible to have screen buttons for all functions. At any moment, only some relevant functions can be shown on the screen and the display of relevant functions itself provides implicit guidance, showing what functions should be considered. For user recovery and command reuse support, its very general functionality and the importance of its role in error recovery suggests it is better to have a screen undo button at most times (Norman [1983]; Perlman [1984]). A designer must analyse the task environment to decide the position and the times for displaying an undo button. Where user recovery and command reuse support is not switched off but is not able to be displayed as a button in its own right, it can be made less directly accessible via a pop-up menu picked by a general function screen button or in very crowded displays by an indirect method.

Recently, HCI research has stressed the need for interfaces to be adaptive (Mason [1986]). The main idea of adaptation is that system interfaces should automatically adjust themselves to the needs of the user in facilitating more effective human-computer interaction. Ideally, the system should automatically tell a user about user recovery and command reuse support when the user needs it. Unfortunately the capacity to realise and organise intelligence in an interface system for recognising such a need does not exist. A designer has to balance all trade-offs and try to build as ideal a system as can be realised without such intelligence. A designer may decide that as the need for an undo button cannot be recognised automatically, the user may need to be prompted by the salience of a permanent screen button that it is there to meet the user's need.

Besides the above issue about input/output representations, what context information a user needs to know and how to present such information to the user are important. According to the results of the inquiry, context information should inform the user what commands have been issued, what commands have been executed and what commands have been undone. Context information serves two purposes. One is to tell a user where he is so that he can find out how he got into the unintended situation and can find out a desired state for the system to return to by undoing. The other purpose is to support the processing of undoing itself.

One responder to the informal survey suggested that a way to organise the presentation of context information would be for a window to be brought to the screen which contains numbered lines of key sequences or command/function names. Another way to organise context information would be to present what has been achieved by commands. An example suggested by Harold Thimbleby of the second method would be a text editor that changes text from black to green as it is deleted. Thus green indicates lost information. Undoing becomes a matter of changing the colour green back to black. The advantage of this method is that all deleted green information is present to the user, although the information about the time it was deleted is not preserved. The position of the cancelled information is the same as it was in the original text. Unfortunately, this method is not as good in practice as it is in theory because maintaining what has been achieved such as the lost information without recording when and how it was achieved would be very wasteful of space both on the screen and inside machine memory.

The command recording method is better at using the space on the screen and inside machine memory because commands occupy less space than what is achieved by these commands. When using a command recording history, several issues have to be considered. The first one is what level of detail the history records, keystroke level or legal command level. A keystroke level history would be a literal record of everything the user submits to the system. It contains legal and illegal commands. One example of keystroke level histories is the history mechanism of the Emacs. A legal command level history only records legal commands. Obviously, the keystroke level of history is more suitable for post-mortem evaluation. The legal command level is more suitable for user recovery and command reuse support. Since editing an illegal command and then reusing it is important also, a more appropriate method for user recovery and command reuse support would be to keep keystrokes for the last command but only to preserve legal commands before that. The undo relevant characteristics of commands have been analysed in (Yang [1988]). A legal command can either belong to the domain of user recovery support or not. Commands which belong to the domain of user recovery support are those which are reversible in respect of their operational effects. In order to record the interaction between a user and the system in such a way as to let the user know where the user is, it is better to record every legal command a user issues. When a user attempts to reverse the effects of commands which do not belong to the undo domain, the system can employ the following tactics to deal with such situations. For commands whose effects definitely cannot be reversed such as highly memory consumptive commands like system dumps, the system should tell the user that it cannot be undone and ask the user to confirm the command before it executes the command. For commands whose effects do not need to be reversed such as a directory listing command, the system should give the reasons that explain its unnecessity when a user issues an undo command to reverse the effects of such commands. For commands whose effect cannot be reversed completely but may be compensated for, the system should tell the user about the way to compensate for its effects. For example, the side-effects of communication beyond the boundary of an system cannot be undone but can be compensated for. Although once communicated, information cannot be *uncommunicated*, a message directing one to *neglect* information previously received does have some *reversal* effects on the state. Thus, the domain of user recovery and command reuse support should be indicated when user recovery and command reuse support is introduced to users.

Depending upon the complexity of an application environment, a history can be shell-oriented, user-oriented or task-oriented. A shell-oriented history records user-issued commands which are executed by processes under one shell. The history recording mechanism of the Berkeley 4.2 Unix operating system is shell-oriented. A user-oriented history records all commands issued by the same user within a (local) network, no matter which process, which window or which terminal the user uses. A user-oriented history is more complicated than a shell-oriented history because it requires that a user in one machine can reverse the effects of commands which are issued from and executed by a different machine. This means that one machine can command the remove of what another machine has done. A task-oriented history is a history about a task which may be done by several people. This task may involve more than one application at the same time. How to prevent common data from being changed by undoing operations simultaneously by different people is a crucial problem. An undo operation executed in one application may influence another application. Such task-oriented undoing requires consistency checks across applications. All these problems have to be solved if a multi-user task environment is to provide user recovery and command reuse support.

4.3. Internal Function Model Of User Recovery And Command Reuse Support

A conceptual model has to be supported internally by an internal function model. Without the support of an internal function model, a conceptual model is only an *empty* model which cannot be executed. A function in a conceptual model can be supported by several functions in the internal function model. Usually the functions in a conceptual model are more general than the functions in an internal function model. Several internal function models of user recovery and command reuse support are formulated and their properties are formally analysed in (Yang [1987]). The two classic kinds of undo support, *history undo/redo* and *linear undo/redo*, are respectively specified by two models, the **primitive** undo model and the **meta** undo model. Their properties are carefully analysed in terms of formal specifications. A new undo model that addresses general requirements is formally specified and its more powerful functionality is demonstrated. People who are interested in these models can find more information in this paper which will appear in the *International Journal of Man-machine Studies* this year.

5. A Framework Of User Recovery And Command Reuse Support

For an interactive system after function specification design, the design process enters the stage of detailed design which takes the design from concepts to implementation specifications. For user recovery and command reuse support, the situation is slightly different because such support cannot exist independently and is only a component of the whole system. Its detailed design has to be conducted in terms of the detailed design of the whole system. In what follows a possible architecture to embed a user recovery and command reuse support feature into a user interface management system is proposed.

There are four basic components which are directly used in user recovery and command reuse support:

1. *Recovery knowledge base*
    responsible for providing recovery techniques and recovery rules which specify how to reverse the effects of commands.

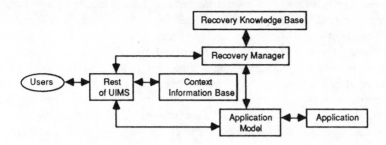

Figure 1. The basic user recovery and command reuse support framework

2. *Application model*
   responsible for bridging the separation between the underlying application and the rest of the system.

3. *Context information base*
   responsible for providing information about data structures, interaction techniques and communication media of executed commands and undone commands.

4. *Recovery manager*
   responsible for handling the recovery process.

The services provided by a user interface management system (UIMS) are handled co-operatively by many of its components. In the last few years, user interface designers have attempted some separation of the semantic component and the user interface component. Unfortunately, this has not worked in practice (Dance [1987]). One important reason for this is that many user interfaces require that semantic information be used extensively for controlling feedback, for generating default values and for error checking and recovery. For user recovery and command reuse support, the above framework can be used to demonstrate how it is embedded into an interactive system. Within a user interface management system, there are editing and filtering components which support the desired interaction techniques and translate user required forms of commands into internal functions. They manage how user commands are specified and how the results of these commands are notified to the user. For user recovery and command reuse support, an undo command can be specified by different interaction styles (Baecker [1987]) such as by command, by menu and by direct manipulation. The results of that undo command can be sent out to different workstations through different communication media from those used to specify the command. This information will be recorded in the context information base. For example, if a user changes a default history form which is process-based to a user-based form, this has to be recorded in the context information base. According to the conclusions drawn from the results of the informal inquiry, information about the different representations between executed commands and undone commands also needs to be recorded in the context information base. The recovery knowledge base and recovery manager stand behind these editing-related and filtering-related components. They are only interested in what recovery commands a user specifies and how these commands are to be executed.

In a typical interactive environment, generally there are two phases in a recovery process, a preparation phase records information needed by recovery and an execution phase carries out the recovery process. In the preparation phase, when a user issues a task-oriented command, the user interface management system handles the syntactic analysis. The desired context information of that command is recorded in the context information base which includes environment information such as the workstation context and the communication media employed and structure information such as the values of data structures and the states of control structures. Then the user-oriented command is changed into a style-independent form and mapped to an appropriate set of calls to the application (if any). After processing the calls, the application sends the results to the interface management system which re-sends the results to the destination workstation through the desired communication media.

In the execution phase, since a user knows which commands have been executed and which commands have been undone according to the representation of this situation by the user recovery and command reuse support facility, he can easily issue a recovery command. If he issues a reuse command, the interface management system will pass the re-used command to the application. If he issues an undo or redo command, after analysing the syntax the recovery command will be passed to the recovery manager. In this aspect, the other components, especially the dialogue manager of the interface management system, take the user recovery and command reuse support component as a *background application* for command recovery. The recovery manager will carry out the recovery process according to the information stored in the context information base. It sends the results to the dialogue manager of the interface management system which sends the result to the destination workstation in the required form.

When an application environment is chosen, the design of user recovery and command reuse support can enter the implementation stage. How other functions of a system affect user recovery and command reuse support and how the machine environment affect it will emerge into prominence. There may be different trade-offs in different situations. Each design alternative has its own set of virtues and limitations. A designer has to balance the trade-offs between various technical, logistical and functional objectives.

6. Conclusions

This paper has discussed a design process for user recovery and command reuse support which involves requirement analysis, conceptual design and function specification. Its detailed design and prototyping stages have to be conducted along with the detailed design and prototyping of its host environment. Since Waldhor has pointed out (Waldhor [1987]) that all users have good reasons for having such support, informal inquiry and questionnaire techniques have to be used for initial requirement analysis to find out who is using such support and which system has such support so that interview and observation methods can be applied to complete requirement analysis. After explaining different considerations for key representation issues about user recovery and command reuse support, a possible architecture to support this facility has been proposed to demonstrate its feasibility. This user oriented design process has further potential. Its approach seems promising for designing other support features of interfaces such as help support.

Acknowledgements

The research reported in this paper was supported by the Alvey grant GR/D 424125. The author would like to thank her husband and people who have responded to her network inquiry. She also would like to thank her colleagues at the Scottish HCI Centre for their valuable comments.

References

R M Baecker [1987], "Interaction Styles and Techniques," in *Human-Computer Interaction: A Multi-Disciplinary Approach*, R M Baecker and W A S Buxton, ed., Morgan Kaufmann.

J M Carroll & M B Rosson [1987], "Paradox of the Active User," in *Interfacing Thought: Cognitive Aspects of Human-Computer Interaction*, J M Carroll, ed., MIT Press, Cambridge MA, 80–111.

J R Dance [1987], "The Run-Time Structure of UIMS-Support Applications," *ACM Computer Graphics* 21, 97–101.

K A Lantz [October 1986], "On User Interface Reference Models," *ACM SIGCHI Bulletin* 18, 36–42.

M V Mason [1986], "Adaptive Command Prompting in an Online Documentation System," *Int. J. Man-Machine Studies* 25, 33–51.

D A Norman [1983], "Design Principles for Human Computer-Interfaces," in *Proceedings of CHI '83 – Human Factors in Computing Systems*, ACM, New York, 1–10.

G Perlman [1984], "Making the Right Choices with Menus," in *INTERACT '84 – First IFIP Conference on Human-Computer Interaction*, B Shackel, ed., Elsevier-Science, Amsterdam, 317–321.

S L Smith & J N Mosier [1984], "Design Guidelines for User-System Interface Software," The Mitre Corporation, Report No. ESD-TR-84-190, Bedford MA.

J S Vitter [1984], "US&R: A New Framework for Redoing," *IEEE Software* 1, 39–52.

K Waldhor [1987], "Some Theses on Undo/Redo Commands," in *INTERACT '87 – The Second IFIP Conference on Human-Computer Interaction*, H J Bullinger and B Shackel, ed., Elsevier Science Publishers B.V., North Holland, 777–781.

Y Yang [1987], *Undo Support Models*, Scottish HCI Centre AMU8727/01, Edinburgh, Accepted for Publication in Int. J. Man-Machine Studies.

Y Yang [1988], "A New Conceptual Model for Interactive User Recovery and Command Reuse Facilities," in *Proceedings of CHI '88 – Human Factors in Computing Systems*, ACM, New York.

Issues Governing the Suitability of Programming Languages for Programming Tasks

Marian Petre & Russel Winder

Department of Computer Science, University College London, Gower Street, London WC1E 6BT.

This research was provoked by assertions in the literature about the 'obvious naturalness' of particular programming languages for general programming. It was intended to uncover principal issues governing the suitability of general purpose programming languages for expressing different types of solutions and to observe factors which obstructed coding or inhibited it altogether. The study required experts to program solutions to a variety of problems in several languages, in order to exercise their opinions and expertise. The general pattern which emerged from the protocols was that experts devised solutions not in terms of a particular programming language, but in terms of a pseudo-language which was a patchwork of different notations and approaches, implying that they found different languages appropriate for different aspects of solution, and that they used a personal computational model which was an amalgam of all their computational knowledge. Solutions so devised were coded into a given programming language, often with heavy translation overheads, particularly for data structures. Once a satisfactory algorithm was adopted, experts resisted a change of algorithm unless provoked strongly. Three sources of irritation in coding were reported consistently: inadequate data structuring tools, inefficiency, and poor interaction facilities.

Keywords: Naturalness, Coding, Computational Model

1. Introduction

The research is provoked by assertions in the literature on programming languages of the sort: 'This language is natural.' [e.g., "...*our 'programming language' enables us to express directly a natural definition of each function and relation.*" (Clark & Darlington [1980])] Despite such claims in the literature, there seems to be mumbled agreement that no one language is a panacea, although some would argue that some languages or styles are generally better than others. All this is the stuff of intuition and legend; relevant empirical work [e.g., (Green [1977]), (Gilmore [1986]), (Soloway, Bonar & Ehrlich [1983])] is scarce and tends to concentrate on aspects of notation, without clarifying the relationship between programming languages and programming.

'Naturalness' is a quality of the relationships between the ways people think about and solve problems and the ways they express the solution strategies. It embodies the directness of translation between internal and external tools and so is not amenable to direct empirical investigation. However, we can recognise that 'naturalness' is relative to its environment — problem, language, and programmer — and can begin to identify factors which affect expression — that is, coding — persistently within the variable contexts of 'programming'.

This paper considers 'naturalness' in the restricted sense of 'what makes a language suitable for expressing a solution'. It reports an investigation intended to uncover principal issues governing suitability and to observe factors which obstruct coding or inhibit it. The work is a knowledge elicitation exercise to evoke expert opinions and experience in order to begin to codify the intuitive and even the obvious. The investigation is an effort to uncover 'received wisdom' about suitability and to gather pointers for experimentation.

2. Approach

The intention was to evoke a rich response from experts, to provoke them to exercise their opinions, arguments, intuitions, biases, and irritations about general-purpose programming languages. The investigation was conceived as a 'Big Shootout', offering experts an arena in which to 'fight it out' among themselves.

Six experts were presented with five problems for solution in three languages each. The problems (see appendix) were chosen to be varied in type and in possible solution strategies, to be non-trivial although small enough for feasibility, and to be familiar but fun. These problems were the backdrop to a questionnaire. The experts chose their own languages, but the study was seeded, minimally, to ensure both a basis for comparison and representation of the major programming styles. All working notes and code were collected, and the questionnaire was supported by interviews.

The questionnaire used the poles 'elegance' and 'awkwardness' to trigger discussion about suitability. Experts were asked, among other things, to rank the given problems in order of the elegance with which their solutions were expressed in each language used. Similarly, estimate rankings for five large problems — TeX, auto-router for printed circuit boards, airline booking system, text editor, small real-time operating system — were requested. We do not equate elegance with suitability, but preliminary investigations suggested that 'elegance' provoked relevant discussion without itself requiring discussion.

Exploratory in nature, the investigation favoured richness over rigour, so that structure and control were loose. Coding and form filling were done at the experts' convenience, without observation. Interviews were driven by the experts, with occasional and careful prompts from the interviewer concerning issues not spontaneously addressed. Partial answers, outside discussion, short-cuts, and variance from the instructions were tolerated, but the experts were pressed to report and justify any liberties they took.

3. Assumptions and Predictions

The experts, of a 'computing generation', are roughly similar in background:

- All have mathematics, physics, or philosophy degrees.
- All have begun programming in an imperative language (although that is not necessarily their current preference).
- All have experience with low-level and machine-oriented problems.
- All are interested in and opinionated about programming languages.
- All are acknowledged by others as 'expert hackers', although few consider themselves experts.

We assumed, based on our own experience, that, given the opportunity, experts would play, would explore solutions and languages for the sake of fun and variety, and that they would be only too happy to exercise and demonstrate their pet notions.

In considering 'naturalness' or suitability, we are interested not in the *process* of solution but with the *nature* of the solution, i.e., not in how programmers reach the algorithm (design and programming), but in what makes the solution amenable to expression in a certain notation (coding or translation). So, problems were chosen to be familiar, in order to lessen the burden on the experts. Nevertheless, the experts were asked to code solutions from scratch so that they would remind themselves of translation issues.

Although it can be and has been shown that problems solvable in one general-purpose programming language are solvable in another, we take it that languages are not uniform in terms of expressive ability and style, i.e., that there is no language that captures all elegant strategies elegantly, and that different languages are suitable for different classes of solutions. Problems were chosen to be as varied in their solution requirements as was feasible. It was assumed that the variety would be sufficient to illustrate differences of expressive ability among the languages used, and that the large-problem rankings would provoke discussion about issues not raised by the coding exercises.

Given the exploratory nature of the research, we did not begin with firm hypotheses about the particular issues we would find. Rather, we set out with general predictions:

- that differentiation among languages, and among language styles, in terms of the solution constructs they express easily or well, would be possible;

- that issues governing suitability of language to solution would emerge;

- that the patterns discerned would coincide only partially with the usual teachings about 'what matters' and 'what matches what';

- that the choice of language would influence the choice of solution, and/or vice versa.

4. Results

11 languages were used by the experts for coding: Ada, BASIC, BCPL, C, C++, FORTH, KRC, Miranda, Pascal, PROLOG and Scheme. 4

more were included in comments: COBOL, FORTRAN, LISP and Occam.

50% of solutions were at least partially coded.

The data was considered as three bodies:

1. objective information from the questionnaires: rankings, records of solution order and time, etc., which was tabulated;

2. code: both pseudo-code and implementations, for which algorithm and data structures were identified, incompleteness and bugs noted, and a quick, subjective mark for clarity or comparative elegance given;

3. commentary and explanation: transcripts of interviews, questionnaire commentary, notes and general code comments, which underwent a two-phase analysis:

    i. keywords were extracted from paragraphs and then assembled, rationalised, and used to 'code' the transcripts and to identify themes or trends.

    ii. transcripts were reviewed for instances of the perceived themes, to check interpretation, determine breadth of occurrence, and note whether each instance was prompted or spontaneous.

Correspondence between the first two categories and the third was investigated. Unsurprisingly, there were discrepancies (Welbank [1983]), although some experts were more consistent than others. Where code and commentary disagreed, particularly as concerned algorithms, the code was considered in preference.

A number of themes or patterns emerged. These are presented below and are illustrated by quotations from the interviews and questionnaires. Where the theme was not unanimously exercised, the proportion of experts who expressed it is given in parentheses (e.g., n/6).

4.1. Elegance

To provide a basis for calibrating 'elegance' rankings, the experts were asked, in the follow-up interviews, to expound their understanding of 'elegance'. They offered comparable and overlapping catalogues of qualities:

— clarity of structure; the ability to control and express the perceived 'natural' structure; coherence (remarked upon by 5/6)

- lack of clutter; 'saying just that which is interesting'; lack of avoidable redundancy (5/6)
- simple things represented simply (4/6)
- economy of expression; conciseness — while retaining necessary information; 'clean syntax' (4/6)
- beauty; lack of ugliness (4/6)
- appropriate mapping; suitable notation; the structure of the expression reflects the structure of the expressed (3/6)
- readability; maintainability (2/6)
- correctness (2/6)

Subtlety was not excluded; 'elegant' was not taken to mean 'obvious' or 'simple'. 'Elegance' was not related to efficiency.

4.2. Relative Importance of Coding and Algorithm-Finding

The experts were provoked by the nature of the investigation itself. They speculated and argued freely, both in the interviews and sometimes on the questionnaires, about what they believed were the underlying assumptions. They were concerned particularly that the research was misguided, that 'coding' was not the 'important bit'. All asserted, without prompting, that finding an algorithm is the more important and more demanding task. [e.g., "*...the problem lies in finding the algorithm, so once I had a working...program, I just translated it, rather than repeat the hard bit of finding a suitable algorithm.*" and "*...the solution itself is far more important than the language in which it is written.*"]

4.3. First Language

Consistent with the valuation of algorithm-finding over coding were the opinions that the choice of language for the first coding of a solution affects expectations about possible algorithms. All of the experts considered important the first language used to express a solution. [e.g., "*I think that solving a problem in any language makes the subsequent reprogramming, in any other language, much easier.*" and "*In Scheme, your expectations about doing I/O, because of the way it just happens to be in most of the world for LISPs, that changes the way you think...*"] However, particular languages or language types did not correspond to particular solution strategies.

There was a suggestion of correspondence between languages and oversights. For example, experts coding the lazy merge solution to Hamming's problem in Scheme tended to seed their multiplication streams with 2, 3, and 5, without actually introducing 1, 2, 3, or 5 to the merged stream, hence missing the beginning of the sequence. Similarly, the stream-oriented Scheme approaches to the next permutation problem mishandled cases containing repeated characters. In some cases, bugs were not discovered until the solution was re-coded in another language. Only half of the experts used a particular language first for all problems.

4.4. Resistance to Change of Algorithm

Contrary to our prediction, but consistent with the reported opinions and with notions of conservatism, was the experts' tenacious resistance to a change of algorithm, reflected in both code and comments. All used a single algorithm for all encounters with a problem, not just during this study, but during their remembered experience with the problem. Unless provoked strongly, the experts did not look beyond the first algorithm 'good enough' to satisfy the problem. [e.g., *"...so, having seen a solution, there's very little incentive to try and find a different one."*] They were not tempted to experiment. In some cases, the same logic errors appear in all versions of the code.

Only a few provocations were strong enough to warrant finding a new algorithm:

1. outright failure: the algorithm did not satisfy the problem or was flawed; [e.g., *"Deciding how you're going to do it is potentially hard. You can get that wrong. You can either produce no solution at all or a solution that doesn't work..."*]

2. inefficiency in time or space; [e.g., *"Discovering that what I had done in C and Pascal was, to all intents and purposes, not a solution, so they wouldn't execute in a reasonable amount of time. That made me look at other strategies."*]

3. to prove a point in an argument; [e.g., *"...I also did this sort of thing in BCPL a long time ago, because there was a fellow ... So I did that in BCPL, as an argument."*]

4. for verification, particularly if the first solution is suspect in terms of appropriateness (1) or performance (2).

In the cases of strong enough provocation, the change of algorithm was undertaken in the first language. Provocation usually arrived during the first coding. When a fatal bug was not discovered until re-coding, the replacement algorithm was coded first in the first language. In no case did a change of language itself provoke a change of algorithm.

In contrast to their tenacity regarding algorithms, experts were willing to change languages 'for the sake of variety' or 'as a party piece', as well as under provocation. [e.g., *"...just for the record, the kind of thing which would cause me to do that sort of computation, to start off with something like Scheme and finish up with something like BASIC, is a situation where you design something, whoops, alright, it runs out of space."*]

4.5. Algorithmic Elegance vs. Elegance of Data Structure

The clarity of evidence about the experts' resistance to a change of algorithm hinges on their consideration of the algorithm in isolation. All of the experts distinguished algorithm from representation, so that a change of data structure was not perceived to entail a change of algorithm. [e.g., *"...there were crucial differences in the way you represent the data; the algorithm is the same..."* and *"...yes...same algorithm. Again, only minor differences in the representation."*] Similarly, the elegance of algorithms was considered separately from the elegance of associated data structures; one might be regarded as elegant while the other was deemed awkward. [e.g., *"...if you ripped out all the bits around and you just left the algorithm, it might look perfectly OK."*]

Although the criteria determining 'elegance' were the same for both algorithms and data structures, and irritations about coding either were described in similar terms, experts were less tolerant of inadequacies in data structuring tools. Irritation about expression of algorithms concerned clutter, whereas irritation about data structures was stronger, concerning obstructions to expression. [e.g., *"[noughts and crosses] is naturally a 2D problem, where Scheme has no 2D utilities or data structures."* and *"...require much work on building utilities to handle the obvious data structures, since BASIC does not support or encourage them."* and *"But... actually implementing sets would be a real drag, lots and lots of work."*]

4.6. Obstructions to Coding

In the interviews, once diverted from comparing the relative importance of algorithm-finding and coding, the experts vociferated spontaneously about irritations and obstructions in coding. Individuals reported being *"...annoyed — absolutely infuriated..."* about shortcomings of programming languages. Most (4/6) expressed insecurity about solutions not yet implemented and felt that a solution was not complete until the code had been compiled and run. [e.g., *"Despite the instructions, I felt I had to use a computer before I was happy with a solution..."*]

Some obstructions to coding were unanimously deplored:

1. inefficiency; [e.g., *"If I came to a situation where...I decided on*

a certain data structure, let's say a list in Scheme, and then I felt irritated because it was inefficient..."]

2. lack of data structuring tools; must distort data structure to contrive its expression; must distort language to construct data structure; [e.g., *"So, how do you arrange, in a purely array world, to imitate a list?"* and *"...that's one of the main problems, where the language doesn't quite support the nice sort of data structures..."*]

3. lack of low-level device handling; lack of memory management; [e.g., *"I'd love to see someone try and do that in Scheme; you can't. You can't get at the bits."* and *"I would never dream of writing a communications protocol in a functional language...Because you can't normally get at those sorts of things..."* and *"Pascal can't interface to hardware."* and *"The thing which Scheme can't do so straightforwardly is give you efficient memory management."* and *"There's a lot of...design decisions which you can't easily express in a language which doesn't allow you to control storage."*]

4. poor input/output or interaction facilities; [e.g., *"Interactive I/O is messy and badly integrated..."* and *"Scheme is not sensible in interaction."* and *"KRC is bad at I/O and anything that requires fast handling of data."*]

5. textual complexity; verbosity; muddy/complicating/cluttering syntax; [e.g., *"Problem 1 requires a data structure so simple that it is hard to represent simply in Scheme!"* and *"PROLOG...doesn't have the same clean syntax (or, indeed, semantics)."* and *"...one of the biggest difficulties I have with this family of languages is...the fact that they're quite verbose. I find that clutters things up, so that I can't easily see what's going on."*]

6. can't reflect 'natural' structure (esp. recursive structure) of algorithm; 'can't see what's happening'; gross/appalling/ugly/ unnatural; [e.g., *"The natural recursive method of solving 5 is about as far from the BASIC style as possible, and inventing an unnatural method for it so that BASIC can then be used is painful."*]

Other were disparaged by at least half of the experts:

1. excess ability to abstract; abstraction facilities lead to 'getting carried away' (4/6); [e.g., *"The problems with something like Ada are severe...because once you start on this track of building up...then you don't know how far to go."* and *"In C, one would have not been tempted to try and do...something too*

complicated...Whereas in C++ you start writing them all down
and you have to cross things out which is ridiculous." and
"And in Ada, the way you go overboard...can...get in the way
of solving the problem."]

2. inability to package or abstract; poor locality (3/6); [e.g.,
   "...you were losing on things like no recursion and poor abstraction." and "...you can actually manage to package up
   control structures in Scheme, whereas you can't really in C++
   or Pascal. Now, the lack of that is something I've felt for a long
   time..." and "ISO-standard Pascal is bad for large programs
   (poor control of visibility, poor locality)..." and "Only C++...
   allows the memory management to be efficient and hidden from
   the 'ordinary programmer'."]

3. had to search around for information; 'couldn't be bothered
   to learn' facilities of language (3/6); [e.g., "Again, it was
   at that which I got stuck, because I didn't know anything
   about streams...and I couldn't be bothered learning it." and
   "I couldn't remember, in the permutations problem, whether
   Ada had sets as a base type or not."]

Although the experts generally presented themselves as willing to 'curse
and carry on', and although they demonstrated a tolerance for overheads
in translation [e.g., "I don't mind going through that level of preamble.
That's not very much; it doesn't take much time."], there were languages
they refused outright to consider (COBOL being the usual example).
[e.g., "...the sheer textual complexity was enough to stop me even
trying."]

4.7. Programming in Pseudo-language

All of the experts claimed, without prompting, often during spontaneous
expostulations about the shortcomings of some programming language,
that they program, not in a particular programming language, but in
some personal 'pseudo-code'. [e.g., "...the interesting thing is, I could
worry about the algorithm; it didn't matter whether I was going to code
it in C, Scheme, or Ada." and "...with the unfamiliar problem, it doesn't
matter what language you do use."] Note the possible conflict between
this notion and the asserted importance of the first programming language used for coding (reported above).

Prompted to enlarge on their 'pseudo-language', each described a composite language, not necessarily coherent or consistent, which borrows
from other disciplines and notations.

e.g.: "I always tend to sketch solutions in pseudo-language which is a mixture of all the bits of language I know, actually."

"...so essentially it's a question of having a working language. I will tend to use a right mixture of notation and ideas I've come across from various places..."

"I find Algol-like pseudo-code useful for control-structure problems, together with arrays, sets, etc. from mathematics. This doesn't, however, cope well with control abstraction — e.g., lazy lists, etc. — for which I tend to use Scheme and Miranda-like notations (but Scheme is rather verbose for use as a working design notation)."

4.8. Machine Model

Unsurprisingly, in view of their backgrounds, all of the experts have a general or reasoning model of the physical machine. [e.g., "...once you've got past the question of specifying what you're going to do, all of the design stuff can't be done without having some model of the machine. Now...I don't worry usually too much about the bottom end details of the machine, how the registers and stuff like that...but it does affect my designs whether I know I'm doing them for say an SIV array or a multi-processor array or a single computer. And it affects it quite early on..."]

4.9. Rankings

The experts were asked, in the questionnaire, to rank the given problems in order of the elegance with which their solutions were expressed in each language used. Although provocative of informative discussion, the rankings were not themselves informative. Where a language was used by more than one expert, enabling comparison, the rankings were idiosyncratic. The justifications of the rankings suggested that the disparate rankings were based on different dimensions, and that each ranking emphasised one characteristic rather than weighing many, so that comparison between experts was inappropriate.

4.10. Coding Time

The experts argued that re-coding a solution in a new language is faster than finding a solution. [e.g., "...I finished up doing the same thing in three languages, on the grounds that I could do it faster that way and therefore I could get more done in the same time." and "...having seen a solution, it's much quicker to recast something, even though it may not be totally appropriate in the language."] First-coding timings reflect the major portion of solution-finding, whether original or reconstructive.

[e.g., "*I only recorded the time I was actually working on the problem, since I couldn't measure the (many) odd moments thinking about it.*"] Although the problems had been chosen to be familiar, only one of the experts had previously solved more than two of them, and the best known problem, telephone directory, was the least coded in this investigation.

However, the expert's own informal timings for the given problems indicate that re-coding is notably faster than first coding only half the time.

5. Patterns and Hypotheses

We draw the results into general patterns, which can be treated as hypotheses for further investigation.

5.1. Computational Model

There was consistent evidence, in the interviews, questionnaires, and work notes, that the experts devise solutions — program — in a personal pseudo-language which is a collage of convenient notations from various disciplines. Their direct claims to a 'working language' are supported by performance: the variation by half of the experts of the language used for the first coding of a problem; the lack of correspondence between solution strategies and languages; the comparable coding times, in half the cases, for all versions of a solution. It seems that programming languages are used, not for 'programming', but for 'coding' or translating a program.

It is likely that the pseudo-language is the surface reflection of a computational model, also a composite of models borrowed from many sources. Hence, each expert has a personal computational model which is used in devising algorithms, and that model is mapped onto a given language, often at the expense of the model embodied by the language. The predominantly-used computational models do not necessarily correspond to programming language styles. Rather than guiding algorithm choice, programming languages may be distorted into conformance with a design.

The pseudo-language and computational model notions imply that experts have an abstract model of the algorithm apart from its expression in a particular programming language. The algorithm is language independent, but not model independent. It is relevant that the algorithm was perceived as separate — nearly independent-from the data representation, with which the bulk of translation overheads between languages was associated. Data is the link to the real world; it is shaped less by the programmer's computational model than by its own internal relationships. And so the quality of the data structuring tools, and the ability to express directly the structure as perceived, contribute strongly to suitability.

There is an apparent conflict between these notions of an abstract algorithm first captured in a pseudo-language and the asserted importance of the first coding language. There need not be a discrepancy. The programmer's computational model may well incorporate the model underlying the coding language. Even if the computational model and pseudo-language algorithm are independent of the first coding language, it may be that the pseudo-code solution is rough or incomplete, so that details and representations are resolved in the first coding, allowing the programmer to observe the particular constraints of, and hence give importance to, the first coding language. This would account for the coding timings. Where the first coding takes longer, either the translation is more difficult or there are details to be settled. Where the timings are comparable for all codings, the solution formulation was perhaps more complete.

It might be interesting to examine coding and re-coding timings produced by programmers of different backgrounds. All of the experts had encountered computational models elsewhere (e.g., in mathematics or physics) before they met programming-related ones. Are they less likely to be first-language bound than programmers without similar background, for whom the first computational model is the one provided by the first programming language?

5.2. Levels of Information

All of the experts claimed an awareness of the underlying machine; all have a reasoning model of the computer. This reflects their backgrounds, the sorts of problems they have encountered, and the fundamental pragmatism of 'programming', the point of which is to produce a program which runs on a machine. The predominance of concern about efficiency underlines both the experts' machine-awareness and the persistence with which reality constrains computing problems. There is a tension between the importance of the abstract algorithm and practical demands.

The experts want, on the one hand, the ability to manipulate hardware, 'to get at the bits', and, on the other, the ability to abstract, to hide or ignore the bits. There is no contradiction. Experts want to look at different things at different times; in particular, they want to *choose* how much they see at any one time. The ability to select the level of information appears within the characterisation of elegance: *"Elegant in the sense that you've got all the details that you want at that level of interest but without too much else, and that it stands out fairly clearly...what that's led to as a notion of elegance depends upon why you're reading something."*

Desirable as abstraction is [e.g., *"Whatever one feels about elegance, it's definitely most 'comfortable' to use Miranda — when you have to worry about low-level details programming is much more stressful."*], detail is needed as well [e.g., *"So my suspicion is the Miranda-like stuff will be useful for the sort of outer levels of the design, and that what I really ought to do if I was being systematic about this is to integrate that with a language which does allow you extra hooks — which does allow you to specify all your control operations, that is to say — so that you can then be free to design."*] Moreover, there is danger from too much abstraction. [e.g, *"I think it actually looks more comprehensible with explicit queue manipulation than the smart lazy version."*]

The desire for abstraction facilities extends from the desire for structural visibility. Partitioning and structuring a solution properly or finding the right abstractions is critical to success and comprehensibility. [e.g., *"In other words, the language structure is a kind of insurance in itself. You will either get the answer and it will be coherent, because of the way the problem is partitioned, or you'll get stuck and you'll realise it."*] Unsurprisingly, the experts want structuring tools, both for expressing strategy and for representing data. Further, they want tools for abstraction, so that they can package structures. Yet such tools are dangerously seductive and can lead users into confusing excess. It is not clear that the languages which offer abstraction facilities actually help in choosing abstractions.

5.3. Matching Languages to Problems

Finding a suitable language relies on an ability to partition a problem well, to recognise the major components of its solution, and to weigh those requirements against the attributes of the language. The idiosyn-chratic rankings, particularly for the large problems, suggest that the experts do not consider all aspects of a problem, but concentrate on one they select as important, perhaps without weighing the alternatives. There was a strong emphasis on the algorithm not accounted for by the problem set. Regardless of the relative intellectual importance of algorithms and coding, coding is expensive of time and emotion. Given that disgruntled programmers will change language, and that the first coding language may affect design details, suitability is important.

Only one expert had codified his language selection strategies: *"I've tried to make my comments here as general as possible, i.e., to abstract from my experience in order to give some heavy hints about how I match problems to languages. Roughly, it's like a table look-up, for which each language is mentally tabulated along with some key concepts or phrases that say what the language offers that is especially distinctive or efficient. When I see a problem, I try to tag the first algorithm that I think of for its solution with an appropriate choice of words from the set used to describe languages. Then the matching is simple."*

6. Further Study

Work is underway to capture a matching strategy as clear as the one quoted above. Particular investigations concern data structuring tools, solution partitioning, and computational models.

7. Summary

The general pattern which emerged was that experts devised solutions not in terms of a particular programming language, but in terms of a pseudo-language which was a patchwork of different notations and approaches, implying that they found different languages appropriate for different aspects of a solution, and that they used a personal computational model which was an amalgam of all their computational knowledge. Solutions so devised were coded into a given programming language, often with heavy translation overheads, particularly for data structures. Once a satisfactory algorithm was adopted, experts resisted a change of algorithm unless provoked strongly, as by inefficiency or failure, or for the sake of argument or verification. A number of irritations to coding were identified, including inefficiency, inadequate data structuring tools, poor interaction facilities, lack of low-level device handling, poor abstraction facilities, and textual complexity, some of them strong enough to cause experts to avoid a particular language.

Acknowledgement

We would like to acknowledge the help, enthusiasm and patience of our experts, without whom there would be nothing to report.

References

K L Clark & J Darlington [1980], "Algorithm Classification Through Synthesis," *The Computer Journal* 23, 61–65.

D J Gilmore [1986], "Structural Visibility and Program Comprehension," in *People and Computers: Designing for Usability (Proceedings of the Second Conference of the BCS HCI SG, York, 23-26 September 1986)*, M D Harrison and A F Monk, ed., Cambridge University Press, 527–545.

T R G Green [1977], "Conditional Program Statements and Their Comprehensibility to Professional Programmers," *Journal of Occupational Psychology*.

E Soloway, J Bonar & K Ehrlich [September 1983], "Cognitive Strategies and Looping Constructs: An Empirical Study," *Communications of the ACM* 26, 853–860.

M Welbank [1983], *A Review of Knowledge Acquisition Techniques for Expert Systems*, Martlesham Consultancy Services, BTRL, Ipswich.

Appendix: The Problems

Noughts and Crosses:

Create an interactive noughts and crosses player.

Next Permutation:

Given a sequence of characters (not the alphabetically last permutation of the string), produce the alphabetically next permutation of that sequence.

For example:

> 'end' is succeeded by 'nde'
>
> 'permute' is succeeded by 'pertemu'

Telephone Directory:

Write an interactive program to maintain a simple telephone directory containing both private and business entries. All entries include:

> name,
>
> one or more addresses,
>
> one or more telephone numbers.

Business entries include, in addition, one or more business classifications.

It should be possible to add, delete, and modify entries; to access an individual entry by name; to give a complete directory listing in name order; and to give a business directory listing sorted by classification and name.

Hamming's Exercise:

Generate in increasing order the sequence 1, 2, 3, 4, 5, 6, 8, 9, 10, 12, ... of the first 1000 numbers divisible by no primes other than 2, 3, or 5.

Making Change:

Compute all the ways of making change for a given amount of money using common English coinage (1p, 2p, 5p, 10p, 20p, 50p, £1).

SEE: A Safe Editing Environment; Human-Computer Interaction for Programmers

J. Rodger Harris

Department of Computer Science, Heriot-Watt University, 79 Grassmarket, Edinburgh EH1 2HJ, U.K.

User-centred design of interactive systems requires many iterations of design and implementation. Software engineering methodologies for software development base their approach on the life cycle and stepwise refinement which, it is assumed, dictate an orderly development.

One of the problems software engineers must overcome is the control and review of multiple versions which are needed for comparison purposes as the development proceeds. The programmers' support provided by system designers, even when used by experts, often leads to misuse and loss of vital information. Even sophisticated source code control systems are not used consistently when developing alternative versions, so leading to loss of working examples for demonstration to users.

This user-centred source code control for programmers is based on stepwise refinement and allows the development of alternative prototypes to be controlled by the programmer(s) in any available language. A number of design principles have been developed and put into practice; a working version has been added to an existing programming environment and evaluated with a user population of novice, intermittent and expert programmers. The system is called the Safe Editing Environment (SEE) and is implemented in the Unix[1] operating system.

Keywords: Programming environment, software engineering tool kit, rapid prototyping, user centred programmer support, interactive design, stepwise refinement.

1. Introduction

All software development can suffer from the 'unknown version' syndrome or the "it worked yesterday before I made a change, and I can't remember what I did!" problem. The Safe Editing Environment (SEE) system was written under the Unix operating system to develop and evaluate a non-intrusive, and normally automatic, system to eliminate these kinds of problems for programmers.

As an encouragement to its use, the SEE system was designed from the start to be operationally simplistic so allowing easy learning and remembering. One objective was to reduce the complexity of controlling versions and change histories, and to make it very difficult to destroy information about previous versions.

The work described here is directed principally at programmers who find out only too late that they should have taken back-ups of their information and kept samples of previous versions; stepwise refinement of any text file benefits from the SEE system by allowing historical developments to be viewed easily.

2. The Motivation

The motivation for developing and using SEE comes from the repeated failure by many programming experts to take adequate precautions in safeguarding their work. This is like the cobbler's children having the worst shoes. For programmers, it is difficult to believe that they will

---

[1] Unix is a trademark of AT&T Bell Laboratories

ever lose or destroy information by their own carelessness, but it does happen to even the best of us.

One common problem for programmers is to keep track of the many back-up versions of their files – how often do they lose control of that situation! It is then excessively time-consuming deciding which to keep or retrieve, or to determine which previous version was working in that 'particular' way.

2.1. Software Development

It has long been apparent that software is difficult to write and almost impossible to write correctly. The methodology which has proved to be most successful for (large) commercially viable software is based on a life cycle. Generally speaking, the first part of the cycle is for requirements specification and design; the second part of the cycle is for implementation and testing. This has the dual purpose of: (a) separating the various activities; and (b) controlling changes that may be required for different reasons by forcing the development always to follow the same direction round the cycle.

This methodology has been used successfully on very complex systems including real-time programs like operating systems; in fact it was because of the obvious deficiencies of existing styles of software development, especially for large software projects (Brooks [1975]), that the life cycle was developed. However, the life cycle is essentially for imposing top-down control, and does not dictate an orderly approach at all levels of development – especially when experimenting with different ideas of implementation. The programmer may be aided by various software tools to keep track of the progress of each module; but these tools are usually at the discretion of the programmer, allowing *laissez-faire* at the detail development level. This PCI (programmer-computer interaction) issue should not be distinct from HCI: programmers are human too.

2.2. Interactive System Design

With the development of highly interactive systems, it has been recognized that there is a new and difficult problem to overcome in software development: that is, taking account of the user. It is no longer sufficient for the designer to adopt rigorous program verification and validation techniques. The kinds of interface acceptable to the modern user are not merely functionally correct; they must be efficacious when used by humans. This is measured in terms of user-centred qualities such as: learnability, memorability, performance, error rate and satisfaction (Shneiderman [1987]). These are, collectively, what is commonly known as 'user-friendliness'.

Thus, new specification techniques are being evolved based on guidelines from psychological experimentation and experience with interactive system performance. Currently, the system definition is carried out by expert designers and programmers able to interpret all the accumulation of knowledge about the proposed system and its potential users. The task of specifying the requirements involves evaluation of some part of the software being used, albeit in a fragile and incomplete form. The results of the evaluation must be incorporated into the software and re-tried, perhaps iterating many times before a satisfactory interaction is achieved. This is not controllable using the traditional software engineering life cycle.

One technique that has been used for interactive system design is prototyping. This is one of the claimed strengths of a programmable operating system (like Unix), with many pre-written and well supported software tools. Other prototyping tools have been developed which allow a look-see at how a system would work. For example, using a form generator, the screen layouts can be displayed without developing any underlying functionality. This knowledge is invaluable for the user-interface designer, providing that the design is participatory – that is, involves a representative population of users (Harris & Parker [1987]). These tools have varying degrees of success. Regrettably, the code they produce will not suffice for any finished commercially viable software product. It must be re-worked and made robust, often involving complete re-definition of all components in the system and consequent added complexity.

Another example of this form of creative activity was experienced in the Scottish HCI Centre when developing a front end for Replay (Howell [1988]; Miller [1987]), a text manipulation tool. Many different versions of parts of the front end had to be tried, changed and sometimes recovered. The tools for achieving this were provided in the Unix environment, but they had to be explicitly invoked by the programmers, and some omissions and over-sights were inevitable. This added complexity to an already difficult task.

3. The Existing Techniques

The two examples of existing techniques described here are both available under Unix and are, in some sense, extremes. They represent firstly a limited, straightforward system for amateurs, and secondly a more comprehensive system for professionals. I use the terms 'amateurs' and 'professionals' here to give a flavour of the sophistication and robustness rather than to indicate any degree of worthiness or otherwise of those people who use these tools. Some of my best friends are professionals.

These two examples, like all the SEE system represented here, rely on

he Unix diff program, which is based on a fast algorithm for finding
common sequences (Hunt & Szmanski [1977]). This tool allows files to
be compared and any differences either reported in a human-readable
form, or stored in such a way as to allow the automatic reconstruction
of one file from the other.

3.1. Get and put

One mechanism that allows programmers to keep histories of file versions
is the get and put command pair developed in (Kernighan & Pike [1984]).
The put program puts the current version of a file into a history file,
together with the differences (diffs) from the previous version, a time
stamp and a short user-specified comment. The get program allows the
programmer to get a previous version by using the diffs for an editor
script file to re-create the appropriate version. Every time a file is
put, a summary, supplied by the user, together with the time and date,
are added to the history file for reference later. This system is useful,
provided the summaries are meaningful and the programmer takes the
trouble to use it. Recovery is a little difficult as the version number has
to be calculated backwards from the latest copy.

The get and put pair are rarely used because the mechanism relies on the
user having to remember to put the current version before the changes
are made, or after a suitable stable version has been reached. In either
case, a simple back-up copy would be easier for the user to visualize and
retrieve. As there is no mandatory checking mechanism, the putting is
soon forgotten.

3.2. Source Code Control System

The source code control system, SCCS (Rochkind [1975]), implemented
under Unix is a system which controls source code by imposing mandatory 'check in' and 'check out' of the source files. This very deliberately
inhibits the look-see approach of software development. Following the
way of the life cycle – starting at the requirements specifications – the
source code control mechanisms guarantee that the changing of code
will be an orderly affair. The differences between each version are
stored rather than the complete version. Versions can be identified by
annotations in the source control file which give sequence numbers and
short user-specified comments. The RCS system was developed to make
version control more convenient (Tichy [1985]).

The SCCS is all too rarely used in Unix environments. My belief, based
on surveys and interviews of Unix users, is that it appears too difficult to
learn, even to experienced by programmers. The check-in and check-out
procedures have been automated in a trial project (Marthins [1988]),

and this made a very welcome improvement. However, ease of viewing
of changes and fast interactive restoring of distinguished versions are not
made available by simply automating the check-in and check-out.

4. The Principles of SEE

The principles propounded in this section were developed for the SEE
system, and in some cases with hindsight, but are in the spirit of Ivan
Illich's conviviality (Illich [1973]) adapted by Donald Norman (Norman
[1986]). They form a useful set of guide-lines which, I believe, can be
adapted to other interactive software designed for, and by, interactive
system users. Section 7 returns to this interesting suggestion after the
design and evaluation of SEE are brought into context in sections 5
and 6.

4.1. Do not impinge on universally available software

First of all, in terms of target usage, the SEE system should not preclude
the following of the software life cycle, adopting rapid prototyping tools,
or imposing rigorous source code control. Thus, it ought not to impinge
on other universally available software tools that are more suited to carry
out their designed functions.

4.2. Be non-intrusive

It should be as non-intrusive as possible, except when invoking its 'safety'
mechanisms for recovery, history, etc.

4.3. Use standard protocols

It should use standard Unix shells and command line operation so as not
to add an extra burden of learning on its users.

4.4. Use standard naming and option conventions

The commands should have as much consistency as possible based on
naming conventions, parameter options and actions. Of course, the
implementation is coloured by the standard Unix names and conventions
and governed by the non-destructive design.

4.5. Do not add complexity

It should eliminate the need for multiple versions of files to be explicitly
maintained by the user, but not add to the complexity more than
necessary.

4.6. Be non-destructive, except when asked

It should be non-destructive of files in all instances, except when specifically instructed to be destructive by the programmer.

4.7. Make default actions non-destructive

It should have default actions which are always non-destructive. This is particularly important when we remember that Unix has full type-ahead on terminals: if carriage-return is repeated inadvertently, the user should not, as a consequence, have destroyed any files.

4.8. Cater for all user populations

It should recognize the distinctions in expectation between the novice, intermittent and frequent user.

4.9. Give feedback to the user

There should be feedback of actions showing the user how the command was interpreted. For prolonged system activity, there should be some indication that all is well.

4.10. Record the history of what was done

It should have automatic history logging so that all changes can be reviewed in sequence, with the ability to select sub-sets of any activity where appropriate.

4.11. Design and evolve help with the command structure

On-line help should be developed at the same time that the system evolved, and be built into command structure. Various functional groupings and alphabetic listing of command options should be tried for best performance. By adopting the policy of evolving the help with the system, the design should be capable of being evaluated continuously. Any updating of help information should be convenient and easily verified.

4.12. Seek early and continuous evaluation from appropriate users

By continuously evaluating the performance of the system with actual use by a typical user population, unnecessary and unwanted commands or options should be spotted from the history mechanism and informed feedback. This should result in a small number of residual commands and options being adopted from a much greater and cumbersome set.

5. The Design of SEE

I believe, along with others, that design itself is a process, is non-hierarchical, involves the development of partial solutions and the discovery of new goals (Carroll & Rosson [1985]). It follows from this point of view that the design of a system inevitably interacts with its evaluation, and design decisions are based on selection and validation during the evolution of the system.

The concepts used in SEE are those that would be known to the users: files and directories; file names, time and date stamping; version numbers; saving, retrieving and archiving; logging and histories. Note that these are both computer and task concepts – we are dealing with the use of the computer system as a task here.

The principal constraint was that the SEE system should work in the standard Unix environment using a glass terminal – that is, a VDU without graphics. Keyboard-based command language was chosen rather than imposing a false layer of full-screen based menus with pointing devices or other direct manipulation style interfaces; this was because command language is the usual style for Unix users when dealing with the file system at the operating system command level.

A form of menu is given on the prompt line. This shows the available options directly or can be expanded by choosing the help option.

The differences in user ability are met by allowing default, silent short-cuts in some instances. SEE does not pretend to be adaptive; this variable response is automatic, but always consistent and controllable from the user's viewpoint.

SEE does not replace any existing editor, source code control, or other tool; it simply allows the stepwise development of any part of the system to be conducted with minimum effort devoted to file maintenance, history recording and recovery or rapid look-see.

The viewing of changes and histories can normally be accomplished with single keystroke commands.

5.1. Logging

SEE automatically logs actions on files, including removing, moving, copying, editing, archiving and recovery in the user's logfile. The log program allows the user to review anyone's logfile – providing the permissions are set correctly! This not only allows single programmer operation to be recorded without any effort by the user, but also allows multiple programmer teams to view any changes that have been introduced into any files. The programmer or any colleague can check any logged command selectively – that is, all the edits or all the removes, etc. The user can elect to review a single command's entries in the logfile, for example:

log −rm   list all remove operations (user's)
log −rm rodger   list all rodger's remove operations

This command is in the style of many Unix commands where there are default actions taken when using just the command name: in this case, it shows the latest screen-full from the log. The command's action is modified by adding an option; as with all the SEE commands, the −h option will give on-line help describing the available options and the action of the command. It was found that functional ordering and grouping of the help list was far easier to read than alphabetic listing. During development, functional ordering is also easier to keep up-to-date and encourages consistency in the design of the options across the range of commands.

5.2. Back-ups

Whenever any editing is done on a file, a back-up is made of the current version (but only when necessary). This is done for all edits except when explicitly refused by the programmer and the back-ups are all kept until they are explicitly removed. The whole file is copied rather than the differences. This was a design decision which allows much easier viewing of changes – space was not a problem and, in any case, the differences can be as long as, and even longer than, the different versions of the file! The underlying computer concept matches the task concept here, so there is absolutely no complexity loading for the user: if a previous version is required, it can be reviewed immediately and directly, or compared to any other version just as easily, without tedious manipulations. This was found to be an enormous comfort to users, completely justifying the overhead on space. Besides, this can be handled by other system functions kept quite separate from the users' needs of accessing previous versions.

5.3. Listing versions

All versions can be viewed using a single command. They are normally automatically listed by name in reverse time order (youngest, most recent, first) and their version date, time and number are easily read.

The feedback to the user is thus quite helpful: the order of listing shows the history of the development, and the name of each file contains a direct indication of the time and date it was written, plus the version number for easy reference and confirmation, illustrated below under 'naming'.

5.4. Naming

The names of the back-ups include the the file name, directory name, date string and version number:

        name.dir.15Sep87@09:06:29.#3

Thus the time and number information stays with the back-up as part of its name, so that it can be referred to when checking historical changes.

5.5. Comparison of versions

To view the actual changes made to any file, it is a single command. The versions are normally always compared with the current version in the current directory. All versions are reviewed one-by-one so that the history of changes unfolds before the programmers eyes. The version number and modification time are always displayed. It is trivial to be able to compare any two versions, should that need arise.

5.6. Recovery

To recover any file from any version is a single command. The programmer is offered the choice of all versions, starting with the most recent. A copy of the current version is added to the back-ups, thus avoiding any loss of information due to overwriting.

5.7. Removing

When the time comes to remove the back-ups, this can be done interactively or globally. The default action at any point is always non-destructive, so that the programmer cannot inadvertently remove all the back-ups.

5.8. Archiving

There is a separate archiving mechanism which saves favourite versions for quick identification and recovery. These can be reviewed historically too. The point at which an archive is taken would normally be when a version of the file has satisfied some criterion of success – possibly for demonstration later. The programmer is then free to make any change, safe in the knowledge that this 'correct' version can be recalled at any time. This also allows multiple versions to be demonstrated with minimum logistic effort.

5.9. Help

At all user input points in the operation of the SEE commands, there are prompt messages for next action to be taken by user. Any unusual happenings are reported when they occur, and if a file is in danger of destruction, the SEE command will offer a non-destructive default action. In addition there is an on-line help program describing what commands are available and what they do.

5.10. Errors

There are no error messages in SEE, only help messages. This is a deliberate policy decision. The only 'error' that the user could make would be to destroy information when it was not the intention to destroy it. This is made difficult for the user to do.

5.11. Implementation Details

SEE is for developing software and other text files by providing a convenient back-up system, and by replacing potentially destructive operations on files with explicitly prompted instructions. All the destructive commands (e.g., removing files) are replaced by safer versions. Some systems do automatically back-up files in case of user error, but they do not all incorporate easy recovery, reviewing and selective deletion of those back-ups. SEE was designed to make use of the relatively common availability of large, fast Unix machines, and to overcome the dangers of self-destruction which Unix allows. SEE is written under Unix in Bourne shell (Bourne [1982]), C shell and C (Kernighan & Ritchie [1978]). The only SEE program written in C is used to abstract the last modification time from the file descriptor and convert in to a string of the form 15Sep87@09:06:29. The only C shell used is for the .login, .logout and .cshrc (or .tcshrc) files for the system environment. Everything else is written in Bourne shell and therefore both portable and easily adjusted as dictated by evaluation in use.

6. Evaluation

There are a number of perspectives to the evaluation of any system, and it is neither necessary nor desirable to depend on any one method.

6.1. Surveys and interviews for requirements

Surveys can give some insight, but in this case, were conducted through informal discussion and observation of programmer frustration expressed in a variety of ways. It appeared from open anedotal sessions that more people made catastrophic mistakes with the manipualtion of their files than anyone realized. My favourite catastrophy in Unix was when a friend tried to remove a file named '??>??' using the '*' to match the presumably unprintable characters marked by '??'. This resulted in creating an empty file called '*' and removing everything else! This cannot happen with SEE.

6.2. Recording of Development

The SEE system itself was developed, in true compiler writer tradition, using itself. It has been invaluable on a number of occasions already for recovering from operator error, and is extremely instructive in displaying what stepwise development really looks like. The current SEE has been the result of over one hundred different versions of the editor back-up program, and about fifty versions of the recovery program, together with many attempts at the other modules. As the versions were not destroyed, the reason(s) for each one being replaced could be reviewed: it was found that most changes were based on interaction problems. Thus, recording developments in a workable form provided tremendous insight into the interaction process itself. The resulting version was obviously the most favoured by users.

6.3. Discussion of subjective user satisfaction

Subjective satisfaction was indicted by the obvious pleasure the users exhibited when showing the changes they made to their files. Instead of feeling that there has been a lot of wasted effort in developing a piece of code or text, the design process is translated into a teaching experience, with all the ideas and changes easily demonstrated and explained.

6.4. Recording of Usage

History and time stamping of commands were used as evaluation tools to determine usage. This logging is made available to users as a source of knowledge, so that the memory load of remembering what they have been doing is reduced. It was not appropriate to seek task completion times for normal operation as most of the SEE system is non-intrusive. If recovery ever were required, any time taken to complete the task of recovery was, in the context of the alternative of not being able to recover, would be, indisputably, acceptable to the users. The major criterion was whether the user could actually recover from apparent disaster.

6.5. Command names and abbreviations

Abbreviation and command defaults for SEE are assessed by the user population only when they have to recover. The standard Unix command names and abbreviations were implemented so that the user did not have to learn any new information to operate normally. Thus, the evaluation of extraordinary commands involved the efficacy of the on-line help and manual. In the same way, any protocol analysis would be in two parts: normal operation and recovery. Normal operation followed the Unix protocol. Recovery is itself non-destructive, and the protocol is based on prompting the user to decide on any action, giving the default and options available. Based on interviews, all this worked without confusion for both novice and expert users, and error rates diminished rapidly with usage.

6.6. Amount of feedback to users

The safe editor program went from being very verbose – to keep track of what was happening – down to being very succinct. It now has a slower and more gentle response for novice users who do not use the default mechanisms, but speeds up when the default options are used. Any extraordinary requests – e.g., those that require careful interaction – are provided with deliberate and confirming feedback. This avoided any tendency of non-experts to race through tasks to match the speed of response, whilst giving subjective satisfaction to those expert users who got to know the defaults.

6.7. Range of function: feedback from users

Evaluation was being done all the time. One general problem encountered was the temptation to include more and more options. Ultimately, most of them have been removed because of the added complexity could not be justified by the usage. However, there was one example that showed that redundant information held in the file name could be utilised automatically and be of benefit to the interaction. This was the comparison program, which was modified to allow the version number to be specified rather than wading through all existing back-up versions – despite the difficulty of conveying that option in a command line. There is fine balance between comprehensiveness and simplicity, and these two goals are different when viewed from the system's functionality and its interaction. It is only by continually evaluating during the design process that this balance can be achieved.

7. Principles as Guide-lines for Software

Engineering

In section 4, I put forward twelve principles which were derived before and during the development of SEE. In this section I argue that they can, and should, be applied as guide-lines for software development in general.

7.1. Do not impinge on other universally available software

In the evaluation of SEE with a user population of Unix programmers, it became apparent that 'not invented here' and 'not part of our standards' are attitudes that are major obstacles in the acceptance of software. Any new system or tool will have to overcome the inertia of the recognized and understood patterns of behaviour. New ideas must offer some perceived improvement in which it is worth investing the effort of change. This applies to programmers as well as to general computer users, and not only in a Unix environment.

7.2. Be non-intrusive

To gain acceptance, software should be non-intrusive. Users should be able to perform their tasks as though the software were part of their normal universe of discourse. In the case of SEE, that means no extra thinking. Generally, intrusiveness occurs when something or someone is noticed as not being part of normal events. Thus, software should aim to be the accepted the norm as quickly as possible. This is part of what others have called 'learnability'.

7.3. Use standard protocols

Using standard protocols is another manifestation of learnability. The adage "I know what I like and I like what I know" applies equally to protocols as it does to classical music. Keep software familiar and it will be popular.

7.4. Use standard naming and option conventions

Command structure should be consistent, which is yet another form of learnability.

7.5. Do not add complexity

A solution to any problem should be seen as no more complex than the original problem. For example, if the problem were not to lose information, the solution may be to keep multiple versions. In SEE, multiple versions are easy to control, even if it is at the expense of space. To generalize: no software should add unnecessary complexity for the user, even if this is at the expense of time, space or programming effort.

7.6. Be non-destructive, except when asked

Interactive software should not be capable of destroying user information, unless this is specifically and deliberately requested by the user.

7.7. Make default actions non-destructive

Any default action must be non-destructive. If the default is, for example, to remove files, then there must be a recovery procedure available for the user.

7.8. Cater for all user populations

The interactive system design should cater for the range of expected user populations. Thus, novice users would need more help, recovery and tutorial mechanisms than experienced users.

7.9. Give feedback to the user

Any interaction between people and machines benefits from 'confirmative' information. In the case of computer systems, this is easily implemented with the aid of feedback of actions. Such a simple idea, but gives enormous assurance to users, and even experienced ones too.

7.10. Record the history of what was done

An interactive session also gains credibility from the user if their, or the system's, actions can be reviewed. A history mechanism can also form part of documentation or notification for other collaborators on the same project. It very quickly becomes an accepted norm.

7.11. Design and evolve help with the command structure

With SEE, as is the case with all other software, first-time users are all novices. Sufficient assistance should be available, but not compulsory. In general, help messages will have more than two levels of verbosity: i.e., not simply on or off, but will have terse, and various levels of detail of accounts of what is happening.

7.12. Seek early and continuous evaluation from appropriate users

Evaluation has been the missing link in software engineering methodologies. Although it is sometimes difficult to find a representative population, consult an expert in the field, conduct surveys, questionnaires, benchmarks, or perform task analysis, etc., etc., it seems absolutely pointless to design and implement software without some form of evaluation. I would now argue that it is essential to have continuous evaluation by a representative user population in order to have learnable, memorable and non-intrusive software.

8. Footnote

As a result of the demonstration of SEE, the standard source code control system (SCCS) provided in Unix has been modified to be almost transparent. This was a major step forward in our environment as SCCS had not been used consistently before. However, the ease with which users of SEE can review history and the subjective programmer satisfaction have yet to be challenged.

Acknowledgements

Many of my colleagues and students have contributed to the ideas in this paper and acted as willing subjects to try out even the most baroque user-aids.

References

S R Bourne [1982], *The Unix System*, Addison-Wesley, Reading MA.

F P Brooks [1975], *The Mythical Man Month*, Addison-Wesley, Reading MA.

J M Carroll & M B Rosson [1985], "Usability Specifications as a Tool in Iterative Development," in *Advances in Human-Computer Interaction 1*, H R Hartson, ed., Ablex, Norwood NJ, 1–28.

J R Harris & D W Parker [1987], "Evaluation of Rapid Prototyping Methodology in a Human Interface," in *INTERACT '87 – The Second IFIP Conference on Human-Computer Interaction*, H J Bullinger and B Shackel, ed., Elsevier Science Publishers B.V., North Holland, 1059–1063.

G Howell [March 1988], "Design and Implementation of Replay," Scottish HCI Centre, Internal Report, Edinburgh.

J W Hunt & T G Szmanski [May 1977], "A Fast Algorithm for Computing Largest Common Sequences," *Communications of the ACM*.

I Illich [1973], *Tools for Conviviality*, Harper and Row, New York.

B W Kernighan & R Pike [1984], *The Unix Programming Environment*, Prentice-Hall, New Jersey.

B W Kernighan & D M Ritchie [1978], *The C Programming Language*, Prentice Hall, New Jersey.

J Marthins [1988], "Software Development Environment," Internal Report, Computer Science Department, Heriot-Watt University Edinburgh.

C D F Miller [1987], *Replay*, Mara Ltd, Edinburgh.

D A Norman [1986], "Cognitive Engineering," in *User Centered System Design*, D A Norman and S W Draper, ed., Lawrence Erlbaum Associates, Hillsdale, New Jersey, 31–61.

M Rochkind [December 1975], "The Source Code Control System," *IEEE Trans. on Software Engineering*.

B Shneiderman [1987], *Designing the User Interface: Strategies for Effective Human-Computer Interaction*, Addison-Wesley, Reading MA.

W Tichy [July 1985], "RCS – A System for Version Control," *Software – Practice and Experience*.

Systems Support

User-driven Adaptive Behaviour, A Comparative Evaluation And An Inductive Analysis

A. Brooks & C. Thorburn

Scottish HCI Centre, Department of Computer Science, University of Strathclyde, Glasgow G1 1XH, U.K.

The comparative effectiveness of user-driven adaption has remained unevaluated until now. An experiment is reported in which two groups of subjects made use of separate text-based interfaces to an operating system environment. One group made use of a traditional interface with a help system, the other made use of a user-driven adaptive interface. The latter group of subjects could move between three different interface styles by a single function key-stroke at any request for input. Both interfaces were built using CONNECT and the experiment was carried out within a research paradigm promoted by Brooks. The group using the traditional interface was found to have requested help significantly more often than the number of times the other group pressed the function keys and four of the subjects commented negatively on the entry/exit nature of the help system. User-driven adaption was otherwise found not to enhance interaction. Interpretations are placed upon subjects' behaviour at the user-driven adaptive interface

and compared with those made of the results of an earlier experiment.

Keywords: user-driven, adaption, evaluation, help system, induction

1. Introduction

1.1. Background

User-driven adaptive interfaces allow the user, at any request for input, to choose a different interface style. Very little was known about such interfaces until only recently. Earlier work was deficient. Palme (Palme [1983]) and Mozeico (Mozeico [1982]), whilst reporting successful use of user-driven adaptive interfaces, gave few experimental details. Maskery's work (Maskery [1984]) cannot be considered of great value since within a session users could NOT change level once allocated to either the 'system leads' or 'user leads' levels. Potosnak (Potosnak [1984]) has reported in some detail on an experiment with a user-driven adaptive interface. Unfortunately, the usual product measures of performance – time and accuracy – are not presented, nor it seems were subjects asked about overall ease-of-use of the interface or their reasons why they chose to interact the way they did. Recently, Brooks *et al* (Brooks, Alty & England [1987]) have reported in detail on an experiment with a user-driven adaptive interface. It was found that two-thirds of the subjects completed the tasks correctly (in the sense that final disk directories were correct) and only one subject from seventeen commented that the interface was not easy to use. The comparative effectiveness of user-driven adaption, however, has remained unevaluated until now. This paper reports on an experiment in which two groups of subjects made use of separate text-based interfaces to an operating system environment. One group made use of a traditional interface with a help system, the other made use of a user-driven adaptive interface. By studying user-driven adaption, rules for successful automatic adaption may, or may not, emerge. (For a review of the current state of knowledge of the effectiveness of automatic adaption, see (Brooks, Alty & England [1987]).) It is noted here that within Bergman and Keene-Moore's (Bergman & Keene-Moore [1985]) taxonomy of help systems, a user-driven interface can be viewed as a help system of the 'integrated' type. The study reported here could therefore be viewed as a comparison of help systems. Borenstein (Borenstein [1985]) has carried out a comparative evaluation of help systems and his results and methodology in relation to the work of this paper are discussed in the final section. A design decision recommendation is also given in the final section.

1.2. CONNECT

Both the user-driven adaptive interface and the traditional interface with a help system were implemented on an IBM PC/AT using a user interface management system called CONNECT (Alty & Brooks [1985]). CONNECT specifies the human computer interface as a transition network. For each network node visited by a subject, CONNECT records, in a trace file, information on node number, time, user input and user reaction times.

1.3. Experimental Paradigm

The experiment was carried out within an research paradigm promoted by Brooks in (Brooks, Walker & Boardman [1987]). Briefly, the paradigm encourages venturesome experiments (unplanned and planned) in naturalistic (i.e., complex) domains, with a view to determining places in the state-space of human-computer interaction at which greater experimental effort is justified and/or where the greatest benefits to users may be realised. The paradigm promotes an inductive analysis of both unplanned and planned experiments, expedited by automatic rule induction techniques – rule learning techniques more commonly used in expert system building. This implies that with more planned experiments, as was the case reported here, data collection remains unrestricted (e.g., comments made by subjects should be noted and interpreted). With more planned experiments, the paradigm does not forbid the application of traditional statistics. The first application of rule induction techniques to multivariate experimental data was reported by Brooks and Alty (Brooks & Alty [1985]) and has since been applied on several occasions (e.g. (Brooks, Alty & England [1987]; Brooks, Walker & Boardman [1987]),). Note that rule induction can manipulate both numeric and logical attributes (variables). In this paper, both a comparative evaluation (partly based on the use of traditional statistics) and an inductive analysis (expedited by the use of rule induction techniques) are reported.

2. The Two Interfaces

2.1. Introduction

In designing the interfaces every effort was made to keep the information content of both interfaces the same and to follow Galitz's (Galitz [1985]) guidelines for screen design – consistent component locations, symmetrical balance, provision of essential information only, provision of all data related to one task on a single screen, use of plain simple

English, an orderly clutter free appearance and cohesive element groupings. According to Perlman (Perlman [1984]), sorted menus are easier to search and compatible letter selectors produce the best performance – these conclusions were also followed as guidelines. Eight commands were available to the users of the interfaces. The chosen command mnemonics consisted of three letters (all of which were required to be typed at menus) and were loosely modelled on the CP/M operating system commands. CP/M's command mnemonic for copying – PIP – was replaced. (Unfortunately, due to the fact that subjects had prior experience of the DOS operating system, some subjects experienced difficulties due to negative transfer. No pre-test of the chosen command mnemonics was given, but subjects could have guessed up to three answers correctly on the basis of their knowledge of DOS.)

2.2. The Traditional Interface With A Help System

The design of the help system was modelled on the help system available on the CP/M operating system. Upon requesting help, with no arguments, subjects were presented with a help menu which listed topics available and some information about help itself. Topics and/or subtopics (in this case EXAMPLES) were specifiable at this point – they were also specifiable as arguments at the opening help request. Once in the help system a special prompt was displayed – HELP>. An exit from the help system was made by pressing the return key. The help screen texts were contained in boxes to remind users that they were within the help system and could not perform tasks.

2.3. The User-driven Adaptive Interface

Three different interface styles or levels were provided – 'expert', 'intermediate' and 'novice'. The expert level presented a simple prompt (A>) and was a normal scrolling interface. The intermediate level presented a screen of examples of command usage and was also a direct command input level presenting the simple prompt (A>) beneath the examples – in this case, the screen did not scroll but was refreshed. The third level presented a totally menu-driven level in which the menu screen was followed by a screen which explained in detail the chosen command, which displayed examples and which also prompted for the command arguments. At the intermediate and novice levels, command output remained on the screen until another command was initiated. Subjects could move between levels by a single function key-stroke (and return) at any request for input. At start-up, the interface was initialised to the expert level. The menu screen text was contained in a box to remind users that they were at the opening menu of the novice level and could not perform tasks. The chosen number (three) and style (expert, intermediate, novice) of interface levels was perhaps arbitrary. In retrospect, however, the three levels may be viewed as providing three different learning styles - learning by trial and error, learning by example only, and learning both by example and by rote.

3. The Experiment

Subjects were asked to carry out twelve tasks ranging in difficulty – one of the simplest tasks was to find the system time and date – one of the most difficult, to delete files greater than a certain size. The simpler tasks came first on the task sheet. The task sheet for the user-driven adaptive interface also had an explanation of the three interface levels and how to access them – for the traditional interface it had an explanation on how to access the help system. There were twenty-two subjects (eleven for each interface) who were all MSc students in Information Technology, who had all recently completed several months of common coursework and who all had experience of using IBM PC computers i.e., they formed a potentially homogeneous group. Briefly, the procedure adopted for each subject was as follows.

(a) Brief subject details were solicited.

(b) Each subject was allowed a few minutes to read the task sheet and ask questions to resolve any misunderstandings. Depending on the subject's group, the function keys were pointed out, or it was stated that tasks could only be performed at the A> prompt.

(c) The subject was left to attempt the tasks (in naturalistic surroundings). Subjects were not advised to complete the tasks as quickly or as accurately as possible (in order that they would respond in a naturalistic way).

(d) On completion the subject was given a post-test and asked for comments. Unsolicited comments by the subject were also noted. The post-test involved asking the subject to look again at the twelve tasks and to state what commands would be used to perform them. The final disk directory was checked to see whether or not it was correct – this provided a measure of the accuracy with which all twelve tasks were attempted. The trace file was examined to determine the frequency of function key presses or help requests.

Unfortunately, data collection problems arose on three occasions and data for subjects A, K and L are incomplete.

Table 1a. User-driven adaptive interface

	time	acc	post	freq
A	*	*	11	*
B	14:48	N	12	12
C	13:58	Y	10	1
D	13:44	Y	12	5
E	14:54	Y	12	4
F	30:29	N	8	6
G	18:18	Y	12	9
H	12:10	N	7	6
I	10:03	Y	11	9
J	16:25	N	10	7
K	20:00	N	11	*

Table 1b. Traditional interface with help

	time	acc	post	freq
L	*	*	12	*
M	11:41	N	12	13
N	11:07	Y	11	7
O	14:18	N	11	13
P	14:09	Y	12	12
Q	19:50	Y	12	9
R	16:20	N	11	12
S	16:02	N	11	10
T	26:39	N	12	22
U	17:12	Y	12	12
V	13:13	Y	11	14

4. Comparative Evaluation

4.1. The Data

In the first instance, four product measures of performance – time, accuracy, post-test and function key/help request frequency scores – were chosen to form the basis of the comparative evaluation. Tables 1a and 1b give these data for all twenty-two subjects (A-V). Missing data is signified by asterisks in the tables. The time is given in minutes and seconds, the **accuracy** is given as a **Y**es or **N**o depending on whether or not the final disk directory was correct, the **post**-test score is given as the number of correct answers out of twelve and the **freq**uency is given as the number of times the function keys were pressed (at the user-driven adaptive interface) or how often help was requested (at the traditional interface). Note that requests for further help from within the help system were not included in the help request frequency scores.

4.2. Analysis and Interpretations

Only the time and access frequency scores were amenable to a traditional statistical analysis. These data passed both skewness and kurtosis tests for normality – tables for which are given in (Brooks [1984]). Subsequent two sample t-tests found no significant difference between the mean times taken by the two groups of subjects but did find a significant difference between the mean function key/help request frequencies for the two groups at the 5% level – indicating that the group using the traditional interface requested help significantly more frequently than the other group changed interface levels by pressing the function keys. This result is easily interpretable and not entirely unexpected – by presenting more information at the outer level of an interface, the less the interface user needs to move around the lower levels. Equal numbers of subjects (five) from the two groups finished with an incorrect final directory – this is indicative of no great differences between groups regarding the accuracy with which the tasks were performed but is suggestive of the ease with which incorrect file operations can be made. It can be seen that interface type had no measurable impact on the usual product measures of performance – time and accuracy. Aside from the two lowest scores by subjects F and H, post-test scores for the two groups were also similar. Note that both subjects concerned had, on more than one occasion, answered a post-test question by giving a command name for another system i.e., they experienced difficulties due to negative transfer.

5. Rule Inductive Analysis

5.1. Rule Induction And Induction Data

The rule induction software used was IRIS (Arisholm [1987]). IRIS automatically provides the number of cases (subjects) falling into each of the rule outcomes. Note that rule induction tends not to be a one-shot process – it is often necessary, as was the case here, to describe attribute data at various levels of detail and observe the effect on the resulting rules. Table 2 and Appendix A, giving all the attributes and all the attribute values represent the final data used in the rule inductions. (Data for subjects A, K and L were excluded because of incompleteness.) In all, three sets of inductions were performed – over all common attribute data (attributes numbered (1)-(13)), over attribute data for subjects who had used the user-driven adaptive interface (adding attributes numbered (14)-(16)), and over attribute data for subjects who had used the traditional interface with help (adding attributes numbered (17)-(23)). In the inductions, each attribute was taken in turn as the rule outcome. Table 2 contains a short description of each attribute and the possible values of logical attributes. In the table 'yes' and 'no'

Table 2.   Attributes

attribute	description	logical values
(1) time	time taken (rounded to the nearest minute)	
(2) post	post-test score of command knowledge (max. 12)	
(3) tday	time of day	morn, afte
(4) lang	native language	eng, neng
(5) sex	sex of subject	m,f
(6) sys	system used	adapt, help
(7) easy	easy to use ?	y, n
(8) rest	computer response time ?	gd, ok, sl
(9) freq	function key/help request frequency	
(10) errt	error type in post-test	none, nbdg, negt
(11) acc	accuracy – final disk directory correct ?	y, n
(12) age	age of subject	
(13) exam	exam score	
(14) novt	percentage of time at novice level	
(15) intt	percentage of time at intermediate level	
(16) expt	percentage of time at expert level	
(17) enex	mention of entry/exit nature of help	y, n
(18) reas	mention of help used for reassurance towards end	y, n
(19) negt	mention of difficulties due to negative transfer	y, n
(20) exex	mention of more EXAMPLES explanation required	y, n
(21) exno	mention of EXAMPLES not used/not needed	y, n
(22) wild	mention of problems with wildcard characters	y, n
(23) less	mention of less use of help towards end	y, n

are abbreviated to 'y' and 'n'. For clarification some extended attribute descriptions follow. Computer response time (rest-(8)) was graded as good (gd), (ok) or slow (sl). The error type (errt-(10)) in the post-test was graded as none (none), no answer or bad guess (nbdg), or no answer and negative-transfer answers (negt). Mentions of the entry/exit nature of help (exex-(17)) in the traditional interface refers to explicitly negative comments and/or comments regarded as being negative implicitly, for example, comments suggesting a separate help window.

In the analysis that follows, only the rules considered to convey the most meaning will be discussed. Note that Appendix B lists the comments made by subjects at the user-driven adaptive interface. These comments are accounted for separately, later, when the resulting interpretations are compared with the earlier interpretations of user-driven adaptive behaviour reported in (Brooks, Alty & England [1987]).

5.2. Common Attribute Data – Rules And Interpretations

Induced rules (not reproduced here), for post (2) and sys (6) as rule outcomes, produced similar findings to the comparative evaluation i.e., they showed that the two lowest post-test scores were due to negative-transfer answers by subjects F and H and that subjects using the traditional interface with help generally had greater function key/help request frequency scores (in fact, eight of the nine highest). The induced rule (not reproduced here) for lang (4) showed that of the eight longest times taken, four were by those subjects whose native language was not english - there may have been a cultural effect. The induced rule (not reproduced here) for easy (7) showed that the one subject (subject B) who did not find the system easy to use had pressed the function keys the most at the user-driven adaptive interface. On inspection of the subject's trace file, it was found that the subject had often made the mistake of entering a command only at the intermediate level. This serious misconception would explain the subject's extreme behaviour (in terms of the number of function key presses) and her unfavourable comment regarding ease of use.

5.3. User-Driven Adaption Data – Rules And Interpretations

Rules for attributes (2), and (7) had similar meaning to those discussed above. Interesting rules, however, were induced for acc (11) – whether or not the final disk directory was correct – and expt (16) – the percentage of time spent at the expert level. These rules are given in Fig. 1.

Figure 1. Induced rules for acc (11) and expt (16)

(11) rule for acc (accuracy – final disk directory correct ?)
IF freq

        < 6 THEN y (3)

        $>= 6$ AND IF exam

                  $>= 76$ THEN y (2)

                  < 76 THEN n (4)

(16) rule for expt (percentage of time at expert level)

IF errt

      negt   THEN $10 <= $ expt < 70 (2)

      none   THEN expt < 10 (4)

      nbdg   AND IF time

                 $>= 14$ THEN expt < 10 (2)

                 < 14 THEN expt > 70 (1)

The rule for acc (11) draws attention to the fact that the two most able subjects in the user-driven adaption group (subjects G and I, in terms of their exam score) had a correct final disk directory. The rule also draws attention to the three subjects (subjects C, D and E) who had pressed the function keys the least and who also had a correct final disk directory. Two of these three had, in fact, spent most of their time at the novice level, where perhaps there was less likelihood of error. The suggestion is that the less able subjects who moved more around the interface were prone to making errors. The rule for expt (16) draws attention to the fact that the two subjects who gave negative-transfer answers in the post-test were two of only three subjects who had spent an appreciable amount of time at the expert level. Both subjects concerned had also incorrect final disk directories. All this suggests that these subjects had moved too quickly to working at the expert level. The rule also draws attention to the one subject (subject I) who spent a considerable time at the expert level. With a correct final disk directory and the minimum time taken to his credit, this subject can only be described as 'a natural expert'. Further enquiries revealed that this subject had amassed considerable computer know-how prior to his course and that he was known as an achiever.

5.4. Traditional Interface With Help – Rules And Interpretations

Interesting rules were induced for acc (11) and reas (18) – mention of help used for reassurance towards the end of the experiment. These rules are given in Fig. 2. The rule for acc (11) draws attention to the fact that the two most able subjects in the traditional help group (subjects P and V, in terms of their exam score) had a correct final disk directory – a similar finding to the one above for the adaption data.

The rule also draws attention to the two subjects (subjects N and Q) who had requested help the least and who also had a correct final disk directory. The suggestion is that the less able subjects who moved more around the interface (by using the help system more), were prone to making errors – a similar suggestion to the one made above for the adaption data. The rule for reas (18) shows that those subjects who had said that they had used help for reassurance towards the end of the experiment and those subjects who had said that they had used help less towards the end of the experiment were mutually exclusive. A check of the trace files, however, revealed that subject N is an exception, as he had used help less towards the end as well as mentioning its reassurance role – the check also revealed that two subjects (subjects N and Q) went several minutes without using help at the end of the experiment. The latter behaviour could be interpreted as successful progression from the level of novice user.

Figure 2. Induced rules for acc (11) and reas (18)

(11) rule acc (accuracy - final disk directory correct ?)

IF freq
```
    < 10    THEN y (2)
    >= 10   AND IF exam
            >= 71 THEN y (2)
            < 71    AND IF time
                    < 17    THEN n (4)
                    >= 17 AND IF time
                            >= 27 THEN n (1)
                            < 27    THEN y (1)
```

(18) rule for reas (mention of help used for reassurance towards end)

IF less
```
    y       THEN n (4)
    n       AND IF exam
            < 70    THEN y (4)
            >= 70 AND IF TIME
                    >= 16 THEN n (1)
                    < 16    THEN y (1)
```

6. Comparison With Earlier Results On User-driven Adaption

6.1. Earlier Results

Brooks *et al* (Brooks, Alty & England [1987]) found that there were three main competing interpretations of subjects' behaviour at a user-driven adaptive interface – maintaining a passive role (cognitive style interpretation), learning style preference (by rote and example and by example alone), and circadian effects. Note that all three interpretations may have held but with regard to different subjects. One of the main results of the paper was the major differences found in patterns of subject behaviour despite subjects having similar amounts of computer knowledge.

6.2. Function Key Behaviour, Interpretations And Comparison

Appendix B lists the comments (paraphrased) made by subjects regarding their use of the three different interface levels and other unsolicited comments made by them. From this data and the data in Appendix A on time spent at each interface level, subjects C, E, and G could be said to have maintained a passive role. In addition, learning by example could be said to to have played an important part for subjects B, D, and J. There are, therefore, at least two competing interpretations of the data. (Those viewed as maintaining a passive role could also be viewed as expressing a preference for a particular style of learning.) It is worth noting here that the three subjects who came in the morning all pressed the function keys at least six times – circadian effects may also have played a part. Both the earlier results (described above) and those reported here can be seen to have been interpretable in a similar way. A notable difference between the two sets of results is the behaviour of subjects F and H who made an orderly progression from the Novice level to the Expert level. (Such clear progressions were not present in the earlier work.) It has already been noted that these subjects may have progressed too quickly. The comment by subject F, to the effect that he had tried to enter filenames with spaces (!), provides another example of how a serious misconception led to extreme behaviour (in this case, the longest time taken.)

7. Summary And Further Discussion

7.1. Impact Of Interface Type

Interface type had no measurable impact on the usual product measures of performance. Aside from the differences in the function key/help request frequency scores (interpretated previously by stating that "by providing more information at the outer level of an interface the less the interface user needs to move around the lower levels") and the fact that four subjects commented negatively on the entry/exit nature of the traditional interface with help, user-driven adaption was otherwise found not to enhance interaction. Four subjects (two from each group) could be said to have progressed to working at an expert level and correct final disk directories were achieved by the four most able subjects (two from each group) and those subjects who moved less around either interface. Interestingly, these two groups of four subjects were comprised of different subjects – the experimental results cannot solely be interpreted in terms of ability effects. The major differences in interpretations of subjects' behaviour points to significant subject variablity and this may have been why interface type was found to have no measurable impact on the usual product measures of performance. Extreme subject behaviour was attributed to serious misconceptions (subjects B and F) and in the case of subject I, attributed to extensive previous computing experience combined with personal drive. (Is there such a thing as a homogeneous group of subjects ?)

7.2. The Work Of Borenstein

Borenstein (Borenstein [1985]) implemented a multi-windowed, multi-faceted help system called ACRONYM, and evaluated it against other help systems using traditional experimental designs and statistics. One of his conclusions was, "the most important determining factor in the goodness of a help system seems to be the quality and nature of texts it presents, rather than details of the help access mechanisms". The results of the experiment reported here could have provided a 'widening' confirmation of Borenstein's conclusion, if it were not for the suspicion that subject variability may well have been why interface type had no measurable impact on the usual product measures of performance. Whilst Borenstein claims to have accounted for subject variability, his work can be criticised for the lack of insight into individual subject behaviour – it has been shown here that an inductive analysis, expedited by rule induction techniques, provided very useful insights into subject behaviour both collectively and individually.

7.3. Future Work

The fact that interpretations could be placed on the user-driven adaption data similar to the interpretations made by Brooks *et al* (Brooks, Alty & England [1987]), encourages harder science to be done in this area. However, according to McKenna (McKenna [1984]), the most common measure of cognitive style correlates substantially with standard ability tests and according to Kircaldy (Kircaldy [1984]), circadian effects "not only depend on the parameters of the task, but on individual differences, and on factors related to sleep-wakefulness rythms". Doing harder science to disambiguate the various interpretations will be very resource demanding and difficult. Given that this is so, it is suggested here that easier gains are to be made by ensuring the goodness of the quality and nature of text and by detecting and correcting users' misconceptions.

7.4. Design Decision Recommendation

Given the greater overheads of designing and implementing a user-driven adaptive interface it is recommended here that interactive help be provided through a traditionally designed help system running in a separate window – until it is more firmly established that user-driven adaption is superior.

References

J L Alty & A Brooks [1985], "Microtechnology and User Friendly Systems: The CONNECT Dialogue Executor," *Journal of Microcomputer Applications* 8, 333–346.

G Arisholm [1987], "IRIS: Integrated Rule Induction System," Department of Computer Science, University of Strathclyde.

H Bergman & J Keene-Moore [1985], "The Birth of the Help System," in *Proceedings of the ACM Annual Conference*, ACM New York, Denver, Colorado.

N S Borenstein [1985], "The Design and Evaluation of Online Help Systems," Department of Computer Science, Carnegie-Mellon University, Doctoral Thesis.

A Brooks [1984], Internal Report, University Observatory, Department of Astronomy, University of Glasgow.

A Brooks & J L Alty [1985], "The Use of Rule Induction, a Knowledge Acquisition Technique for Expert Systems, to Interpret HCI Experiments," in *People and Computers: Designing the Interface*, P Johnson and S Cook, ed., Cambridge University Press, Cambridge.

A Brooks, J L Alty & D England [1987], "An Inductive Analysis of Behaviour at a User-Driven Adaptive Interface," Scottish HCI Centre Report No. AMU 8722/01S, Department of Computer Science, University of Strathclyde.

A Brooks, A Walker & C Boardman [1987], "At the Interface of Shell Built Expert Systems," in *Proceedings of the Third International Expert Systems Conference, London, (2-4 June)*, Learned Information, Oxford.

W O Galitz [1985], *Handbook of Screen Format Design*, QED Information Sciences Inc..

B D Kircaldy [1984], "Performance and Circadian Rhythms," *Eur. J. Appl. Physiol.* 52, 375–379.

H S Maskery [1984], "Adaptive Interfaces for Novice Users – An Experimental Study," in *INTERACT '84 – First IFIP Conference on Human-Computer Interaction*, B Shackel, ed., Elsevier-Science, Amsterdam.

F P McKenna [1984], "Measures of Field Dependence: Cognitive Style or Cognitive Ability?," *Journal of Personality and Social Psychology* 47, 593–603.

H Mozeico [1982], "A Human/Computer Interface to Accommodate User Learning Stages," *Communications of the ACM* 25, 100–104.

J Palme [1983], "A Human-Computer Interface Encouraging User Growth," in *Designing for Human-Computer Communication*, M E Sime and M J Coombs, ed., Academic Press.

G Perlman [1984], "Making the Right Choices with Menus," in *IN-TERACT '84 – First IFIP Conference on Human-Computer Interaction*, B Shackel, ed., Elsevier-Science, Amsterdam, 317–321.

K M Potosnak [1984], "Choice of Interface Modes by Empirical Groupings of Computer Users," in *INTERACT '84 – First IFIP Conference on Human-Computer Interaction*, B Shackel, ed., Elsevier-Science, Amsterdam.

Appendix A. Values Of Attributes (1)–(23)

	(1)	(2)	(3)	(4)	(5)	(6)	(7)	(8)	(9)	(10)
B	15	12	afte	eng	f	adapt	n	ok	12	none
C	14	10	afte	eng	m	adapt	y	sl	1	nbdg
D	14	12	afte	eng	m	adapt	y	sl	5	none
E	15	12	afte	eng	f	adapt	y	ok	4	none
F	30	8	afte	eng	m	adapt	y	sl	6	negt
G	18	12	morn	eng	m	adapt	y	ok	9	none
H	12	7	morn	eng	m	adapt	y	gd	6	negt
I	10	11	afte	eng	m	adapt	y	sl	9	nbdg
J	16	10	morn	eng	m	adapt	y	ok	7	nbdg
M	12	12	afte	eng	f	help	y	sl	13	none
N	11	11	afte	eng	m	help	y	ok	7	nbdg
O	14	11	afte	eng	f	help	y	gd	13	nbdg
P	14	12	afte	eng	m	help	y	gd	12	none
Q	20	12	morn	nen	f	help	y	ok	9	none
R	16	11	afte	eng	m	help	y	ok	12	nbdg
S	16	11	afte	nen	m	help	y	ok	10	nbdg
T	27	12	afte	nen	m	help	y	ok	22	none
U	17	12	afte	nen	m	help	y	ok	12	none
V	13	11	afte	eng	m	help	y	ok	14	nbdg

	(11)	(12)	(13)	(14)	(15)	(16)
B	n	25	60	44	56	0
C	y	25	69	100	0	0
D	y	23	63	36	64	0
E	y	23	65	98	1	1
F	n	26	70	80	8	12
G	y	22	76	93	7	0
H	n	25	55	71	2	27
I	y	31	77	20	5	75
J	n	43	64	41	59	0

	(11)	(12)	(13)	(17)	(18)	(19)	(20)	(21)	(22)	(23)
M	n	24	55	y	n	n	n	n	n	y
N	y	34	69	y	y	y	y	n	y	n
O	n	23	59	n	n	n	n	n	n	y
P	y	23	71	y	y	n	n	y	n	n
Q	y	29	58	n	n	n	n	y	n	y
R	n	27	70	n	n	y	y	n	n	n
S	n	27	67	n	y	n	n	n	y	n
T	n	40	62	n	y	n	n	n	n	n
U	y	24	67	y	y	n	n	n	n	n
V	y	36	75	n	n	n	n	n	n	y

Appendix B. Comments On The Adaptive Interface Levels And Other Comments

Subject B
Novice : didn't explain enough about commands, not any more than Intermediate
Intermediate : fine
Expert : never used
Other : didn't like USE command

Subject C
Novice : fine
Intermediate : didn't use at all, forgot was there
Expert : didn't use, no need for
Other : better to display previous data on screen, windows? [†]

Subject D
Novice : slower than Intermediate, so just used at start, then moved to Intermediate
Intermediate : liked
Expert : didn't use
Other : didn't like date being wiped off screen, would have liked directory to remain [†]

Subject E
Novice : easiest to use, therefore stayed at this level
Intermediate : didn't use at all
Expert : didn't use
Other :

Subject F
Novice : quite good, used at beginning
Intermediate : examples of COP not clear, quicker than Novice, but didn't need on hindsight
Expert : after practice at other levels moved to Expert
Other : Couldn't do tasks 11 and 12, was entering filenames with spaces and file not found error, therefore gave up

Subject G
Novice : stayed there because it was easiest to use and didn't find it necessary to use the other two levels
Intermediate : just looked, but found wasn't as easy as Novice level so returned
Expert : didn't use at all
Other :

Subject H
Novice : good to start with but was too easy once the commands were familiar
Intermediate : only looked at once, didn't like the look of it so went back to Novice
Expert : graduated onto Expert after Novice, missing out Intermediate
Other :

Subject I
Novice : for novices, but found it useful
Intermediate : didn't find this useful at all
Expert : used that all the way, only using Novice at times
Other : use of wildcards not as extensive as it could be, should be able to use them for all commands

Subject J
Novice : didn't spend time reading screens
Intermediate : used this first, found this more useful than Novice, found that towards the end was using Intermediate without needing to look at menu
Expert : wasn't confident of commands to use this, perhaps with more time would have used it
Other : should have given information on use of wildcards

[†] Recall that command output at the intermediate and novice levels remained on the screen until the next command was initiated.

Contextual Structure Analysis of Microcomputer Manuals

Hiroyasu Chimura, Hiroshi Kato, Hiroyuki Mitani & Takahiro Sato

C&C Information Technology Research Laboratories, NEC Corporation, 1-1, Miyazaki 4-Chome, Miyamae-Ku, Kawasaki, Kanagawa, 213 Japan.

With the rapid diversification and popularization of microcomputers, the necessity for good manuals is increasing. Manuals play an important role in human computer interaction. Most manuals, however, are hard to understand. It is necessary to develop methodologies, methods and technologies for improving the quality of manuals.

The authors considered that contextual structure plays an important part in readability. From this point of view, a method was developed for manuals contextual structure analysis and evaluation applying ISM (Interpretive Structural Modeling) method which is one means for structurally modeling a system. Use of the method helps manual developers to graphically express the whole contextual structure for manuals and to find any logical inconsistency.

This paper describes the basic idea and the method, and then demonstrates the feasibility of using the method through actual applications.

Keywords: Human Computer Interaction,Microcomputer Manuals, Improving Quality Of Manuals,Contextual Structure Analysis, ISM (Interpretive Structural Modeling)

1. Introduction

With the rapid diversification achieved in microcomputers, the necessity for improving the quality of manuals (user documentation) is increasing. Up to this time, engineers and programmers with computing expertise were main users of manuals. They read manuals, which may have been insufficiently explicit, while making up for defects in the manuals with their knowledge or expertise. As microcomputers have come into wide use, various persons, who are not always skilled in computer operation, have become users of manuals, also. Consequently, readability and easy understanding of manuals became a serious problem.

Manuals play an important role in human computer interaction. Most manuals, however, are hard to understand, especially for novices. It is necessary to develop methodologies, methods and technologies for improving the quality of manuals. Several studies on this area (called 'documentation engineering') have been reported. Negishi and Yoshida proposed a method for standardization and systematization of the manual production process to improve the quality of manuals (Negishi & Yoshida [1986]). Jensen and Osguthorpe identified principles of effective design for microcomputer manuals (Jensen & Osguthorpe [1985]). There also are a number of books and articles describing how to produce good manuals (e.g., (Kaiho [1987]; Shneiderman [1987])).

The authors examined factors pertinent to readability and appropriate understanding of manuals and considered that contextual structure plays an important part in achieving the desired readability level. From this point of view, the authors developed a practical method for contextual structure analysis and evaluation for manuals. Use of this method helps manual developers to graphically express the overall contextual structure of manuals and to easily find any logical inconsistency.

This paper describes the basic idea and the method, then, demonstrates the feasibility of using the method through actual applications.

2. Contextual Structure Analysis Of Manuals

2.1. Basic Idea

Various factors pertinent to readability and appropriate understanding of manuals have been cited. They can be summarized as follows:

- Contextual structure,
- Writer's skill in technical writing,
- Whether writer recognizes what the users want to know, and
- Editing style.

The authors considered that the contextual structure should be the first factor to be investigated, for the following reasons. Typical layout and presentation patterns for manuals, which are hard to understand, are represented by:

1. Too detailed contents often appear here and there in the manual.
2. Technical terms and abbreviations are used without their explanations.
3. Prerequisite contents often appear in sequentially later pages than their superior contents (logical inconsistency case).
4. Contents related to each other are widely separated.

The reason that such problems arise is that logically prerequisite relationships among constituent elements of manuals are not regarded in the manual designing process. This is a problem in contextual structure. For this reason, the authors considered that an appropriate method is necessary for manuals contextual structure analysis and evaluation to improve the manual's readability and understanding on the part of the reader.

This study proposes a method for contextual structure analysis and evaluation for manuals, in order to give writers or manual designers information pertinent to improving or reconstructing manuals.

Manuals are normally grouped into the following three categories.

1. Tutorial Manual: Users' purpose is to acquire general knowledge about functions and operations.
2. Reference Manual: Users' purpose is to acquire knowledge on specific subjects, when problems appear in regard to equipment.
3. Index Manual (Quick-Reference Manual): Users' purpose is to look up meanings of terms or usages of commands.

Each category has a characteristic structure. Figure 1 shows a model of the structures for the three manual categories. When analyzing the contextual structure for a manual, it is important to understand into which category the manual falls.

2.2. Method For Contextual Structure Analysis Of Manuals

A manual can be viewed as a system composed of a number of complicatedly related elements and as having characteristics similar to those found in social systems. It is therefore thought that it is possible to effectively apply the social systems engineering technologies to contextual structure analysis for manuals. The authors applied 'The ISM Teaching Objective Structure Chart Analysis Method' (Sato [1979]; Sato [1980]; Sato [1987]) which was developed within the field of the Educational Information Technology, to analyze the contextual structure of manuals (Chimura & Sato [1985]; Chimura & Sato [1987]). The above method is based upon the ISM (Interpretive Structural Modeling) method, which was developed as one means for structurally modeling a system (Warfield [1976]).

The basic procedure for the method proposed in this paper is to first subdivide the manual contents into a number of constituent elements, determine the logically prerequisite relationships among the elements as shown in Fig.2, graphically express the entire structure of the elements as a hierarchical network chart as shown in Fig.3, and then examine whether or not the elements are adequately located in the page sequence while observing the chart.

To carry out the last step in the above procedure, a 'page sequence chart', which corresponds to the hierarchical network chart, is produced and used, also. Figure 4 shows a model of the page sequence chart. In Fig.4, the vertical positions of the elements are just the same as those in the corresponding hierarchical network chart. On the other hand, the horizontal positions of the elements are rearranged according to the order of pages in which the elements appear. The page sequence chart is helpful to find logically inconsistent points. The usage of the chart is described later in detail.

2.3. Procedure Of Contextual Structure Analysis Of Manuals

This section describes a procedure of contextual structure analysis in detail. The method process is shown in Fig.5. The step number given to each of the following paragraphs corresponds to the frame number in Fig.5. In practice, the authors use the ISM Teaching Objective Structure Chart Analysis System, which was developed and implemented on microcomputers (Chimura & Sato [1984]), in support of using this method.

(1) Tutorial Manual

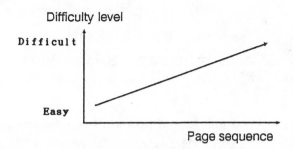

(2) Reference Manual

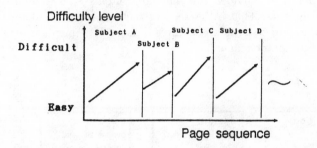

(3) Index Manual
(Quick – Reference Manual)

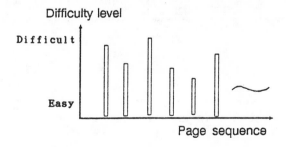

Figure 1. Structures for three manual categories

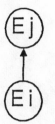

: logically prerequisite relationship
between superior element Ej
and subordinate element Ei.

**Figure 2.   Determining logical prerequisite relationships
among elements**

(1) Abstracting constituent elements

First, an analyst subdivides the manual contents into a number of
constituent elements. That is, he/she abstracts pertinent elements from
the manual. Figure 6 shows an example of a set of elements abstracted
from a microcomputer manual.

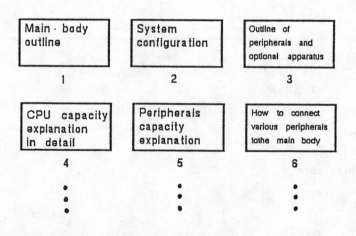

Figure 6.   A set of elements example

(2) Classifying the elements

The analyst classifies the elements according to their difficulty level. For

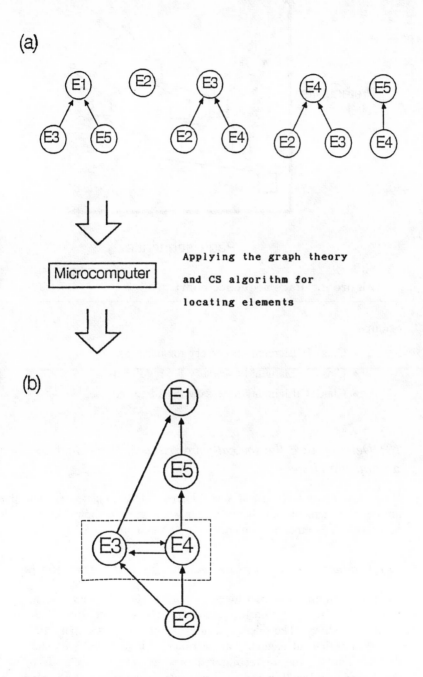

Applying the graph theory
and CS algorithm for
locating elements

Figure 3. A hierarchical network chart for elements

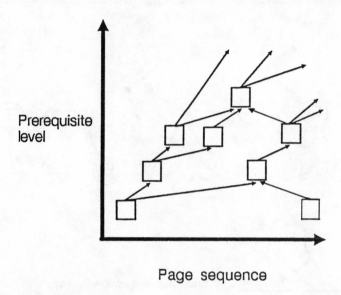

Prerequisite level

Page sequence

Figure 4. Page sequence chart

example:

- Class 1: Elements necessary for basic use.
- Class 2: Elements necessary for regular use.
- Class 3: Elements necessary for advanced use.

(3) Determining the logically prerequisite relationships among the elements

Next, the analyst determines the logically prerequisite relationships among the elements as shown in Fig.2. Figure 7 shows an example of relationships among the elements in the manual.

(4) Producing a hierarchical network chart for elements

After determining the relationships among the elements, the analyst inputs the direct relationships data into the microcomputer program mentioned above. The microcomputer prints a network chart automatically, in which all elements are arranged hierarchically, as shown in Fig.3b. That is, the microcomputer produces the hierarchical network chart shown in Fig.3b based on direct relationships among the elements shown in Fig.3a. The reader may refer to Sato (Sato [1979]) and Warfield

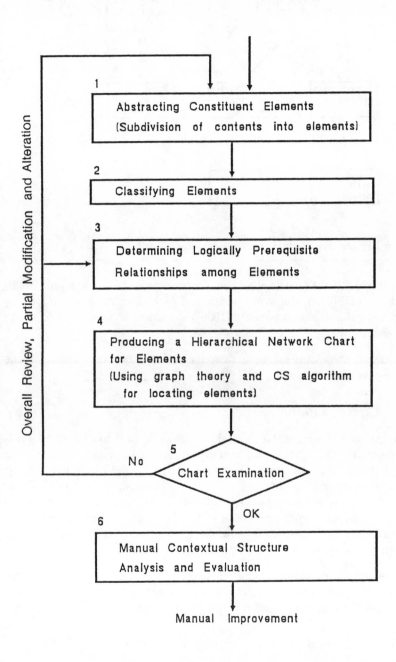

Figure 5.   Contextual structure analysis process

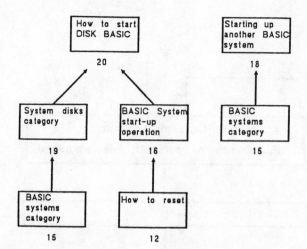

Figure 7. Relationships among elements

(Warfield [1976]) for the algorithm for arranging the elements hierarchically. In addition, the exact position of each element is determined by CS algorithm (Chimura & Sato [1980]) to reduce the number of crossings of the arrows.

Figure 8 shows an example of a hierarchical network chart for the elements of the manual.

(5) Chart examination

The analyst examines the hierarchical network chart to determine if it is acceptable. The chart is prepared in a visually interpretive manner, such that it is easy to determine the overall structure and examine it closely. If it is necessary, he/she can modify the relationships, add new elements and/or delete some elements. After revising, the analyst returns to Step 1 and/or Step 3 and repeats the above steps to obtain a revised chart. In many cases, an acceptable chart is obtained by repeating this loop two or three times.

After obtaining an acceptable hierarchical network chart, analyst produces the page sequence chart which corresponds to the chart obtained. The microcomputer program prints out the page sequence chart, also.

(6) Contextual structure analysis and evaluation for a manual

The analyst analyzes the contextual structure of the manual while

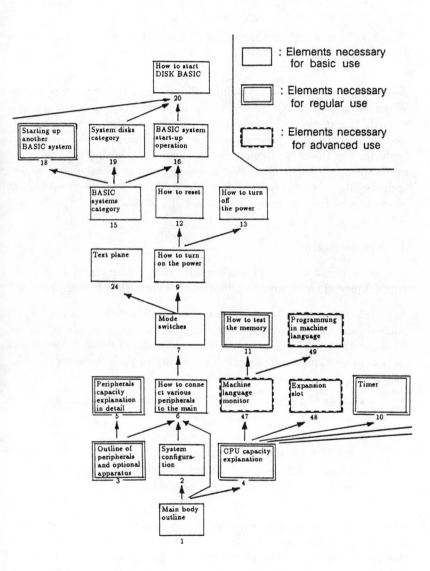

Figure 8. Elements hierarchical network chart

observing the hierarchical network chart and the page sequence chart. Viewpoints for analysis are as follow:

- To find logically inconsistent points in the page sequence. (To find prerequisite elements which appear in sequentially later pages than their superior elements.)
- To observe whether elements, segregated into various difficulty level classes are adequately located or not.
- To observe whether or not elements related to each other are located close together.

A page sequence chart is very helpful to find logically inconsistent points. When an arrow which connects two elements is pointing diagonally towards the upper right-hand corner, it means that the prerequisite element appears before the superior element. This situation involves no problem. On the other hand, when an arrow is pointing diagonally towards the upper left-hand corner, it means that the prerequisite element appears after the superior element. In this way, logically inconsistent points can be found merely by glancing at the chart.

3. Application

Actual manuals were analyzed by applying this method to test its applicability. This section describes one case of such actual applications.

A 'User's Manual' for a microcomputer was chosen as a subject. This manual was for one of the most popular microcomputers in Japan. 49 elements were abstracted from the manual. 36 of these elements were section titles. They were classified according to their difficulty level, as follows:

- Class 1 (Elements necessary for basic use); 22 elements. Such as 'How to turn on the power'.
- Class 2 (Elements necessary for regular use); 21 elements. Such as 'Graphic coordinate system'.
- Class 3 (Elements necessary for advanced use); 6 elements. Such as 'Programming in machine language'.

The logically prerequisite relationships were determined among the elements, and a hierarchical network chart and a page sequence chart of them were obtained. The page sequence chart in this case is shown in Fig.9.

By analyzing this chart, much pertinent information was obtained about the contextual structure of this manual. Data are as follows:

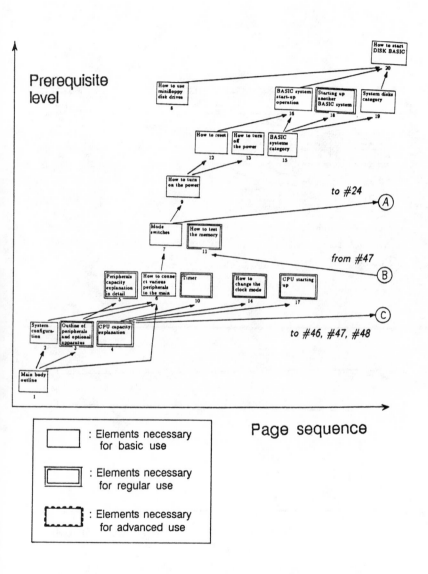

Figure 9a. Case study page sequence chart (1/3)

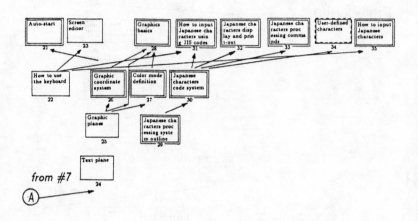

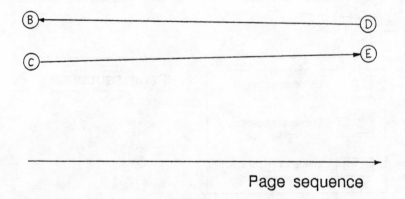

Page sequence

Figure 9b. Case study page sequence chart (2/3)

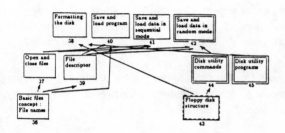

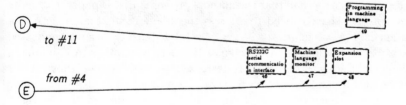

Page sequence

Figure 9c. Case study page sequence chart (3/3)

1. A few advanced elements which belong to class 2 or class 3 are located right after basic elements. For example, elements #3, #4 and #5, which belong to class 2, are located right after elements #1 and #2, which belong to class 1. If users are novices, they may be confused at this point. However, when this manual is used as a reference manual, the sequence is reasonable because elements related to each other are located close together. So, it is required to make adequate direction to assist users, such as, 'If you are a novice, skip these advanced sections'.

2. A few elements related to each other are separately located. Element #8, which is a direct subordinate of element #20, is located far from its superior element. If there was no special reason for the present location of element #8, it should be moved to immediately before element #20. Element #24 is also in such a case.

3. A few prerequisite elements appear after their superior elements. Element #11 and Element #21 are in this category. The sequence should be modified.

The authors judged that the contextual structure for this manual is almost adequate on the whole, except for a few defects described above.

4. Discussion

To sum up the method that the authors proposed in this paper, a visually interpretive chart is used to express the whole contextual structure of manuals. A visual chart is very useful to easily grasp complicated relationships among many elements. However, when there are too many elements, the merit of a chart is decreased, because human beings find it inherently difficult to grasp an overall structure which consists of many elements at one time. As a result of having examined this method, it is deemed difficult to understand an overall structure, whenever the number of elements exceeds 60 or more. For this reason, when a subject manual has large contents, analysis should be carried out according to the following process. First, an analyst abstracts elements from a macro-level point of view. For example, he/she regards a chapter and/or a section as an element. After producing a relational structure chart of these elements, he/she analyzes the composition of the overall contents of the manual. Then, he/she goes to a phase of the contextual structure analysis within each chapter and/or section.

The main purpose of this method is to analyze and evaluate existing manuals in order to improve them for use by effectively untrained personnel as well as experts in the field. The method can also be applied in the following ways:

1. Writers elaborate the composition of a manual by applying this method before they begin to write.

2. Instructors, who teach microcomputer use, employ a hierarchical network chart to determine the instructional sequence.

3. Manual designers analyze manuals of good reputation and/or those of poor reputation, to acquire know-how for producing good manuals.

5. Postscript

The authors proposed a method for contextual structure analysis and evaluation for manuals and demonstrates the feasibility of using the method through actual applications.

Recently, the study of electronic manuals or on-line manuals has been activated. The authors consider that contextual structure analysis plays an important part in designing these manuals, also. To develop a method for contextual structure analysis for electronic manuals is the authors' next subject.

Acknowledgments

The authors would like to thank Masao Managaki and Yoshihiro Nagai of C&C Information Technology Research Labs, NEC Corporation, for their suggestions and help with the production of this paper. Thanks are also owed to the referees who commented on an earlier draft of this paper. Their comments have led to improvements in the structure of the final paper.

References

H Chimura & T Sato [1980], "A Layout Algorithm of Teaching Units Arranged by Using the ISM Method," in *Transactions on Educational Technology of the Institute of Electronics and Communications Engineers of Japan* #ET80-9, 5–10, In Japanese.

H Chimura & T Sato [1984], "Computer-Assisted Analysis and Determination of Instructional Sequences," in *Proceedings of Ed. Comp. Conference*, IEEE Computer Society, 29–37.

H Chimura & T Sato [1985], "Contextual Structure Analysis of Manuals Applying the ISM Instructional Sequences Analysis Method," in *Transactions on Educational Technology of the Institute of Electronics and Communications Engineers of Japan* #ET85-3, 39–44, In Japanese.

H Chimura & T Sato [1987], "Analysis and Evaluation of Contextual Structure of Manuals – Proposal of a Method in Documentation Engineering," in *Transactions on Fundamental Information: Information Processing Society of Japan* #FI 7-3, 1–8, In Japanese.

R P Jensen & R T Osguthorpe [1985], "Better Microcomputer Manuals: A Research-Based Approach," *Educational Technology Research* 3, 42–47.

H Kaiho [1987], *How to Write Manuals*, Kyoritsu Syuppan, Tokyo, In Japanese.

H Negishi & T Yoshida [1986], "Manual Production Based on Documentation Engineering," in *Transactions of the 27th Programming Symposium: Information Processing Society of Japan*, 169–180, In Japanese.

T Sato [1979], "Determination of Hierarchical Networks of Instructional Units Using the Interpretative Structural Modelling Technique," *Educational Technology Research* 3, 67–75.

T Sato [1980], *Data Analysis Methods for Instruction, Design and Evaluation*, Meiji Tosho, Tokyo, In Japanese.

T Sato [1987], *The ISM Structural Learning Method*, Meiji Tosho, Tokyo, In Japanese.

B Shneiderman [1987], *Designing the User Interface: Strategies for Effective Human-Computer Interaction*, Addison-Wesley, Reading MA.

J N Warfield [1976], *Societal System*, Wiley, New York.

Information Flow in a User Interface: the Effect of Experience and Context on the Recall of MacWrite Screens

J. Terry Mayes*, Stephen W. Draper, Alison M. McGregor* & Keith Oatley

Department of Psychology, University of Glasgow, Glasgow G12 8QQ, U.K.

*Scottish HCI Centre, University of Strathclyde, Glasgow G1 1XH, U.K.

A major theoretical and practical concern in HCI is to discover and characterise what it is that users know – of what their expertise consists. We have tested what users remember of the detailed content of the MacWrite interface. We found that even experienced users can recall little of the menu contents, even though during use those menus are the instruments of their successful performance. It seems that the necessary information is picked up, used, and discarded; it is not learned in the sense that commands are learned. More exactly, users retain only enough information for recognition, not the much greater amount required for recall. This has implications for predicting learning times (not having to learn commands even for skilled performance should

make for fast skill acquisition), and for writing documentation (no need to teach what won't be learned): thus
the 'information flow' view of human action (Norman &
Draper [1986]) can be used to re-interpret the findings
and recommendations of the 'minimal manual' approach
developed by Jack Carroll and his associates (Carroll
[1984a]; Carroll [1984b]).

Keywords: HCI, information flow, learning, recall, interface
design, documentation, MacWrite, minimal manual

1. Introduction

A major theoretical and practical concern in HCI is to discover and
characterise what it is that users know – of what their expertise consists.
This seems a fundamental thing to know, with obvious implications
for the design of interfaces, documentation, prediction of expert performance, and prediction of learning times. For instance, the work on
mental models (Gentner & Stevens [1983]), and the use of Task-Action
Grammars (Payne & Green [1986]) to predict learning times depend
on this. At first common-sense seems to suggest that expertise means
knowing the commands a system offers to users: their names, what they
do, and how to use them to carry out useful tasks. This paper contributes
to the growing number of reasons for suggesting that the matter is not
that simple.

In discussing the nature of expertise in UNIX, Draper (Draper [1984])
found that experts on that system did not in fact know more than a
fraction of the commands, but were characterised rather by skill at
discovering information as and when they needed it, for instance by
successful use of the help facilities. This paper reports a study of
knowledge of a very different kind of interface – MacWrite – which
nevertheless also rejects the simple view that expert users know the
commands a system offers, and again suggests that expertise consists
in the fluid use of a flow of information rather than in its permanent
retention as 'knowledge'. The experiment probed what users of various
degrees of experience could recall about the MacWrite interface.

2. The experiment

2.1. Subjects

Fifteen subjects, with varying levels of Macintosh experience, participated in the experiment. Two were students on an Information Technol-

ogy course, the others could all be classified as computer professionals, being research staff in the Turing Institute or the Scottish HCI Centre. All 15 subjects were male and, except for the two students, all had been using the Macintosh for at least a year. Subjects were divided into three groups of five, according to the amount of prior experience with MacWrite. In the *Occasional users* group (to call them *novices* would be misleading for three of this group were experienced users of other computers) were the two students who had used MacWrite only for a few hours altogether, and the other three subjects who used it about once every two months. The five *Intermediate users* had used Macwrite more often than every two months but less than twice a week. *Frequent users* were those subjects who used Macwrite more than twice a week. Four of the five subjects in this group used MacWrite every working day.

2.2. Procedure

A questionnaire was developed which led subjects through the whole process of using MacWrite to create a document, from switching on the computer through creating, formatting, editing and printing. At several steps through this process subjects were asked to recall exactly what would be on the screen and to record this, on paper, in as much detail as possible. In the first part of the questionnaire, details were elicited of subjects' prior experience with the Macintosh. Subjects gave details of their length of experience and frequency of use of the Macintosh, the applications they used with the frequency of each, and in particular their frequency of use of MacWrite. Subjects were then required to work systematically through the booklet, without referring to previous pages. The experimenter monitored the completion of the questionnaire to ensure that this instruction was complied with. The average time spent on the questionnaire was about an hour and a quarter.

2.3. Results

The overall result was that the recall performance of every subject was worse, in *almost* every respect, than either they or we had expected. Some of the subjects with extensive MacWrite experience expressed considerable surprise that they had so much difficulty recalling what they were sure, in a functional sense, they knew. In the following section we summarize the main results under each of the questions.

1. When you switch on what appears on the screen? Please try to draw it below.

Six of the fifteen subjects correctly drew a small box with a blinking questionmark. Three of these were occasional users, one an intermediate and only two were frequent users. None of subjects were able, even when prompted, to draw the icon in any detail and none seemed to be able to recall that it was really a representation of a disc. Seven subjects, however, recalled the smiling Macintosh icon that appears for a second or so when an acceptable disc is inserted. This time one was an occasional user, four were intermediate and two were frequent users.

Overall there seemed to be no obvious trend towards more accurate representation of these icons with increasing frequency of use. This point was confirmed by copying each subjects' drawing and placing it in a group with the drawings from the four other subjects in the same experience category. Three independent judges were asked to look through these groups of drawings and indicate which belonged to which category of user. While the intermediate and occasional groups were each correctly identified once, none of the judges correctly identified the frequent users' group.

2. When you insert your disc with MacWrite on it what appears on the screen? Assume that your 'desktop' has been left clear. Please try to draw the whole screen below.

Here a totally correct recall would have involved the following items appearing in some form that was recognisable on the subject's drawing: menu bar, menu titles (**'Apple'**, **File, Edit, View, Special**), disc icon, wastebasket icon. The mean proportion of these items successfully recalled by each of the three groups is shown in Table 1. A Kruskal-Wallis test confirmed that differences between groups fell well short of significance. The menu titles were particularly poorly recalled, with only three subjects correctly recording the existence of all five menus (one subject from each group). The most notable point about these results is that if we take only the menus, then the occasional users recalled exactly the same number as the frequent users (a mean of 2.9), with the intermediate users producing slightly fewer still (2.2). Interestingly, all 11 subjects who remembered the menu bar remembered the **'Apple'** menu. The worst remembered menu was **View** with only four subjects recording it. Two subjects included items from the MacWrite menu bar and two others included items from the MacDraw menu bar.

3. When you open the disc a window appears on the screen. Can you draw the form of the window in as much detail as possible. Indicate the contents of the window (no need for every detail here).

Eight items were sought here. These were close box, disc title, scroll bar (right), scroll bar (bottom), zoom box, size box, disc information, title bar.

Here the pattern was rather different. While both occasional and intermediate groups were able to recall less than half of the required details the frequent user group now performed significantly better. A Kruskal-Wallis test revealed a significant effect at $p < 0.05$. Even so, only three subjects remembered all the items. One subject omitted only the size box. Three of these subjects were in the frequent user group whilst the other was in the intermediate user group. No one item was recalled by everyone. The best remembered items were the right-hand scroll bar (13 subjects) and the close and size boxes (each 12 subjects). Disc title was the worst recalled detail (5 subjects).

4. At this stage along the top of the screen, in the menu bar, are titles of the menus you can choose from. These are **'Apple' File Edit View Special**. *Now please list in order the choices you have from each menu after it is pulled down from the menu bar.*

Table 1 summarizes the results of the attempts to recall details of these menus. (The **'Apple'** menu was not scored because of the variability in its contents across users.) Not a single menu was correctly specified by a single subject, even by those in the frequent user group who had been using Macwrite daily for over a year (three in one case). This was not because just one or two items were particularly difficult to recall. Average performance was surprisingly poor and there were several instances of complete inability to recall anything at all. Six subjects, for example, could recall no items at all under **View**.

The memorability of the Finder menu across the three groups was subjected to statistical analysis. A Kruskal-Wallis test revealed that the frequent user group did recall significantly more items than those subjects in either of the other two groups ($p < 0.05$).

5. If you select MacWrite what appears on the screen? Please draw it in as much detail as possible.

Here the subjects were required to attempt to recall the following 14 items: Menu bar, 'untitled', close box, scroll bar, size box, ruler, left margin marker, right margin marker, indentation marker, tab marker, regular tab well, decimal tab well, space boxes, alignment boxes.

Results are also summarized in Table 1. There was considerable individual variability in how well this task was performed within each of the three groups. Overall, the best performance here was by the intermediate users but this time a Kruskal-Wallis test revealed no significant difference between the groups.

Again, recall of the titles on the menu bar was poor. None of the subjects recalled all of them and only four subjects recalled 6 (out of 7). However, all of the subjects who remembered the menu bar at all included **File** and **Edit**.

6. The menu bar is now as follows: **'Apple'** **File Edit Search Format Font Style**. *Now please list the choices you have from each menu when it is pulled down.*

These results (also summarized in Table 1) again reveal surprisingly poor memory for menu choices. There was considerable confusion evident here between the Finder and MacWrite menus. Even one of the subjects classified as a frequent user thought that the **File** and **Edit** menus did not vary in the two interfaces. The scoring of the **Font** and **Style** menus was based on a basic set, present in all such menus. Again, a Kruskal-Wallis test revealed no significant difference between the three groups.

7. Assume you have created a nicely typed and formatted letter using MacWrite. You now want to move a picture from the Scrapbook to the bottom of your text. What is the routine? Please list selections from menus.

This question produced quite a different pattern of performance from that seen in all other questions so far. Now subjects were required only to recall an operation rather than specify the name (or even the existence) of the menu from which it is chosen. Here subjects seemed to have no difficulty at all in specifying the correct routine. Seven subjects claimed never to have used the Scrapbook so they were permitted to describe the normal cut or copy (to the Clipboard) and paste. All but one of the subjects gave a correct account, which included the recall of menu items, although those required were only **'Apple'**, *Scrapbook*, **Edit**, *Copy* and *Paste*.

8. You are satisfied with your document and therefore save it. You now want to organise the layout, size of paper, etc., ready for printing using either the ImageWriter or the LaserWriter. Please try to draw what appears on the screen under Page Setup.

Although a score of 12 was possible (printer heading, OK button, cancel, paper type (4), reduction, orientation, pagination or printer effects (2))this question produced the worst recall performance across the board. It is probing users' knowledge of rather infrequently required functionality and while all subjects had used Page Setup, and understood its functions, only five subjects claimed that they used it at all frequently. These subjects (three frequent users and two in the intermediate group) did not obviously reveal better visual memory for Page Setup than other subjects who claimed to use it infrequently. While subjects in the frequent users group did produce more detail than other subjects this difference did not reach statistical significance. Without exception all subjects drew this dialogue box in a highly confused way. The mean number of items remembered was less than 3.

Table 1. **Proportion of items recalled under Questions 2, 3, 4, 5, 6 & 8**

	Desktop	Finder Window	Finder Menu	MacWrite Screen	MacWrite Menus	Page Setup
Occasional	.52	.40	.31	.41	.31	.21
Intermediate	.57	.42	.37	.59	.33	.18
Frequent	.59	.79	.58	.54	.43	.33

9. You print out your document and now want to finish your session on the Macintosh. What is the procedure?

All of the subjects correctly recalled the various routines they use for finishing a session.

2.4. Conclusions from the Recall Test

There is a trend in the results from the above questionnaire for better recall of the details of the interface to be associated with increasing experience of MacWrite. Of course the interest in these results lies not in the observation of that effect itself but rather in its marginal nature when considered in relation to overall performance. The fact that the difference between the performance of the three groups reached statistical significance on two of the tests but not on the others should not be given undue weight. The sample sizes were small, individual variation was high and we are in any case not attempting to prove the null hypothesis. Nevertheless the striking point remains that overall recall performance of even our frequent users was surprisingly poor. For subjects who use MacWrite every working day to be able to recall only about 50% of the rather gross details scored, such as the names or even the existence of menus or menu choices, was not predicted by either us or our subjects.

A rather different, and potentially important, point was suggested by the apparent ease with which almost all subjects were able to respond successfully to questions 7 and 9. Is it the case that memory for details of the interface is context-dependent in a way that allows detail to be easily recalled as part of a *procedure* but otherwise only with difficulty?

2.5. Follow-up study

A subsequent study was conducted on five of the subjects. The purpose of this was to see to what extent a failure to recall some feature of the interface was reflected in the subjects' use of that feature in actual performance.

The subjects who were also tested in this part of the study were: Subjects A and B: *Occasional users*; Subject C: *Intermediate user*; Subjects D and E: *Frequent users*.

2.6. Procedure

Each subject was asked to create a short document using MacWrite. It was convenient to use Page 1 of the memorability questionnaire for this purpose. At first our intention was to devise a tailor-made routine for each subject. In the event the same routine was suitable for all subjects except Subject A (who was asked to copy a picture from the scrapbook and to paste it at the bottom of the text instead of looking at the clipboard).

The task sheet gave the following instructions:

1. Ensure 12 point is selected.
2. Type in text.
3. Move the heading 'PART TWO' to the centre of the line.
4. Change heading to Courier.
5. Select 'DO NOT WORRY'; underline these three words.
6. Select the last three lines 'PLEASE WORK ... ANSWER'; change these lines to bold.
7. Hide ruler.
8. Open header.
9. Drag page number icon to side of page. Type in 'memorability questionnaire' and press return 3 times.
10. Close header with close box.
11. Show ruler.
12. Select 1.5 spacing.
13. Hide ruler.
14. Find all occurrences of 'important'; change to 'essential'.
15. Select 'PART TWO' and copy it; look to see if it is on the clipboard; paste it on to the bottom of your text.

Subjects were instructed simply to perform these tasks as they normally would. All actions on the screen were recorded in real time using *Tempo*. These could then be replayed at a slower rate for data recording. Using this software in real time mode records all of the mouse movements, including any meanderings and hesitations between the point at which a mouse button is pressed and the point at which it is released.

2.7. Results

The results of this observational study can be illustrated by considering the performance of each of the five subjects individually, contrasting aspects of their performance on the memorability questionnaire with their equivalent in the follow-up task. (The latter is given in italics).

Subject A:

1. Put point sizes under *Font*. *Went straight to Style menu to check point size.*
2. Put fonts under *Style*. *Went to Courier under Font menu with no hesitation.*
3. Did not recall existence or contents of *Format* menu. *Went straight to the Format menu and selected Hide Rulers (2 sec. hesitation).*
4. Did not recall any contents of *Search*. *Correctly used Change without hesitation.*
5. Omitted the Spacing boxes on the ruler. *Went straight to the correct Spacing box.*

Subject B:

1. Omitted *Format* on menu bar, did not remember *Align* commands. *Selected the heading and went straight to Align Centre.*
2. Did not recall any of the upper part of the *Format* menu. *Opened, set up and closed the header without hesitation.*
3. Did not recall any contents of *Search*. *Correctly used Change but first looked for this under the Edit menu.*

Subject C:

1. Did not recall any of the upper part of the *Format* menu. *Opened, set up and closed the header without hesitation, found Show Rulers without any apparent searching.*

Subject D:

1. Put point sizes under *Font*. *Went straight to Style menu to check point size.*
2. Forgot *Copy* and *Show Clipboard*. *Demonstrated no hesitation in finding and selecting both.*

3. Only recalled *Insert Page Break* from *Format* menu. *Opened, set up and closed the header without hesitation; found and selected Align Centre without hesitation.*

Subject E:

1. Put point sizes under *Font*. *Went straight to Style menu to check point size.*
2. Did not recall any of the upper part of the *Format* menu; omitted *Align Centre*. *Carried out all the tasks involving Show Rulers, Open Header, Align Centre without hesitation and without any apparent searching.*

2.8. Summary of results

The main conclusion was that subjects had very little difficulty in carrying out the tasks. All produced an error-free document. Items that could not previously be recalled, or items that were put in the wrong place, or confused in some other way, were generally found without hesitation and used with ease when creating the document. One of the two *occasional users* (Subject B) displayed more hesitation, and some searching of the menus to find the required commands. Even with this subject, however, the only real problem was with finding a menu item (*Change*) never previously used. The most striking finding for our present purposes was the frequency with which these subjects went smoothly and without hesitation to select an item that had not previously been recalled. In several cases the existence of the entire menu had been previously forgotten but the subject's performance at the interface itself now revealed an effortless functional memory for the items within it.

Overall, the main findings from our study can be summarized as follows. First, memory for the visual detail of the Macintosh interface was far worse than expected, even by very experienced users. Second, there was some tendency to associate increasing experience with better memory for detail but this effect failed to reach significance in four of the six tests we carried out. More interesting was the exception to the generally poor performance demonstrated when subjects were asked to recall *action sequences*, rather than visual details of what would be on the screen. That subjects, in a sense, 'knew' what they were unable to recall was demonstrated in the follow-up study in which subjects experienced no difficulty in performing with aspects of the interface they had previously 'forgotten'.

3. Discussion

3.1. Incidental learning

To some extent the results of this study go against our commonsense feeling that being familiar and skilful within some situation comes from knowing it well, and that this knowing should allow easy recall – a feeling shared by the subjects who were surprised by the difficulties they had. On the other hand, studies of incidental learning have shown that people often remember rather little about familiar objects. For instance, the study by Nickerson and Adams (Nickerson & Adams [1979]) demonstrated the remarkably poor visual memory most subjects had for the detailed features on the face of a familiar coin. A plausible explanation is that such detailed features are quite incidental to the functionality of a coin, receive only shallow processing and are therefore poorly remembered. This argument suggests that although it may contradict our model of our own minds that we seem to notice so little about the environment we 'know', it is functional not to learn unnecessary detail.

However our study of MacWrite differs from such previous studies because the learning which our subjects seemingly failed to do was not incidental but central to their purposeful and skilful behaviour. In other words, it seems that users do not learn even things which are vital to their performance if they reliably find them in the environment when needed. Much of the 'knowledge' that underwrites their performance seems to be left in the world, which is thus used as a kind of extended memory.

One consequence should be a reduction in the requirement for cognitive effort, and hence an increase in the usability of an interface. The main rationale for direct manipulation is that the user's attention should be focussed directly on the application ('directly engaged'); cognitive resources that must be assigned to processing tasks at the interface are simply a diversion. Thus the 'invisibility' of an interface may be taken as a mark of successful design. We propose that one, previously neglected, way of evaluating the cost of an interface in human information processing resources (that might more profitably be directed to the application it serves), is to assess its *memorability*. Though it may seem a paradoxical idea, the most effective interfaces will be eminently forgettable, or more accurately, will never be learned in a recallable form. While Maclean, Barnard and Hammond (Maclean, Barnard & Hammond [1984]) have experimented with recall measures as a way of determining an index of the 'goodness' of alternative command sets, we suggest that the difference between recognition and recall may be a useful measure of the 'goodness' of a menu-based or direct manipulation interface at avoiding cognitive load on the user.

Eventually, of course, many experienced MacWrite users regard it as a worthwhile investment of cognitive effort to learn keyboard commands and to dispense with the use of the equivalent menu items. This no doubt reflects the cost of continually taking a hand from the keyboard and picking up the mouse. Recall of the detailed commands must now be good or this strategy would not bring any benefit. However, with extended practice even keyboard commands may well come to be poorly recalled away from the computer as this knowledge becomes 'compiled' into sequences of actions. Thus one issue in interpreting these results is that of the accessibility of users' knowledge.

3.2. Accessibility of knowledge

A simplistic view of the questionnaire results might simply equate failure to recall with absence of knowledge. However it is apparent that away from the computer, or outside the context provided by a task, the knowledge is simply less accessible. There are several aspects to this. The first is exemplified by the observation that some skilled touch typists are not aware at a conscious and reportable level of the layout of the keyboard: if asked where, say, 'X' is located they have to imagine typing it and follow the finger movement. Since they must have originally learned the finger movement by using visual search of the keyboard, we might interpret this as a 'compiling-in' of action sequences and the dropping (eventual forgetting) of the visual representation they were derived from. That is, the visual representation *became* 'incidental' and hence is forgotten, even though it was once a necessary part of performance. Since subjects with all degrees of experience showed quite similar poor recall in our experiment, this does not seem the explanation for our findings.

The second point about accessibility, however, is that the knowledge may be coded in a highly specific form and cannot be reproduced away from the interface itself. This would therefore represent an example of *encoding specificity* (Tulving [1974]) where recall is only possible when the retrieval cues present at learning (at the interface) were also present at recall. This kind of explanation might be tested by a version of the experiment in which subjects would be interrupted when about to make a menu selection while actually using MacWrite, and would be asked at that moment to describe in detail what they were about to see. An important issue is whether the context is provided mainly by general cues from the interface itself, or whether it is specific to the current task and that memory for detail is embedded in a sequence of actions. In so far as our data throws light on this issue at all, the ease with which subjects were able to describe the details of the procedures sought by Questions 7 and 9 gives support to the latter idea.

A slightly different approach to the present results is to suggest that the knowledge is encoded in the form of spatial patterns of mouse movements. In terms of Baddeley's (Baddeley [1983]) account of the structure of working memory, handling the MacWrite interface may occupy the capacity of the *visual-spatial scratchpad*. A series of experiments in which subjects used MacWrite while performing a variety of secondary tasks should enable us to specify the nature of the coding processes involved here, and would clarify the question of whether the resources involved in direct manipulation are essentially visual or spatial.

3.3. Recall, Recognition, and Information Flow

Although further studies are needed to address these issues directly, there is a theoretical reason for believing that it is not simply a question of accessibility. It is clear that although our subjects could not recall parts of the interface, their smooth performance of procedures implies that they were able to recognise them. Therefore they could be said to 'know' the features of the interface in an important sense. It should be pointed out however that not only is recognition normally easier than recall (and so is consistent with a saving in cognitive load), but the forced-choice recognition demanded by the MacWrite menus involves much less information in the information theoretic sense than the task of recalling command names from some space of possible names. Thus a user whose skill is based on remembering only enough to make the right choices accurately and swiftly has a relatively small memory load. More work is required to identify what exactly a MacWrite user retains, but it seems clear that their 'knowledge' is much less than the mental replica that would support recall. This point connects with the minimal manual technique (Carroll [1984a]; Carroll [1984b]) for designing training documentation. Again the basic idea is to avoid the fully descriptive style of manual writing in both content and organisation by concentrating on how the user is to make choices, rather than describing what they will see anyway. This technique has been shown to reduce bulk while increasing effectiveness.

In itself, the study described here only shows a greater-than-expected failure of memory for spatial organisation and menus of commands in a visual interface given rather general recall cues. We have used the results to support a particular point of view but in itself the evidence is merely suggestive and other interpretations are possible. Our frequent users *were* better at recall than our occasional users. It is our contention here, however, that the difference was considerably less than would be expected from the usual view about learning at interfaces. Our data does not prove this point. To test the interpretation argued here, future studies should investigate what knowledge users have that supports recognition (perhaps by varying the names on menus and observing the effects of distractors). To test alternative interpretations, future studies should explore recall from semantic cues: given a description of a needed function (e.g., leaving the editor, or changing font size), can subjects describe how to invoke it? Failure to recall from semantic cues would more directly indicate that the visual cues given by the interface remain important to performance and are not necessarily internalised by learning.

Semantic knowledge is also the subject for an important possible extension to this study of the content of users' expertise. Menus relieve users of the need to remember command names, but not of the need to know what functions can be performed by some command: users still need to know how to decompose their goals into actions. To avoid search, users must presumably learn what functions are available, even if they do not learn how to invoke them without visual prompts. Future studies should therefore also study the semantic knowledge users have about the existence of functions as opposed to the 'lexical' knowledge of how the functions are invoked. Users might thus be asked whether a command exists for various functions, as well as how they would go about invoking it.

The present study implies a rather different view of human action from the one predominant in cognitive science so far. Rather than being based on 'knowledge' consisting of mental models that replicate substantial aspects of the external world and support detailed advance planning, human action may be organised around a flow of information picked up from the environment during execution. This is not merely feedback: people often *decide* what to do on the basis of information flow, and embark on activities expecting to find out how to succeed as they go (acting on faith rather than on knowledge). This kind of activity is common in our lives. It seems also to be the basis of how we interact with computers, particularly modern interfaces that minimize memory load. Observing new users of some interface shows how their behaviour is guided from moment to moment by what they take to be clues. The study reported here suggests that this can also be characteristic of experienced users, whose expertise may consist simply of a more reliable knowledge of which clues are useful and what they signify.

References

A D Baddeley [1983], "Working Memory," *Phil. Trans. of the Royal Society* B302, 311–324.

J M Carroll [1984a], "Designing Minimalist Training Material," IBM York Town Heights NY, Technical Report RC10438.

J M Carroll [1984b], "Minimalist Training," *Datamation* 30, 125–136.

S W Draper [1984], "The Nature of Expertise in UNIX," in *INTER-ACT '84 – First IFIP Conference on Human-Computer Interaction*, B Shackel, ed., Elsevier-Science, Amsterdam.

D Gentner & A L Stevens [1983], *Mental Models*, Lawrence Erlbaum Associates, Hillsdale, New Jersey.

A Maclean, P Barnard & N Hammond [1984], "Recall as an Indicant of Performance in Interactive Systems," in *INTERACT '84 – First IFIP Conference on Human-Computer Interaction*, B Shackel, ed., Elsevier-Science, Amsterdam.

R S Nickerson & M J Adams [1979], "Long-Term Memory for a Common Object," *Cognitive Psychology* 11, 287–307.

D A Norman & S W Draper [1986], *User Centered System Design*, Lawrence Erlbaum Associates, Hillsdale, New Jersey.

S J Payne & T R G Green [1986], "Task-Action Grammars: A Model of the Mental Representation of Task Languages," *Human Computer Interaction* 2, 93–133.

E Tulving [1974], "Cue-Dependent Forgetting," *American Scientist* 62, 74–82.

Can Cognitive Complexity Theory (CCT) Produce an Adequate Measure of System Usability?

Christine Knowles

Department of Computer Science, Queen Mary College, London E1 4NS, U.K.

Superficial interface characteristics alone (e.g., mouse movements, command names, syntax) cannot adequately explain novices' learning difficulties. A source of error in user/system interaction can occur when there is a mismatch between the system and the user in terms of the way in which *the domain* is being represented by the system and the user's ability to carry out tasks which effect changes in the domain.

Kieras and Polson (1985), proposed that *cognitive complexity theory* (CCT) could provide some *quantitative measure* of the *usability* of an interface. CCT represents job-task knowledge using production rules, which in conjunction with a task-to-device mapping structure attempts to provide a formal description of both *user knowledge* and device behaviour. *CAD systems* in the fashion industry provide an interesting opportunity to assess CCT by focusing on the highly skilled design activity of pattern cutting. This study tests the basic tenets of CCT and its ability to predict errors and learning difficulties when using CAD tools for pattern cutting, and goes on to suggest that the quality of the system's representation of the domain can, in part, determine *interface complexity* such that a purely quantitative measure of user-task knowledge (e.g., counting production rules) is both limited in application and inappropriate as a reliable metric for evaluating sources of complexity in an interface.

Keywords: Cognitive Complexity Theory (CCT), User knowledge requirements, Domain representation, CAD systems, Interface complexity.

1. Introduction

Cognitive complexity (CC) is the complexity of a device from the point of view of the user. This complexity is dependent on "the amount, content and structure of the knowledge required to operate the device successfully". An added source of complexity for a new user is that of the ease with which s/he can acquire the new knowledge to operate the device.

Kieras and Polson (Kieras & Polson [1985]) state that they are attempting to provide a **quantitative** measure of user complexity. This poses two questions. First, is a quantitative approach the most appropriate one for HCI research? Secondly, do Kieras and Polson actually produce a valid measure of complexity?

Kieras and Polson put forward a theoretical framework within which cognitive complexity could be assessed by identifying and quantifying possible sources of complexity. Usability can thus be measured using Cognitive Complexity Theory (CCT). The account of complexity given by Kieras and Polson specifically mentions the content and structure of knowledge and thus implies more than simple quantity as a measure of CC. However, Kieras and Polson place an emphasis on the **amount** of knowledge involved and not on the **type or content** of such knowledge. Kornwachs (Kornwachs [1987]), in a paper examining measures of system complexity and CC suggests that the simple addition of elements in a system does not necessarily make it inherently more complex, only more complicated. To suggest that something may be difficult to learn simply because of the number of facts or rules to be remembered cannot explain all the problems that new users have in their earliest encounters with a system.

In assessing knowledge CCT makes use of GOMS (Card, Moran & Newell [1983]) and production rule systems (Anderson [1983]) to describe the knowledge the user has about the tasks to be performed and the methods of accomplishing those tasks available to him/her using the system. It is argued that it is this reliance on such restrictive forms of knowledge description which inevitably reduces the scope of application and power of CCT as an evaluative tool for interface design.

2. Criticisms of the Kieras and Polson approach to CCT

Memory load is one possible source of complexity, using measures such as 'peak number of items in memory, average number of items in memory and integrated number of items in memory'. The focus on memory load as portraying some psychological properties of the user is not only inadequate but more importantly inaccurate. CCT equates memory load with the number of productions held in working memory (WM). The assumption that productions are equivalent is a major criticism of CCT. By counting the number of production rules to represent knowledge requirements, CCT suggests that two alternative interface designs to a system can be evaluated in terms of their usability. CCT assumes that productions are equivalent in meaning, the level of detail expressed in both sets of rules is equal, and that the assumed knowledge requirements are equivalent. Studies on short term memory capacity would also support the argument against using production rules as measures of memory load (Rumelhart & Norman [1985]). For example, short term memory capacity is thought to be determined not by the absolute amount of information to be learned but on its meaningfulness to the subject (again, the idea of quality rather than quantity of information is portrayed).

Although focusing on amounts of knowledge, CCT does not mention the sources of such knowledge. It can be argued, and is to some extent supported by those advocating the use of 'blackboard models' (Hayes-Roth [1984]), that different types of knowledge are recruited from different sources. This can be illustrated using an example taken from pattern cutting in the fashion industry.

When deciding how to adapt block patterns to a particular style, factors such as fabric type, fabric pattern, fashion etc. will affect the initial choice of block. For example, it would be inappropriate to use a stretch fabric bodice block, which has a relatively tight fit and which relies on the elastic properties of the fabric itself to produce the closeness of fit, if the fabric chosen is a stable woven one such as a wool material. The resulting garment would be very uncomfortable to wear and the person might experience some difficulty in moving their arms. To choose the correct block pattern depends on utilising knowledge of fabrics, fit, blocks etc. To design a swimsuit a stretch fabric could be used. A swimsuit not only uses the characteristics of the fabric as part of the design but also as part of the function of the swimsuit, i.e., to lower drag in water. Not only is knowledge derived from particular subject areas, but has to be **combined** with other elements to produce the appropriate answer. Therefore to adapt a block to produce such a garment would necessitate accessing knowledge from several sources to arrive at the right answer. My thesis in this paper is that **it is the association between the knowledge sources that more closely reflects the meaning of the term complexity**. The GOMS model, and consequently CCT as used by Kieras and Polson, do not reflect these features and differences in knowledge and hence are inadequate metrics of usability.

Although one problem with CCT is the forms of representation used, another point concerns the identification of the different sources of knowledge discussed by Kieras and Polson. It is not clear from Kieras and Polson's descriptions what part of their goal structure model refers to **device independent** and **device dependent** knowledge. These are two sources of complexity suggested by Kieras and Polson to be present in the user's task representation, however, the two are not separated out and therefore are not individually measured.

In CCT the behaviour of the device is modelled using a Generalised Transition Network. From this it is possible to derive a device behaviour hierarchy. This structure can then be compared to the user's goal hierarchy, derived from the production rule system, to give some indication as to the degree of mapping between the user's behaviour and the device's behaviour when carrying out the task. Green, Schiele and Payne (Green, Schiele & Payne [1985]) suggest that using a GTN raises problems such as where to include nesting of components. This process is 'essentially arbitrary' and therefore, any conditions based on mismatches in the goal structure are not well founded. They may be 'intuitively plausible' but not necessarily valid. Despite these limitations the mapping of the user's goal hierarchy to the device behaviour hierarchy part of CCT shows potential for assessing usability and is described in more detail later.

CCT suggests that if the two hierarchies map well then the device will not impose any additional memory load on the user and will not, therefore, increase the overall degree of complexity in the interface. What constitutes a 'good' mapping? It can be argued that it is not necessarily the **number of mismatches** that determines the quality of the mapping, but the **type of mismatches**. For example, does the system view parts of the task in the same way as the user. An example of when this situation might occur is given later. Kieras and Polson have not developed this mapping idea further. Using the degree of correspondence between structures to highlight possible sources of complexity can be achieved by assessing device dependent and device independent knowledge. This approach has been used in the present study.

Remember, the only measure of CC given by Kieras and Polson is that of counting the number of production rules used to represent the user's task knowledge. If, as Kieras and Polson suggest, CC can be determined by several sources why are there no metrics for assessing the relative contribution of each of these factors to the overall degree of complexity in an interface. While **complexity** of the user's task representation is said, by CCT, to be a source of complexity, no rules are given for determining what makes the task complex.

In summary, CCT, as put forward by Kieras and Polson, can be seen to have several major flaws, namely :

1. No underlying theory of knowledge sources and their interaction.

2. Restricted in application, by virtue of its reliance on GOMS, to tasks involving no problem solving.

3. No empirical validation of the hypotheses Kieras and Polson put forward in the paper.

4. There is no clear separation of the components of CC, if they cannot be identified how can they be measured.

5. An over reliance on quantitative aspects of representing knowledge at the expense of qualitative aspects.

With all these criticisms can CCT still be a useful tool for HCI researchers to evaluate interface designs?

3. The future for CCT?

The introduction to this paper suggested that user difficulties arise from several sources, most notably presentation characteristics of the interface (e.g., mouse movements, need to have keyboard skills to enter commands etc.) and a disparity between knowledge of a domain as represented within a system and as represented by the user. It is also suggested that the psychological characteristics of the user if in conflict with the system's mode of operation will result in a further source of complexity.

With its reference to device behaviour, task knowledge, user behaviour and cognitive processing demands, CCT would, at first glance, appear to provide an ideal framework within which to identify and quantify the possible sources of CC inherent in an interface and which might therefore, present problems to the novice user. CCT is an attempt to resolve the problem of 'formally' representing device characteristics and user characteristics in such a way that facilitates a direct comparison. Each representation could be broken down further to reveal the individual parts which constitute sources of complexity. For example, device independent and device dependent knowledge is seen as part of the CC within the **user's task representation**, device layout knowledge and how-it-works knowledge are seen as sources of complexity within the **user's device representation**.

A more detailed study of CCT reveals that the initial promise of an all encompassing theory is not met and, as it stands it does not provide an adequate method of evaluating interface complexity. The attempt to provide a 'quantitative' measurement of complexity is in conflict with the original ideas put forward by Kieras and Polson and predictions made on the basis of the approach have found only limited support (Ziegler, Vossen & Hoppe [1986]). Vossen *et al* (Vossen, Sitter & Ziegler [1987]) suggested that production system models "as put forward by CCT provide ... only ... a first order approximation for predicting learning times in HCI". In other words, to predict ease of learning the knowledge required has first to be described in terms of production rules. Having derived these rules it can be demonstrated that in general, the more rules describing the task, the longer it will take for the user to learn to use the system. This relationship is, however, not a truly linear one and as such is only an approximation not a hard and fast rule.

In its present form CCT is not a viable way of identifying the different sources of complexity in the interface. If, however, a slightly different approach is taken, whilst still retaining **some** aspects of CCT it proves to be more applicable. This adaptation of CCT has been used with some success in a study currently being undertaken which is an attempt to identify possible sources of CC in an interface to a pattern cutting system used in the fashion industry.

4. Applying a modified version of CCT to an interface evaluation

The pattern cutting system being evaluated is called a Pattern Design System (PDS) and is a computer aided design system (CAD) for use by skilled pattern cutters in the fashion industry. To apply CCT effectively necessitates the use of a task which characterises the most important skills in pattern cutting, to pick a task which is very simple (i.e., uses very little domain knowledge) would not give a very informative test of CCT (in a modified version) applied to a real-world task. The task chosen (following advice given by senior fashion tutors) was that of designing a raglan sleeve top.

There are three main stages to the raglan construction.

1. Construction of the basic draft.
2. Addition of a style line.
3. Tracing off resulting blocks.

The hypotheses put forward in this study were based on the assumption that by altering specific parts of CCT representations it would be possible to separate out the different types of knowledge required of the user. The modified version of CCT concentrates on identifying sources of complexity within the user's task representation. The two most easily identifiable sources are **device dependent** knowledge and **device independent** knowledge. A mapping scheme is used to identify the two sources mentioned. A model of how the task is carried out using the particular device is developed. This provides a model of the job-task knowledge defined by CCT.

5. Device dependent and device independent knowledge

To represent device independent knowledge a 'manual' version of the raglan design task was used. An analysis of the task was derived using fashion texts and demonstrations given by fashion tutors. The manual version of a task is seen as being the most device independent method of raglan design possible. Although it can be argued that the manual version relies on its own system and devices, namely using pencils, tracing wheels etc., because the 'standard' method of construction is manual it is considered an acceptable assumption. PDSs are a relatively expensive outlay for a small firm (small firms being the main employers of fashion designers) and have only recently been available to medium sized fashion companies. Only two colleges in England have established training courses in using PDSs and it is this lack of skill in using new technology which is a very serious problem in the fashion industry. As such the 'normal' way to design a raglan is manually. Therefore, the manual method of design is put forward as reflecting the most device independent version possible.

What of device dependent knowledge? This can be reflected by the PDS version of the raglan construction task. The user has to be skilled in pattern cutting to use the PDS. (The PDS is not a teaching aid and is aimed at enabling skilled pattern cutters to work more effectively). As such it can be assumed that the PDS user has the same pattern cutting skills as the person carrying out the task without the PDS. By adopting this view it enables an analysis of the differences between the two versions to be undertaken and hence, an identification of the device dependent knowledge to be made.

In order to carry out such a comparison it is necessary to describe both versions of the task using the same notation. The initial analysis of the two versions of the task resulted in two goal structures. The goal structure for the manual version of the task is shown in Figure 1, the PDS version of the task is shown in Figure 2.

GOAL - CREATE RAGLAN TOP
- GOAL - CONSTRUCT BASIC DRAFT
- - GOAL - MARK FRONT PITCH POINTS
- - GOAL - POSITION BLOCKS
- - - GOAL - MATCH SLEEVE TO PITCH POINTS
- - - GOAL - MATCH SLEEVE TO GAP AT SHOULDER POINT
- GOAL - ADD STYLE LINES
- - GOAL - MEASURE NEW POINT
- - - GOAL - SELECT START POINT
- - - GOAL - SELECT DISTANCE
- - GOAL - DRAW STRAIGHT LINE
- - - GOAL - MARK START POINT
- - - GOAL - MARK END POINT
- - - GOAL - JOIN START PT, END PT.
- - GOAL - DRAW CURVED LINE
- - - GOAL - MARK BOUNDARY/MID POINT
- - - GOAL - JOIN ST.PT, MID PT, END PT.
- GOAL - TRACE OFF NEW BLOCKS
- - GOAL - TRACE OFF BODICE BLOCK
- - - GOAL - SELECT BODICE LINES
- - GOAL - TRACE OFF SLEEVE BLOCK
- - - GOAL - SELECT SLEEVE LINES

Figure 1. Goal Structure Of Manual Raglan Design

It could be argued, on the basis of the number of goals in each description, that the PDS version of the task involves much device dependent knowledge simply because it has more goals in it than the manual version does, and that if the goals common to each description are cancelled out then the remaining goals are the ones reflecting device dependent knowledge. As mentioned earlier when criticising Kieras and Polson for their approach to complexity, if the goals were directly translated into production rules and compared, the problem of goal equivalence would arise. It is not sufficient to argue that the PDS provides a more difficult environment within which to carry out the design task, simply because of the number of goals involved, it is far more important to look

GOAL - CREATE RAGLAN TOP
- GOAL - CONSTRUCT BASIC DRAFT
- - GOAL - MERGE BODICE UNDERARM LINE POINTS
- - - GOAL - DELETE MID POINTS
- - GOAL - SPLIT SLEEVE ARMHOLE LINE
- - - GOAL - SELECT SPLIT POINT
- - GOAL - POSITION BLOCKS
- - - GOAL - ADD JOINING LINES
- - - - GOAL - MEASURE SLEEVE UNDERARM LINE
- - - - GOAL - MEASURE BODICE UNDERARM LINE
- - - - GOAL - DIGITISE NEW SLEEVE LINE
- - - - - GOAL - PLOT START POINT
- - - - - GOAL - PLOT END POINT
- - - - GOAL - DIGITISE NEW BODICE LINE
- - - - - GOAL - PLOT START POINT
- - - - - GOAL - PLOT END POINT
- - - GOAL - MAKE JOINING LINES BOUNDARY LINES
- - - - GOAL - SWAP SLEEVE LINE
- - - - - GOAL - SELECT NEW BOUNDARY
- - - - - GOAL - SELECT NEW INTERNAL
- - - - GOAL - SWAP BODICE LINE
- - - - - GOAL - SELECT NEW BOUNDARY
- - - - - GOAL - SELECT NEW INTERNAL
- - - GOAL - SET BLOCKS TOGETHER
- - - - GOAL - SELECT SLEEVE MATCHING LINE
- - - - GOAL - SELECT SLEEVE MATCHING POINT
- - - - GOAL - SELECT BODICE TARGET LINE
- - - - GOAL - SELECT BODICE MATCHING POINT
- GOAL - ADD STYLE LINES
- - GOAL - MEASURE NEW POINT
- - - GOAL - SELECT LINE
- - - GOAL - SELECT START POINT
- - - GOAL - SPECIFY DISTANCE
- - GOAL - PLOT START POINT
- - GOAL - PLOT MID POINT(S)
- - GOAL - PLOT END POINT
- GOAL - TRACE OFF NEW BLOCKS
- - GOAL - CREATE NEW BLOCK
- - - GOAL - SELECT BOUNDARY LINES
- - - GOAL - SELECT INTERNAL LINES
- - - GOAL - DETACH BLOCK
- - GOAL - SELECT BODICE BLOCK
- - - GOAL - SELECT BOUNDARY LINES
- - - GOAL - SELECT INTERNAL LINES
- - - GOAL - DETACH BLOCK
- - GOAL - SELECT SLEEVE BLOCK
- - - GOAL - SELECT BOUNDARY LINES
- - - GOAL - SELECT INTERNAL LINES
- - - GOAL - DETACH BLOCK

**Figure 2.   Goal Structure For PDS Version Of Raglan
Design (continued)**

at the differences in the type of goals in the two descriptions. What are the common elements in the goal structures, what elements are different and why, where do goals map onto one another, which have equivalence in each description and how can a mapping of such goals

Figure 3. Correspondence between goal structures

Number Of Goals		
Level	Manual version	PDS Version
ONE	1	1
TWO	3	3
THREE	7	10
FOUR	11	17
FIVE	0	10
SIX	0	8
TOTALS	**22**	**49**

say anything about complexity? This is the point at which the Kieras and Polson version of CCT and the modified version most obviously part company, the modified version of analysis becoming more qualitative and less quantitative in approach.

There are two stages involved in formulating answers to the questions raised. The first stage is to look at the structure of the task and identify which levels have some degree of correspondence. The second stage is to re-express the goals in terms of the actions and objects involved at each level. This will provide some measure of the number of elements common to various stages in the two task descriptions and also refine the informal levels of correspondence analysis produced in the first stage.

6. Analysis of goal structures - first stage

The number of goals and sub-goals present in each task description is shown above in figure 3. The term level refers to the level within the hierarchy the goal is described. For example at level one there is one goal, namely that of creating a raglan top. This goal has three major sub-goals, constructing a basic draft, drawing in a style line and tracing off the resulting blocks. This is the second level in the hierarchy. The lower levels describe the sub-goals which are part of those higher level goals. The idea of levels is to show the structure and number of goals and sub-goals within the task hierarchy. But, concentrating on the number of goals alone is not very informative, i.e., are the methods of accomplishing the goals described in level four of each version equivalent in function? Do they have the same number and type of sub-goals, are they, in turn, equivalent in structure? To answer these questions the next step is to consider the structures within the two versions.

The analysis of similar and different goal structures within the two versions of the task does not, at this stage, go into great detail. The comparison is essentially superficial picking out commonalities in terms

Figure 4   Goal structures at levels 2 and 3

CONSTRUCT BASIC DRAFT		TRACE NEW BLOCKS	
Manual version	PDS Version	Manual Version	PDS Version
Mark f.p.p			Whole block
	Adjust bodice	Bodice block	Bodice block
	Adjust sleeve	Sleeve block	Sleeve block
Position block	Position block		

Figure 5.   Goal structures at levels 2 , 3 and 4

ADD STYLE LINES		Add Style lines – level 4	
Manual version	PDS Version	Manual Version	PDS Version
Measure new pt	Measure new pt		
		Mark st pt	Select ln
		Select distance	Select st pt
			Specify distance
Draw st line		Mark st p	
		Mark end pt	
		Join pts	
Draw curved ln		Mark mid pt	
		Join pts	
	Plot st pt *		
	Plot mid pt(s)*		
	Plot end pt *		

*Together they produce a curved line.

of order of construction. The order in which a goal's sub-goals have to be satisfied can be thought of as a procedure. Although two procedures may appear to have the same or similar function at one level, in order to determine if they are truly identical in structure and meaning the analysis has to be taken to a lower level. This continues until the lowest levels have been examined. This process is exemplified in figures 4 and 5.

The tables serve to illustrate where procedures, part of the manual version, are not replicated in the PDS version, and vice versa. For example, the process of adding style lines (Figure 5). This sub-goal is common to both versions of the task, but if the next level of detail is given differences between the two versions emerge, these differences, on further analysis, prove to be important in identifying the additional types of knowledge required of the PDS user.

In order to check that the procedures described at each level are equivalent in function, some method of analysing the procedures is required. A process in level five of the manual version may be directly mappable to a process in level six of the PDS version. If just numbers of goals at each level was examined, then this might be missed. The procedure in the PDS version may have to be a lower level goal, simply because of the constraints imposed by the system when the user is carrying out a specific set of actions. (I.e. the procedure is dependent on the setting up of a new condition.). Therefore, by looking only within goal levels, such subtleties would be missed. The method of analysing the goal structures and the mapping between such structures has to be applied both **within** levels and **between** levels.

7. Analysis of goal structures - second stage

This stage concentrates on the details within a procedure, i.e., the commonality of **actions and objects**. To this end the task goals are re-expressed in terms of the actions and objects involved at each stage of the task. This allows common action/object sequences to be identified both across and within levels. This analysis is currently in progress and it is hoped that confirmation concerning the accuracy of this analysis will be obtained very shortly. The results are derived from studies using the raglan design task given to fashion students and tutors, to perform using a PDS.

During a video taped session of a subject carrying out the raglan task using a PDS a subject made several comments concerning the system's 'view' of the blocks being manipulated. When using a PDS a 'whole new language ' had to be learned and the way in which the system regarded blocks, lines and points was very different to the view of these concepts in a manual domain. For example, the PDS does not allow curved lines to be matched together. It will only allow straight lines to be joined. In the manual version of the task the subject is able to match two curved lines easily using the balance points as position indicators. It is not necessary to draw in new straight lines. Another example of the difference in attitude is that of how blocks are perceived. The PDS views a block as an enclosed shape with external 'boundary' lines and 'internal' lines within the block shape. If a new line is to be drawn outside the block shape it is then very difficult to direct the system into accepting it as an external line, changing the old boundary line into a new internal line. This is not a problem in the manual version as the idea of there being boundary lines and internal lines does not exist. The second stage of evaluation should result in differences of this nature being identified.

The mis-representation of the pattern cutting activity (in terms of the actions which can be carried out on the different objects involved) inevitably leads to the user making errors. The errors identified in the pilot study were most commonly ones of a conceptual nature. As stated previously, it should be remembered that subjects carrying out the task using the PDS are skilled pattern cutters, any problems which arise are not because of a lack of understanding about what the task involves in terms of the principles of pattern cutting. The type of error most often reported was due to the system view of the objects involved, for example the subject made statements such as "why didn't it let me do that I wonder", or "I know I have to do this, but I don't know why". Comments such as "you wouldn't have to do this if you were doing it by hand", were also recorded.

The errors noted in the pilot study did support the hypothesis put forward that the underlying representation of a task by a system is the major source of complexity in an interface.

By the end of the second stage of analysis the following complexity sources should have been identified :

1. Goals which are part of the task in its manual form.

2. Goals which are part of the task using the PDS (**job-task** knowledge).

3. Goals which are common to both versions of the task in terms of function and object/action sequences. (**Device independent** knowledge).

4. Goals which are not part of the manual version and which are present in the goal structure solely because of the device being used. (**Device dependent** knowledge).

5. The overall degree of correspondence between the two goal structures.

8. Discussion

CCT is, in the form originally proposed by Kieras and Polson is open to many criticisms. It attempts to cover a wide area by suggesting different sources of complexity as well as methods of representing them. It can in this respect be considered to have been over ambitious. It is too heavily based on the intuition of the analyst in describing the goal structures at the appropriate level, the corresponding production rules and the GTN model of device behaviour. There is not enough evidence to support the hypotheses Kieras and Polson put forward. The only evidence from empirical studies available seems to have been where CCT is used only in part, namely as listing production rules to describe tasks using specific systems, and only then to predict learning times. These studies have not attempted to separate out each source of complexity and model it (e.g., device dependent, device independent knowledge and device behaviour knowledge), indeed, it may be suggested that only the 'easy' bits of the theory have been instantiated and applied, while the more interesting and meaningful parts of CCT have not been developed by Kieras and Polson.

The modification to CCT suggested here retains the original notion of different sources of knowledge being important in learning to use a system, but concentrates on the identified sources of complexity and suggests an appropriate method of representing those knowledge requirements. Kieras and Polson use GTNs to model device behaviour. This technique been criticised on the grounds of its susceptibility to subjective interpretation and is not considered to be a necessary part of modelling CC. The modified version of CCT put forward in this paper derives the device hierarchy from observational and interview data from subjects carrying out given tasks. This hierarchy is empirically valid and not simply constructed on the basis of assumptions of user performance.

The degree of correspondence between goal structures can be represented using a very general mapping idea. It allows the analyst or researcher to describe what sources of knowledge are 'missing' and to identify those which need to be acquired by the user to enable him/her to operate a device successfully. For example the situation where there is a good mapping between the system's view of objects and actions and the user's view will result in there being a need to learn only device knowledge. This device knowledge would be that of learning how the controls in the device map onto its external behaviour. It is, therefore, only related to task knowledge in the sense of it being necessary to know in order to accomplish goals using a particular system, but is not the same as device dependent knowledge as it does not constrain the goal structure or procedures being used to fulfill those goals. This more 'simple' device knowledge might be acquired by encouraging the user to develop a mental model of the device (Young [1983]).

In Kieras and Polson's CCT mapping, a device behaviour hierarchy is compared with the user's goal hierarchy. As stated previously, the goal hierarchy is composed of the user's task knowledge, which is an amalgamation of job-task knowledge, device independent knowledge and device dependent knowledge, but without any method of separating out the different knowledge types. The mapping in modified CCT, refers to the degree of correspondence between concepts in the manual and system versions of the same task. The comparison is essentially between device independent (as identifiable in the manual task version) and device dependent knowledge (as manifested in the system task version).

The comparison is carried out at two levels. The first identifies the goals and goal sequences (procedures) which comprise the goal hierarchy. The second stage introduces the notion of actions, objects and simple action/object sequences which constitute the finer detail of the analysis. In the case of a 'good' mapping both the high level detail (goals and procedures) and the lower level detail (actions and objects) correspond well. In a 'poor' mapping condition there would be marked differences between the goal structures and the action/object sequences, these differences illustrating the 'conceptual' disparity between the device independent version of the task and the device dependent version.

An example of this can be seen in the raglan design task. At a high level of analysis the goal structures of the manual and PDS version of the task correspond fairly well. There are three clearly identifiable sub-goals within the overall goal of constructing the raglan draft. But the device dependent knowledge becomes evident when the goal structures start to differ. For example, in the case of tracing off the new blocks, there is an additional sub-goal in the PDS version of the task which is not present in the manual version. Here the constraints imposed on the user by the system begin to emerge. A more detailed level of analysis reveals differences in the perception of lines, blocks and points in the two task versions. This two stage analysis is more informative than the mapping in Kieras and Polson's CCT providing tangible results from which it is possible to point out possible areas of user difficulty.

9. Conclusions

The bulk of the criticisms levelled at Kieras and Polson's CCT suggest that the focus of CCT should not be on the **amount** knowledge required to operate the device, but on the **type and content** of such knowledge.

To reduce the degree of cognitive complexity in an interface it is necessary to identify the disparities between the knowledge the user **has** and the knowledge s/he **needs**. CCT, in its original form, requires modifications if it is to be generally applicable in HCI research. Tasks using CAD systems can rarely be described as non-problem solving. Therefore, any technique to evaluate usability cannot itself be useful if it has to be restricted to a very limited type of task environment.

The modified version of CCT put forward in this paper changes the emphasis from representing amounts of knowledge to representing the type and content of knowledge requirements. It uses manual versions of a task to represent device independent knowledge and thus allows identification of device dependent knowledge by examining the discrepancies between the two versions. Information as to how to reduce interface complexity in terms of button presses, icon selection and menu design etc. is well documented. What is not so well recorded is information as to how to evaluate domain knowledge as modelled in a system. The modified version of CCT should help the interface designer in assessing if a system has retained the concepts from the manual domain and correctly transcribed them to the system domain.

In conclusion, CCT in its modified form can be more appropriately used to assess system usability, but this is accomplished by using only some of the ideas in the original version of CCT **and** by adopting a qualitative approach to analysing knowledge requirements not a quantitative one.

Acknowledgements

I would like to thank Dr. Peter Johnson for his helpful comments, advice and support during the writing of this paper, Miss Alison Beazley and her colleagues at Manchester Polytechnic and Mr. Peter Rhodes and Julie Lewis of Gerber-Scientific, Bradford.

This paper is based on work being carried out as part of a Ph.D. linked studentship funded by the Economic and Social Research Council (ESRC) at Queen Mary College, Department of Computer Science.

References

J R Anderson [1983], *The Architecture of Cognition*, Harvard University Press.

S K Card, T P Moran & A Newell [1983], *The Psychology of Human-Computer Interaction*, Lawrence Erlbaum Associates, Hillsdale, New Jersey.

T R G Green, F Schiele & S J Payne [1985], "Formalisable Models of User Knowledge in HCI," Draft Report.

B Hayes-Roth [December, 1984], "BB1: An Architecture for Blackboard Systems that Control, Explain and Learn about their own Behaviour," Stanford University, Technical Report HPP-8 4-16.

D Kieras & P G Polson [1985], "An Approach to the Formal Analysis of User Complexity," *Int. J. Man-Machine Studies* 22, 365–394.

K Kornwachs [1987], "Quantitative Measure for the Complexity of the Man-Machine Interaction Process," in *INTERACT '87 – The Second IFIP Conference on Human-Computer Interaction*, H J Bullinger and B Shackel, ed., Elsevier Science Publishers B.V., North Holland, 109–116.

D E Rumelhart & D A Norman [1985], "Representation of Knowledge," in *Issues in Cognitive Modelling*, A M Aitkenhead and J M Slack, ed., Lawrence Erlbaum Associates, Hillsdale, New Jersey.

P H Vossen, S Sitter & J E Ziegler [1987], "An Empirical Evaluation of Cognitive Complexity Theory with Respect to Text, Graphics and Table Editing," in *INTERACT '87 – The Second IFIP Conference on Human-Computer Interaction*, H J Bullinger and B Shackel, ed., Elsevier Science Publishers B.V., North Holland, 71–75.

R M Young [1983], "Surrogates and Mapping: Two Kinds of Conceptual Models for Interactive Devices," in *Mental Models*, D Gentner and A L Stevens, ed., Lawrence Erlbaum Associates, Hillsdale, New Jersey, 35–52.

J E Ziegler, P H Vossen & H U Hoppe [1986], "On Using Production Systems for Cognitive Task Analysis and Prediction of Transfer of Cognitive Skill," in *Proceedings of the Third Conference on Cognitive Ergonomics*, Paris, To be published.

Training for Optimising Transfer between Word Processors

Clare Pollock

Ergonomics Unit, University College London, 26 Bedford Way, London WC1H 0AP, U.K.

This paper describes research which aims to develop a type of training programme for users changing from one word processor to another. The training seeks to maximise the positive and minimise the negative transfer of knowledge about one system to another and thus improve the users' performance on the second system. Evidence is first presented which indicates that transfer may be a problem for such users. A model is, then, described which is used to interpret this evidence and to develop different training solutions. Three types of training which can be related to the model were tested and all were found to reduce the problem. On the basis of these results, further training programmes were developed which were more efficient. The results of an experiment which compared the second set of programmes, are next described. The experiment showed that one type of training was superior to the others. This training gave the subjects low level information about the second system as well as relating it to the first. However, this effect was not consistent over all of the tested functions. The differences between the functions are interpreted in terms of the model and the utility of the model in aiding the development of training is discussed.

Keywords: Transfer, training, word processors, frames

1. Introduction

The increased use of computers means that more people are trying to use a new computer system who have already had experience of another system ('system' is used here in the computer sense, to refer to the hardware and software; it is not used in the ergonomics sense to refer to the combination of computer, user and environment). In such circumstances, there is a need to consider the effect of transfer of knowledge about the previous system on performance on the new system.

The transfer of knowledge about one system to another can be either positive or negative. Positive transfer improves the performance of a user experienced on one system when they use a different system compared to that of a user who had no previous experience of any system: negative transfer will have a detrimental effect on performance. It is important to maximise the positive effects whilst minimising the negative; hence the aim must be to optimise transfer.

It may be possible to optimise transfer by training the users on the new system. Training is currently widely practised, as shown by the fact that 87% of UK staff involved with New Technology have to be trained when they join a company; 17% of these staff have previously been trained, but need to be re-trained to use the new company's systems (Limited [1984a]) (sometimes referred to as cross-training). Such training is not cheap. In 1984 the mean cost per employee of attending a word processor training course was £217 (Limited [1984b]). Given the cost of cross-training, it would be advantageous to design the training to achieve optimal transfer as quickly as possible. This exploitation of knowledge about a previous system is not widely used at present. Most of the available training programmes make no concessions to the trainees' previous experience, except to allow them to proceed through the training more quickly. One company standardises the structure of the training programme in an effort to aid transfer, however this may only encourage transfer of knowledge about how to use a training programme; it does not directly attempt to transfer the knowledge about the previous system to the new one.

Word processors were chosen as the area of application for the study because transfer was expected to be relevant and problematic. Word processors are widely used and there is a range of them available which differ in the knowledge required for their operation.

To summarise, the aim of this research was to investigate the type of training programme which optimises the transfer of knowledge for users changing from one word processor to another.

2. Evidence

It was expected that transfer would be a problem. In order to adduce evidence which would support this claim and to identify where training might be required, a study was conducted to identify the problems facing a user experienced on one word processor when trying to learn how to use a second. To obtain a clear view of the need for training, minimal training was given on the new system. This study is reported for the purpose of illustrating the problem which is to be solved by training in the subsequent experiments, hence it is not described in full detail.

The subjects were all experienced WordStar users who had worked as WordStar operators for an average of 20 months. WordStar, from MicroPro, was chosen as it was one of the first word processors developed for business use and is currently the most widely used system (Micropro International Limited [1988]). The system which the subjects attempted to use was WordPerfect, from Sentinal. This was chosen as it is marketed for use in similar situations to WordStar (on a personal computer for business use); it has been more recently developed and is becoming more popular (Tebbutt [1987]). Both systems were installed on the same IBM PC XT.

The tests which the subjects undertook were based on a survey conducted by a leading employment bureau of the tasks which its word processor operators would be expected to perform and the functions associated with these tasks. A representative set of these functions was selected for the tests. The subjects performed one test on WordStar and three tests on WordPerfect over a four hour period. The tests were separated by periods during which the subject could practise the functions.

Measures of performance included the number of functions which subjects executed correctly, the time taken to complete the test and the number of errors made. A deviation from the optimal keystroke sequence constituted an error. The optimal sequence was defined as that which produced a complete and correct operation in the fewest keystrokes. Errors, therefore, indicate those operations which the subject is not performing optimally. These errors were also classified according to a model of 'ideal', errorless user performance, thus producing a set of functions on which training is required.

The measures showed that the subjects experienced a problem in transferring to WordPerfect, illustrated by a failure to complete all the functions and a low efficiency for those functions which were completed, (efficiency was calculated as the ideal number of keystrokes divided by the actual number of keystrokes that the subject made). The majority of the errors consisted of three main types:

1. typing errors (10% of total),
2. cursor movement errors (24% of total) and
3. 'change text function' errors (55% of total).

The cursor movement errors most frequently occurred when attempting to move the cursor either a character or a word at a time. The 'change text function' errors mainly occurred during either deleting or moving a block. When deleting, most errors occurred either when deleting a character with the backspace key or when deleting a word. When moving a block, most errors occurred during the initial attempts to identify the block.

These errors (typing, move cursor word/character, delete with backspace/word and move block) accounted for 41% of the total number of errors committed. Making these operations more efficient would greatly improve the overall efficiency of performance. Hence, these six functions were chosen to be addressed by the training programmes.

3. The Model

The above evidence was used as the basis on which to develop a model of transfer. Only those details which are necessary for the understanding of the experiments to be reported later will be presented here. The model is based on the concept of Frames (Minsky [1975]). Frames were chosen as a framework for the model as they capture two aspects of knowledge representation identified from the transfer and training literature as being important for such a model: namely, the ability to represent different levels of knowledge and to represent the knowledge in 'packets' (Rumelhart & Norman [1983]).

Frames were originally developed to account for the process of visual analysis of a scene and were later applied to language analysis (Winograd [1975]). In these contexts, a frame represents data connected with a stereotyped situation. In this respect, it is similar to a schema (Rumelhart & Ortony [1977]). However, unlike a schema, a frame has a defined structure with areas (called 'nodes') which contain different types of information about the subject of the frame. The frames are linked together by a frame system which creates a hierarchical organisation.

In the model of transfer, frames are a structure for representing a 'packet' or unit of knowledge. In the case of word processing, a frame might contain the information about one function, such as Delete Text. Each frame contains information about the characteristics of the frame, specifies examples of the frame and the parent frame for which this frame is an example. The parent and example information is contained in nodes and these nodes provide links to more general, higher level, and more specific, lower level frames respectively. This creates a structure of frames at different levels. In the word processing example, the parent node for deleting might be Change Text and the example node might be Delete Character.

In terms of this model, learning occurs when new frames are created or old frames altered. This process is controlled by a mechanism which can assess the frames for their ability to match a goal, and create new frames if necessary. A similar mechanism controls the production of performance, where performance is the operationalising of the frames. New frames are made by creating an empty frame and then filling in the nodes. The content of the nodes is developed from either, only incoming information, the incoming information plus information from old frames, or only information from old frames. In terms of the model, transfer is represented as this application of information from old frames to new frames: positive transfer occurs when an old frame is applied appropriately and negative transfer occurs when this application is inappropriate. Information from old frames can be used in three ways:

    i. an old frame can be copied to another at the same level, with nodes added or deleted,

    ii. an old frame can be generalised, with the old 'parent' node becoming the new 'example' node, or

    iii. or an old frame can be instantiated, with the old 'example' node becoming the new 'parent' node.

Training can now be expressed as facilitating the acquisition of a new set of frames by the trainee. The trainer can vary the level of the frame which is provided, the order of presentation of the frames and the level at which old frames are related to the new frames. All these options can be expressed in terms of the model. Training for transfer means using the process of training to optimise the use of old frames.

In terms of the model, when the WordStar operators from the first study changed to WordPerfect, they were unable to develop the appropriate frames for moving the cursor, deleting and moving a paragraph. The aim of the following experiments was therefore to improve the performance on these elements by training. The model suggests that the new frames for Word Perfect can be related to the WordStar frames at a high or a low level. Relating frames at a high level would involve the successive generalisation of WordStar frames to produce a high level frame. The WordPerfect frames would then be produced by instantiation of this frame. This is similar to the use of models in training (Young [1981]). For example, "You delete a character to the left of the cursor in WordStar, by pressing the 'Del' key. You can delete a character to the left of the cursor on most word processors by pressing a key or combination of keys." (Generalisation from specific WordStar frame). "In WordPerfect, you delete the character to the left of the cursor by pressing the 'Backspace' key." (Instantiation). Relating WordStar to WordPerfect at a low level involves the copying of a WordStar frame, with appropriate nodes added or deleted. This is equivalent to using an analogy: it uses an 'is like' comparison. In addition, it defines the limits of this similarity by adding and removing nodes; for example, "deleting a character on WordPerfect is like deleting a character on WordStar" (copied frame), "except that you use the 'Backspace' key" (added node) "and not the 'Del' key" (removed node).

4. Developing the Training

The functions which showed poor performance in the first study were used as the basis for developing a training programme. The programme attempted to train the user of the new system to perform more like an ideal user, as defined in the first study. The model was used to develop the different methods of training for WordPerfect. In order to control for prior training, all subjects received the same training and experience on Word Star, before using WordPerfect.

Although the main functions for training had already been identified, training in those areas alone would not have made sense to naive users without some introduction to the system. Hence, a pilot subject was run to identify the minimum amount of extra information that was required to understand the training. The minimum was: an overview of what the system could do (that it could create, change, save and print text), and an explanation of what was on the screen (status line, ruler, cursor). For the functions which were not explained in detail, the training stated that the information would not be needed to perform the tasks. For example, the training explained that a file had a name, but added,

> "There are certain rules concerning the name of a file, but
> you need not learn these".

The details of the training programme were developed on the basis of the list of functions to be taught. In terms of the model, these functions corresponded to the frames that the subject was to acquire. The training was divided into sections corresponding to the ideal set of high level frames for this information. These were Creating Text, Moving Cursor and Changing Text. The sections were then broken down into the next level of frames which described the functions, for example, Changing Text was split into Deleting, Inserting and Moving Text. This process was continued until the information concerning the correct keystrokes for the required functions was identified. This represented the basic information to be given to the subjects in the training. Each part of this information (which corresponded to the content of one frame) was typed on a card. These cards were used as the medium for providing the information to the subjects. Cards were used in order to reduce the variability in training which could result from an experimenter telling different subjects the same information. They also provided a useful source of reference for the subjects' later use. (Note that the cards were not used as 'Guided Exploration' cards (Carroll et al. [1985]) during the training, as subjects were required to proceed through the cards in a pre-determined order.)

In order to standardise the subjects' experience on each system, additional cards were produced which instructed the user to try out the command they had just read about. These cards were inserted into the set of cards after the card with the details of the correct keystroke for a particular function. For example, in the Moving Cursor section there was a card which stated:

"striking the right-pointing arrow moves the cursor one character to the right".

This was then followed by a 'do' card which said:

"Try this on the top line. Move along five characters".

'Do' cards were marked with a prominent asterisk to help subjects recognise when when an action was required. Wherever possible, the required action was performed with text which had already been created by following the instructions on preceding 'do' cards.

The same method of training development was used for both WordStar and Word Perfect. Cards could be added or removed as required. The structure and the examples used were the same in both sets of training.

5. Evaluating the Training

5.1. Experiment 1

A first experimental study was conducted to test the usefulness of high or low level references to WordStar for subjects learning WordPerfect. This study was not completely successful and it will only be reported briefly in order to indicate the rationale for the second experiment. Three versions of the training were used:

1. the basic training, with no references to WordStar (unrelated),
2. the basic training, plus WordPerfect related to WordStar at a low level (low) and
3. the basic training, plus WordPerfect related to WordStar at a high level (high).

The three versions were tested by using them to train different groups of WordStar trained subjects on WordPerfect. The subjects' performance was measured in terms of the time taken to complete the tests, the number of errors made, the number of test operations completed correctly and the efficiency of the operations.

Results. Each version of the training enabled the subjects to complete the tests efficiently. This means that each training programme enabled the subjects to solve the problem which was identified from the first study. However, there were no differences between the three groups in terms of the subjects' performance. This could have been due to several reasons, for example, the subjects might have only used a subset of the training which was common to all three programmes to perform the tasks; alternatively, there could have been a ceiling effect, which obscured true differences between the groups. This second alternative is supported by the fact that there were differences between the groups in a post-experiment questionnaire. Subjects in the two related groups were able to state more about the differences and similarities between WordStar and WordPerfect than subjects in the group which received non-related training.

Discussion. Whatever the reason for the failure to obtain significant differences between training programmes in this experiment, it can be claimed that it produced a series of training solutions to the initial problem. However, all versions of the training presented a large amount of information for the areas they covered. Using a similar amount of information for the whole system would result in a long and expensive training programme. As one of the aims of this research was to increase the efficiency of training, these solutions were inappropriate. They raise the question, however, of how to reduce the training while maintaining the same level of performance. This would involve reducing the information about Word Perfect which the subjects receive, thus making the need to use knowledge about WordStar (perhaps) more important.

In the first experiment, all the training programmes contained the basic high and low level information. In the second experiment, it was decided to compare the effect of giving just the high level or the low level information, in addition to the effect of relating these levels to Word Star. Therefore, four types of WordPerfect training were developed:

i. high level WordPerfect information, unrelated to WordStar (High, Unrelated),

ii. the same high level information, but related to high level WordStar information (High, Related),

iii. low level WordPerfect information, unrelated to WordStar (Low, Unrelated), and

iv. the same low level information, related to low level WordStar information (Low, Related).

5.2. Experiment 2

5.2.1. Design

Subjects. 20 subjects were tested, 5 in each of four groups. All subjects had little or no computing experience, and they were all familiar with a typewriter (although they were not trained typists). The mean age was 38 years (range 20 to 62). All subjects were either students or members of university staff. They were not paid for participating in the experiment.

Procedure. Subjects attended two sessions, each of which lasted approximately 2 hours. The two sessions for any subject occurred within a 36 hour time period, with a minimum of 2 hours between sessions. In the first session, the subjects learned WordStar and in the second they learned Word Perfect. Each subject was tested individually, with the experimenter present throughout all the sessions. The considerable time required to test each subject limited the number of subjects which could be used, given available resources. At the beginning of the first session, each subject was asked for details of their computing and typing experience to ensure that they met the criteria for participation. They then proceeded through the WordStar training cards at their own pace. Upon completing the training they were allowed a short time to review the cards and practise the functions, until it was time for the first test (50 minutes after starting the training). This ensured that all subjects had equal exposure to the system at the time of the first test. After the first test, they were again allowed time to practise on the system, and to refer to the cards if required. Subjects were not allowed to refer to the cards during the tests. If the subject appeared to be not attempting to learn a function, they were prompted to do so by the experimenter. This was to try to ensure that all subjects were capable of executing the same functions by the end of the WordStar session. A second test was administered after 105 minutes, or later if the subject had still to learn some functions. In the practice sessions, the subjects were free to practise whatever they wanted (provided they tried all the functions at some time). They were allowed to create their own text if they wished, or they could request the experimenter to call up a piece of text that had been created previously.

The procedure for the second session was identical to the first, except that the initial questions were omitted. The first test on WordPerfect was administered after 40 minutes and the second after 90 minutes following the start of the session, regardless of how much the subject had learned. Finally, the subjects were de-briefed as to the purpose of the experiment and were given a questionnaire which concerned their opinions on the training and the similarities and differences between the systems.

The tests were divided into four sections: Move Cursor, Delete, Insert and Move Paragraph. The subjects had to complete 10 operations in each section, except for the Move Paragraph section where they had to complete five. Each operation was performed on separate statements or paragraphs, with the statements numbered and separated from each other by blank lines. Subjects were instructed to work through the operations in the order in which they were presented, as quickly and efficiently as possible. They were told to leave any operations which they were unable to complete and go on to the next. The test pieces were stored on the computer and retrieved by the experimenter at the beginning of the test. The subjects were given a hard copy of the tests, with the required changes marked in red and highlighted. Four versions of the test were developed using a single source for the statements (a national newspaper). In each version, the operation was placed at the same position within the text, so that each test could be completed with the same number and type of keystrokes. Each subject encountered a different version at each test point and the order of presentation of the versions was counterbalanced.

Data. During the test periods a video recording was made of the computer's visual display. This was later analysed to obtain the performance data. The practice sessions were not recorded. The measures taken were: time; errors (where an error was a deviation from the ideal keystroke sequence); number of operations completed (where the function had been carried out); number of operations correct (where the end result was perfect, with no typing or spacing errors); and efficiency of the completed operations. The efficiency of the completed operations was used, rather than overall efficiency, because subjects would often make no keystrokes at all if they could not perform an operation. This tended to increase the overall efficiency. The efficiency was expressed as a percentage and calculated as follows:

$$\frac{\text{Ideal no. of keystrokes for completed operations}}{\text{Actual no. of keystrokes for completed operations}} \times 100$$

5.3. Results

The order of the presentation of the test pieces was not significant and this will not be discussed further.

Performance Measures-Overall (See Graphs 1, 2 and 3 and following paragraphs)
Graph 1 shows the performance of the four groups in terms of the number of operations which were completed. Graph 2 shows the performance in terms of the number of these completed operations which were correct and Graph 3 shows the efficiency of the completed operations. Note that the performance on all these measures tends to increase from Trial 1 to Trial 2 (the WordStar trials). Upon transfer to WordPerfect (Trial 3), the number of operations which were completed and correct tends to fall, before increasing again on Trial 4. The efficiency on Trial 3 does not appear to fall to a great extent for the two Low groups (solid marks), while it does for the two High groups (open marks). Further the two High groups do not appear to improve from Trial 3 to Trial 4.

A two way repeated measures ANOVA revealed no differences between groups on the WordStar trials. Subjects completed a mean of 32 operations. No subject failed to complete more than two operations in any section; if an operation was not completed at one point in the test, it was completed successfully at another point in the test. This was a prerequisite for the subjects to continue on to the WordPerfect training. On Trial 2, the performance, in terms of the efficiency of the completed operations, was the same for these subjects as for the WordStar experts described in Section 2.

On the first WordPerfect trial (Trial 3), there were significant differences between the groups in terms of the number of completed operations $(F(3, 16) = 4.599, p < 0.025)$, the number of correctly completed operations $(F(3, 16) = 3.286, p < 0.05)$ and their efficiency $(F(3, 16) = 5.485, p < 0.01)$. Tukey comparisons showed that the Low, Related group completed and correctly completed significantly more operations

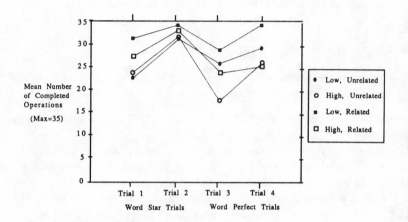

**Graph 1.   The number of completed operations on
WordStar and WordPerfect**

than the High, Unrelated group. The Low, Related group was significantly more efficient than both of the High groups. Hence the Low,
Related group is initially better on WordPerfect than the two High
groups.

On the second WordPerfect trial (Trial 4) there were significant differences between the groups on the number of completed operations and
their efficiency, $(F(3, 16) = 3.494, p < 0.05; F(3, 16) = 4.628, p < 0.01$,
respectively). Tukey comparisons showed that the Low, Related group
completed more operations than the High, Related group and completed
these more efficiently than both High groups. This means that after
practising the functions, the Low, Related group still performed better
than the High groups.

There were no differences between the groups in the time taken or the
number of errors which they made. This was the case even if the time and

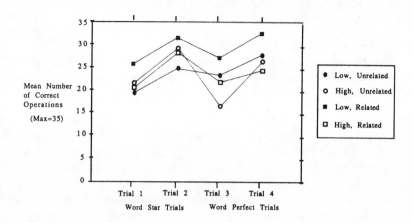

Graph 2.   The number of correct operations on WordStar and WordPerfect

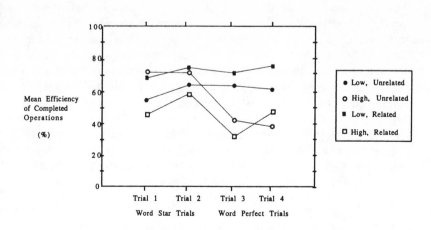

Graph 3.   The efficiency of the completed operations on WordStar and WordPerfect

errors were corrected to allow for those subjects who did not complete all the sections. This may be of note when considering an appropriate measure of performance on similar tasks.

These findings indicate that the Low, Related group achieved better performance on Trials 3 and 4 than the two High groups.

Performance Measures-Individual Sections
The details of the performance of subjects on two of the sections will be described. The details of the Move Cursor and Insert Text sections do not contribute to the discussion and have been omitted due to space limitations.

Delete. There were significant differences in the number of completed operations made by the groups on Trials 3 and 4 ($F(3, 16) = 5.312, p < 0.01$; $F(3, 16) = 3.932, p < 0.05$, respectively). On Trial 3, the difference was due to the Low, Related group completing more operations than the High, Unrelated group, and on Trial 4 to the Low, Related group completing more operations than the High, Related group. Again, it appears that the Low, Related group is specifically better than the High groups in the Delete section.

Move Paragraph. Graph 4 shows the performance of the four groups in terms of the number of completed Move Paragraph operations. The solid triangle marks show the performance of one of the groups from Experiment 1. This comparison with Experiment 1 will be described in more detail later.

The graph shows that all of the Experiment 2 groups performed very poorly on the first WordPerfect trial. Differences between the groups on this trial became apparent when the performance was analysed in more detail. There are seven stages for moving a paragraph in WordPerfect; of these the Low, Related group completed an average of 6.2 stages, the Low, Unrelated group completed 4.6 stages, the High, Related group completed 1 stage and the High, Unrelated group completed no stages. The stages which most of the Low group subjects failed to complete were the Cut stage (two subjects managed this in the Low, Related group, none in the Low, Unrelated group) and the Retrieve stage (four subjects completed this in the Low, Related group, two in the Low, Unrelated group). Hence, although all the groups performed poorly, the Low groups still performed better than the High groups.

On the fourth trial, this performance had improved slightly, although only the Low, Related group showed good performance by completing the maximum number of Move Paragraph operations. Trial 4 gave significant differences between the groups for the number completed ($F(3, 16) = 7.004, p < 0.001$), due to the Low, Related group completing

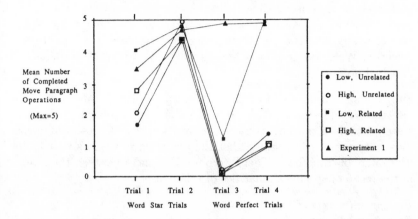

Graph 4. The number of completed Move Paragraph operations on WordStar and WordPerfect

more than all of the other groups. Again, this shows the difference between the groups, although it also indicates that the performance of the Low, Related group was poor on the first WordPerfect trial.

Move Paragraph is the function classified as the most advanced of those studied, according to the classification of word processing functions used to develop the original set of tasks (see Section 2). This may indicate that complexity is an additional variable in the selection of the training. Alternatively, or in addition, the two sections of the Move Paragraph section with which the Low groups had most difficulty, Cut and Retrieve, are not used in WordStar in order to move a paragraph. Hence, similarity may also be a consideration.

Questionnaire
The questionnaire asked subjects whether knowing WordStar had affected them when they learned WordPerfect. Fifteen of the twenty subjects stated that they had been affected in some way. Seven of the ten High subjects and five Low subjects said that WordStar helped them learn WordPerfect; three Low subjects stated that WordStar hindered their WordPerfect learning. Subjects were also asked whether the training had helped them learn Word Perfect. All Low subjects stated that

it did, however, only three High subjects stated this and five stated that the training did not help in any way.

When the subjects were asked which word processor they found easier to use, most High subjects preferred WordStar, while most Low subjects preferred WordPerfect. The High subjects also expressed a strong preference for the WordStar training although the Low subjects did not show any differences in their preferences (three of the ten subjects preferred WordStar training, three preferred WordPerfect training and four had no preference.)

Subjects were also asked to comment on the similarities and differences between WordStar and WordPerfect. The High subjects made more statements than the Low subjects, however, many of these statements were not specific: they stated that the two word processors were either 'the same' or 'different'. There were no differences between the groups in the recall of specific similarities or differences.

Experiment 1 versus Experiment 2
Experiment 2 was designed to enable these subjects to perform as well as the subjects had in the first experiment, but with less training. A reduction in training was achieved, indicated by the fact that all groups in Experiment 2 took significantly less time to complete the WordPerfect training than all the groups in Experiment 1 (16.9 mins. versus 33.3 mins. $(F(7, 32) = 6.179, p < 0.001))$

The performance of the best Experiment 2 group (Low, Related) will now be compared with the best group from Experiment 1 (Unrelated) in order to assess whether this decrease in training time was associated with a decrease in performance. There were no differences between these groups in the number correct or the efficiency of the completed operations. However, the Experiment 2 group did complete significantly fewer on the first WordPerfect trial than the Experiment 1 group $(F(1, 8) = 16.760, p < 0.01)$ This difference had disappeared by the second WordPerfect trial. When the individual sections of the test were analysed separately, this difference between Experiment 1 and 2 was only significant on the Move Paragraph section $(F(1, 8) = 30.083, p < 0.001)$. Graph 4 illustrates this difference between Experiment 1 and 2. The Experiment 1 group (solid triangles) did not show a decrement in performance upon transfer to WordPerfect (Trial 3), whereas the best Experiment 2 group (solid squares) did show a decrement, although this decrement had disappeared by Trial 4.

6. Discussion

It can be concluded that the group which received the low level, Word-

Star related training, performed better on the tests than the groups which received any of the other training types. The Low, Related training is also significantly shorter than the training used in Experiment 1, yet it enables the trainees to perform tasks almost as well as subjects who had received the best Experiment 1 training. The function which the Low, Related group does not perform as well, is the Move Paragraph function. The Low training also appears to be preferred to the High training by the subjects.

In terms of the model, the failure of the High groups implies that they cannot successfully generate a complete set of low level frames from the high level frames. However, their performance was not a complete failure; the High subjects did manage to identify some keys correctly, hence they can generate some low level frames. They could be generating these frames by guessing which keys to hit, or by using prior knowledge. If they used prior knowledge, then the low level frames which would be hardest to generate would be those where the WordStar low level frames were very different to those required for WordPerfect. The low level frames which the subjects were least successful in generating were those for deletion using the backspace key and moving a paragraph. Both of these functions are performed using different keys on the two systems. The backspace key is used to move the cursor in WordStar, but most subjects failed to try this for deleting in WordPerfect. Most subjects did find out how to use the Delete key on WordPerfect: on WordStar the Delete key is also used for deleting, but it is used in a different situation. These two facts would imply that the trainee does not randomly try keys, but tries those which previous experience would suggest might be appropriate. An appropriate low level frame would be one which was derived from a high level frame that was related most closely to the new function. Hence, when trying to delete, the subjects applied those frames which were used to delete on WordStar, before applying the frames associated with another function.

The success of the Low groups suggests that the required low level frames can be constructed from the Low training. However it is unclear whether these subjects had also formed a successful high level frame. This high level frame would have provided a means of organising the low level frames and recalling them correctly; this would be most beneficial when performing a complex function, such as move paragraph. By the second WordPerfect trial, the Low, Related group was better at moving paragraphs than the Low, Unrelated group. This would suggest that relating the systems at a low level enabled the Low, Related group to utilise features of the WordStar high level frame for moving paragraphs. A high level WordPerfect frame for moving paragraphs could then have been generated more easily.

The failure of the Low, Related group to move paragraphs on the first Word Perfect trial suggests that the possible utilisation of WordStar high level frames does not occur immediately. This can be compared with the Experiment 1 group which received both high and low level WordPerfect information and which performed well on the first WordPerfect trial. It would appear from this that some high level information is beneficial for complex tasks, although this can be achieved by relating two systems at a low level. This second option is shorter, but does not produce correct performance as quickly.

It is possible that the High, Related group performed poorly because the subjects had not had sufficient experience on WordStar to enable them to have developed the required high level WordStar frames. If these high Word Star frames were not available to the subject, then they would have had difficulty relating the two systems at a high level. However, two facts militate against this. Firstly, all the subjects received WordStar training which contained both high and low level information. All subjects were therefore able to develop the required high and low level frames by the end of their experience on WordStar. Secondly, the efficiency of all the groups on WordStar at Trial 2 was equal to that of the WordStar experts on the same tasks. Although it is still possible that the subjects were performing the WordStar tasks using only low level frames, the fact that these subjects could perform as well as experts, having been given the low and high level information would suggest that this is not necessarily the case.

7. Conclusion

The aim of the research was to investigate how to design a better cross-training programme. The results indicate that this has been achieved, in that several different training programmes were developed which were effective in reducing a particular instance of a transfer problem. A further programme was also developed which was more efficient than the previous programmes, but which enabled the standard of performance to be largely maintained. However, these results are only specifically applicable to the design of WordPerfect cross-training for WordStar operators. The generality of these results is a function of the similarity between the other systems to those studied.

The development of the experiments has shown that the model is useful for relating the areas which the users of a system cannot learn without help, to options for training which might be able to provide relevant instruction. Its use suggests that it could be helpful in the development of a tool for the use of training programme designers. This possibility has been explored as part of the research, with the model and experimental findings being re-expressed in a form which would be suitable for the training developers. This form was derived from a study of the task of training programme design and the problems which designers encounter.

Acknowledgements

The work reported here is part of research for a Ph.D. thesis funded by SERC and supervised by Professor John Long at the Ergonomics Unit, UCL. I would like to thank members of the Ergonomics Unit for helpful comments and advice especially Dr. Andy Whitefield and Andrew Life.

References

J M Carroll, R L Mack, C H Lewis, N L Grischkowsky & S R Robertson [1985], "Exploring Exploring a Word Processor," *Human-Computer Interaction* 1, 283–307.

Alfred Marks Bureau Limited [January 1984a], "Word Processing Training," Statistical Services Division, Alfred Marks Bureau Limited, Internal Report.

Alfred Marks Bureau Limited [October 1984b], "The International Impact of Office Automation," Statistical Services Division, Alfred Marks Bureau Limited, Internal Report.

Micropro International Limited [1988], *Company Profile*.

M Minsky [1975], "A Framework for Representing Knowledge," in *The Psychology of Computer Vision*, P Winston, ed., McGraw-Hill.

D E Rumelhart & D A Norman [1983], "Representation in Memory," Centre for Human Information Processing, University of California, CHIP Technical Report No. 116, San Diego.

D E Rumelhart & A Ortony [1977], "The Representation of Knowledge in Memory," in *Schooling and the Acquisition of Knowledge*, R C Anderson, R J Spiro and W E Montague, ed., Lawrence Erlbaum Associates, Hillsdale, New Jersey.

D Tebbutt [July 1987], "Flying Start-Nought to 15% in Three Years," *PC Dealer*.

T Winograd [1975], "Frame Representations and the Declarative Procedural Controversy," in *Representation and Understanding: Studies in Cognitive Science*, D G Bobrow and A Collins, ed., Academic Press, New York.

R M Young [1981], "The Machine inside the Machine: User's Models of Pocket Calculators," *Int. J. Man-Machine Studies* 15, 51–85.

Measuring User Satisfaction

Jurek Kirakowski & Mary Corbett

Department of Applied Psychology, University College, Cork, Ireland.

The Computer User Satisfaction Inventory (CUSI) is a system independent evaluation metric questionnaire. It provides an indication of the individual's feelings of satisfaction along two dimensions: competence and affect. This paper presents data on the relationship between CUSI scores and other, more system dependent, metrics and discusses the role of user satisfaction in the development of user ability.

The relationship between the CUSI profiles and other metrics indicates that CUSI measures aspects of users in a way that is neither context sensitive nor labour intensive, unlike other measures derived from, for example, console logs, interviews, and diaries.

CUSI's two subscales of affect and competence work in accordance with what is hypothesised on the basis of the self efficacy theory of Bandura. When we look at a longtitudinal profile of user adaptation to a computer system we find an initial period of rapid development characterised by increase in satisfaction ratings, followed by a relative plateau during which feelings of competence lag behind those of affect. After this plateau stage users begin to try experimenting with more advanced features of the interface.

Keywords: Evaluation, Metric, User Development

1. The Assessment of Usability

If we allowed a person to freely interact with a computer system, and made no impositions on him or her to come back for a second session, we presume that the most important variable that would predict the probability of return would be the *user friendliness* of the system. This behavioural definition, as most such definitions, is in fact circular, and it is the circularity of such definitions of *user friendliness* that has led to the term being abused in HCI research of recent years.

1.1. A Background Model for Usability Assessment

We have, in the past few years, worked with the concept of user satisfaction rather than friendliness. We have adopted the theoretical framework of Albert Bandura (e.g., (Bandura [1986])). In this framework, thought affects action through the exercise of personal agency. The consequences of action, in turn, affect the nature of thought. This model can be called one of reciprocal causation: people are neither autonomous agents, nor are they automatically shaped and controlled by forces from their environment: people, rather, make a causal contribution to their own motivation and behaviour.

Increases in levels of motivation arising out of what Revesman and Permutter call *environmental control* (Revesman & Permutter [1981]) have been shown to have important effects on learning and performance and the feeling of well-being. In a series of papers, Permutter and his colleagues have shown that *environmental control* can be successfully operationalised as the subject's ability to exercise choice and control. In other words, the greater your feelings of mastery over an environment, the better you will feel about your performance, and the more likely you are to persevere at the activity.

1.2. The Computer User Satisfaction Inventory

In order to develop an instrument that would measure a person's feelings about a computer system, we have developed the Computer User Satisfaction Inventory (CUSI). CUSI is still a research instrument, and currently consists of 23 questions that can fairly evenly be divided into questions that tap an individual's feelings of mastery over the computer system they are using (called the *competence* subscale), and their feelings of fear or pleasure (called the *affect* subscale.)

Statements in CUSI are of the form of declarative statements of opinion, which express either affirmatory (positive) or negative attitudes towards the object being rated. The instructions ask the users to indicate the strength with which they agree or disagree with each statement with reference to the computer system they most often use using a five-point Lickert-type scale.

In psychometric research, we judge each research instrument by its reliability (does it measure consistently) and validity (does it measure what it is supposed to measure).

The reliability of version 3.1 of CUSI, as measured by the Kuder-Richardson formula 20 coefficient, stands at 0.95.

The research we are going to report in the present paper throws light on the validity of CUSI, by comparing the scores of subjects on CUSI with other, more labour-intensive methods of assessing satisfaction and with performance.

2. Description of the Study: Measuring User Development

The data was collected as part of ESPRIT project 385, HUFIT, area A6: *User development with flexible interfaces*. Our concern in this part of the project was to discover how users developed their computing competence with a system that offered a number of styles of human-computer interfaces, from those which relied on recognition memory at the most (i.e., menus) to those which relied on direct recall (i.e., abbreviated commands). Data on the validity of CUSI also involves us in interpreting the results of the experiment to some extent, but our main focus in this paper is to present CUSI as a measuring instrument.

2.1. The Test Application

The computer software on which we studied user development was a procedural spreadsheet type of application, which used colour extensively. It is called PVS (for a more technical description of PVS, see (Kirakowski et al. [1987b])).

The main feature of the PVS software as far as we are concerned in this paper is that the interface enabled the user to communicate with the computer using at least three different interface styles: a menu-style, a long command style, and a brief command style. There was also an extremely context-sensitive *help* facility.

Being an experimental HCI tool, PVS has a keystroke log facility which records each keystroke of the user. Subsequent programs can re-run this log producing an *animated* run-through, or can output this log to a printable file with additional information such as time stamps, and readable indications of what part of the interface environment the user is at, at any particular moment.

2.2. Design of the Study

Users were required to do ten sessions using PVS; each user had to solve a particular problem at each session. On the basis of preliminary work, each of these problems was a financial calculation known as a *break even analysis*, and there were four blocks of trials in which problems of increasing complexity were presented. The rationale for presenting these four blocks was the finding from educational psychology research that learning is most effective when more complicated elements are introduced gradually with a logical stepwise refinement of ideas (see, for instance (Gagne [1975]),). The blocks were arranged as follows: sessions 1-3 (block 1), 4-6 (block 2), 7-8 (block 3), and 9-10 (block 4). 12 Subjects (*Ss*) participated in this study. None of the *Ss* had substantial experience of computers before. They received no training in how to use PVS before their first session, but the briefing beforehand checked that they knew how to do a break even analysis.

The outputs from each session that will be discussed in this paper were: a completed CUSI questionnaire; an annotated log; and a tape recording of the *Ss*' simultaneous verbalizations. *Ss* also filled out diaries with probe items at each session; these are not reported here. For further details, the reader is directed throughout to (Kirakowski et al. [1987a]).

3. Data Obtained

The CUSI data will be presented first, then the data from the objective (behavioural) record of the experiment, and finally the data from the console logs and tape recordings, which are extremely labour-intensive to score and to analyse but which can give extremely detailed data. These measures will be compared with CUSI as we go along.

3.1. CUSI Data

The results of the CUSI questionnaire over the ten trials are shown in figure 1. Affect and competence are graphed separately. Our main way of analysing the data was to use a ranks test method that finds a vector of integers that best fits the order of average ranks of the observed data (Meddis [1984]). With each such vector we can calculate the probability that it could have occurred by chance, and express this as an area on a normal (*Z*) distribution.

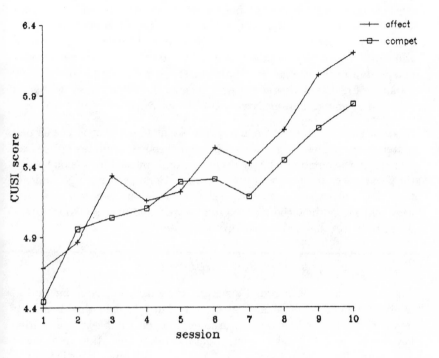

Figure 1. Average scores on the Affect and Competence subscales of CUSI for each of the ten sessions of the experiment

Looking at the feelings of competence dimension first, we find two plateaux in the *Ss*' development: the first plateau lasts from sessions 2 to 4, and the second 5 to 7 ($Z = 4.682$, $p < 0.001$). Now taking the affect dimension, we find the same two main plateaux, but time-lagged by one session: the first occurs at sessions 3 to 5, the second at sessions 6 to 8 ($Z = 4.551$, $p < 0.001$).

3.2. Behavioural Data and CUSI

We may correlate this attitudinal data with the behavioural data. PVS enables *Ss* to switch between menu and various command styles, within the building up of a command if desired. All *Ss* started by using menu interface styles. At what stage did they begin to switch to command styles? The data is best analysed using a *command advantage* metric that ranges from 1.00 (commands used exclusively) to −1.00 (menus used exclusively). Figure 2 displays the command advantage averages over the sessions. The best fitting vector indicates a plateau for sessions 1 to 7, and thence a steady increase in the use of commands to the end of the experiment ($Z = 3.637$, $p < 0.001$) Designers of systems which rely exclusively on menus may take note here that our users began to spontaneously change to command styles after approximately 150 minutes of distributed practice with menus. This figure also held good in another more ambitious series of trials not reported here.

It seems this switch to command styles begins to occur after the second plateaux as defined by the two CUSI dimensions. We also noticed an increase in the number of help calls at session 7, but not at session 8 when the changeover to command styles began. Comments from *Ss* indicate that they only wish to start switching styles when they feel sure that they understand how the menu system works, and have got to the stage when they feel the menus take up their time.

3.3. Console Log Data and CUSI

The console logs tell a broadly similar story, but since our method of analysing them is not a familiar one, we must explain this in a little detail first. Taking the tape recordings first, on the basis of a scoring key we are able to classify each spontaneous verbalization into one of four mutually exclusive categories: confused, rational, knowledgeable, and expert. The inter-rater reliability of such a categorization scheme is high, once raters have been trained. We tendentiously perceive these categories as ordinated on a scale from little to much competence over the interface under study.

When these categorized verbalizations are linked with the annotated console log output, we then transfer our rating of the verbalizations to a rating of the behaviours exhibited. Occasions where there is an obvious mismatch between what we have inferred from the verbalization and what we could infer from the behaviours are rare, but in these cases our rule is to go by the verbalization. Although this technique is only briefly descibed here, it must be stressed that it is an extremely labour-intensive activity. It is discussed in greater detail in (Kirakowski et al. [1987a]).

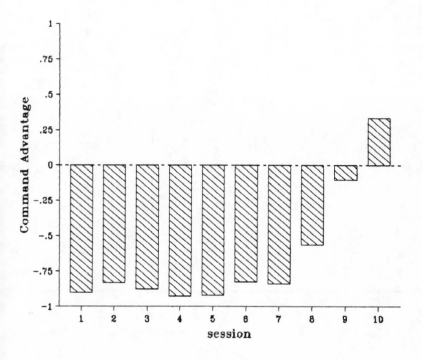

Figure 2. **Average Command Advantage for each of the
ten sessions of the experiment (+1.0 =
commands only used, −1.0 = menus only used)**

Taking the confused state as numerically equal to 1, and so on, we find
the average state per session as given on figure 3 (medians, and smoothed
maxima and mimima are given). The best fitting vector to this data
indicates a gradual increase in ability over sessions 1-5; a small decrease
at sessions 6 and 7, and thence a steady increase from session 7 to the
end of the experiment.

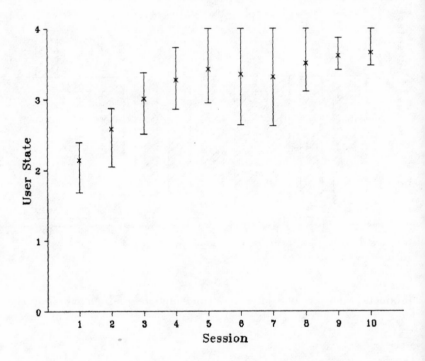

**Figure 3. Average scores for user states for each of the
ten sessions of the experiment**

Note that *Ss* begin to increase in competence before they begin to change
interaction styles, and that their actual competence mirrors fairly closely

their profile on the CUSI data on the competence dimension (most importantly the rise from session 7 to the end).

4. Conclusion: CUSI as an Efficient Metric of Usability

We have shown in this paper three sorts of measures we were able to take during the course of our experiment: objective data from the environments and the help messages the *Ss* were using; questionnaire (CUSI) data; and the labour-intensive console log data. These three are typical sorts of user data that the modern HCI laboratory may be expected to produce: however, they vary drastically in terms of amount of effort to be expended by the analysing team, and also in terms of the specificity to the studied application of the measures used.

The most general purpose measure is also the least time-consuming to use: CUSI. The research reported in this paper shows that CUSI does in fact have a strong relation to these other, more specifically orientated measures and can be safely used as a first approximation, at least.

Although we have shown how CUSI can be used to plot the development of user satisfaction in the course of interacting with one product, clearly, CUSI can also be used to compare the level of user satisfaction offered by different products if the pool of user subjects is kept relatively homogenous with respect to computer experience and task expectation. It therefore offers a useful opportunity to test out the market at a prototype or beta test stage.

At present no standardizations of CUSI exist which can be used as benchmarks. All CUSI comparisons have to be relative to other *brand X* products. This is of course not time- and effort- efficient, but the development of norms is beset with a number of conceptual problems which are best left for further research to unravel.

References

A Bandura [1986], "From Thought to Action: Mechanisms of Personal Agency," *New Zealand Journal of Psychology* 15, 1–17.

R M Gagne [1975], "Military Training and Principles of Learning," *American Psychologist* 17, 83–91.

J Kirakowski, J Good, M Corbett & T O'Sullivan [1987a], "Learning by Doing in Systems of Varied Flexibility," ESPRIT Project 385, HUFIT/HFRG-3-7/87, Department of Applied Psychology, University College, Cork.

J Kirakowski, J Good, A Dillon, M Corbett & M Sweeney [1987b], "A Flexible Interface to a Real Task and its Reception by Naive and Non-Naive Users," ESPRIT Project 385, HUFIT/HFRG-1a-1/87, Department of Applied Psychology, University College, Cork.

R Meddis [1984], *Statistics Using Ranks: A Unified Approach*, Blackwell, Oxford.

M E Revesman & L C Permutter [1981], "Environmental Control and the Perception of Control," *Mot. and Emot.* 5, 311–321.

Input/Output

A Review of Human Performance and Preferences with Different Input Devices to Computer Systems

N.P. Milner

Advanced Man-Machine Interface Group, British Telecom Research Laboratories, Martlesham Heath, Ipswich, Suffolk IP5 7RE, U.K.

A large number of studies exist which compare different computer input devices. Under experimental conditions no single device has been found to be consistently more appropriate than any other for Human-Computer interaction.

An extensive literature review has been undertaken of papers which compare the performance of different input devices. In the studies reviewed, all the devices have been compared on either speed, accuracy or subjective preference or a combination of these three measures. Whilst it is accepted that there are studies which contradict one another, the following general conclusions can be drawn.

1. For fixed choice, low resolution applications the most direct input device (e.g., a touch sensitive screen) is quickest and most liked by subjects.

2. For quick and accurate selection or manipulation

of high resolution objects indirect input devices
are better than direct devices.

3. There is no clear evidence to support the mouse,
joystick or trackball as being the best high resolution indirect input device.

4. In comparative studies, cursor keys and function
keys perform poorly against other input devices.

5. Experimental tasks and the specific design of the
input device have a large effect on the empirical
results.

Keywords: Input Devices, Speed, Accuracy, Subjective Preference, Literature Review

1. Introduction

A number of sources have compared different input devices to determine
which is the most appropriate for a particular computer function (Card,
English & Burr [1978]; Haller, Mutschler & Voss [1984]; Thomas & Milan
[1987]). The latter two references and others have (Greenstein & Arnaut
[1987]) reviewed the literature and drawn up tables which compare the
reported performance of different devices against one another.

The studies and the literature reviews show a good deal of conflict as
to which input device is best. The simple reason for the conflicting
conclusions is because no single device is better than any of the others.
Differences in the experimental task, the environment and the particular
design of the input devices used have a large effect on the findings.
This means that there are likely to be differences in performance and in
user opinion not only between categories of device (e.g., trackball versus
joystick, but within *categories* as well (e.g., directional joystick versus
isometric joystick).

Other reviews have sought to provide detail about the experimental
task. Thomas and Milan (Thomas & Milan [1987]) divided input tasks
into 'Object Manipulation', 'Target Location', 'Data Selection', 'Data
Entry' and 'Artwork'. Greenstein and Arnaut (Greenstein & Arnaut
[1987]) divide input test into different generic sections for their reviews.
Essentially there are four broad categories of input tasks:

Data Entry

Object Selection

Object Manipulation

Drawing/Tracking

Data entry refers to its tasks that require the entry of data. Object selection refers to positioning the cursor to select an object on the screen. Some authors have drawn differences between the alternative types of selection by calling them target selection, menu selection and large or small object selection. In some cases, experiments have been carried out on the first part of the selection process only i.e., cursor positioning. For the purposes of summarising the literature all the selection categories, as well as cursor positioning, will be reported under 'Selection'.

Object manipulation refers to the process of moving objects about on the screen by selecting them and dragging them into place. Drawing and tracking tasks have been grouped because they both require smooth cursor movements and accurate positioning. Whilst it is accepted that the tasks have some differences, it is felt that the similarities and the paucity of information are sufficient to make it worthwhile grouping them together.

In this paper each of the four broad categories will be referred to, but not necessarily for each device. The input tasks cited depend on those used in the particular study. The input devices considered are:

1. Keyboard   6. Function Keys
2. Mouse   7. Tablet (touch pad)
3. Trackball   8. Touch Sensitive Screen
4. Joystick   9. Light pen.
5. Cursor Keys

For each device, the format will include an introduction, a section on the performance of the input device against other devices of the same category (e.g., keyboard versus keyboard) and a section on the performance of the input device against other input devices (e.g., keyboard versus the rest). After all devices have been considered, the findings will be presented in a large summary table. Now to the first of the nine input devices.

2. The Keyboard

2.1. Introduction

It was over a century ago in 1866 that the first typewriter, developed by Americans Sholes and Glidden, became a commercial success (Noyes [1983]). Many will have heard the rumour that the ubiquitous QWERTY layout of keys was designed to slow down typing speed to prevent the early typing machines from jamming. Whilst it is true that the layout was designed to fit around the short-comings of the typewriter, it was not designed to slow the operator down *per se*. Studies of keying performance on the QWERTY layout compared to alternative layouts support the notion that it was not deliberately designed to be inefficient to use to slow the user.

2.2. The Performance of different Keyboard Layouts

The expected typing rate for a layout may be estimated (Card, Moran & Newell [1983])by applying the following equation.

$$\text{Typing Rate} = \Sigma_i f_i t_i$$

where $f_i =$ the frequencies with which two-letter combinations (or digraphs) appear in English,

and $t_i =$ time for the keystroke for all but the most infrequent letter keys

Applying the formula to the QWERTY layout and an alphabetic layout (and compensating for the fact that they had an incomplete set of digraph times) Card, Moran and Newell (Card, Moran & Newell [1983]) calculated that the alphabetic (66.5 words/minute) was about 8% slower than the QWERTY (72 words/minute).

The Dvorak keyboard (Dvorak [1943]) was designed to be faster than the QWERTY but according to Kinkead (Kinkead [1975]) the improvement in speed would only be in the order of 2.6%. Yamada (Yamada [1980a]; Yamada [1980b]) has disputed some of Kinkead's assumptions and Yamaha (Yamaha [1980]) has claimed increases in speed of 15-20% as well as reduced fatigue.

2.3. The Performance of Keyboards against other Input Devices

The keyboard is the best means of inputting text into a machine at present. The evidence for this is the lack of any viable alternative to the keyboard on the market. Other text input devices do exist for special groups such as the handicapped but these are very slow. Where very high keying rates need to be sustained chord keyboards offer keying rates of 300 words per minute. Shneiderman (Shneiderman [1987]) points out that it takes months of learning and continuous practice to retain the complex pattern of chords which allow such high keying rates.

For other tasks, such as menu selection, Karat *et al* (Karat, McDonald & Anderson [1986]) found that although the keyboard was more popular than the mouse, the mouse was a faster selection device. Goodwin (Goodwin [1975]) reported that a light pen and a light gun "were four to five times faster than the keyboard for [an] arbitrary positioning task, and about twice as fast for the other tasks" (which were sequential cursor positioning and check reading). Speed, accuracy and subjective rating were all poor compared to other input devices according to (Albert [1982]). He reported that direct input devices (touch screen and light pen) resulted in the highest speed and preference and the trackball and tablet were the most accurate. Thomas and Milan (Thomas & Milan [1987]) reported that a 'Concept Keyboard' performed as fast as a touch screen and faster than a trackball, joystick and cursor keys. However, in this experiment the Concept Keyboard was a touchpad with a paper outline of the salient screen features laid over it. For this reason it may be viewed less as a keyboard and more as a touchpad.

3. The Mouse

Huckle (Huckle [1981]) described the mouse as "a small device, about the size of a cigarette packet, with [one to] three buttons on top. This is attached to a display terminal by a thin cord". The forerunner of today's mechanical mouse was invented by Douglas Engelbart of SRI (Menlo Park, PA) in 1964. The device had two wheels underneath it, set at right angles to each other, which were translated, via potentiometers, to X and Y movement on the screen. The commercial optical mouse was invented by Steve Kirsh of Mouse Systems Corporation in 1982 (Comerford [1984]).

3.1. The Performance of Different Mice

To date, it appears that there have been no studies of different mice despite the wide range of shapes, sizes and number of buttons. Although no research has been carried out on the optimum number of buttons, Price and Cordova (Price & Cordova [1983]) suggest that the performance of the mouse is faster and more accurate using different buttons rather than different number of button clicks.

3.2. The Performance of the Mouse against other Input Devices

The mouse is an extremely popular input device in industry and academia. One of the major advantages of the mouse is that it is is quick to learn. Apple Computer Inc. reported that computer-naive users could become familiar with the mouse in 15 minutes. In contrast, it required an average of 20 hours to operate similar software using a keyboard. The reasons given for the difference are the time taken to learn to use a keyboard and the time required to learn long command sequences to perform functions with a keyboard. Generally the mouse is a popular input device. It allows the user to work in a comfortable position with the hand supported. Engelbart (Engelbart [1973]) also noted that working with a mouse allowed the user to change posture easily which is important during long interactions.

Card *et al* (Card, English & Burr [1978]) compared the positioning time and the error rate of selecting text using four different pointing devices (cursor keys, function keys, rate-controlled isometric joystick and a mouse). The mouse used in the experiment was an old design (English, Engelbart & Berman [1967]), consisting of two wheels at right angles to one another on the underside of the mouse. As the mouse moved over the table one wheel coded the amount of movement in the X-direction, the other the movement in the Y-direction. The experimental results showed that the mouse was quicker to position and resulted in fewer errors than the other devices investigated. In addition, it was reported that as the target distance increased so did the positioning time. However, the effect of the target distance had a much lesser effect on the overall positioning time for the mouse than it did for the other devices (see figure 1).

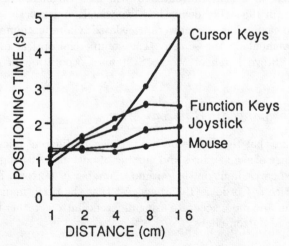

Figure 1.   The effect of distance on positioning time for four different input devices. (From (Card, English & Burr [1978]))

In a number of other studies (Haller, Mutschler & Voss [1984]; Karat,

McDonald & Anderson [1986]; Ritchie & Turner [1975]; Thomas & Milan [1987]) the mouse has been outperformed by direct input devices.

4. The Trackball

The trackball (or roller ball) is a cursor control device in the form of a mechanical rolling ball set into a work surface near the display terminal. Rotating the ball causes the cursor to move on the screen. The direction and speed of the cursor is determined by the speed and direction of the trackball. For those who have not had experience of a trackball but who have used a mouse, the trackball could be described as a static, up-turned mouse. The trackball only positions the cursor. A further feature (e.g., a button or a keyboard) is required to perform any action on the object located. Due to the method of operating the trackball, it would be difficult to operate the ball and a button simultaneously.

4.1. The Performance of Different Trackballs

Most authors reporting on the trackball have commented on the ease and speed with which most subjects have learnt to manipulate a pointer using a trackball (Huckle [1981]). Another attribute of trackball operation is its 'feel'. Feel refers to the inertia and damping of the ball which varies between models due to the size and weight of the ball used and the way that it is mounted in its holder. Reporting on the literature, Jackson (Jackson [1982]) concluded that users adapt very quickly to the different feel of different trackballs.

The trackball is often used as input device in potentially stressful environments such as air traffic control (Shneiderman [1987]), radar and other military applications (Greenstein & Arnaut [1987]). However, no research exists to suggest that an operator performs quicker or more accurately under stress with a trackball than with any other input device.

4.2. The Performance of the Trackball against other Input Devices

Some input devices make use of a proprioceptive relationship between the user and the equipment to facilitate speed and/or accuracy (e.g., touch typing on a keyboard and operating a mouse). It is interesting to note that although the mouse makes use of both tactual and proprioceptive perception and the trackball only the tactual component, empirical evidence suggests that there is no significant decrement in cursor positioning time for the two devices (Haller, Mutschler & Voss [1984]). In fact some authors claim that the trackball is one of the fastest target selection devices (Gomez et al. [1982]; Mehr & Mehr [1972]).

Others have reported that their empirical results show the trackball to be one of the most accurate input devices (Albert [1982]; Ball, Newton & Whitfield [1980]; Gomez et al. [1982]; Mehr & Mehr [1972]; Ritchie & Turner [1975]) although more recent studies disagree (Haller, Mutschler & Voss [1984]; Thomas & Milan [1987]).

5. The Joystick

The joystick concept has a long history which began in car and aircraft control devices (Shneiderman [1987]). The notion of using a joystick to control cursor movements on computer systems has been accepted for a long time too and this is reflected in the variety of devices that are currently available. Although there are three basic types of joystick; the displacement joystick, the isometric (or force-operated) joystick and the switch activated joystick, they all look essentially similar. They consist of a short lever mounted in a base. Movement of the stick results in a movement of the cursor or arrow on the screen. The differences between the three types of joystick become apparent when the user attempts to move the stick.

5.1. The Performance of Different Joysticks

Displacement Joystick
The displacement joystick allows the user to move the stick in any direction and the cursor moves proportionately. Depending on the design of the joystick, the stick (and cursor) will either remain in the same place when the user removes his/her hand from the stick or will self-centre itself if it is spring loaded.

Isometric Joystick
The isometric joystick (or force-operated joystick) looks the same as the displacement joystick but when the user applies pressure against the stick it does not move. However, strain gauges located in the device sense the pressure and translate this into cursor movement. When the user stops applying pressure to the stick, the cursor stops moving.

Switch-Activated Joystick
Unlike the other two joysticks, the switch-activated (or digital) joystick only detects movement in eight directions (north, north-east, east, south-east, south, south-west, west, and north-west). This is because the stick is in contact with eight switches at its base and when the user moves the joystick it closes one or more of the switches. The switch status information is simply converted into cursor movement.

Fixed Velocity or Rate-Controlled
There are two joystick/cursor relationships. Firstly, they can have a fixed

velocity relationship where, no matter how fast one moves the joystick or how much pressure one puts on it (in the case of the isometric joystick) the cursor will move at a fixed velocity. The second type of relationship is termed rate controlled. In this case the cursor speed can be controlled by moving the joystick at different speeds or applying more or less pressure against the stick.

5.2. The Performance of the Joystick against other Input Devices

There have been no reports in the literature of users finding it difficult to learn to operate joysticks. The widespread use of joysticks for various home-computer games is testimony to the ease with which people can learn to use the device as well as its relative cheapness.

There is minimal learning required in the use of a joystick especially if one is familiar with the control display relationships of the mouse or trackball. Difficulties will occur if the joystick encodes rate or higher order information as opposed to absolute distance information (Poulton [1974]).

As with mice and trackballs, the gain of the joystick may be changed. Jenkins and Karr (Jenkins & Karr []) found that the optimal control to display movement ratio was approximately 0.4 (i.e., for each 10 units of joystick movement the cursor moves 4 units of the same scale on the VDT screen). However, the size of the joystick that is required for this level of accuracy would be impracticable for most modern VDT screen and keyboard sizes. The alternatives are i) to increase the gain of the joystick or ii) to introduce rate controlled displacement joysticks. The first alternative would entail large magnifications of hand movements in the display and so reduce accuracy.   (Foley & Dam [1982]) It is therefore suggested that the joystick is better utilised when movements control velocity or rate of cursor displacement, in addition to direction, as opposed to absolute distance.

It is generally reported that the joystick is not a very accurate input device and has low resolution (Rubinstein & Hersh [1984]; Scott [1982]; Thomas & Milan [1987]). For computer applications, joysticks are thus most suited to grosser pointing or tracking tasks which do not require a great deal of precision. It is interesting to note that support for the accuracy of the joystick comes from work carried out at an earlier time and (Mehr & Mehr [1972]; Ritchie & Turner [1975]) underlining the need to consider the relative technical development of the input devices in the experiment at that time. In the case of Ritchie and Turner they concluded that the joystick was more accurate than a graphics tablet, a mouse and a light pen.

6. Cursor Keys

On some keyboards the movement of the cursor on the screen can be controlled by special keys. These cursor keys are usually located to the right of the alpha keys (an international standard will shortly be produced to encourage this standard location). There are usually four keys to control cursor movement – up, down, left and right.

6.1. The Performance of Different Cursor Key Layouts

Comparison between different Cursor Key layouts have been carried out in the United States by Foley (Foley & Dam [1982]) and Emmons (Emmons [1984]). They reported that cross (figure 2a) and inverted T-shaped (figure 2b) layouts were quicker than linear alternatives except for frequent users who could become proficient with any layout. Emerging international standards will also accept corruptions of the cross layout as shown in figures 2c and 2d.

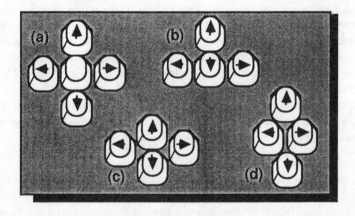

Figure 2.   Alternative Cursor Key Layouts

6.2. The Performance of Cursor Keys against other Input

Devices

The general performance of cursor keys has been found to be poor compared to other cursor positioning devices (Card, English & Burr [1978]; Haller, Mutschler & Voss [1984]; Thomas & Milan [1987]; Usher [1982]). Card et al reported that where the distance that the cursor needed to moved was very short, the cursor keys (which they termed "step keys") were quickest. As the distance increased the performance deteriorated rapidly.

7. Function Keys

Many keyboards contain a set of additional keys for special functions or programmed functions. The keys are usually positioned above the row of numbers at the top of the keyboard or down the left hand side and are often labelled PF1, PF2...PF10 (indicating a programmable function) or, more simply F1, F2...F10. The advantage of the function key is that it can reduce a function to a single key press as opposed to typing in the whole command. The disadvantage is that it increases the memory load on the user who may have to remember the function of each key and it also requires the user to remove their fingers from the home row.

7.1. The Performance of different Function Key Layouts

It does not appear that different function key layouts have been compared. Imminent ISO standards will identify the areas of the keyboard where function keys should appear to ensure some consistency of design which will generally enhance user performance.

7.2. The Performance of Function Keys against other Input Devices

The Card et al (Card, English & Burr [1978]) study is one of a limited number of studies which look at function keys. They used function keys which positioned the cursor at the end of the PARAGRAPH, LINE, WORD, or CHARacter and allowed forward movements as well as a function to REVerse. Positioning time was slower than the joystick and mouse (except for very small movements) but performance did not deteriorate as badly as the cursor keys (see figure 1).

Usher (Usher [1982]) compared a series of function keys (two groups of sixteen 9 × 9mm keys set 3mm apart) with a touch screen. Using forty seven subjects performing a process control task he reported that the touch screen was easier to learn, faster to use, made the task easier to control (and therefore more accurate) and was five times more popular with subjects (this increased to ten fold in long term subjects).

8. The Tablet (including the Touch Pad)

The tablet (or graphics tablet as it is sometimes called) is a touch sensitive area separate from the screen usually placed flat on the work surface. The tablet may have an overlay of options on it which can be selected by a finger, pen, puck or stylus using acoustic, electronic or contact positioning sensing (Shneiderman [1987]). Alternatively, the tablet may allow free input to the screen (drawing) or selection of objects on the screen as one might with a touch screen or light pen. The advantage that it has over the latter two devices is that the arm may remain in a relaxed, supported position. Where the tablet works on the pressure of the finger or pen to indicate its position, it may be known as a touch pad.

8.1. The Performance of different Tablets

Within the scope of the review no studies which compared the performance of different tablets were located.

8.2. The Performance of the Tablet against other Input Devices

Albert (Albert [1982]) compared a number of input devices in a selection task. The results suggested that the tablet was as accurate as the trackball and faster than all the other input devices which included a touch sensitive screen, a light pen, a joystick and a keyboard. Thomas and Milan (Thomas & Milan [1987]) found that their Concept Keyboard (a touch pad with an overlay) to be as quick as a touch sensitive screen and faster than a trackball, a joystick and cursor keys. Haller *et al* (Haller, Mutschler & Voss [1984]) disagree about the speed of the tablet and reported that the light pen was not only faster but more accurate and more popular with subjects. Ball *et al* (Ball, Newton & Whitfield [1980]) and Ritchie and Turner (Ritchie & Turner [1975]) also disagree with the accuracy of the tablet. Both research teams found that the trackball was more accurate than the tablet.

9. Touch Sensitive Screens

There are several different types of Touch Sensitive Screen (TSS). Although the enabling technology differs between devices, they all operate in the same way from the user's point of view. With a TSS a series of options is presented on the visual display terminal screen. The options are often framed in touch sensitive boxes (called light buttons). The user indicates his/her choice by touching the appropriate box on the screen with one of their finger's and a new or revised set of choices appears on

Table 1.   Characteristics of Touch Sensitive Screen Technologies. From (Greenstein & Arnaut [1987])

Characteristic	Touch Sensitive Screens				
	Touch Wire	Infrared	Acoustic	Pressure Sensitive	Conductive
May obscure display	X				
Unreliable detection	X				
Limited resolution		X			
Parallax		X	X	X	
Sensitive to ambient lighting		X			
Inadvertent activation		X	X		
Does not use whole screen		X			
Awkward drawing device	X	X	X		X
Extra training required				X	
Reduced light from screen					X
Relatively easily damaged					X

the screen. There are a number of different enabling technologies. These include; Acoustic Touch Sensitive Screens, Conductive and Capacitive Touch Sensitive Screens, Infrared Touch Sensitive Screens, Pressure Sensitive Touch Sensitive Screens and Touch Wire Touch Sensitive Screens. For a review of how Touch Sensitive Screens work see Greenstein and Arnaut (Greenstein & Arnaut [1987])

9.1. The Performance of different Touch Sensitive Screens

Greenstein and Arnaut (Greenstein & Arnaut [1987]) summarised the relative weaknesses of the different touch sensitive screen technologies in table 1.

9.2. The performance of Touch Sensitive Screens against other Input Devices

The literature suggests that touch sensitive screens perform very well against other input devices in selection or manipulation tasks (Albert [1982]; Karat, McDonald & Anderson [1986]; Ritchie & Turner [1975]; Thomas & Milan [1987]; Usher [1982]). One of the consistent findings is that the device is particularly quick.

An indication of the relatively low load imposed by the act of pointing was described by Martin *et al* (Martin, Long & Broome [1984]). As a pilot study of the effects of pointing or speaking on a primary tracking task, they compared the time taken to locate an object on a screen by pointing to it (using a stylus) or speaking its co-ordinates into a voice recogniser. The total speaking response time was comprised of two distinct elements; a silent period where the cognitive elements occurred followed by a period of articulation. The two periods were found to be of the same duration. Martin *et al* (Martin, Long & Broome [1984]) reported that pointing took half the time of speaking i.e., that the cognitive *and* motor components of pointing took the same time as the cognitive or articulation element of speaking. This may be interpreted as evidence that pointing is a more compatible low-resolution system input, requiring only limited cognitive processing and imposing a minimal cognitive load.

Where touch sensitive screens have not done well (Ball, Newton & Whitfield [1980]) in experiments it is usually due to the very high resolution of the task. The smallest object that can be accurately pointed to on a screen is determined by the finger size, the error due to parallax and the width of the non-sensitised area around each sensitive button.

One of the major problems with using touch sensitive screens for extended periods of time is the fatigue caused by regularly reaching out and touching the screen. The regular action of pointing causes local fatigue and discomfort not only in the muscles of the active arm but often in the muscles of the shoulder and neck which are in a state of contraction to support the arm. With the advent of flat screens, there will be a commercial possibility of angled or even horizontal (desktop) TSSs. Subjects have reported a preference for declinated touch sensitive screen surfaces (Beringer & Petersen [1985]; Long, Whitefield & Dennett [1984]) with no significant performance differences (Beringer & Petersen [1985]). It appears that, provided appropriate anti-glare lighting is installed, there could be serious commercial advantages to declinated TSSs because of the reduction in operator fatigue.

10. Light Pens

Light pens are pens which are attached to the VDT via a cord and are used to point to areas or objects on the screen. Most light pens include a button to indicate when the user is pointing at the right area on the screen. Light pens vary enormously in size, shape, weight and button position. One extreme variation is the light gun, which is shaped like a small pistol and has a trigger instead of a button.

10.1. The Performance of different Light pens

Within the scope of the review no studies which compared the performance of different light pens were located.

10.2. The Performance of Light pens with other input devices

Despite the fact that the light pen (and its variations) is tiring in extended use, that the hand may cover the critical part of the screen during use and that the operator must remove their hands from the keyboard it has still done well against other input devices. Several authors have reported that it was most liked by subjects and was the quickest to locate the target (Albert [1982]; Goodwin [1975]; Haller, Mutschler & Voss [1984]). Experiments carried out over a longer period of time would probably support the anecdotal evidence that using a light pen repeatedly during the day is fatiguing.

A further short-coming of the device is that it is not very accurate (Foley & Dam [1982]; Greenstein & Arnaut [1987]). The only exception to this were Haller *et al* (Haller, Mutschler & Voss [1984]) who found the light pen to be the most accurate device, with the mouse and trackball amongst the worst. As Greenstein and Arnaut (Greenstein & Arnaut [1987]) note "light pens are highly dependent on the hardware and software with which they are used, and any problems or inaccuracies in either of these components may lead to inaccuracies in light pen performance".

11. Discussion

The literature reviewed in the nine previous sections is summarised in Table 2. The table shows the main task types and the different input devices. Each study is identified and the input devices used in each study are denoted using a tick or a cross. The cross indicates that a device was used in the study and a tick (in conjunction with a number) specifies whether it was quickest, most accurate and/or most popular.

Selecting the fastest input device depends largely on the task. For high resolution applications, trying to select objects by pointing at them with the end of one's finger may be slow due to repeated attempts to activate the right area and, in some cases, impossible because of the relative sizes of the user's finger and the sensitive area on the screen. However, many experimenters have reported that for low resolution applications, the most direct input device (e.g., a touch sensitive screen) is quickest (Albert [1982]; Goodwin [1975]; Haller, Mutschler & Voss [1984]; Karat, McDonald & Anderson [1986]; Thomas & Milan [1987]; Usher [1982]) and often most liked by subjects (Albert [1982]; Haller, Mutschler & Voss [1984]; Usher [1982]). Of course speed is rarely a criteria on its own.

Most real tasks require a high level of accuracy to make them worth doing. It is interesting to note that the literature suggests that it is not an "either ... or... " choice; one does not have to decide whether the input device has to be either fast or accurate. A number of studies have shown that a single device can be both quickest and most accurate for a particular task; the Mouse (Card, English & Burr [1978]; English, Engelbart & Berman [1967]), the Trackball (Gomez et al. [1982]; Mehr & Mehr [1972]), the Lightpen (Haller, Mutschler & Voss [1984]; Karat, McDonald & Anderson [1986]), Touch Sensitive Screens (Usher [1982]). The problem is that when it comes to choosing between the alternative indirect input devices, the literature does not give any clear indication about which device is most appropriate.

The only finding which is consistent amongst all those who studied indirect input devices it is that cursor keys are slower, less accurate and not liked by subjects compared to other indirect input devices (Card, English & Burr [1978]; Haller, Mutschler & Voss [1984]; Thomas & Milan [1987]; Usher [1982]). The empirical support for the ubiquitous mouse input device is poor in the literature. Only Card et al (Card, English & Burr [1978]) and English et al (English, Engelbart & Berman [1967]) reported that the mouse out-performed other input devices. Both papers are at least a decade old and were spawned by the Xerox development programme. Support for the trackball and joystick is varied and neither of them emerges as the stronger device. So, for quick and accurate selection of high-resolution objects there is no clear evidence to support the use of the mouse, the joystick or the trackball in preference to either of the others.

Also interesting is the fact that direct input devices were sometimes quicker *and* more accurate than indirect devices (Haller, Mutschler & Voss [1984]; Karat, McDonald & Anderson [1986]; Usher [1982]). In these studies the task resolution was not high and the duration of the tasks were short. For quick and accurate selection or manipulation of high-resolution objects, indirect manipulation devices appear better than direct devices. They also place less load on the body's musculo-skeletal system because the actual indirect input devices rest on the desktop. This position allows the hand and forearm to rest on the device during use and thereby reduce the onset of fatigue.

One of the noticeable things about the most commonly used input devices is that they are manual. Voice input might be considered as input device but, as yet, it has still failed to deliver a robust, useable and popular system. Other non-manual input devices which use eye-movements or limb movements have only been considered for the disabled or in speculative research fields.

Another observation is that the commonly used input devices only

Task	Reference	Input Device — Indirect							Direct	
		Keyboard	Mouse	Trackball	Joystick	Cursor Keys	Function Keys	Touch Pad	Touchscreen	Light Pen
Selection	Albert 1982	✗		✓2	✗			✓2	✓1.3	✓1.3
	Ball et al. 1980			✓2				✗	✗	
	Card et al. 1978		✓1.2		✗	✗	✗			
	English et al. 1967		✓1.2							
	Gomez et al. 1982			✓1.2				✓1		
	Goodwin 1975	✗					✓			✓1.4
	Haller et al. 1984		✗	✗		✗		✗		✓1.2.3
	Karat et al. 1984	✓3	✗						✓1.2	
	Mehr & Mehr 1972			✓1.2	✓2					
	Ritchie&Turner 1975		✗	✓2	✓2			✗	✓	✗
	Thomas&Milan 1987	✓1.5		✗	✗	✗			✓1	
Manip- ulation	Thomas&Milan 1987	✗			✗	✗			✓1	
	Usher 1982						✗		✓1.2.3	
Tracking	Ball et al. 1980			✓2				✗	✗	
	Irving et al. 1976			✗	✗					✓2

Key to Numbers
1. Fastest Device
2. Most Accurate Device
3. Most Liked by Subjects
4. Light Gun
5. Concept Keyboard

Table 2.   Summary of studies of Input Devices

require one hand to operate them. The keyboard is the exception where the user wants higher input rates. However, most users know many unskilled keyboard users often use just one hand during their early experiences with the keyboard. Skilled keyboard operators can reach very high rates of input – the Guinness World Record for typing on an electric IBM typewriter is 9316 words (with 40 errors) in an hour which corresponds to 149 words per minute with the error penalties. The implications are clear. Where speed and volume are important, then devices need to make greater use of both hands and the fingers. In the case of skilled audio typists, their feet often control the rate at which the information reaches the ears. Whilst the feet are not strictly being used as an input device to the word processor, they are being used as part of the input process.

12. Future directions

The future will demand greater use of the ways that a person can communicate with a computer. Computer systems are getting faster and memories larger. People are sending more and more information to one another via computers and storing information on them. Graphics and other three dimensional interfaces will mean that the control and manipulation of these large and powerful systems will need more than simple one finger input devices. Both hands, both feet, the position of the eyes, the voice and possibly facial expressions are all going to be needed to provide the level of subtlety and complexity needed for people to exploit tomorrow's powerful computers to their full benefit. It may be that we have to abandon our ideas about designing 'easy to use' devices. Controlling the new computing power and navigating through vast data banks may require input devices that require significant amounts of training and have more similarities with a car or aircraft cockpit controls than a Microsoft mouse or a Tandy joystick.

It does not mean that the information about current input devices is obsolete. It is useful providing general conclusions can be abstracted from the specific experiments. The conclusions drawn from the literature reviewed in this paper are at the device level (i.e., comparing different input devices) which is its aim. It is likely that the information will need to be made more device independent (i.e., focussing on the principles underlying input from human to computer) for it to be used in the design of future input devices.

13. Conclusions

The current literature makes it difficult to select an input device for a specific task because of the differences in the individual studies reported in the literature. Whilst it is accepted that these differences make it difficult to generalise, the following broad conclusions may be drawn.

1. For fixed choice, low-resolution applications direct input devices (e.g., touch sensitive screens) are faster and usually subjectively preferred.

2. For quick and accurate selection or manipulation of high-resolution objects, indirect manipulation devices are better than direct devices.

3. For quick and accurate selection of high-resolution objects there is no clear evidence to support the use of the mouse, the joystick or the trackball in preference to either of the others.

4. Cursor keys and function keys perform badly against other input devices.

5. Experimental tasks and the specific design of individual input devices have a large effect on empirical results.

Acknowledgements

Acknowledgement is made to the Director of Research of British Telecom plc for permission to publish this paper. My thanks to my colleague Tony Lo who kindly read my manuscript.

References

A E Albert [1982], "The Effect of Graphic Input Devices on Performance in a Cursor Positioning Task," in *Proceedings of the 26th Meeting of the Human Factors Society*, 54–58.

R G Ball, R S Newton & D Whitfield [January 1980], "Development of an Off-Display, High-Resolution, Direct Touch Input Device: The RSRE Touchpad," *Displays*.

D B Beringer & J G Petersen [1985], "Underlying Behavioural Parameters of the Operation of Touch-Input Devices: Biases, Models and Feedback," *Human Factors* 27, 445–458.

S K Card, W K English & B J Burr [1978], "Evaluation of Mouse, Rate-Controlled Isometric Joystick, Step Keys and Text Keys for Text Selection on a CRT," *Ergonomics* 21, 601–613.

S K Card, T P Moran & A Newell [1983], *The Psychology of Human-Computer Interaction*, Lawrence Erlbaum Associates, Hillsdale, New Jersey.

R Comerford [July 26 1984], "Pointing-Device Innovations Enhance User/Machine Interfaces," *EDN*.

A Dvorak [1943], "There is a Better Typewriter Keyboard," *National Business Education Quarterly* 12, 51–58.

W H Emmons [1984], "A Comparison of Cursor-Key Arrangements (Box versus Cross) for VDUs," in *Ergonomics and Health in Modern Offices*, E Grandjean, ed., Taylor and Francis, London and Philadelphia, 214–219.

D C Engelbart [1973], "Design Considerations for Knowledge Workshop Terminals," in *Proceedings of NCC AFIPS #42*, 9–21.

W K English, D C Engelbart & M L Berman [1967], "Display Selection Techniques for Text Manipulation," *IEEE Trans. on Human Factors in Electronics* HFE-8, 21–31.

J D Foley & A van Dam [1982], *Fundamentals of Interactive Computer Graphics*, Addison-Wesley, Reading MA, Reprinted with corrections 1984.

A D Gomez, S W Wolfe, E W Davenport & B D Calder [1982], "LMDS: Lightweight Modular Display System," Naval Ocean Systems Center, NOSC Technical Report No. 767, San Diego CA.

N C Goodwin [1975], "Cursor Positioning on an Electronic Display Using Light Pen, Light Gun or Keyboard for Three Basic Tasks," *Human Factors* 17, 289–295.

J S Greenstein & L Y Arnaut [1987], "Human Factors Aspects of Manual Computer Input Devices," in *Handbook of Human Factors*, G Salvendy, ed., Wiley Interscience, New York, 1450–1489.

R Haller, H Mutschler & M Voss [1984], "Comparison of Input Devices for Correction of Typing Errors in Office Systems," in *INTERACT '84 – First IFIP Conference on Human-Computer Interaction*, B Shackel, ed., Elsevier-Science, Amsterdam, 218–223.

B A Huckle [1981], *The Man-Machine Interface: Guidelines for the Design of the End-User/System Conversation*, Savant Institute Studies, Lancashire, UK.

A Jackson [1982], *Some Problems in the Specification of Rolling Ball Operating Characteristics*, RSRE UK.

W L Jenkins & A C Karr, "The Use of a Joystick in Masking Settings in a Simulated Scope Face," *Journal of Applied Psychology* 38, 457–461.

J Karat, J E McDonald & M Anderson [1986], "A Comparison of Menu Selection Techniques: Touch, Panel, Mouse and Keyboard," *Int. J. Man-Machine Studies* 25, 73–88.

R Kinkead [1975], "Typing Speeds, Keying Rates and Optimal Keyboard Layout," in *Proceedings of the 19th Meeting of the Human Factors Society*.

J Long, A Whitefield & J Dennett [1984], "The Effect of Display on the Direct Entry of Numerical Information by Pointing," *Human Factors* 26, 3–18.

J Martin, J Long & D Broome [1984], "The Division of Attention between a Primary Tracking Task and Secondary Tasks of Pointing with a Stylus or Speaking in a Simulated Ship's-Gunfire-Control Task," *Human Factors* 27, 397–408.

M H Mehr & E Mehr [1972], "Manual Digital Positioning in Two Axes: A Comparison of Joystick and Trackball Controls," in *Proceedings of the 16th Meeting of the Human Factors Society*, 110–116.

J Noyes [1983], "The QWERTY Keyboard: A Review," *Int. J. Man-Machine Studies* 18, 265–281.

E C Poulton [1974], *Tracking Skill and Manual Control*, Academic Press, New York.

L A Price & C A Cordova [1983], "Use of Mouse Buttons," in *Proceedings of CHI '83 – Human Factors in Computing Systems*, ACM, New York, 262–266.

G J Ritchie & J A Turner [1975], "Input Devices for Interactive Graphics," *Int. J. Man-Machine Studies* 7, 639–660.

R Rubinstein & H M Hersh [1984], *The Human Factor: Designing Computer Systems for People*, Digital Press, Burlington MA.

J E Scott [1982], *Introduction to Computer Graphics*, Wiley, New York.

B Shneiderman [1987], *Designing the User Interface: Strategies for Effective Human-Computer Interaction*, Addison-Wesley, Reading MA.

C M Thomas & S Milan [1987], "Which Input Device Should be Used with Interactive Video?," in *INTERACT '87 – The Second IFIP Conference on Human-Computer Interaction*, H J Bullinger and B Shackel, ed., Elsevier Science Publishers B.V., North Holland.

D M Usher [1982], *A Touch-Sensitive VDU Compared with a Computer-Aided Keypad for Controlling Power Generated Man-Machine Systems*, IEE Conference Pub. No. 212.

H Yamada [1980a], "An Analysis of the Standard English Keyboard," Department of Information Science, Faculty of Science, University of Tokyo, Technical Report No. 80-11.

H Yamada [1980b], "A Historical Study of Typewriters and Typing Methods: From the Position of Planning Japanese Parallels," *Journal of Information Processing* 2, 179–202.

H A Yamaha [1980], "A Historical Study of Typing and Typewriter Mechanics," *J. of Information Processing* 2, 175–202.

A Gesture Based Text Editor

L.K. Welbourn & R.J. Whitrow

Department of Computing, Trent Polytechnic, Burton Street, Nottingham, U.K.

This paper describes a text editor which has been designed to mimic the usual pen and paper type of editing. Hand-drawn gestures are used to specify the editing task. The use of gestures as an interface becomes more important with the advent of the electronic paper. The user specifies the editing task and its range by drawing the gesture on a tablet. The 'ink' of the pen appears on a screen, allowing the user to see what is drawn. The recognition of the gesture is on-line in its nature and the results of the edit are displayed immediately. Typically, two horizontal lines drawn through a word will be recognised as a delete operation, and the word will be removed from the display . The editing operations described include deletion, insertion, new paragraph, block moves and page formatting. The editor has been designed to work on both cursive and ascii text. The output document from the editor is directed to a character recogniser for recognition purposes. The choice of gestures and their recognition is described and discussion of the user acceptability given.

Keywords: Gestures, Text editing, Electronic paper

1. Introduction

The classic method of interaction with the computer is the keyboard. However, this does not provide a very natural human-computer interface, and so there has been increasing interest shown in 'drawn' and 'pointing' input. These have been developed following the belief that user productivity is enhanced by the ability to operate directly on graphical objects by touching them (Shneiderman [1987]). Although these methods of input go some way to providing a more natural interface, they all fail when some unpredictable input is required. Therefore, in an editing situation, use is limited, and the only method of inputing new text is via the keyboard. The use of gestures may cause a further increase in the user productivity since it will allow a command to be indicated along with its arguments (Wolf & Morrel-Samuels [1987]). However, if it were possible to mix the gestural input with handwritten input, the result would be an even simpler and much more natural interface between the user and the machine. The present editor has been designed with the above ideas in mind. It uses a set of symbols similar to those used in paper editing, that are drawn on to a data tablet using a stylus.

Previous work done in this field has been limited, but also very varied in the approaches to the solution.

Doster and Oed (Doster & Oed [1984]) have developed a word processing package. Their tablet and stylus combination allows input of characters, commands and cursor control. The cursor is positioned and then a command or text input. Any symbol input via the stylus is translated into the keyboard sequence associated with the word processing package.

Konneker (Konneker [1984]) describes a simple syntactic method for on-line recognition of gestures. These gestures are made with a stylus on a tablet. The implementation of the gestures to an editing system is then shown.

Coleman (Coleman [1969]) implemented a simple text editor based on hand-drawn proofreaders symbols. The symbols are drawn on a data tablet and recognised by passing various characteristics through a decision tree.

More recently a group at IBM have started to study the use of hand-drawn gestures for simple editing tasks. Wolf and Morrel-Samuels (Wolf [1986]; Wolf & Morrel-Samuels [1987]) have done a pen and paper study of editing gestures. They believe that people behave in a way that makes gesture-driven interfaces feasible. Their experiments showed a good intra-subject consistency and fairly high inter-subject consistency, when using gestures for editing paper documents. Rhyne (Rhyne [1987]) explains some of the results obtained by the group as they undertake to build a prototype system.

The editor presented in this paper differs significantly from the majority of those described above. Like the IBM system it is designed to be used by anyone regardless of their expertise. It uses only input from a pen moving across a datapad to avoid the necessity of the user switching back and forth between the pen and the keyboard. The editor works in real time, the updated version of the document appearing immediately, after the symbol has been recognised and acted upon. There are some differences from the IBM system, in this editor we have attempted to relax the constraint on the user to make very accurate marks. For instance, our tests showed that users found it easier to mark the start and the end of an irregular area of text, than to circle it.

2. Data Input

The ideal system for the editor is the electronic paper – a thin flat display on which the stylus is used directly. However, at present our system is based on a datapad/stylus combination together with a conventional display. All input to the editor is made by the stylus moving on the surface of the data pad. This combination is used like a pen and paper. The text is displayed on the screen, together with a small cursor that tracks the stylus's movement. The user can therefore see the position of his pen in relation to the script. The position of the stylus at any given time is recorded as a co-ordinate pair. Therefore, a stroke is a string of these pairs.

3. The Editing Symbols

To help decide on the symbols a small experiment was carried out. Each of 38 subjects were given a copy of a document and asked to carry out a number of editing operations. These included delete word, insert word, insert character, move block plus some others.

The most popular symbols used for each of the editing tasks are shown in Figure 1, in their context. Some of the others symbols used are also indicated.

To make the system as user friendly as possible other symbols have been included in the recognition procedures. For instance, a double line and a cross will also be recognised as delete symbols.

Figure 1. Editing Symbols.

4. Symbol Recognition

The software that collects data from the tablet is designed to recognise when the stylus is off the tablet. This information is recorded as a negative co-ordinate, the magnitude of which is representative of the time that the stylus is raised. As a symbol is drawn, the co-ordinates of its strokes are stored in an array. The completion of an edit is at present signaled by a pause. If after a time, t, from the moment when the stylus left the surface of the tablet, there has been no further input, the data stored in the array is tested. At present t is approximately 3 seconds, i.e., the user must wait 3 seconds after drawing a symbol before it is recognised and acted upon. The time delay t, is partly machine dependent since the system is being developed on a multi-user machine with all the associated overheads. The time has been chosen after making observations of people creating and editing documents. Whilst it is relatively easy to mark a delete, when inserting some text the user may pause between writing words to consider what to write next. Also it can give the user time to change his mind and cancel the symbol and therefore its effect. It is expected that when such a editor is implemented on a single user microcomputer that the time t will be less than the value chosen at present.

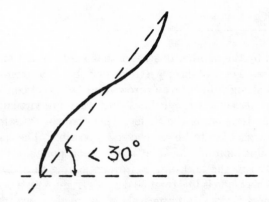

Figure 2. Horizontal Strokes.

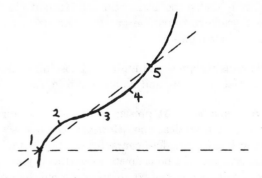

Figure 4. Segment Gradient.

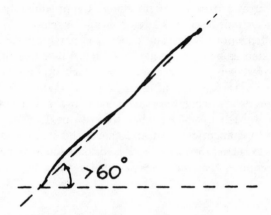

Figure 3.   Vertical Strokes.

Symbols are recognised by the number of strokes that they contain and the types of the strokes. For instance, a stroke may be a horizontal straight line, a vertical straight line, or an arrow head. In practice the symbols cannot contain perfectly straight lines since they are virtually impossible to draw using the pen on the tablet. Therefore the tests for recognising the stroke types have to be as relaxed as possible. The test horizontal and vertical lines initially looks at the two end points of the strokes. The angle, taken to the horizontal, of a line joining these two points is calculated. If this angle is less than 30 degrees (Figure 2), a test for horizontal straightness is done, alternatively if the angle is greater than 60 degrees, a test for vertical straightness is carried out (Figure 3). The tests for straightness consider segments within the stroke. A stroke segment is taken to be five consecutive co-ordinates. In the horizontal test, if all the segment gradients (Figure 4) are less than or equal to 45 degrees then the stroke is said to be horizontal and straight. In the vertical test, all segment gradients must be greater than or equal to 45 degrees to be classified as straight.

At present the set of symbols recognised is limited. Those allowed are catagorized in terms of stroke numbers, and details given in Table 1.

Considering the one stroke symbols. At present it is just a matter of testing for a horizontal line or a vertical one. However, the new set of symbols will use a vertical line for a delete character symbol as well as a split symbol. A horizontal line will be a delete as well as a join. To distinguish between these pairs some context information will be used. The position of the symbol in relation to the characters and words gives this information. If a vertical stroke is found that covers a character the user is trying to delete that character, whereas if the stroke is between

Table 1.   The Set of Recognised Editing Symbols.

No. of Strokes	Editing Symbol
1 stroke	join ——
	split
2 strokes	delete word
	insert one stroke
	new paragraph
3 strokes	insert two strokes
4 strokes	insert three strokes
5 strokes	delete phrase
	move phrase
	insert four strokes
6+ strokes	insert five+ strokes

two characters a split is implied. With the horizontal line, the position of the end points of the stroke in relation to the words is used. For a join symbol, the stroke ends will appear close to the end of one of the words and close to the start of the next adjacent word

DEVEL~~OP   ME~~NT

whilst for a delete

~~DEVELOP   MEN~~T

the stroke must cover a larger part of the words. Context will be used in a similar way for the identification of the other sets of symbols.

Figures 5 and 6 are screen dumps taken during an editing session. In Figure 5 the user has drawn two strokes through the word 'development'. Figure 6 shows the result of the edit, the strokes have been recognised as a delete symbol and the word removed.

5. Conclusion

The system at present has been used by six users. Their reactions have been noted. It was found that the system was easy to use once they became accustomed to the fact that they must write on the tablet and watch the results appear on the screen. This problem will obviously be overcome by using the system on an electronic paper. This would more nearly mimic the pen and paper operations by allowing the display of input and output simultaneously beneath the pen. This paper describes a system which is not yet complete. It is designed to work with text files containing ascii characters, cursive script or a mixture of both. The idea is to be able to write a piece of script cursively, make any necessary

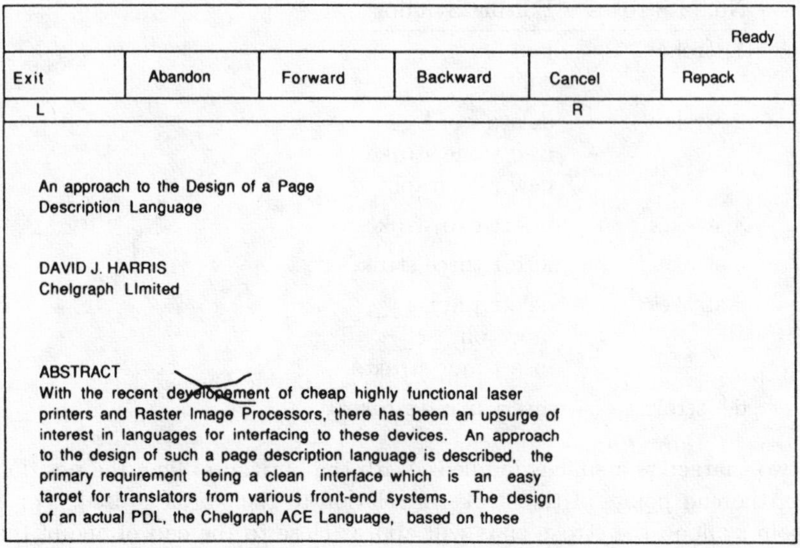

					Ready
Exit	Abandon	Forward	Backward	Cancel	Repack

L   R

An approach to the Design of a Page
Description Language

DAVID J. HARRIS
Chelgraph LImited

ABSTRACT
With the recent development of cheap highly functional laser
printers and Raster Image Processors, there has been an upsurge of
interest in languages for interfacing to these devices. An approach
to the design of such a page description language is described, the
primary requirement being a clean interface which is an easy
target for translators from various front-end systems.   The design
of an actual PDL, the Chelgraph ACE Language, based on these

Figure 5.

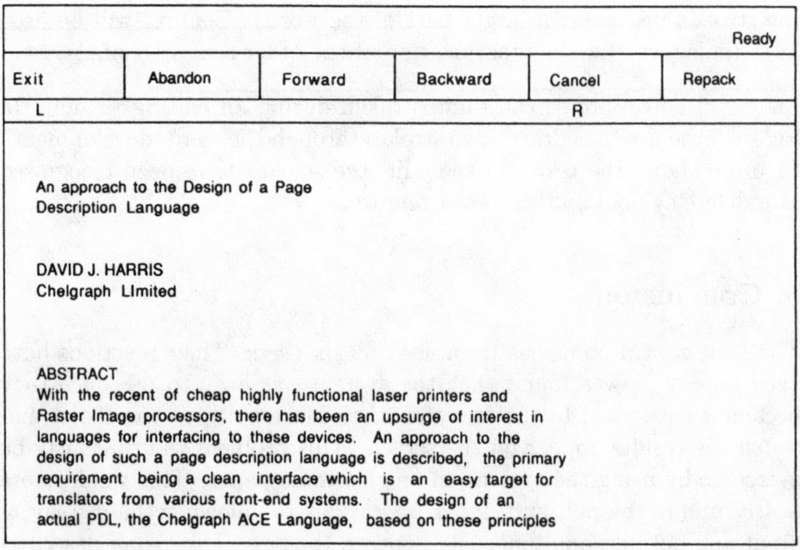

					Ready
Exit	Abandon	Forward	Backward	Cancel	Repack

L   R

An approach to the Design of a Page
Description Language

DAVID J. HARRIS
Chelgraph LImited

ABSTRACT
With the recent of cheap highly functional laser printers and
Raster Image processors, there has been an upsurge of interest in
languages for interfacing to these devices. An approach to the
design of such a page description language is described, the primary
requirement being a clean interface which is an easy target for
translators from various front-end systems.   The design of an
actual PDL, the Chelgraph ACE Language, based on these principles

Figure 6.

corrections and pass the result to a character recogniser. The output from the recogniser can then be edited again using the same editor and the process repeated until the text file is in the required form.

Acknowledgment

This work was supported by the European Strategic Programme of Research in Information Technology (ESPRIT) Project 295, entitled "The Paper Interface".

References

M L Coleman [1969], "Text Editing on a Graphic Display Device Using Hand-drawn Proofreader's Symbols," in *Proceedings of the 2nd Univ. Illinois Conference on Computer Graphics*, 282–290.

W Doster & R Oed [October 1984], "Word Processing with On-Line Script Recognition," *IEEE Micro*.

L K Konneker [December 1984], "A Graphical Interaction Technique Which Uses Gestures," *IEEE 1st Int. Conference on Office Automation*.

J Rhyne [1987], "Dialogue Management for Gestural Interfaces," *ACM Computer Graphics* 21, 137–142.

B Shneiderman [1987], *Designing the User Interface: Strategies for Effective Human-Computer Interaction*, Addison-Wesley, Reading MA.

C G Wolf [October 1986], "Can People Use Gesture Commands?," *ACM SIGCHI Bulletin* 18, 73–74.

C G Wolf & P Morrel-Samuels [1987], "The Use of Hand-Drawn Gestures for Text Editing," *Int. J. Man-Machine Studies*.

Towards The Construction of a Maximally-Contrasting Set of Colours

Darren Van Laar & Richard Flavell

Colour In Displays Unit, The Management School, Imperial College, London SW7 2PG

Two experiments are reported. The first investigates the relationship between hue, lightness and saturation in determining colour contrast in displays, the second examines the effect of surrounding and adjacent colours on the perception of stimuli in colour displays. All subjects taking part in the experiments had normal colour vision. Hue difference between stimuli was found to exert the biggest single effect on colour contrast, with similar hues being discriminated significantly more slowly than different hues. Lightness difference also produced a significant effect in the same direction. Saturation effects were surprising in that more similar saturations were associated with significantly faster reaction times. In the second experiment strong brightness and hue context (induction) effects were observed but effects due to target size and saturation did not reach significance. The relevance of these findings to designers of colour displays is discussed.

Keywords: Colour Displays, Contrast Effects, Information Display, Psychophysics

1. Introduction

In order for the design of colour information displays to be effective, designers of both quantitative and qualitative colour displays need access to a perceptually maximally-contrasting set of colours. Such a set would allow colour codes to be easily distinguished and reduce the number of errors arising from confusions of colour codes.

Whilst colour contrast effects have been extensively studied this work is not usually applicable to the use of colour on Cathode Ray Tube (CRT) displays for two main reasons. Firstly, many experiments exploring colour perception have not used CRT screens but monochromatic light sources or paper and ink stimuli. These differ markedly from the emissive display technology used in CRTs. Many workers cast doubt on the unqualified use of results from such experiments (Mollon & Cavonius [1984]; Murch, Cranford & McManus [1973]; Walraven [1984]).

Secondly, more recent work employing emissive displays often does not precisely specify the colours used, so that the work is simply not replicable. It is insufficient to describe a displayed colour as 'red' for example, because a colour generated by a particular display system will vary from that seen on other systems, and even from other monitors within the same product range. The work carried out in the present series of experiments is being completed under carefully controlled conditions, with the colours employed being measured with precision using a telespectroradiometer.

1.1. The Discrimination Of Contrasting Colours

Stimuli which have a high contrast ratio are discriminated faster than those which have a lower contrast ratio (Coren, Porac & Ward [1979]; Hemnon [1906]). One way to make information sets more easily distinguishable is to ensure a high colour contrast between them. Performance in both quantitative and qualitative colour tasks may in theory be improved if contrast between colour codes is kept high. Contrast effects will influence many tasks and types of tasks. These are summarised in Table 1.

There are two major perceptual factors affecting colour contrast on displays in people with normal colour vision, these are 'magnitude' effects and 'context' effects.

Table 1   Tasks affected by contrast effects

1. **Qualitative tasks** (coded by differences in type)
   a. Highlighting   (e.g., coding error messages)
   b. Discrimination   (e.g., reading text)
   c. Relating   (e.g., using colour-coded columns in tables)

2. **Quantitative tasks** (coded by differences in kind)
   a. Absolute colour judgements   (What value is this colour ?)
   b. Relative colour judgements   (By what value do these
                                                        colours differ ?)

1.2. Magnitude Effects

Any colour can be specified precisely by values along three dimensions. Taken together these dimensions describe a colour space. One way of describing a colour space is in terms of hue angle (H°), lightness (L%), and saturation (S%) (Murch [1987]). The relative distance between two colours in this space will determine the colour contrast of these colours. That is, the more two colours differ along one or even all three of these dimensions, the more discriminable they become. Note that 'lightness' as defined in HLS space is not correlated exactly with 'brightness', which is the perceived intensity of a stimulus.

Studies looking at the rate and extent of perceived differences along these dimensions have given rise to a number of colour spaces which are in theory perceptually uniform (Hunt [1987]). However these spaces, such as the C.I.E. L u'v' space do not accurately predict the discrimination time between colours on CRTs (Mollon & Cavonius [1984]). Display designers need evidence of the relative effect of hue, lightness and saturation on colour contrast in order to provide easily discriminable information sets for colour displays.

1.3. Context Effects

A major problem with complex colour coded displays is that the perceived colour of any particular code member is determined not only by the voltages applied to the electron guns, but also the colour and size of surrounding or adjacent colours. It is especially important to be able to gauge the effects of surround colours on a screen when dealing with absolute colour judgements, or cases when fine colour discriminations are necessary.

Colour context effects, sometimes called chromatic induction or colour contrast effects, are due to a number of different processes often operating at the same time (Walraven [1973]; Werner & Walraven [1982]). The two dominant context effects are known as simultaneous colour contrast effects, and colour adaptation effects. Whilst the first of these is an instantaneous neuronal response to coloured edges, the second is due to prolonged fatigue in the colour response of the eye.

An example of a brightness context effect would be an object which appears to be brighter or darker because it is viewed on a dark or light background respectively. Hue contrast effects tend to make an object appear to take on the complementary hue to that of a surrounding or adjacent colour (Jameson & Hurvich [1964]). In this way blue colours will induce a change towards yellow, red colours towards green. The actual extent to which this effect occurs is related to the size and separation of the adjacent or 'inducing' area of colour (Walraven [1973]).

1.4. Summary

In order to determine exactly how a colour will be perceived on a CRT display it is necessary to collect two types of data. The first type is the effect of the magnitude of hue, saturation and lightness of an object in a display, the second the context effect of other colours in the display.

2. Experiment 1: Magnitude Effect Experiment

At least one widely quoted study (using 8 unspecified CRT colours) has suggested that legibility of coloured text on VDUs is primarily determined by brightness contrast (Bruce & Foster [1982]). However the conclusion seems inappropriate as this, and other studies, have not systematically considered the effects of hue, lightness and saturation, but only unknown mixtures of all three. The aim of this experiment is to determine the extent to which the response time to coloured objects in a forced-choice discrimination design would be related to the hue, saturation, and lightness differences between pairs of coloured stimuli. Another aim is to discover the effect of target size on colour contrast, with differences in colour between smaller sizes hypothesised as being less easily perceived than those with larger sizes.

2.1. Design

The experiment was of a $3^7 \times 81 \times 27$ factorial design, with all main effects and 2 factor interactions unconfounded with subjects and times. There were 27 ($3 \times 3 \times 3$) different colours used in the experiment. The experimental conditions consisted of:

      a.   3 levels of target size (small, medium and large).

For the left-hand side there were,

      b.   3 levels of saturation, (25%, 50%, 75%),

    c.   3 levels of lightness, (25%, 50%, 75%),

    d.   3 levels of hue, (120°, 240°, 360° (or 0°)),

and for the right-hand side,

    e.   3 levels of saturation, (25%, 50%, 75%),

    f.   3 levels of lightness, (25%, 50%, 75%),

    g.   3 levels of hue, (120°, 240°, 360° (or 0°)).

This gives 7 display variables each at 3 levels, one subjects variable with 27 levels, and a time or trials variable with 81 levels. The subjects' task was to respond to pairs of coloured stimuli presented to them by pressing one of two keys, labelled 'SAME' or 'DIFFERENT' according to whether the pair of colours were exactly the same (in terms of H, L and S) or not. The time taken to respond to each of the combinations was recorded, as were the type and number of errors made by each subject.

The target size was set at 0.5° of horizontal visual field for the small size condition, 2.5° of field for the medium condition, and 5° for the large condition. Each target had a horizontal to vertical length ratio of 1 : 1.5. Figure 1 shows a schematic diagram of the experimental display. Pairs of stimuli were always of the same target size. The background colour in all cases was a medium grey, (H° = undefined, L% = 50, S% = 0).

2.2. Subjects

27 (16M, 11F) colour normal (as measured by the Ishihara colour blindness test) volunteer subjects took part in the experiment. The mean age of these subjects was 29.26 years old, with a standard deviation of 7.07 years. All subjects were either students or staff at London University. Every subject had satisfactory or corrected eyesight for the task. Subjects were assigned randomly to conditions.

2.3. Apparatus

Conditions under which colours were viewed were designed to be a compromise between typical psychophysical laboratory study conditions and an office-like environment. The pairs of colours were presented on a 14″ Mitsubushi AT14 high-resolution monitor, driven by a Pluto graphics driver and illuminated by Northlight 55 flourescent tubes. The chromaticity coordinates for the three phosphors (and white), are shown in Table 2.

All colour measurements were made under experimental illumination conditions using a Bentham M300E telespectroradiometer. Illuminance, measured by an AVO 4 illuminance meter held in front of the display, was approximately 280 lux.

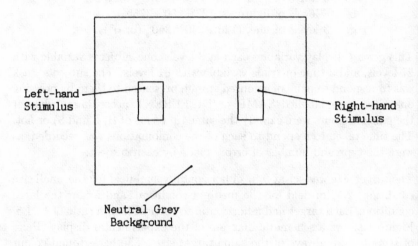

Figure 1   Schematic diagram of display setup, showing medium sized target condition

Table 2	Phosphor chromaticity coordinates		
Phosphor	x	y	$Y(log_{10}Cd/M^2)$
Red	0.63	0.33	1.56
Green	0.20	0.70	1.88
Blue	0.155	0.06	0.96
(White)	0.31	0.33	1.99

2.4. Procedure

Each subject was presented with 81 pairs of colours of which approximately 40% were the same. The whole experimental session lasted about 30 minutes, with approximately 15 minutes being taken up with training, 10 minutes with the experimental presentations. After 40 trials subjects were given a break of 1 minute.

3. Results: Magnitude Effect Experiment

The overall average time taken to respond to the pairs of colours was 778 milliseconds (msec), with a standard deviation of 349 msec. Errors were of two types: clerical errors (1.28% of all responses) where the subject had pressed the wrong key by mistake, and true errors (1.37% of all responses) where subjects did not realise that their response was inaccurate. A significant difference was found with a t-test between 'SAME' (mean = 888 msec) and 'DIFFERENT' (mean = 703 msec) responses overall, t with 2185 df = 12.56 ($p \leq 0.001$). Only the 'DIFFERENT' response data was employed in the rest of the analysis as the experiment is primarily concerned with the response to relative colour differences between stimuli.

3.1. Subjects And Trials Effects

There was a significant difference in response time observed between subjects, (F (26.1291) = 17.53, $p < 0.001$), but a non-significant difference over trials, (F (80.1237) < 1, $p > 0.05$). This indicates how subjects differed in their basic reaction times, but probably did not experience systematic learning or fatigue effects over time (i.e., over the 81 trials).

3.2. Colour Conditions

The principle summary results are presented in Table 3. No significant differences occur between left or right hue conditions nor between left or right lightness or saturation conditions. However the elements on the principal diagonal, (those in bold) in Table 3 differ significantly from the off diagonal elements. That is, significant differences are observed between those conditions where the SAME condition level occurs in both members of a stimulus pair, (e.g., where left saturation = 25% and right saturation = 25%), and those where levels of left and right conditions differ. These results are considered in detail below.

When hue conditions are the same for both sides the average reaction time (798 msec) is significantly longer than when the hue condition differs on each side, (662 msec), (F (1.1316) = 55.56, $p < 0.001$). When lightness conditions are the same (mean = 772 msec), they are also significantly longer than when lightness differs on each side (mean = 673 msec.), (F (1.1316) = 29.4, $p < 0.001$). However with saturation data the opposite effect occurs, as the same saturation conditions in both of the stimuli pair are significantly faster (mean = 667 msec) than when saturation differs between sides (mean = 719 msec), (F (1.1316) = 8.05, $p < 0.0046$).

Overall the Hamming distance between left and right side conditions shows a highly significant difference, with more similar pairs of colours associated with longer response times, (F (2.1315) = 20.46, $p < 0.001$).

Table 3   Average reaction times in milliseconds by left and right hue, saturation and lightness conditions

		Right Hue Condition		
		120°	240°	360°
Left	120°	**805**	647	652
Hue	240°	690	**835**	661
Condition	360°	653	670	**753**

		Right Lightness Condition		
		25%	50%	75%
Left	25%	**842**	670	668
Lightness	50%	662	**713**	706
Condition	75%	642	690	**763**

		Right Saturation Condition		
		25%	50%	75%
Left	25%	**682**	722	717
Saturation	50%	726	**650**	719
Condition	75%	752	675	**668**

Table 4   Average time by target condition with *post hoc* comparison differences

	Target Condition (TCond)		
	Sml	Med	Lge
TCond. Code	0	1	2
Mean (msec.)	770	676	664
SNK code	1,2	0	0

Key: SNK - Code of target significantly
from the present target condition.

3.3. Target Size Conditions

A significant difference was observed between target size conditions (F (2.1315) = 15.62, $p < 0.001$). Table 4 shows the means and significance of results between conditions, as calculated using the Student Newman-Keuls procedure at the 5% level of significance.

4. Experiment 2: Colour Context Experiment

The aim of this experiment is to confirm whether or not colour contrast effects actually occur with CRT screens. This is operationalized by determining what effect differing surround colours have on matching the colour of two displayed inner rectangles. From evidence available from previous work in the literature the hypotheses were as follows:

1. That colours surrounded by a lighter background would be seen as darker than they actually are, and that those colours surrounded by a darker background should appear brighter than they really are.

2. A target surrounded by a coloured background should be perceived as taking on the properties of the complementary hue of that background.

3. The changes in lightness and hue will be related to the relative size of the background and target colours, with perceived differences being greater with smaller targets than larger targets.

4.1. Design

The design of the experiment was based on a $9 \times 3^4 \times 2$ factorial experiment, with all main effects and certain 2 factor interactions unconfounded with subjects and times. There were 81 ($3 \times 3 \times 9$) different surround colours used in the experiment and three target colours. Note that the colour combinations used in this experiment are a superset of those used in experiment 1. The independent variables consisted of:

a. 2 levels of screen side, (left or right).

b. 3 levels of target size, (small, medium and large).

c. 3 levels of target colour, (grey, green and purple).

d. 3 levels of surround colour saturation, (25%, 50%, 75%).

e. 3 levels of surround colour lightness, (25%, 50%, 75%).

f. 9 levels of surround colour hue, (360° (or 0°) to 320° in 40° steps).

The dependent variables in this experiment were time taken to match the colours in seconds, and the difference in hue, lightness and saturation between each matched pair.

4.2. Subjects

36 subjects with normal colour vision (27M, 9F), took part in the experiment. The mean age of these subjects was 28.97 years old, with a standard deviation of 6.66 years. All subjects were from the same subject pool as experiment 1.

Table 5   Chromaticites and HLS values of target colours

	Target Colour		
Metric	Grey	Green	Purple
x	0.32	0.36	0.29
y	0.30	0.41	0.22
$Y(log_{10} Cd/M^2)$	1.13	1.01	1.40
H	undefined	85°	265°
L	45%	36%	64%
S	0%	18%	28%

4.3. Apparatus

All apparatus and materials were the same as, or variations upon that used in experiment 1. The colour graphics monitor and software were set up to provide descriptions of screen colours in terms of H, L and S (Foley & Dam [1982, p 617]). The subject could change the amount of hue, lightness and saturation in the match square. See Figure 2.

The matching rectangle at the start of each trial was set to a medium sized white rectangle on a neutral grey background, (the same background colour as used in experiment 1). The three target colours were picked to give a wide sample of hue, saturation and lightness effects. These colours approximated to a medium grey, a purple, and a brown-green (see Table 5).

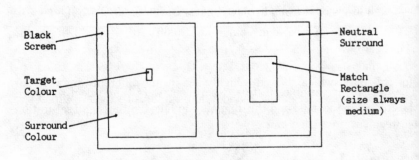

Figure 2   Schematic representation of typical matching screen arrangement showing small target size

4.4. Procedure

The training phase of the experiment lasted approximately 30 minutes, during which subjects were taught how to use the computer to change the colour of the matching rectangle in HLS space. Between each match presentation subjects were given 10 seconds for their eyes to readapt to a neutral grey coloured piece of card.

All subjects completed 18 trials in all, and had a 4 minute break between trials 9 and 10 in order to decrease fatigue effects. The time from when subjects entered the cubicle, to when subjects left after debriefing was approximately 90 minutes.

5. Results: Colour Context Experiment

Because of space limitations only the results for one target colour, grey, will be described in this paper. In the first section data concerning brightness contrast will be discussed and in the second section the hue shift results will be reported.

5.1. Brightness Contrast Data

Table 6 shows the matched lightness values, in L%, for each condition. Note that the grey target subjects were trying to match to had an associated lightness value of 45%.

There was a highly significant difference between surround lightness conditions, $(F(2.207) = 9.82, p < 0.001)$. An inspection of Table 6 shows that with dark surrounds, targets were matched as lighter than medium backgrounds, which in turn were matched as lighter than matches for those with light surrounds. The range of match scores between target size conditions (range = 1.78%) was very small when compared with those between surround lightness conditions, (range = 15.2%).

The greater variation between lightness conditions is borne out by a 3×3 analysis of variance (ANOVA) with unequal group sizes calculated for this data, which showed a highly significant difference between surround lightnesses (see above), and a non-significant value for target size, $(F(2.207) < 1, p > 0.05)$. An ANOVA for the interaction between surround lightness and target size was also non-significant, $(F(4.207) < 1, p > 0.05)$. The overall mean lightness match was calculated as 43.39%. The smallest lightness change possible in the experiment was by 1%.

5.2. Hue Difference Data

When colours are totally unsaturated no hue can be identified. The grey target colour was totally unsaturated, $(S = 0\%)$. Of the 216 grey target

Table 6   Mean lightness matches (L%), to grey targets for all surround lightness and target size conditions

Size		Surround Lightness Dark	Medium	Light	$\bar{X}$	Σ_n
Sm	$\bar{x}$	52.0	41.96	33.28	42.41	72
	sd	4.4	4.0	7.0		
	n	18	29	25		
Med	$\bar{x}$	52.25	41.1	37.42	43.59	72
	sd	5.27	3.12	3.57		
	n	31	20	21		
Lge	$\bar{x}$	50.78	43.08	38.73	44.19	72
	sd	2.71	2.55	2.55		
	n	23	23	26		
	$\bar{X}$	51.67	42.0	36.47	$X_{..}$	=43.388
					N	=216
	Σ_n	72	72	72		

colour matches, 91 (42%) were saturated to some extent. This means that the subject had needed to incorporate some hue in order to achieve a match to the grey target colour with coloured surround.

Differences in hue between the surround and the subjects' matches were calculated. These figures were in turn transformed into differences from 180°, (this being the predicted difference in hue, as complementary colours will appear on opposite sides of the hue circle). A frequency distribution of this data is given in Figure 3, which shows the highest number of scores, (84, or 92.3%) falling between 0° and ± 90° from 180°. In the other half of the circle between ± 91° and ± 180° (i.e., towards the actual hue of the surround), only 7 scores were observed (7.7%).

As the hue difference data was made up of only those matches with greater than 0% saturation, the number of cases observed for each condition was unbalanced. Table 7 shows the number of observed saturated matches to grey targets for surround lightness, surround saturation and target size. A χ^2 test was carried out on the frequency data in Table 7 pooled into a 3 × 3 matrix, but was non-significant, (χ^2 with 4df = 0.37, $p > 0.05$).

6. Discussion

The discussion will first consider the results of the magnitude effects experiment, then go on to look at the colour context experiment before ending with general comments.

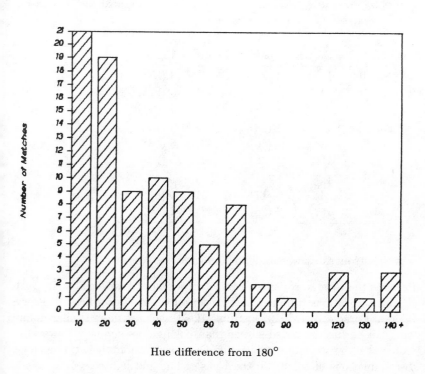

Hue difference from 180°

**Figure 3   Frequency histogram to show the spread of
hue matches about 180°**

6.1. Magnitude Effects Experiment

The discriminability of the pairs of colours presented to subjects was very
highly related to the magnitude of the difference in hue, lightness and
saturation between stimuli. There is a marked difference between mean
response times when the hue, lightness and saturation conditions are the
same and when these conditions are different between left and right sides.
The difference between means for when hue is the same on both sides
and when hue is different on both sides is 135 msec, for lightness 99 msec
and for saturation 52 msec. It may be concluded from these figures that
differences in hue are the biggest potential factor in determining colour
contrast effects, followed by lightness then saturation differences. This
result goes against the findings of Bruce and Foster (Bruce & Foster
[1982]), who, in a more limited study, suggested that brightness contrast

Table 7   **Frequency of saturated matches by surround lightness, target size (Size), and surround saturation (Surr S) with low, medium, and high saturation levels.**

N.B. Figures in brackets are frequencies of saturated matches as a percentage of total matches for each combination

Size	Surr S	Surround Lightness Dark	Medium	Light	Σ
Small	L	3 (37)	5 (63)	3 (37)	
	M	2 (50)	7 (54)	6 (67)	38
	H	4 (67)	5 (63)	3 (37)	
Medium	L	4 (33)	1 (33)	3 (33)	
	M	4 (50)	5 (63)	5 (63)	35
	H	2 (18)	8 (89)	3 (75)	
Large	L	1 (11)	3 (37)	1 (17)	
	M	1 (17)	2 (25)	1 (8)	18
	H	2 (25)	3 (43)	4 (50)	
Σ =		23	39	29	91

was the strongest factor in determining colour contrast.

Perhaps the most surprising result of experiment 1 was that pairs with similar saturations produce faster reaction times. According to theory, (Coren, Porac & Ward [1979]; Hunt [1987]), colours more similar in any way will be discriminated slower than colours less similar. However it seems that if two stimuli have the same saturation then this enables discriminations of colour on the basis of hue and lightness to be made faster. This has implications for current colour use guidelines in that it should not matter what saturation level colours possess when displayed on a screen, as long as they have the same level of saturation. That is, similar saturation levels will enhance the discriminability of colours based on hue and lightness dimensions. Although there is no previous evidence to support this finding the effect was strongly significant ($p < 0.0046$) which at least seems to recommend that the phenomenon should be studied in greater detail.

The observation that target size is related to ease of discrimination holds with our initial hypothesis that smaller targets should be associated with slower reaction times than larger targets.

6.2. Colour Context Experiment

The effect of surround lightness on the perceived lightness of the target was dramatic, ($p < 0.001$). Dark surrounds made the target in all 3 size conditions appear lighter than they were in physical terms, as predicted.

The light surround condition caused targets to appear darker than they were in reality for every target size, again this is in agreement with the first hypothesis. The medium surround was set at 50% lightness, which is lighter than the target by 5%. According to hypothesis 1, targets in this condition should be seen as darker than they actually were, but not by such a large factor as occurred with the light surround condition, (where L = 75%). This part of the hypothesis was also supported, with all three target size means for medium lightness backgrounds being within 4% of the target, and with each one darker than the actual target lightness. The first hypothesis is therefore supported for all three surround lightness conditions.

Hypothesis 2, which stated that the target should be perceived as taking on a hue complementary to that of the surround is also supported. 92.3% of all observed differences were between 0° and ± 90° away from 180°. The third hypothesis is split into two parts. The first postulates differences in perceived lightness due to target size, the second differences in perceived hue due to target size.

In an analysis of variance conducted on the lightness data, target size was not found to significantly affect lightness matches. An inspection of the means of the data did show a trend within the data toward the predicted result. For example, smaller target sizes should increase the magnitude of the effect due to surround lightness. This does occur with light backgrounds, the darkest mean match being observed with small targets, the least dark, (and therefore the least affected), being with large target sizes, as predicted.

In a 3×3 χ^2 test there were no significant differences between frequencies of the number of saturated matches for target size or surround lightness. However, there were almost twice as many small targets matched with saturated colours than large targets. This shows that targets surrounded by relatively smaller induction fields tend to be less affected by lightness and hue contrast effects, although these tendencies are not significant. Hypothesis 3 must therefore be regarded as not supported.

The lightness contrast effect observed was very strong, even though lightness does not correlate exactly with brightness, with which this type of effect is usually associated. Possible explanations for this are that people intuitively had a feel for the lightness dimension in HLS space, or that lightness and brightness are highly correlated, at least with the particular equipment used. Where subjects did require some non-neutral colour to match the target, there is good evidence to suggest that the matched hue will be approximately complementary to the hue of the background. This effect was well represented across all surround hues.

Whilst target size was not significantly associated with hue contrast or lightness contrast effects, the data did tend in the direction of the hypothesis. It is possible that target size effects were swamped by the much stronger lightness contrast effect within the data. Another explanation could be that the viewing conditions, or colour stimuli were not especially suited to target size effects. However the large effects of lightness and colour contrast did not seem to be adversely affected by viewing conditions.

6.3. General Discussion

Given that tasks may be improved by the appropriate use of colour in displays the next step should be to determine which particular colour or colours, out of the total colour gamut available on a display, should be used. Here, a knowledge of colour contrast effects is important to ensure that the colours displayed are easily distinguishable from each other (where this is desired). Application of this knowledge should improve the effectiveness of the colour coding technique used.

The major objective of this series of experiments has been to derive guidelines for determining perceived colour contrast effects and how they ought to be used to colour code information.

The findings for experiment 1 suggest that colours that need to be discriminated quickly should be as far apart in hue and lightness as possible, but near in saturation. The size of the stimuli to be discriminated should also be as large as is practicable.

It seems from experiment 2 that previous findings about brightness and hue context effects can be generalised to colour visual displays. We may conclude from the colour context experiment that perception of the lightness and hue of objects on a display by people with normal colour vision is affected greatly by the lightness and hue of surrounding and adjacent colours.

The next step in this work is to use the data gained from this and other experiments to produce a comprehensive theory of colour use on VDUs. This theory will be based on knowledge of magnitude and context effects as well as principles of information design. This will allow the designer not only to choose from a palette of maximally-contrasting CRT colours, but also to identify the tasks in which the use of colour coded information is likely to be beneficial.

Acknowledgement

Thanks are due to Dr. Linda White of the Department of Mathematics, Imperial College, for help with the experimental design.

References

M Bruce & J J Foster [1982], "The Visibility of Coloured Characters on Coloured Backgrounds in Viewdata Displays," *Visible Language* XVI, 382–390.

S Coren, C Porac & L M Ward [1979], *Sensation and Perception*, Academic Press, London.

J D Foley & A van Dam [1982], *Fundamentals of Interactive Computer Graphics*, Addison-Wesley, Reading MA, Reprinted with corrections 1984.

V A C Hemnon [1906], "The Time of Perception as a Measure of Differences in Sensations," *Archives of Philosophy, Psychology and Scientific Methods* 8.

R W G Hunt [1987], *Measuring Colour*, Ellis Horwood, Chichester.

D Jameson & L M Hurvich [1964], "Theory of Brightness and Color Contrast in Human Vision," *Vision Research* 4, 135–154.

J D Mollon & C R Cavonius [1984], "Derivation of a Uniform Colour Space from Discriminative Reaction Times," in *IERE International Conference on Colour in Information Technology and Visual Displays*, University of Surrey, 27–31.

G M Murch [1987], "Color Displays and Color Science," in *Color and the Computer*, H J Durrett, ed., Academic Press, 27–62.

G M Murch, M Cranford & P McManus [1973], "Brightness and Color Contrast of Information Displays," in *SID International Symposium*, Society for Information Display, Philadelphia, 168–169.

J Walraven [1973], "Spatial Characteristics of Chromatic Induction: The Segregation of Lateral Effects from Straylight Artifacts," *Vision Research* 11, 1739–1753.

J Walraven [1984], "Perceptual Artifacts that may Interfere with Colour Coding on Visual Displays," in *Proceedings of the Workshop on Colour Coded versus Monochrome Electronic Displays*.

J S Werner & J Walraven [1982], "Effect of Chromatic Adaptation on the Achromatic Locus: The Role of Contrast, Luminance and Background Color," *Vision Research* 22, 929–943.

Gripe: A Graphical Interface to a Knowledge Based System which Reasons about Protein Topology

Kathryn Seifert and Christopher Rawlings

Biomedical Computing Unit, Imperial Cancer Research Fund, Lincoln's Inn Fields, London WC2A 3PX, U.K.

GRIPE is an interactive graphical interface to a knowledge based system which reasons about the topological structure of proteins. The knowledge based system, TOPOL, derives symbolic, declarative representations of protein topology from the underlying three-dimensional coordinates of protein structural elements. The use of the topological representation rather than the complex three-dimensional displays provided by most molecular graphics systems is intended to make it easier for a biologist (or a computer program) to perceive certain kinds of structure and symmetry in proteins, thus easing analysis and comparison. In particular, the topological representation is useful for the detection of topological motifs, which are common folding patterns taken by the proteins. GRIPE was developed to facilitate the use of TOPOL by molecular biologists as it allows the user to

construct graphical queries about the presence of linear
and topological structures in selected proteins. GRIPE
also provides facilities for viewing the three dimensional
and topological structures of the proteins. The interface
provides an easy and effective way to examine protein
structure.

Keywords: Graphics, Interface, Knowledge-Based, Protein,
Topology, Prolog

1. Introduction

Biochemists make extensive use of graphical representations of protein structure in their work. Computer graphics are often used to
provide scientists with sophisticated three-dimensional representations
which allow them to view and manipulate protein structure (Blundell
& Sternberg [1985]). Special-purpose hardware is frequently required to
support the intensive computations necessary to provide such displays.
However, abstract topological representations of protein structure which
are not supported by conventional molecular graphics programs are also
available. Protein structure is very complex, and simplified, abstract
structural representations have been developed in the domain for illustrative or didactic purposes. Such topological representations are intended
to make it easier for a biologist to perceive certain kinds of structure
and symmetry in proteins, thus easing analysis and comparison. In
particular, the topological representation is useful for the detection of
topological motifs, which are common folding patterns taken by the
secondary structural elements of proteins.

GRIPE is an interactive, computer graphical system for protein examination which makes use of simple topological representations of protein
structure. GRIPE is an interface to a knowledge based system which
reasons about protein topology; this knowledge based system, called
TOPOL, derives symbolic representations of protein topology from the
underlying three- dimensional coordinates of protein structural elements
(Rawlings, Seifert & Saldanha [1987]; Rawlings et al. [1986]). A primary
goal in constructing GRIPE was the facilitation of the use of TOPOL
by domain experts, thereby increasing the acceptance of such advanced
computer tools in biochemistry. The system can reason about the
abstract topological structure of the protein based on this symbolic representation. The representation also makes possible the development of
a graphical query language which forms the basis of GRIPE. The system
enables the user to view the mappings between the simplified, abstract
representations and the more complex three-dimensional representations

of the proteins. The three-dimensional structure of proteins is their most important property, and the problem of automated three-dimensional spatial reasoning is still a largely unexplored and very difficult research issue in Artificial Intelligence. However, it is assumed that providing a way to view the answers to structural queries at different abstraction levels will increase the utility of the underlying system: even though the system cannot itself reason about three-dimensional structural relations, the user can benefit from seeing the relationship between the results of topological queries and the three dimensional structure of the protein.

2. A Graphical Interface for Protein Examination

The TOPOL system provides various levels of declarative description of protein structure, from the linear sequence of amino acids to the complex three-dimensional structure of the path traced by the protein backbone. The TOPOL knowledge base contains Prolog clauses describing the structure of 90 proteins. The system can be queried about the presence of topological patterns in a protein, and provides mappings between the various levels of structural description.

TOPOL is envisioned as eventually being a component knowledge-source of a much larger system which will bring together diverse information from several sources to predict protein structure. However, the system as it stands could also potentially be used by a molecular biologist in order to examine the known structure of proteins in the knowledge base and to make queries about the presence of structural motifs. Towards this end, GRIPE, an interactive graphical interface to TOPOL, has been developed.

Raw Prolog formed the original interface to TOPOL, which required that users be very familiar with Prolog to make queries to the system. For example, the following is a typical Prolog query asking whether a 'meander' motif overlaps a 'hairpin' motif in a protein:

?- meander(X, strands([A, B, C])), hairpin(Y, strands([Q, A])).

The overlapping relationship between the two motifs has been indicated implicitly using Prolog unification on the variables (indicated by capital letters) in the query. Thus, the user has asked whether there is a meander motif whose last strand is the same as the first strand of a hairpin motif (this common strand is indicated by the letter A). However, we cannot expect that most of the intended users of GRIPE will be sufficiently familiar with Prolog (or willing to learn the language) to understand and construct such queries. A linguistic interface to TOPOL was also considered, but linguistic or propositional descriptions of complex physical structures tend to be awkward and unwieldy. In addition, biochemists have become well acquainted with using computer graphics and visual representations to examine complex molecular structures. Thus, the nature of the domain dictated that a graphical interface would be more appropriate (Seifert [1987]).

GRIPE allows the user to construct topological motifs on the screen using icons representing the elements of protein secondary structure. The system can then be queried about the presence of such motifs in selected proteins. The topological relationships between the structural elements is represented using a version of a graphical representation of protein topology originally developed by biochemists. In GRIPE, a protein can be viewed from different grain or resolution levels, that is, the structure can be viewed as being constituted of elements of different sizes. The relationships between structural elements at different levels of resolution are displayed in the interface. The mapping between the graphical and internal representations of protein structure is facilitated by the fact that the topology of the proteins can be described by a few simple linear relations.

In the rest of this paper, some background to the area of protein structure is presented. The graphical representation of protein topology which forms the basis of GRIPE is then described, along with the principles behind the design of the interface, and the set of structural relations that can be represented by GRIPE. This set of structural relations needs to be extended in order to provide a more useful tool for biochemists. Thus, the paper concludes with an outline of these possible extensions to GRIPE and conclusions.

3. Levels of Protein Structure

Biochemists have found it useful to view protein structure at various levels characterised by the size or resolution of the structural elements taken as primitive at each level. These levels of structure can be organised into a hierarchy, with the units from the lower levels making up the units in the higher levels of the hierarchy. In this application, we are interested in three levels of protein structure: primary, secondary, and super-secondary structure.

The primary structural elements of protein structure are the amino acids. Proteins are large molecules made up of simple repeated units, each unit being one of twenty different amino acids. The protein molecule is a linear sequence of amino acids which folds into a complex three-dimensional structure. It is the precise three-dimensional structure which determines a protein's biological function.

Within the amino acid sequence of a protein are repeated structural features. These structural features comprise the secondary structure of the protein, and are characterised by bonding patterns between the amino acids which help to maintain the stability of the protein as whole. The secondary structural elements are α-helices and β-strands, and it is the relative positions of these secondary-structural elements which constitutes protein topology.

β-sheets are formed from β-strands which bond together to form planar sheet structures. Super-secondary structures comprise another level of structure in proteins, and are common topological patterns called motifs, which are formed from β-strands and/or α-helices. A handful of such motifs have been identified. For instance, four linked β-strands can be arranged to form a pattern called a 'greek-key' (Figure 1) after decorations that appear on Greek vases. The higher level of abstraction provided by the concept of motif has helped clarify and aid understanding of protein structure and function. The similarities of topology in different proteins suggest that they might have evolved from a common ancestor. Furthermore, the motifs impose constraints on allowed structural conformations which are exploited in some algorithms to predict structure from amino acid sequence.

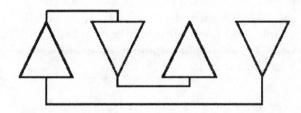

Figure 1. A greek-key motif formed from four linked β-strands

4. Graphical Representations of Protein Topology

Graphical representations of the structure of β-sheet proteins at different levels of abstraction can be generated from the positions of the α-carbon atom of each amino acid which trace a ribbon through the path of the polypeptide chain. Three such representations which have been developed and used by biochemists are shown in Figure 2.

All of these representations depict the same protein (prealbumin), and preserve information about the relative positions of the protein secondary structural elements as well as the order of these elements in the amino

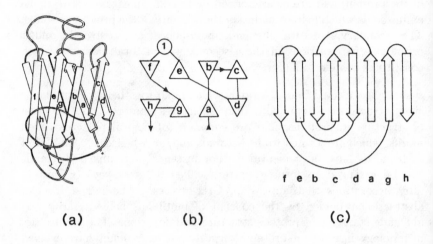

(a)   (b)   (c)

**Figure 2. Abstract representations of the structure of
prealbumin: (a) A simple three dimensional
representation with letters labelling the
separate strands (b) The two-dimensional
topological form with labelled strands and
helix (c) A planar topology diagram with
labelled strands**

acid sequence and the direction of the strands as they lie in their sheets.
The least abstract, simple three-dimensional form (see Figure 2(a))
represents each β-strand as an arrow and α-helices as coils. This form
shows the stacking of one β-sheet formed from strands 'f,e,b,c' on another
β-sheet formed from strands 'h,g,a,d', together with a short α-helical
region just after strand 'e'. The next most abstract two-dimensional
topological form (see figure 2(b)) represents each β-strand as a triangle
with the apex denoting strand direction, and each helix as a circle.
The stacking of the sheets is represented with sheet 'f,e,b,c' above sheet
'h,g,a,d'. In proteins such as prealbumin where there is a stacked pair
of β-sheets, a more abstract one-dimensional topological representation
can be obtained by considering the two sheets as a barrel-like structure
and then unfolding the barrel onto a single plane. For example, strand
'f' on the edge of the top sheet can be viewed as being adjacent to both
strands 'h' and 'e'. Similarly, strand 'c' can be considered adjacent to
strands 'b' and 'd'. From such an abstraction, and ignoring α-helices, the
relative positions of all the strands can be denoted in the most abstract
'planar' form (see Figure 2(c)).

Proteins are relatively unusual physical objects in that their three- dimensional structure can be abstracted into simple linear representations while still retaining many interesting properties. This is because proteins are essentially linear structures and the topological motifs which are an important feature of protein structure are defined by strand direction, linear relations within sheets or the planar form, and linear relations between the positions of secondary structures in the amino acid sequence. Thus, some automated reasoning about protein structure can be made tractable in the form of performing inferences about linear topological relationships.

5. Description of the Interface

It was felt that potential users of GRIPE should not have to go through a great deal of training and acclimatization in order to use the system. The literature on user interface design furnished certain generally applicable guidelines and suggestions on how to make an interface acceptable and usable (Foley & Dam [1982]; Newman & Sproull [1979]; Williams [1986]), and these were adhered to as much as possible. These suggestions and guidelines were mostly appeals to common sense: familiar concepts and objects should be employed to make the interface more acceptable and easier to learn to use; the layout of objects on the screen should be simple and carefully considered, as the ways in which information is displayed and the kinds of feedback utilised will contribute to the system's ease of use; and the information display should make it clear what objects are available to be manipulated in the interface and what actions can be performed on these objects at any time.

The initial requirements for the interface to the topological reasoning program were that it should be a simple to use system allowing biochemists to make queries about the presence of topological motifs in the structure of specified proteins. The users could not be expected to be familiar with the underlying Prolog representations used by the system or to be skilled in the use of computers. Based on these requirements, a decision was made to exploit the graphical representations of abstract protein topology exemplified by Figure 2(b) and Figure 2(c), which should be familiar to target users as they have been developed and used by biochemists in other contexts. In addition, the component symbols of such diagrams are uncomplicated and easily manipulated, which make them amenable to use in a direct manipulation style interface.

The primary objects available for manipulation in the interface are the elements of protein secondary structure (α-helices and β-strands); other objects of interest are the structural motifs which are formed from combinations of helices and strands, the proteins being examined, and the amino acids making up the secondary structures. As in Figure 2(b), strands are graphically represented as triangles (with the apex of the triangle indicating the direction of the strand), helices as circles, and the loops, or undifferentiated links between the strands and helices as lines (see Figure 3). These representations for the elements of secondary structure are derived from methods developed and used by biochemists to graphically represent protein topology. The decision to use this specific representation in GRIPE was made because of the guiding design principles of using representations that would be familiar to the users, and of making the interface as simple and easy to use as possible.

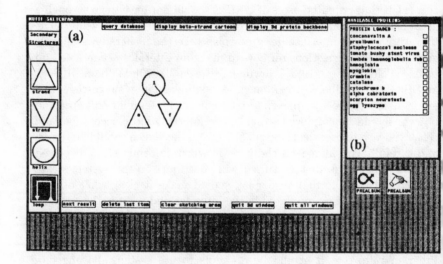

Figure 3. **A GRIPE screen with (a) a motif formed from strands 'b' and 'f' in the 'sketchpad' motif-editing window and helix '1' and (b) the menu of proteins available for inspection**

There are five main windows in GRIPE: three display windows, one which contains the three-dimensional ribbon diagram, one which contains the one- dimensional topology diagram, and one which contains the amino-acid sequence of selected structures, and two user-input windows, one which contains a menu of the proteins available for examination, and one called the 'sketchpad' in which a user may construct sketches of topological structures to be used The user-input windows are always on the screen. The display windows are opened in response to the users' requests.

The functionality of the GRIPE system was very much determined by features of TOPOL and the contents of its protein structure database. These features of TOPOL were developed in consultation with protein structure specialists. Many of the general functions of GRIPE are obvious, e.g., loading data, displaying data, etc., but care has been taken to make them easily carried out. The important operations which are provided to the users of GRIPE include: selecting a particular protein for examination, constructing a representation of a topological motif, finding out if a constructed motif is present in the protein, and finding out the amino acid sequences of the secondary structures which make up a motif. Additional operations which the graphical medium makes possible are the viewing of the one-dimensional topology and three-dimensional α-carbon ribbon diagrams of the currently loaded protein. All of these operations, with the exception of constructing a motif representation and extracting amino acid information, are made available in the interface by the use of screen 'buttons' which can be pressed using the mouse. Motif construction is a slightly more complex operation from the user's point of view, and involves the user selecting, placing, and linking the icons representing secondary structures in the sketchpad window. Users can indicate that they wish to display the amino acid make-up of certain secondary structures in the motif by using the mouse to draw a box around the structures in which they are interested (see Figure 4).

When the system finds a match between a user's query and the structure of the protein, the results are graphically displayed by labelling the query motif with the names of the matching secondary structures in the protein. If the three-dimensional and planar representations of the loaded protein are displayed, then the results of the match are highlighted in these images. This highlighting allows the user to view the correspondence between structures in the different representations. If several matches are found, then these can be iterated through by successive mouse clicks on the appropriate screen button. If no match between the user's query and the structure of the protein is found, then a message to this effect is displayed on the screen; the message is removed as soon as the user clicks a mouse button or types at the keyboard.

6. Graphical and Propositional Representations of Topology

TOPOL represents protein topology in terms of linear relationships.

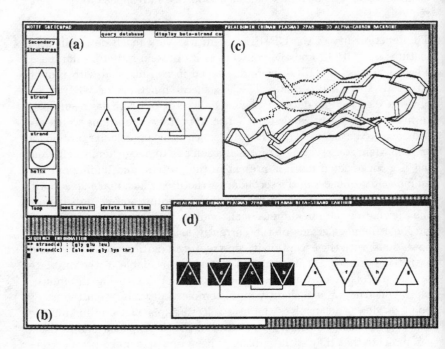

Figure 4. A GRIPE screen showing (a) a greek-key
query motif in the 'sketchpad' motif-editing
window (b) the amino acids forming strands
'c' and 'd' in the 'sequence' window and
highlighting of the results of the to- pological
query in (c) the 3-d ribbon and (d) and planar
representations of prealbumin (d)

These relationships are applicable to primary and secondary structures
of the protein, and at the sequence, plane, and sheet structural abstractions. There are two classes of relations that are of interest: connectivity
relations, which are the relative positions of structures within the amino
acid sequence; and neighbourhood relations, which are the relative
positions of strands within sheets or planes. Both connectivity and
neighbourhood relations are linear relations, but at different abstraction
levels. Thus, the basic vocabulary necessary to describe topological

motifs consists of only two binary relations which express that two structures are immediately next to one another: 'X meets Y' and its converse 'X is-met-by Y'.

The screen representation of these relations is very simple. The connectivity relationship between two objects is indicated by a line from one object to the other. The strand icon to whose apex the link is attached is interpreted as being prior in the protein chain. If a helix is involved in a connectivity relation, then if the line is attached to the edge of the helix icon, it is interpreted as being prior in the protein chain. Since the neighbourhood relation means that two structures are adjacent in a β-sheet or adjacent in the planar representation of two β-sheets, only β-strands can be neighbours. In GRIPE, all strand icons placed in the sketchpad must lie on a single horizontal line, and all the queries are interpreted at the planar abstraction, unless helices form part of the query motif, in which case the queries are interpreted at the sheet abstraction. The neighbourhood relation is represented by two strand icons next to one another, with no intervening strand icons. The icon which is leftmost on the screen is interpreted as preceding the other in the sheet (see Figure 5(a)).

Proteins are naturally segmented into non-overlapping structures – thus their relative positions can be described using the 'meets' and 'is-met-by' relations. However, further structural relations need to be supported by the system in order to provide a more useful tool for biochemists. In particular, imprecise relationships and overlapping segments should be represented. The vocabulary of relations in the current system is a small subset of the linear relationships which have been described by Allen for reasoning about another linear structure, time (Allen [1983]). The augmentation of the current vocabulary to include the full set thirteen relationships proposed by Allen would allow the desired properties between segments to be represented. The way in which some of these relationships could be graphically represented and incorporated into the current system are discussed in the next section.

7. Proposed Extensions to the Graphical Interface

After the initial prototype of GRIPE was constructed, domain experts were allowed to use the system and their comments about the functionality of the system were noted. From this informal user testing, and from further discussions with biochemists, it was found that it would be helpful to users to be able to describe additional relationships between the secondary structures in the proteins. At least part of the basis of this mismatch between user requirements and interface functionality was the existence of interesting properties of the protein that do not follow the di-

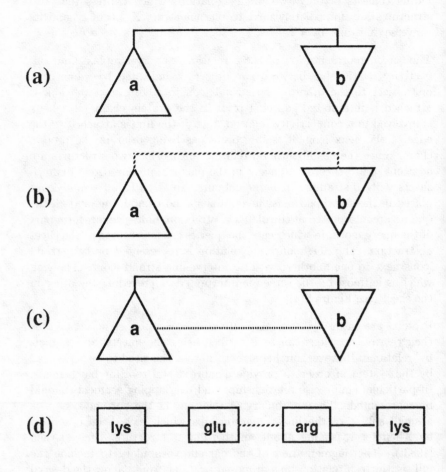

Figure 5.   Representations of spatial relationships in the 'sketchpad' motif-editing window. (a) Strand 'a' meets strand 'b' in the sheet and in the sequence. (b) Strand 'a' is before strand 'b' in the sequence and meets strand 'b' in the sheet. (c) Strand 'a' is before strand 'b' in the sheet and meets strand 'b' in the sequence. (d) A proposed query about the linear relations between residues

visions dictated by the secondary structures. In certain circumstances a biochemist may wish to ask whether or not an arbitrary protein segment overlaps or forms part of another segment. A biochemist may also want to make queries about the relative positions of structures in the protein, rather than constructing the query in terms of absolute positions. For example, the user may wish to ask about a structure where one strand is somewhere before another strand in a sheet, but is not necessarily its immediate neighbour. Allowing the user to ask such questions involves extending the underlying vocabulary of linear relations. An analysis of the possible linear relationships between segments has been done by Allen. His work was in the domain of temporal reasoning, but as time can be reasoned about as a linear ordering of segments, the logic of relations between temporal intervals could be adapted for use in reasoning about the linear ordering of segments in proteins.

Allen's representation of temporal relations allows imprecise statements about the relation between time intervals to be made, e.g., A occurred before B, without reference to specific times or dates for A and B. The representation also supports the relationships between overlapping segments and allows the grain of reasoning to be varied, so that the interval lengths can be varied depending on the problem domain. All of these properties map well onto the protein structure reasoning problem, and in some cases are already part of the TOPOL program.

In GRIPE, the only relationships that are currently represented are 'X meets Y' and 'X is-met-by-Y', for non-overlapping segments. Introducing 'X before Y' and 'X after Y', which are transitive versions of 'meets' and 'is-met-by', for both neighbourhood and connectivity relationships in the topological structures, would allow imprecise statements about the ordering of structures to be made. The introduction of the the relationships which deal with overlapping segments in Allen's temporal logic would make it possible to reason about arbitrary segments that overlap the naturally occurring structures of the proteins. The biochemists who have used GRIPE agree that this would be a useful extension to its functionality.

Proposed extensions to the graphical representations of linear topology in GRIPE to deal with imprecision and to allow the user to make queries about the presence of amino acid patterns are outlined below. These extensions follow naturally from the present representations of connectivity and neighbourhood relationships between secondary structures. Representations of overlap between segments are also being considered, but this would involve a larger modification and reorganisation of the current interface, and the graphical representations of these relationships have not yet been designed.

Representations of the 'before' and 'after' relationships for both connectivity and neighbourhood relationships have been developed in the form of modifications to the original representation of protein topology. As connectivity relationships in GRIPE are represented by a link between two structures, the transitive version of 'meets' can be dealt with straightforwardly by introducing another kind of link into the interface. Figure 5(b) shows the proposed representation of 'strand A is somewhere before strand B in the amino acid sequence'. Neighbourhood relationships present a slightly more complicated problem, as they are not represented explicitly in GRIPE by links, but by two strand icons placed in the sketchpad with no intervening strands. It seems necessary to introduce a 'transitive-neighbour' link; a dotted link can be place between two strands on the same vertical level. Figure 5(c) shows the proposed representation of 'strand A is somewhere before strand B in the sheet'. The current representation of direct neighbours remains the same for simplicity and to reduce clutter.

The links used to represent 'meets', 'before' and 'after' in the connections of secondary structures in the sequence could also be used to represent the same relationships between amino acids in the sequence. Iconic representations of the twenty amino acids need to be introduced so that the user can manipulate them to construct such queries. A way in which this could be done is shown in Figure 5(d). This would provide a general graphical pattern-matching language which can be used to find similar amino acid patterns in several different proteins.

The ability to make more general queries to the system is another way in which GRIPE might be improved. In most graphical query systems, it will probably be the case that user will want to be able to construct general queries, without having to specify all of the properties of the objects involved. To allow for this, generic objects from an object class could be made available for query construction (for example, three different kinds of strand icons might be available: one pointing up, one pointing down, and one generic strand icon with no direction). Another facility that would be useful in GRIPE is a way of grouping and naming objects to form complex objects which can be stored for future use. For example, a user should be able to construct a motif, name it, and retrieve the motif by name later in a session with the system.

8. Conclusions

This paper has described a prototype of an interactive graphical interface which allows users to construct graphical queries about the presence of topological structures in proteins. The user can construct queries to the system using a graphical query language based on a representation of protein topology familiar to protein structure specialists. The development of the graphical query language was made possible by the symbolic representation of protein structure in the underlying knowledge based system, TOPOL. TOPOL derives a declarative description of the topological relations between secondary structural elements using data specifying their absolute three-dimensional coordinates. GRIPE allows various views of the protein to be graphically displayed: the linear sequence of amino acids making up secondary structures, the one-dimensional topological relationships of β-strands, and the three-dimensional structure of the protein's backbone. Users can construct queries to the system at the topological level, and the results of these queries can be displayed, by highlighting and labelling, in the three different views of the protein. Thus, the user can see the relationship between the topological and three- dimensional representations of protein structures.

Various extensions to the functionality of the interface have been suggested. In particular, the ability to represent imprecise linear relationships and to construct queries about overlapping structures should be provided. These extensions would allow GRIPE to provide a graphical pattern-matching language for linear relations between protein substructures. It might also form the basis for the adaptation of the system to other domains where linear relationships are important.

No formal evaluation of the system has been performed, but reactions from biochemists who have used GRIPE have been favourable. Most users find it easy to use and understand with very little introduction. Thus GRIPE satisfies the initial requirements that it should be an easy to use interface allowing structural queries about proteins to be made.

9. Implementation

GRIPE was implemented in POP11 and Prolog in the POPLOG programming environment, and runs on SUN workstations. A prototype colour version of the system, which uses colour-coding to indicate the different secondary structures of the proteins, has been implemented to run on a colour SUN-3. A demonstration version of GRIPE is now in use; extensions and alterations to the functionality of the interface are currently in progress.

Acknowledgements

The authors wish to acknowledge support for this work from the Imperial Cancer Research Fund and the Science and Engineering Research Council through the Alvey programme (project IKBS/140).

References

J Allen [1983], "Maintaining Knowledge about Temporal Intervals," *Communications of the ACM* 26, 832–843.

T Blundell & M J E Sternberg [1985], "Computer-Aided Design in Protein Engineering," *Trends in Biotechnology* 3, 228–335.

J D Foley & A van Dam [1982], *Fundamentals of Interactive Computer Graphics*, Addison-Wesley, Reading MA, Reprinted with corrections 1984.

W M Newman & R F Sproull [1979], *Principles of Interactive Computer Graphics*, McGraw-Hill, 2nd Edition.

C J Rawlings, K Seifert & J Saldanha [1987], "A Large Knowledge Based System for Molecular Biology," in *Proceedings of the First Workshop for the Special Interest Group on Knowledge Manipulation Engines*, Alvey Directorate.

C J Rawlings, W RT Taylor, J Nyakairu, J Fox & M J E Sternberg [1986], "A Large Knowledge Based System for Molecular Biology," in *The Third International Conference on Logic Programming. Lecture Notes in Computer Science*, Springer-Verlag, 536.

K Seifert [1987], "GRIPE: A Graphical Interface for Protein Exploration," Biomedical Computing Unit, Imperial Cancer Research Fund, Technical Report.

F R A Hopgood D A Duce E V C Fielding K Robinson and A S Williams [1986], in *Methodology of Window Management*, Springer-Verlag.

Graphical Prototyping of Graphical Tools

David England

Department of Computing, University of Lancaster, Lancaster LA1 4YR, U.K.

This paper describes a tool set for the interactive specification and construction of graphical user interfaces. It combines a specification method, Object-ATN, with a painting tool to describe interface objects. Interfaces can then be simulated for user testing and evaluation. The tool set is part of the ECLIPSE Integrated Project Support Environment but is not limited to producing user interfaces for that environment.

Keywords: Specification, Prototyping, Evaluation.

1. Introduction

One of the problems with new styles of graphical interfaces, such as that of the Macintosh, is, while such interfaces help the *end user*, they are difficult for the designer to build. Their complex underlying structure requires greater skill and effort on the part of the designer than more traditional, character VDU interfaces. To handle the complexity of graphical interface construction, programming methods and specification methods for user interfaces have been developed. This paper is concerned with an interactive, graphical specification method for the prototyping of graphical user interfaces.

2. Programming Tools

Programming tool kits have evolved which provide designers with a standard set of parts. Examples include MacApp (Shumucker [1986]), which provides a higher level programming interface to the Macintosh ROM-based Toolbox routines, SunView for Sun Workstations (Sun Microsystems [1986]), and the X tool kit (Scheifler & Gettys [1986]). Further, visual programming tools are available which allow the designer to directly manipulate tool kit objects via specialised draughting tools. Some examples are Trillium (Henderson [1986]) within the InterLisp environment and ExperInterface Builder running on the Macintosh under ExperLisp. Within the Eclipse project (Alderson, Bott & Falla [1985]) a window generator has been prototyped (England [1987]) to produce Eclipse control panels (Reid & Welland [1986]). This tool generates an interface Format Description Language (FDL) which describes the window and panel layout. The FDL description is interpreted by the Eclipse UIMS (Smart [1986]). The general aim of all such tools is to provide designers with access to the full range of interface objects, in a usable way. Hence, it is possible to provide end users with richer and more complete interfaces.

3. Specification Techniques

Producing tools by an ad-hoc painting approach answers only part of the problem of interface specification. This approach is insufficient, especially in the large, multi-member teams that Eclipse is intended to support. Specification techniques are required for unambiguous interface description, for validation and quality control, and to assist with interfacing to other system components. Specification techniques also provide a degree of abstraction from the physical implementation which the above programming tools lack. It is thus possible to consider interface characteristics without reference to their physical realisation. This has the advantage that it forces the analysis of the interface and increases the probability of finding problems and inconsistencies.

Four techniques are especially relevant to the development of graphical interaction systems. EPROS (Hekmatpour & Ince [1987]) uses a functional specification notation based on the VDM method to produce an evolutionary prototype. It combines systems functionality and user interface components in one prototyping system – a feature often missing from such systems. SPI (Alexander [1987]) uses a CSP-type notation (Hoare [1985]) to describe the user interface in terms of input events and processes. Sibert (Sibert, Hurley & Blesser [1986]) describes an object-oriented user interface management system for graphical interfaces where the interactive system is decomposed into representational, interaction and application object classes. These classes of object are responsible for the lexical, syntactic and semantic levels, respectively, of an interactive system. In addition the specification language Z (Took [1985]) has been user for the specification of user interfaces.

Another approach used for the specification of user interface dialogues is Augmented Transition Nets (ATN). Here, the dialogue is described as a graph of nodes (dialogue states) and links between nodes (state transitions). For example, a user may be faced in one state with a menu of five choices. Selecting a menu choice causes a transition to one of five possible states. The use of ATN's for the specification of graphical interaction was first expounded by Newman (Newman [1968]). Other tools, for the specification of traditional, user interfaces, have been described by Alty (Alty & Brooks [1985]) and Wasserman (Wasserman et al. [1986]).

Jacob (Jacob [1986]) recognises the inadequacy of traditional ATN's in describing graphical interfaces. Graphical or direct manipulation interfaces usually have more than one possible point of control which is difficult to represent in a single flow of control ATN. For example, when the user selects and manipulates a number of objects as a group. Jacob's solution, which we shall term Object- ATN, is to augment the Object model, as suggested by Sibert, with a private ATN for each class of interaction object. An executive takes input events and passes them to any interactive object which is currently interested (as defined by its ATN syntax diagram). Our tool set is based on Object-ATN but modified for interactive graphical description. It provides advantages over SPI in that the complexity of the notation required for, say, parallel event input, is hidden by the object approach. To illustrate the technique we consider two examples of Object-ATN descriptions.

4. Object-ATN Examples

Consider the Disk Icon of the Macintosh Finder interface shown in figure 1.

If the inputs from the user are given the tokens, **mouseUp**, **mouseDown**, **doubleClick** and **drag**, and the object description (in pseudo-Smalltalk) of a generic Icon is;

> Class named: Icon
>
> instance variables: icon_image
>
> tokens: mouseUp, mouseDown, enter, exit, drag, doubleClick
>
> diagram: IconATN
>
> methods:

DISK LABEL

Figure 1   A Macintosh Disk Icon

---

sOpen	'open the icon to a window'
intersect?	'Does the icon intersect another object'
intersect_op	'Deal with the intersection'
move	'Drag the image with the cursor'
highlight	'invert the image'

Then the description of a Disk Icon is;

Class named: MacDiskIcon

superclasses: Icon Label

instance variables: icon_image label

We have created a class of object *MacDiskIcon* which inherits the properties of two generic objects *Icon* and *Label*. It also consists of two of these generic objects. The valid inputs which cause transitions in this objects ATN diagram are shown after *tokens:*. We will ignore keyboard events in this example for the sake of space. The syntax diagram, *IconATN* is shown in figure 2. Numbered nodes are states between user input events while text labeled nodes represent method invocation.

Referring to the numbered nodes, Figure 2 can be informally expressed as;

"The user moves the cursor over the disk icon and then either;
1) moves it out again (**1-2**),
2) double clicks the mouse opening a window(**2-3**),
or
3) depresses the mouse, drags the icon and releases the mouse (**4-5**).
If the icon intersects another object perform some method else await further user input (**2**)"

The intersect arc shows one advantage of Object-ATN over a single ATN

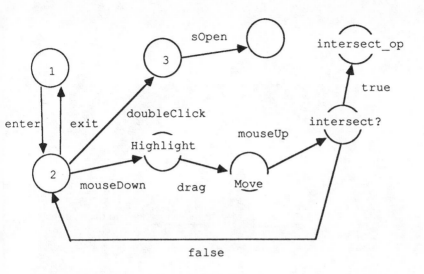

Figure 2   IconATN

description. If two object images intersect e.g., a Disk Icon and a Trash Icon, they are both involved in the user-system dialogue.

It is possible to go on to produce a complete collection of interface objects. More interestingly, novel interaction objects for analysis via an ATN description can be studied, such as, Pie Menus as implemented by Hopkins for NeWS (Callahan et al. [1988]). Pie menus are circular versions of pop-up hierarchical or walking menus where the active segment of the menu item extends beyond the circumference boundary of the menu image. The user selects a menu item by moving the cursor into an item's segment. It is suggested that it is easier to select items as the user remembers which direction to move the cursor. An example is given in figure 3.

The syntax diagram for the parent pie menu is shown in figure 4a while the syntax for subsequent child pie menus is shown in figure 4b. The input tokens are; **exitCentre, enterCentre, enterSeg, exitSeg, rightButtonDown, rShow** and **sShow**. **rShow** and **sShow** are examples of synthetic tokens, that is, tokens sent between objects rather than from the user.

Informally figure 4a can be expressed as;

"Depressing the right button over the root menu pop-ups a pie menu

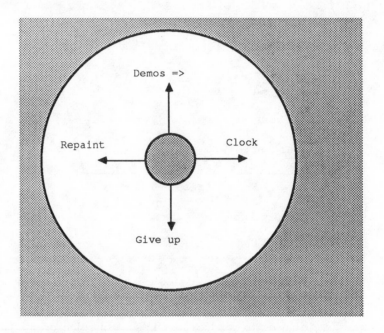

Figure 3   Pie Menu

(**rshow**). The user can then move the cursor out of and into the centre (**2-3**), or into and out of a menu segment (**2-4**). Releasing the mouse in the centre exits the menu dialogue (**3**). Releasing it in a segments invokes the relevant menu action (**4**)."

Comparison of the two diagrams shows an inconsistency (italic labels) in the behaviour between parent and child in that the parent remains visible while the right button of the mouse is *depressed* while the child is visible while the right button is *released*. The bold arcs (**4-5, 5-6**) on the diagrams show alternative behaviours to correct the inconsistency, i.e., pop-up a child menu as soon as the user enters a submenu segment of the parent menu. This demonstrates the advantage of using a formal specification.

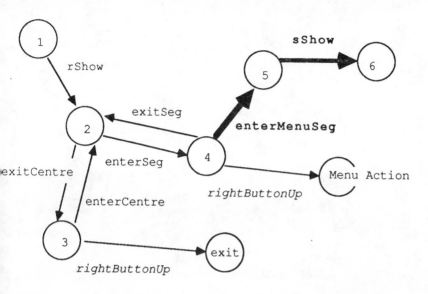

Figure 4a Parent Pie Menu

5. A Prototyping Tool Set

Using Object-ATN user interfaces can be prototyped, using a tool set shown in figure 5. This consists of:

— A layout/painting tool which describes the graphical view of a primitive object and the relationship between objects in a compound object. A complete user interface is merely the highest level compound object.

— An ATN diagram editor.

— An ATN executive to execute the interface.

The tool set attempts to combine the advantages of specification and visual programming tools. The layout tool is a generic version of the window generator described in (England [1987]). The ATN diagram editor is based on the Eclipse Design Editor (Beer, Welland & Sommerville [1987]). Any diagram that can be represented as a directed graph can be represented within the Design editor. The syntax and the components of the diagramming method are presented to the Design Editor, so it is relatively simple to configure the Design Editor to draw ATN diagrams

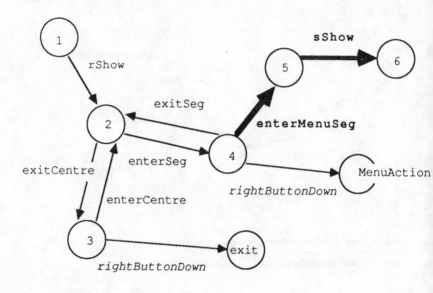

Figure 4b Child Pie Menu

---

such as those shown in figures 2, 4a and 4b.

Typically a designer would begin by drawing the layout of an interface object. A form interface and the Design Editor are invoked from the layout tool to specify object attributes and the ATN diagram, respectively.

6. Simulation

Given adequate graphical and syntactic primitives the application behind a user interface can be simulated, to some degree, by its graphical and syntactic effects on that interface. At an initial stage of tool use the interface *is* the system, as far as the user is concerned (Carroll & Thomas [1980]). This has important considerations for a *user-centred* approach to systems design, when, at an early stage of systems development there is insufficient functionality in the application for any realistic user evaluation.

Such a model is insufficient for multi-team, large scale projects as likely to be supported by Eclipse. Eclipse is also a method-independent support system so the interface tool set should be adaptable (by supporting

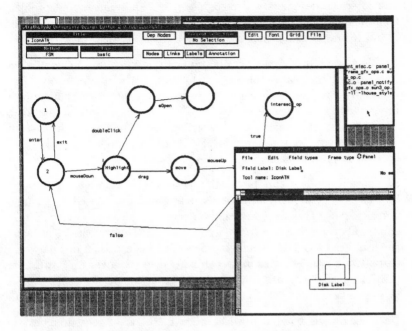

Figure 5   Toolset

different system interface styles) to a particular method. Some possible simulation models that the tool set may support are;

— Automatically generating FDL for interpretation by the ECLIPSE UIMS. This is linked to some user-produced, application code.

— Generating skeleton source code for linking and compilation with application code e.g., Ada skeletons generated from the MASCOT3 tool set.

— Communication with a window server e.g., generating PostScript for NeWS (Henderson [1986]).

Ideally the toolkit should present an abstract interface which can be configured to communicate to a specific window server.

7. Evaluation

A project that carries out proper task analysis and interface specification should produce a user interface that closely meets the user's needs. Undoubtedly though, over the life time of the project, users and interface designers will recognise new requirements and problems. Communication of this information is formalised in evaluation sessions. A full review of evaluation techniques is given by Lea (Lea [1987]).

Problems remain however. Evaluation can often be on too small a scale to represent the real problems met by users. It may also be expensive, especially if the subjects are software engineers rather than undergraduate students. Frohlich (Frohlich [1987]) describes a video studio for the experimental observation and recording of product use. Such studios are expensive and the analysis of video tapes labour intensive. The evaluation process needs further automation.

Simulation models can be used for the basis of user evaluation of interfaces. As shown above, ATN diagrams can be used to formulate and test the syntax of interaction objects. They can also be used to aid empirical evaluation of a completed interface. The transitions caused by the user are logged and time-stamped. The log can then be analysed by statistical packages. This approach is used in (Brooks, Alty & England [1987]) where the data is analysed by an induction package such as ACLS (Paterson & Niblett [1982]) to show patterns in the data as derived rules.

Data logging is combined with other methods of measurement such as questionnaires on user background and user satisfaction with an interface, plus debriefing the user on his/her actions during a study session.

8. Discussion

The ATN executive and the Layout tool are at the prototype stage (implemented in Objective C on Sun 3 workstations) and only perform some of the basic features described here. The prototypes will be developed to produce useful end-user tools for evaluation. The evaluation process and its role in the overall design cycle will be assessed.

At present ATN diagrams have two classes of transitions, user input events and synthetic tokens for graphical feedback. A third class, of time-based transitions, will be added. Pulses, either from the ATN executive or from clock objects inherited by interface components, would fire time-based transitions. This will be used for;

1. Representing graphical clocks,
2. Animated graphics and dynamic icons,
3. Simulating application time delays.

The tool kit as a whole focuses on graphical interaction and this fits in with the Eclipse user interface approach. Other forms of dialogue description could be used; CSP (Alexander [1987]) or production rules (Harmelen & Wilson [1987]), augmented by the object model to handle multi-threaded dialogues. Task analysis is also an important part of interface development and the integration of task analysis and user interface specification needs to be addressed.

Acknowledgements

This work is funded by the Alvey Directorate as part of the ECLIPSE project. I would like to thank my supervisor Ian Sommerville and the HCI '88 referees for their help in getting this paper into shape.

References

A Alderson, M F Bott & M E Falla [1985], "An Overview of the ECLIPSE Project," in *Integrated Project Support Environments*, J A McDermid, ed..

H Alexander [1987], "Executable Specifications as an Aid to Dialogue Design," in *INTERACT '87 – The Second IFIP Conference on Human-Computer Interaction*, H J Bullinger and B Shackel, ed., Elsevier Science Publishers B.V., North Holland.

J L Alty & A Brooks [1985], "Microtechnology and User Friendly Systems: The CONNECT Dialogue Executor," *Journal of Microcomputer Applications* 8, 333–346.

S Beer, R Welland & I Sommerville [1987], "Software Design Automation in an IPSE," in *ESEC '87 – 1st European Software Engineering Conference*, Springer–Verlag.

A Brooks, J L Alty & D England [1987], "An Inductive Analysis of Behaviour at a User-Driven Adaptive Interface," Scottish HCI Centre Report No. AMU 8722/01S, Department of Computer Science, University of Strathclyde.

J Callahan, D Hopkins, M Weiser & B Shneiderman [1988], "An Empirical Comparison between Pie vs. Linear Menus," in *Proceedings of CHI '88 – Human Factors in Computing Systems*, ACM, New York.

J M Carroll & J C Thomas [1980], "Metaphor and the Cognitive Representation of Computing Systems," IBM T J Watson Research Center, Technical Report No. RC 8302.

D England [1987], "A User Interface Design Tool," in *ESEC '87 – 1st European Software Engineering Conference*, Springer–Verlag.

D Frohlich [1987], "Using Video in the Design Process," in *IEE Colloquium – Evaluation Techniques for Interactive System Design*, IEE, Savoy Place, London.

M van Harmelen & S M Wilson [1987], "Viz: A Production System Based User Interface Management System," in *Eurographics '87*, Elsevier Science Publishers B.V., North Holland.

S Hekmatpour & D Ince [1987], "Evolutionary Prototyping and the Human-Computer Interface," in *INTERACT '87 – The Second IFIP Conference on Human-Computer Interaction*, H J Bullinger and B Shackel, ed., Elsevier Science Publishers B.V., North Holland.

A Henderson [1986], "The Trillium User Interface," in *Proceedings of CHI '86 – Human Factors in Computing Systems*, ACM, New York.

C A R Hoare [1985], *Communicating Sequential Processes*, Prentice-Hall.

R J K Jacob [October 1986], "A Specification Language for Direct-Manipulation User Interfaces," *ACM Trans. on Graphics* 5.

M Lea [February 1987], "Review of Evaluation Methods," COSMOS Project Internal Report No. INT/RES/EVAL/24.1.

W Newman [1968], *A System for Interactive Graphical Programming*, SJCC Thompson Books.

A Paterson & T Niblett [1982], *ACLS User Manual*, Intelligent Terminals Ltd, Glasgow.

P Reid & R C Welland [1986], "Project Development in View," in *Software Engineering Environments*, I Sommerville, ed., Peter Peregrinus.

R W Scheifler & J Gettys [April 1986], "The X Window System," *ACM Trans. on Graphics* 5.

K Shumucker [1986], "Object-Oriented Programming for the Macintosh," New Jersey.

J Sibert, W D Hurley & T W Blesser [1986], "An Object-Oriented User Interface Management System," *ACM SIGGRAPH '86* 20.

J Smart [1986], "A Man-Machine Interface Management System for UNIX," in *Proceedings of Uniforum 1986*, Anaheim CA.

Sun Microsystems [1986], *SunView Systems Programmer's Guide*, Mountain View CA.

R Took [1985], "The Presenter – A Formal Design for an Autonomous Display Manager," in *Integrated Project Support Environments*, J A McDermid, ed..

A I Wasserman, P A Pircher, D T Shewmake & M L Kerstein [February 1986], "Developing an Interactive Information System with the User Software Engineering Methodology," *IEEE Trans. on Software Engineering* SE-12.

A Comparison of Hypertext, Scrolling and Folding as Mechanisms for Program Browsing

Andrew F. Monk, Paul Walsh & Alan J. Dix

Departments of Psychology and Computer Science, University of York, York YO1 5DD, U.K.

Hypertext removes some of the constraints of conventional linear text by providing mechanisms for physically realizing the conceptual links between related sections of material. This research examines the use of a hypertext browser with a literate program. A literate program has a sequential structure, in that it is divided into sections presented in a particular order, and a hierarchical structure, in that some sections 'use' other sections.

Two experiments are described which compare the performance of users browsing the same program presented either as a linear or hypertext structure. In Experiment 1 one group used a hypertext browser the other two scrolling and folding browsers. The hypertext browser is shown to be inferior to the scrolling browser under these particular circumstances. In a second experiment two further groups of users were tested, one of which was provided with an overview of the hypertext structure. This manipulation removed the disadvantage demonstrated in Experiment 1. It is concluded that while hypertext presents many new opportunities to the interface designer, it also raises new problems. In particular, the importance of providing an overview or map of the hypertext structure is demonstrated.

Keywords: Hypertext, scrolling, folding, browsing, literate programming.

1. Introduction

This paper presents two experiments which explore the use of hypertext. A hypertext system for program browsing is compared with two alternatives schemes. A typical hypertext system is made up of screens or windows containing 'hot spots'. Selecting one of these hot spots causes some associated screen or window to be displayed. For example, one screen may contain a diagram with labels describing its components. The labels are hot spots. Moving the mouse cursor to one and clicking causes a screen of text expanding the description to be displayed. This screen may also contain keywords which are also hot spots.

Hypertext has been used for teaching (Hammond & Allinson [1988]; Yankelovich, Meyrowitz & Dam [1985]), authoring (Halasz, Moran & Trigg [1987]; Trigg & Weiser [1986]), and programming (Kuo et al. [1986]). There is also the multi-purpose information system ZOG (Akscyn, McCracken & Yoder [1987]). The salient feature of these applications is that they present the user with a physical realization of the conceptual links which can only be symbolized in conventional text. For example, this paper has a hierarchical structure as indicated by the section headings and subheadings, however, that conceptual structure is symbolically rather than physically realized in its printed form.

With printed material and most text editors the underlying object manipulated by the user has a serial or sequential structure. Thus, page one is followed by page two, line one is followed by line two and so on. Hypertext permits the use of hierarchies or any other form of connected network to access related material within the system. Further, if the links between screens can be of different types then it is possible to impose alternative structures on an object. For example, the multimedia system described by Yankelovich *et al* (Yankelovich, Meyrowitz & Dam [1985]). envisages an arrangement where the teacher provided a large data base of linked information. The student may then build a new set of links onto the same screens providing a novel perspective onto the material.

While a number of the papers referenced above discuss the advantages and disadvantages of hypertext systems there has been little systematic empirical work comparing the usability of hypertext with the alternatives. This is unfortunate, not because it is possible to do the definitive experiment showing that hypertext is better or worse than some alternative, but because systematic empirical study is the most effective way of gaining insights about how to design good systems.

2. The Vehicle for Experimentation

2.1. Literate Programming

The experiments to be described in the next section evaluate a hypertext browsing system in comparison with two alternative browsing schemes. Each browser operates on the same material. With the hypertext system the user is constrained to follow a network of links representing one way the information might be structured. In the other two browsers the user operates on a more conventional sequential information structure. The problem area chosen was browsers for literate programs (Knuth [1984]).

Knuth's idea is that computer programs should be regarded as works of literature, in which the software author strives for a program that is comprehensible because its concepts have been introduced in an order that is best for human understanding. To do this a literate program has two additional layers of structure above the procedural and data flow structures provided by the programming language. First there is a sequential structure. The program is divided into numbered sections and the order of these sections is chosen to explain the program as a simple expository sequence. The second layer of structure is hierarchical. The program is divided into sections which may 'use' other sections. This gives the author a mechanism, additional to the procedural structure of the programming language, to conceal inessential detail at each level of exposition (for a detailed discussion and evaluation of literate programming see (Thimbleby [1986]). A literate program is convenient for our purposes as it can have these different structures imposed on it.

In the experiments described in the next section users are asked to answer questions about a program. Each section in that program ends with a statement of in what section the current section is used, which sections it uses and, where global variables and constants are declared, a 'see also' referring to all the other sections where global variables and constants are declared. This indexing information forms the basis of the hypertext structure used in these experiments. These section numbers are 'hot spots'. Users can move from one section to another which uses it or to a section which it uses by selecting one of these numbers. Alternatively, users can move from one section to another referred to in the 'see also' information. This hypertext browser is compared with two browsers based on a sequential model of the documented program as it might be printed out. One uses scrolling to view the document, the other folding.

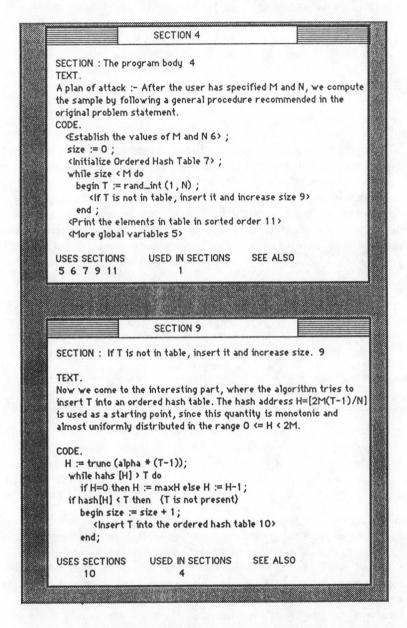

Figure 1.   The Hypertext Browser. The user has opened
            section 9 by clicking on that number in the
            indexing information for section 4

2.2. The Hypertext Browser.

Figure 1 illustrates what a user of the Hypertext Browser might see at some point in time. Positioning the mouse pointer on a number in the indexing information for a section and clicking has the effect of overwriting the text in the other window with the chosen section. Since clicking in one window always causes the material in the other window to be replaced by a new choice there are never more than two sections displayed and there is no need for the concept, commonly found in multi-window environments, of an 'active window'. If the section selected is already displayed then the system beeps to indicate that no change will be visible. Each window is 24 lines deep and so would accommodate the largest section.

2.3. The Scrolling Browser.

The implied user model of the object being inspected in this case is the more conventional sequential one. The user is to imagine that they are inspecting a continuous document. The text in the Scrolling Browser is displayed in a single window (Figure 2). To make it comparable with the Hypertext Browser the window is large enough to display two sections (48 lines). Along the top of this window there is a thumb bar. Clicking in the thumb bar will scroll to the appropriate point in the program. In addition there is a second small window containing an up and a down arrow at the bottom right of the screen which we shall refer to as the scroll box. Clicking on the up arrow scrolls up 30 lines i.e., the text moves up relative to the window. Clicking on the down arrow causes the text to move down. Thus the user has a choice of navigation strategy with the Scrolling Browser. They can either (a) position the mouse pointer in a portion of the scroll box and click to scroll forwards or backwards, or (b) they can position the mouse pointer at a point on the thumb bar and click to scroll forwards to that portion of the text.

2.4. The Folding Browser.

The Folding Browser also has an implied user model which is a single sequential document. Initially there is a single window containing the twelve section titles and below them a grey portion of free space. The user browses sections by positioning the mouse pointer on the section title and clicking. The section is partly unfolded to reveal holophrasts for the 'Text' and the 'Code' subsections, plus the indexing information for that section. The action of unfolding causes the text window to encroach upon the free space slightly. The user can continue the operation of unfolding information by pointing to either the text or the code holophrast and clicking. This unfolds the chosen subsection

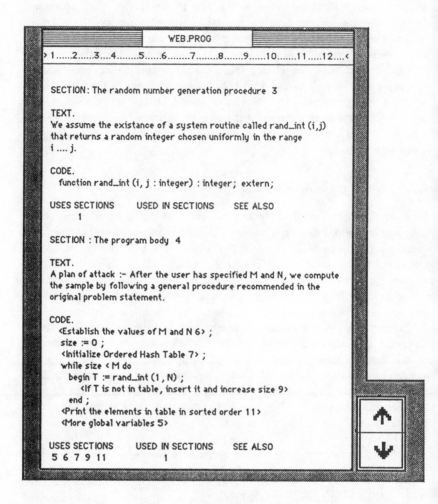

Figure 2.   The Scrolling Browser

and further encroaches upon the free space (see Figure 3). When the free space is exhausted (about two sections or 50 lines unfolded) further unfolding actions result in an error message which takes the form of a beep. The user is now obliged to fold away some of the information in order to release free space. This is done in the same way as unfolding, by positioning the pointer and clicking. If the object chosen is the text or code holophrast that subsection is folded away. If the user clicks on the section title the entire section is folded away. The user can fold away sections in an unfolded or partly-folded state, then when that section is next unfolded it will appear as it was before section folding took place.

Table 1.   Program comprehension questions

1. Only one section has input and output statements in it. Which is it? (Find its number)

2. Only two sections (other than that above) have writeln statements in them. Which are they? (Give their numbers)

3. What checks are carried out on input from the user? (Specify boolean expressions involved).

4. Where is T declared? (Give section number)

5. Where is T first assigned a value? (Give section number)

6. What is T? (Give a few words of explanation)

7. What is the maximum value taken by the variable Size?

8. Where is Size incremented? (Give section number)

9. How big is the hash table?

10. What is the value of alpha? (Give an expression)

11. 11. What does alpha represent? (Give a few words of explanation)

12. T is the new candidate for insertion. Which section contains the code which detects whether T has already been inserted or not?

13. What causes the insertion process to stop? (Specify the boolean expression involved)

14. There are two cases considered when printing the results: the case where 'wraparound' has occurred and the case where it has not. What boolean condition shows whether wraparound has occurred?

15. In what two sections of code does this wraparound occur, that is wraparound in the insertion process, not wraparound in printing out the hash table? (Give section numbers and the relevant lines of code).

3. Experiment 1

3.1. Method

A short program, written by Knuth (Bently [1986]) to demonstrate the

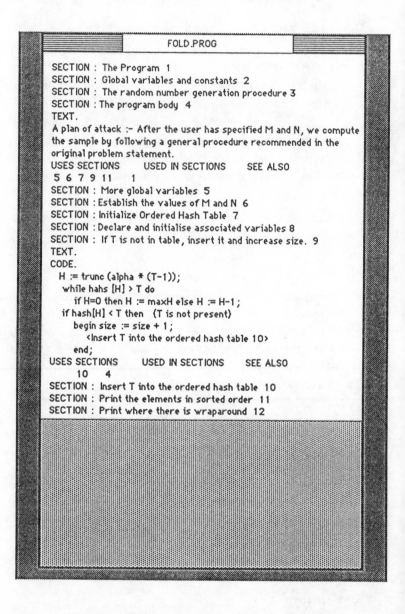

Figure 3.   The Folding Browser. The user has unfolded
             the text portion of section 4 and the code
             portion of section 9

key features of literate programming, was adapted for the purposes of this experiment. The original program is reported in (Bently [1986]). Changes made were to achieve a reasonable degree of equivalence between the three browsing schemes and to adapt Knuth's Pascal-like notation to the dialect of Pascal our users were familiar with. Fifteen questions about this program, of increasing difficulty, were devised for the users to answer (see Table 1). The users tested were thirty computer science undergraduates of at least one year's Pascal programming experience. The program uses an ordered hash table. These students were familiar with the idea of a hash table but had not seen this way of using one before. None were experienced users of mouse-based systems. To avoid any carry over effects which might have arisen if the same individual was trained to use all three browsers a between subjects design was used. Ten users were allocated to each browser condition on a random basis.

After reading some instructions about the aims and methods of literate programming the users were introduced to the browser they were going to work with by means of a practice program. They then worked through the fifteen questions using the browser on the program described above. When the user obtained the answer to a question, they were instructed to tell the experimenter. The answer was recorded, but no feedback was offered. The results described below were extracted from a time stamped log generated by the system for each user.

3.2. Results

Performance data is provided in Table 2. All three groups correctly solve most of the tasks set. The rate at which the 15 tasks were performed is also given in Table 2. The original measurement in seconds was transformed to tasks per hour in order to make it more suitable for parametric statistical tests. The comparisons of interest are Hypertext vs. Scrolling and Hypertext vs. Folding. The former comparison can be shown to be significant ($p < 0.05$) but the latter is not (analysis of variance followed by Dunn's test for two non-orthogonal planned comparisons gives the minimum difference which would be significant as 17.45 tasks per hour).

The advantage experienced by the Scrolling group over the Hypertext group is surprising as examination of system logs indicates that the two groups behave in very similar ways. If the Scrolling group had basically followed the sequential expository structure, which is after all one of the major features of literate programming, then one could see how the Hypertext group might be at a disadvantage because this strategy is not available to them. In fact, both groups rely very heavily on the 'uses/used in' links which are the basis of the hypertext structure. This is

Table 2. Mean performance data for Experiments 1 and 2 (standard deviations in brackets)

	Tasks Correct (out of 15)	Tasks per hour
Experiment 1		
Hypertext	13.5 (.93)	49.2 (13.9)
Scrolling	13.2 (1.2)	68.1 (21.0)
Folding	13.1 (1.1)	56.7 (12.9)
Experiment 2		
Hypertext with map	13.7 (1.3)	69.1 (25.8)
Hypertext with list	13.3 (1.7)	51.8 (11.8)

Table 3. Percentage recall of 'Uses' / 'Used in' links

Hypertext	73
Scrolling	67
Folding	46

perhaps best illustrated in some recall data collected after the users had completed the program comprehension tasks. Each user was given the numbered section titles and asked to indicate which other sections were referenced in each i.e., to recall the hierarchical part of the hypertext structure. Mean percentage recall scores are given in Table 3. It can be seen that the hypertext group recall nearly three quarters of this information and the scrolling group do nearly as well. Clearly these two groups are paying equal attention to this part of the hypertext structure. Interestingly the folding group recall less, indicating that they were navigating through the program in some other way.

The different browsers constrain which sections can be simultaneously visible in different ways. The Scrolling Browser constrains a user to viewing sequentially adjacent sections. A user of the Hypertext Browser can only view sections which are adjacent in the hypertext space i.e., each of the two sections displayed must have a reference to the other in its 'uses', 'used in' or 'see also' indexing information. A user of the Folding Browser is unconstrained as to what sections are open at the same time. There are also different constraints upon the way a user can move about the program. It might be thought that the Hypertext Browser will require many more operations to reach some required state than the Scrolling or Folding Browsers. This is not true because the 'uses'/'used by' hierarchy is very shallow and in addition there are the 'see also' links. Figure 4 presents a map of the hypertext structure. 47% of the changes needed to open some arbitrary section, given some arbitrary screen state can be achieved in one i.e., clicking on one number. 85% can be achieved in 2 and in only one case (opening Section 12 when 2 and 10 already opened) does it take 4. Of course in practice the transitions a user will want to make will depend on the particular strategy used to solve the task in hand.

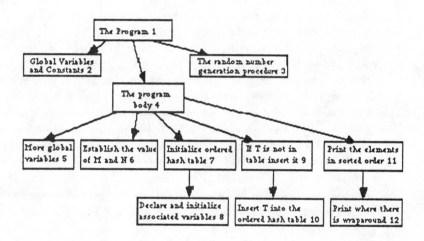

Figure 4. The 'uses/used in' hierarchy. There are also 'see also' links between sections 2, 5, 7 and 10

The better performance of the Scrolling Group when compared to the Hypertext Group could be explained in terms of these constraints. Either they impose a cognitive overhead on users resulting in generally less efficient behavior or, more trivially, the constraints simply mean that users have to engage in more system activity and the extra time taken to perform the tasks can be explained as necessary additional system response time. This latter explanation can be rejected. First, there is no evidence that the Hypertext Browser forces users into additional system activity. The system produced a time stamped record of user actions. This log was processed into a log of section visits. The smallest of the 'sections visited' scores in each group gives an indication of the minimum number of visits necessary to complete the fifteen tasks. This was 27 and 22 for the Hypertext and Scrolling Groups respectively. For a difference of five transactions to explain the observed time difference of 323 seconds implies a system response time of around one minute per transaction! We have to conclude that the Hypertext Browser is interfering with the performance of its user in some more subtle way.

Perhaps the major difference between the Hypertext and Scrolling browsers is that the latter allows random access to the sections. Although we have ruled out the possibility that the results could be explained by the additional system response time engendered when a transition requires one or two intermediate actions to complete, there may be cognitive overheads. It is possible that the additional mental work required to complete the transition distracts the user from the main task of program comprehension and results in generally less efficient behavior. The Hypertext and Scrolling Browsers would have been much more equivalent if the thumb bar for the Scrolling Browser had an equivalent in the Hypertext Browser. This might have been a map of the hypertext structure like Figure 4. Clicking on some node in this diagram would display the corresponding section. It was not practical to generate such a radically different system for the purposes of these experiments. However, the hypothesis was tested by reducing the cognitive effort needed to make transitions within the hypertext structure by providing a non-interactive map of the structure. That is the basis of Experiment 2.

4. Experiment 2 – hypertext browsing with and without a map

4.1. Method

The Hypertext Browser was used with two further groups of subjects. One had a printed map of the hypertext structure displayed prominently to one side of the screen. This this gave the 'uses/used by' indexing information in the same form as Figure 4. This map includes the section titles and so to control for the possibility that this information alone might explain any observed improvement in performance a second control condition was introduced. This second group of 10 users had a printed list of the 12 section headings. There were twenty subjects, none of whom had participated in the first experiment.

The hierarchical map and the list of titles were introduced to the subjects as memory aids that could help them remember where information could be found. Otherwise, the present experiment proceeded in an identical fashion to the first.

4.2. Results

Table 2 includes the results of Experiment 2. Comparing the two new hypertext groups with the original in Experiment 1 we see that the rate of performance is very much improved with the addition of a map but that providing the section titles without any indication of the hypertext structure has very little effect. The former difference can be shown to be significant. Analysis of variance of the complete data set for Experiments 1 and 2 followed by Dunn's test for four non-orthogonal planned comparisons shows that the minimum difference which would be significant is 19.35 tasks per hour. The group with a map also visit fewer sections but this is not significant ($F(4, 45) = 1.34$, n.s.)

It would seem that providing a map or 'overview', to use the terminology of the Notecards system (Halasz, Moran & Trigg [1987]), is of crucial importance. An interactive map, allowing direct access to a section anywhere in the hypertext structure, might have improved performance still further. Without any kind of overview the cognitive effort required to navigate the hypertext network may outweigh the advantages of providing a non-linear text structure conforming to the demands of the task.

5. Conclusions

It would be quite wrong to conclude, on the basis of the results from Experiment 1, that hypertext will always be more difficult to use than the alternatives. Clearly the generality of any one experiment is limited to the tasks used, the user population sampled and the precise nature of the alternatives compared. The performance difference observed in Experiment 1 is interesting because it stimulated further exploration of the use of these browsers. Study of the behavior of users in the scrolling group of Experiment 1 demonstrated the salience of the 'uses/used in' links between sections, thus showing that the links the hypertext structure is based on are the important ones for users doing these tasks.

The final conclusion, that finding your way about a hypertext structure may distract from the primary task, in this case program comprehension, may be much more generalisable. With a hypertext structure of only 12 sections, providing a map resulted in a 25% improvement in performance. The improvement could be very considerable with large hypertext structures.

Hypertext provides exciting new ways of structuring information but it should be remembered that there are already well understood ways for communicating non-linear conceptual structures in conventional linear text (e.g., section headings and subheadings, forward references and so on). While hypertext presents the designer with many new ways of helping the user, it also presents a whole new range of problems for the user and designer to solve. These problems will only come to light through systematic empirical work looking at the behavior of the users of hypertext systems. This paper is a start in that direction.

Acknowledgement

I am grateful to members of the Human-Computer Interaction Group at York who have commented on drafts of this paper, particularly Harold Thimbleby. The work was supported by the U.K. Alvey Directorate through grant GR/D/0231.7. A fuller report can be obtained by writing to the first author.

References

R M Akscyn, D L McCracken & E Yoder [November 1987], "KMS: A Distributed Hypermedia System for Managing Knowledge in Organizations," in *Proceedings of HyperTEXT '87*, Chapel Hill, North Carolina, 1–20.

J Bently [1986], "Programming Pearls: Literate Programming," *Communications of the ACM* 29, 364–369.

F G Halasz, T P Moran & R H Trigg [1987], "Notecards in a Nutshell," in *CHI + GI Conference '87*, ACM, Toronto Canada.

N V Hammond & L Allinson [1988], "Development and Evaluation of a CAL System for Non-Formal Domains: The Hitch-Hikers Guide to Cognition," *Computers and Education* 12, 215–220.

D E Knuth [1984], "Literate Programming," *The Computer Journal* 27, 97–111.

J H C Kuo, K J Leslie, M D Maggio, B G Moore & H C Tu [1986], "Information Structuring for Software Environments," in *Advanced Programming Environments*, G Goos and J Hartm, ed., Springer-Verlag.

H Thimbleby [1986], "Experiences of 'Literate Programming' Using CWEB (a variant of Knuth's WEB)," *The Computer Journal* 29, 201–211.

R H Trigg & M Weiser [1986], "TEXTNET: A Network Based Approach to Text Handling," *ACM Trans. OIS* 4, 1–23.

N Yankelovich, N Meyrowitz & A van Dam [1985], "Reading and Writing the Electronic Book," *IEEE Computer*.

Hypertext Tips: Experiences in Developing a Hypertext Tutorial

Lynda Hardman

Scottish HCI Centre, Heriot-Watt University, Chambers Street, Edinburgh EH1 1HX, U.K.

Hypertext is a next step in the sophistication of presenting text and graphics to users. One of the major HCI issues is how an author presents information to the reader in an easily comprehensible way. This is problematic because designing a hypertext is even more difficult than designing a good linear document, which is already difficult enough. Furthermore, at the present time, there are only a small number of good examples of hypertexts.

This paper examines the development of a hypertext, written using the Guide hypertext system, for presenting a tutorial on the structure of the brain to physiology students. The paper describes a number of points that were raised during the authoring of the tutorial. These points are formed into guidelines which suggest how to structure a hypertext and how to make the layout of the information in a hypertext clearer.

The Guide hypertext system allow links from graphics to text, whereas paper allows only links from text to graphics. The use of this extra dimension is discussed.

The paper is intended to give advice on creating a hypertext for authors new to the concept.

Keywords: Hypertext

1. Hypertext: Why and What?

Hypertext systems allow us to go beyond linear documents and make use of the computer's memory and screen facilities to present information to people in a more useful way.

Jeff Conklin (Conklin [1987]), describes a number of hypertext systems and looks at these in an attempt to get at the essence of hypertext. The property that comes closest to defining a hypertext system is the ability to create links between items and to navigate through the hypertext using these links. These links allow the reader to access different parts of a document in any order, for example, a list of chapter headings could be linked to the chapters themselves.

Some hypertext systems not only allow linking of text, but also linking of graphics (e.g., Guide (OWL International [1986]), HyperCard (Inc. [1987]) and Hyperties (Shneiderman [1987]).) Other systems that incorporate further media, such as video, are known as hypermedia systems.

Hypertext thus introduces two new dimensions of complexity when writing documents:

- using graphics in new ways
- using both text and graphics within a new structural framework.

2. Creating a Hypertext is Not Easy

Systems for creating hypertexts are now readily available to potential authors. However, knowing how to go about producing a finished hypertext that is easy and pleasant to use is another matter. Creating a well-constructed, easy to use linear document (such as a good text book) is a problem in itself. Trying to do that, and more, using a new way of constructing documents is even harder. Davida Charney (Charney [1987]), gives an excellent account of readers' problems when reading non-linear texts. She points out that writers of linear documents have developed techniques to lead readers through the material. They know the reader is going to read from the start to the finish and can use that knowledge to sequence topics. When reading a hypertext the reader is free to choose any sequence of reading. Writers of hypertexts need to develop new ways of giving the reader cues to cope with this.

A particular illustration of hypertext construction 'maturing' can be seen in the progression of documents written using the Guide hypertext system for the Macintosh. Before the product was launched, Guide's help system was produced as a hypertext to be read on-line. These files contained the necessary information, but were not presented in a particularly imaginative way (Figure 1). The help files produced for the second release of Guide are much more graphically based, and are much more deliberate in hiding unnecessary information and retaining context information (Figure 2). The Space Adventure on the Zone Club Disk #1[1](The Saving Zone [1987])(Figure 3) is another step in the graphical direction and moves away from paper analogies – for example, there are various comments, linked to items in the picture, which can only be viewed using the screen.

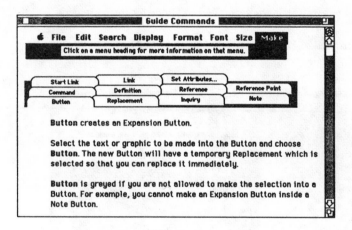

The reader is currently reading about the Button menu item in the Make menu. The reader can click on the section headings in italics at the bottom of the window to go directly to those sections.

Figure 1.   Extract from Guide 1.0 Help

The Zone Club Disk #1 was produced by the Saving Zone primarily as a catalogue of their products (both software and hardware). However, the disk also contains a light-hearted Space Adventure (and a competition) which makes great use of the ability to link graphics in Guide.

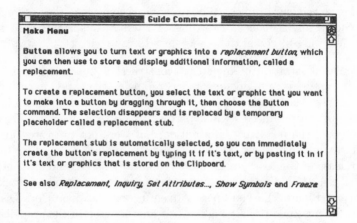

The pictures of menu headings at the top of the window are links to the sections about the menus. Similarly, the tabs on the cards link to the sections about those menu items. Currently, the reader is looking at the Button item in the Make menu. (Button is the term used in Guide for linked items.)

Figure 2.   Extract from Guide 2.0 Help

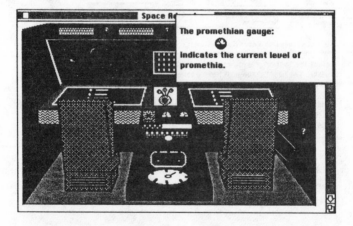

The cursor is over the leftmost of the three gauges at the centre of the picture and appears as an asterisk – indicating a Guide note link. The mouse button is being held down.

Figure 3.   Extract from the Zone Club Disk #1

This paper describes a number of points that were raised during the authoring of a particular hypertext (a neuroanatomy tutorial) and forms these points into more general guidelines. It is intended as a place for authors to start considering how they construct their hypertexts. From the experience gained during the construction of the hypertext tutorial potential authors will be more aware of pitfalls that can cause delay or detract from the inherent advantages of hypertext.

The hope is that, after a few years, guidelines such as these will be overtaken by 'common knowledge' on how to build hypertexts. However, at this stage, where there are only a very small number of good examples of hypertexts, this paper will provide information on the construction of hypertexts for the growing number of authors experimenting with this medium.

3. Cutting the Problem Down to Size

Garrett *et al* (Garrett, Smith & Meyrowitz [1986]), describes a categorisation of hypertexts. These categories[2] are:

- single author, single reader
- single author, many readers
- many authors, many readers

The case of single author, single reader is where the author is using her/his own hypertext database and knows (more-or-less) where things are and what they mean.

The case of single author, many readers is where the author is producing a hypertext to be distributed to a distinct readership.

The case of many authors, many readers can be split into two subcategories. One where the readers are the authors, and the dynamic growth of the material in the hypertext is the end in itself. The other where the readers are distinct from the authors, and a finished hypertext (or finished version) is distributed to a distinct readership.

In this paper I concentrate on the categories where the result is a finished hypertext and the readers are distinct from the author. This is similar to

---

The paper mentions annotators in addition to authors and readers. I am putting readers and annotators in the same category (namely readers) for the purposes of this discussion.

the production of a text book. The author[3] has an expected readership
and is trying to communicate her/his ideas to that readership.

4. The Tutorial Used for this Case Study

The hypertext used as the basis for this paper is designed as an on-
line tutorial for physiology students. The hypertext is being created by
Nikki MacLeod, a physiology lecturer at the University Medical School
in Edinburgh. The goal of the hypertext is to present the complex
information of neuroanatomy to students in a more transparent way
than is normally encountered in neuroanatomy text books.

The hypertext tutorial can be compared in size with a small book. There
are 18 sections, each of which is comparable to the information content
of a chapter in a text book. The hypertext so far contains 5 completed
sections and requires over 300 kilobytes of disk space, which is taken up
mostly by graphical images.

The hypertext tutorial has taken about 2 personmonths (so far) to
construct. A small part of this was spent getting round practicalities
in preparing the tutorial (for example obtaining access to an image
scanner) and creating the basic hypertext structure for the tutorial. The
main part was spent editing and resizing graphical images so they looked
pleasant on the particular screen being used.

The tutorial was produced using Guide version 2.0 for the IBM PC range
of machines. The machine used was the Olivetti M24 (a 'fast' IBM PC
compatible), with 640 kilobytes of RAM, a 20 megabyte disk and an
Olivetti Enhanced Graphics Card (allowing colour graphics to be used).

5. The Guide Hypertext System

The Guide hypertext system allows the reader to move around a hypertext by actioning links, for example by clicking on a linked item with
a mouse. Guide has three different types of links – replacement links,
reference links and note links. Replacement links give a hierarchical
structure to the document. Reference links take the reader to another
part of the same document, or to a different document. Note links bring
a temporary window on the screen to display a short aside[4]. A Guide
hypertext is a collection of documents with links between them.

---

[3] I will not go into the problems of multi-authorship – these are no doubt an
extension of those encountered with multi-author books.

[4] Similar to a footnote in printed documents.

Guide allows a text or graphics selection to be made into a linked item, at either end of the link. When the cursor moves over a linked area it changes shape. Textual links can have properties, such as bold and underline, associated with the different link types.

6. The Construction of the Hypertext Tutorial

The following issues, raised during the construction of the hypertext tutorial, can be grouped into two categories. Those that:

- suggest how to structure the hypertext
- suggest how to make the layout of the information in the hypertext clearer

6.1. Designing the structure of the hypertext

The author has a particular 'chunk' of information s/he wishes to communicate to the reader. This information exists in the author's head as a network of related points. John Smith (Smith [1987]), describes the funnelling process the author goes through in order to construct a linear document. For a hypertext the author is not obliged to cut all the network links to form a strict hierarchy, and then lay out the hierarchy in a linear form. Instead, the information can be put into the hypertext in the same structure as it is in the author's head.

Currently, most hypertexts are essentially hierarchical in nature, with links between items across the hierarchy. This allows the reader to have the feeling of being at the 'beginning' of the hypertext (that is at the top level, or root, of the hierarchy) or at some 'position' within the hypertext. Perhaps this tendency will disappear as authors become more used to creating hypertexts.

A hierarchical structure does not preclude different hierarchies being imposed on the same material. For example, a hypertext of a city tourist guide may have separate contents for places of interest based on location and type.

The hypertext can be viewed as two distinct parts – the subject matter and a collection of links into the subject matter. The subject matter consists of information with links between related items. Other links can be viewed as being above this level, linking into the mass of information, e.g., contents screens and indices. The sorts of decisions the author then has to make are:

- What is the structure of the links within the subject matter?
- Will there be contents screens? What form will they take?
- Will there be a glossary? What form will it take?
- Will there be an index? What form will it take?

Tom Hewett lists some guidelines ((Hewett [1987]), section 4 on Design Principles) that were followed when the Drexel Disk was created. Some of these are relevant when creating any hypertext structure:

- The reader should be able to move around the hypertext easily and quit when finished.
- Any hierarchy should be shallow and wide, not narrow and deep.
- There should be multiple paths through the information.

Ideally, the author should produce a 'naked' structure that contains all the major links necessary for the hypertext, then slot the subject matter in later. (This process is similar to, but more complex than, outlining a text book.)

Once the creation of the hypertext is underway it will become more difficult to restructure the information. Hypertext systems do allow this, but major revisions present a complex editing and restructuring problem, in which the author has to know how the current state relates to both the original and intended structures. In the neuroanatomy tutorial clearcut structural changes were made, while there was little subject matter incorporated in the structure, and these took several hours of editing to complete.

6.2. Linking information

On paper it is not possible to always directly connect a piece of information with all related pieces of information. Hypertext allows much greater flexibility with this, but authors have to consciously seek possible applications.

Two examples of more direct linking were encountered while authoring the neuroanatomy tutorial.

Glossary section: There are at least two uses for a glossary list. One is for readers to check up on the meaning of a word while they are reading the main text. Another is to scan through the glossary, after learning some of the subject matter, to check that they do indeed know the words listed. For the former use, to have to look up the glossary itself is a lengthier process than need be. It is much more convenient to have the definition of every word immediately accessible. (This is possible in Guide by using a note link to display the definition in a temporary window on the screen. In other hypertext systems this type of link could be implemented in slightly different ways.) The glossary section can then be a list of words, each of which is linked to its definition.

Contents screens: Direct access to a contents screen can be provided throughout the hypertext. Different levels of contents can be accessible from different places. In the neuroanatomy tutorial, links to the contents for the current subsection and to the main contents are almost always on the screen.

6.3. Hiding information

Allowing direct access to related information gives another bonus – because it is easy to get to, it does not have to be present on the screen. The author's goal should be to present the reader with an uncluttered screen that the reader can recognise. There can be a large amount of information linked to items on the screen, but the reader is shielded from the immediate confusion of it all. For example, a paper page can look cluttered with diagrams and explanations of the diagrams, but on-screen only the diagrams need be present. Related text can be linked to the diagrams and read in a superimposed window when the reader chooses. This can make up for the currently limited screen space available on cheaper machines.

6.4. Presenting contextual information

When a reader actions a link whose destination is some remote part of a hypertext there should be information there to reorient the reader. This can be explicit by having all the section and sub-section headings present on the screen, although this takes up more screen space as the reader goes to deeper levels in a hierarchy. For example, in figure 2, the menu bar remains at the top of the window with the current menu heading highlighted. Alternatively, the information might be implicit, where there is a link to the contents screen of the current subsection, so the reader can find out where s/he is.

In the neuroanatomy tutorial context is retained by links which allow the reader to go to the contents screen for the current subsection (labelled with the name of the subsection) and to the main contents screen.

The Drexel Disk, a 'one-off' hypertext application, has a particularly nice method of stopping the reader from getting disoriented. A menu gives access to the different levels of contents screens, and the contents screens themselves have distinctive layouts and icons on them. Tom Hewett describes the disk in more detail, and users' reactions to the disk (Hewett [1987]).

Other hypertext systems, such as NoteCards (Halasz, Moran & Trigg [1987]), display a graphical representation of the links in the hypertext. These highlight where the reader is and allow the reader to navigate directly to other sections by selecting items directly. However, these diagrams become very confused for more than a small number of items and links. The wider problems of navigation are discussed in Karen Mahony's paper (Mahony []).

6.5. Avoiding multiple copies of the same information

Links in hypertext mean that information duplication can be avoided by linking to that information wherever it is required. This means that problems with maintaining multiple copies of the same information can be avoided.

This problem was encountered during the construction of the hypertext tutorial, although it was caused by the implementation of Guide. It was decided that a file for each section was more appropriate than one large file. Guide does not allow the description of a note link to reside in a different file from the note link, so that any time a glossary item is used its description needs to be included in the file.

6.6. Designing the layout of the hypertext

Graphics design for paper is hard, but graphics design for the dynamic environment of hypertext is even harder. The layout of any screenful of information should be at least as good as it would have been on paper, and then the way related pieces of information are displayed should be of the same standard. One simple example is not to have a detailed description of an item appear in a window directly on top of that item. Figures 2 and 3 give an idea of what can be achieved. Also see (Kindborg & Kollerbaur [1987]) for ideas on combining text and graphics for good visual communication.

6.7. Using graphical instead of textual references

Hypertext systems with the ability to link graphical items allow the use of graphical images as references. Figures in paper documents are always referred to from the text, and cannot, themselves, refer to the text (unless text is used in the figure to describe this).

The Drexel Disk (Hewett [1987]), and the Domesday Project (BBC [1986]), illustrate two ways in which graphical references can be used.

A contents screen on the Drexel Disk is effectively a list of items which link to different subjects, where each link has a distinctive graphical (and textual) description. The Domesday Project makes use of the graphical image as an organising feature and so allows the reader to select a point on a map to reveal enlarged detail in the neighbourhood of that point.

The latter use can be exploited whenever a continuous space can be mapped onto a more detailed continuous space, but would not work for entwined networks of ideas used in something like literary criticism. In the neuroanatomy tutorial this feature is used to allow the reader to navigate through the different levels of the brain.

6.8. Distinguishing between highlighting items and showing structure

In any hypertext the presence of a link needs to be communicated to the reader. Some hypertext systems have particular graphical icons which indicate the links (e.g., Intermedia (Garrett, Smith & Meyrowitz [1986]), KMS (Akscyn, McCracken & Yoder [1987])). Others use highlighted words to indicate the links (Hyperties (Shneiderman [1987])). Others have no built-in standard (Guide (OWL International [1986]), Hyper-Card (Inc. [1987])).

In Guide, HyperCard, and Hyperties the information describing the link is directly associated with the link. With other systems, such as KMS and Intermedia, the connection is less direct, and a description of the link lies in the neighbourhood of the link icon.

In all these cases the reader should be presented with a screen where it is obvious

- where the links are on the screen,
- what each link's destination is.

The layout of the screen should draw attention to important pieces of subject matter (information content), as well as the links (structure information). When the hypertext system directly associates the link with the description of the link's destination there is a conflict between emphasising the two different types of information (content and structure). The problem is particularly severe using text in Guide because, for example, all replacement links are bold by default, and when the author introduces a new term it is convenient to make it bold to stand out. The reader can only distinguish by moving the cursor over the bold word and noticing whether the cursor shape changes.

The solution to this conflict is simple. The author needs to decide on style standards from the beginning. A simple example would be to use bold, underline or italic for highlighting important words, but use underline *and* italic to denote a replacement link. This consistency can be continued into graphical links, so that any graphical link containing text would have the text in the required style.

Style refers not only to text format, but to colour, font and size as well. Similarly, graphical items emphasising important details should have a style which is not used to denote linked items. Graphical styles could include properties such as colour, size, shading, pattern, outline, shape and orientation.

Johnson and Beach (Johnson & Beach [1988]), discusses styles in (linear) document editing systems.

6.9. Distinguishing between navigation links and subject matter links

Having made clear to the reader the difference between content and structure information, further distinctions within structure information can be made. Links always take the reader somewhere else, but do so for different reasons. For example, they may lead to a small piece of information directly related to the current context, to a remote place in a different subject (with some relevant connection), or to a contents screen. The author should design standard styles for these, and other, reasons for links.

Even greater consistency can be achieved by placing certain types of linked items in similar places on the screen. For example, in the neuroanatomy tutorial, items which link to the current subsection contents screen are always the same style (white text on a purple oval), and are to be found at the bottom left of the window.

In Guide there are already 3 different types of link – the reference, replacement and note as mentioned previously. Further distinction can be made within these types according to the information accessed via the link. Care should be taken, however, to keep the number of different styles small so as not to overload the reader.

7. Conclusion

The complexity of creating a hypertext lies somewhere between writing a text book and software engineering. The author needs to make initial decisions on the subject matter, the readership and then go on to design the hypertext itself. The author should be prepared to spend time on the design as well as the construction of the hypertext.

The process can be thought of in much the same way as a software design cycle, where the design decisions taken early on become harder to change as the amount of information in the hypertext increases.

The issues the author has to face are:

- designing the overall structure of the hypertext – including the links external to the subject matter, as well as major internal subject matter links;

- designing the structure of the subject matter – being aware of linking information, hiding information, presenting contextual information and avoiding multiple copies of information;

- designing the layout of the material – deciding where graphics would be more suitable than text, or even where other media such as video would be suitable, and on style conventions for the various link types used in the hypertext.

After the design stage comes the construction (or 'implementation') stage. Ideally this should be planned out in advance. The plan should allow for 'prototypes' of the hypertext to be shown to potential readers for evaluation as early as possible in the construction.

If creating the whole hypertext at once seems too daunting, then, as in good software engineering practice, it can be broken down into parts, each part created separately, then linked together as necessary.

The purpose of stressing the complexity of creating a hypertext is not to dissuade potential authors, but to make explicit, before they embark on such a project, the decisions they will have to make. Others have already created and used hypertexts, for example the Intermedia hypertext system has been used successfully in teaching courses on English and Biology at Brown University (Beeman et al. [1987]). For authors to benefit most from the guidelines in this paper they should consider them along with examples of well-constructed hypertexts. Readily available examples of these are the help hypertexts for Guide (version 2.0) and HyperCard.

References

R M Akscyn, D L McCracken & E Yoder [November 1987], "KMS: A Distributed Hypermedia System for Managing Knowledge in Organizations," in *Proceedings of HyperTEXT '87*, Chapel Hill, North Carolina, 1–20.

BBC [1986], "The BBC Domesday Project.

W O Beeman, K T Anderson, G Bader, J Larkin, A P McClard, P McQuillian & M Shields [November 1987], "Hypertext and Pluralism: From Lineal to Non-Lineal Thinking," in *Proceedings of HyperTEXT '87*, Chapel Hill, North Carolina, 67–88.

D Charney [November 1987], "Comprehending Non-Linear Text: The Role of Discourse Cues and Reading Strategies," in *Proceedings of HyperTEXT '87*, Chapel Hill, North Carolina, 109–120.

J Conklin [1987], "Hypertext: An Introduction and Survey," *IEEE Computer* 20, 17–41.

L N Garrett, K E Smith & N Meyrowitz [December 1986], "Intermedia: Issues, Strategies and Tactics in the Design of a Hypermedia Document System," in *Proceedings of the Conference on Computer-Supported Cooperative Work*, Austin, Texas, 163–174.

F G Halasz, T P Moran & R H Trigg [1987], "Notecards in a Nutshell," in *CHI + GI Conference '87*, ACM, Toronto Canada.

T Hewett [1987], "The Drexel Disk: An Electronic 'Guidebook'," in *People and Computers III*, D Diaper and R Winder, ed., Cambridge University Press, Cambridge, 115–129.

Apple Computer Inc. [1987], "HyperCard," Cupertino, CA.

J Johnson & R J Beach [1988], "Styles in Document Editing Systems," *IEEE Computer* 21, 32–43.

M Kindborg & A Kollerbaur [1987], "Visual Languages and Human-Computer Interaction," in *People and Computers III*, D Diaper and R Winder, ed., Cambridge University Press, Cambridge, 175–187.

K Mahony, "Navigation Around Hypertext," The Alvey Fortune Project, Working Paper K7, University of Kent, Canterbury, UK.

OWL International [1986], *Guide Users Manual*, Bellevue, Washington, USA.

B Shneiderman [November 1987], "User Interface Design for the Hyperties Electronic Encyclopedia," in *Proceedings of HyperTEXT '87*, Chapel Hill, North Carolina, 189–194.

J Smith [November 1987], "A Hypertext Writing Environment and its Cognitive Basis," in *Proceedings of HyperTEXT '87*, Chapel Hill, North Carolina, 195–214.

The Saving Zone [1987], *Zone Club Disk #1*, Redmond, Washington, USA.

Optimum Display Arrangements for Presenting Visual Reminders

John M. Findlay, Simon P. Davies*, Robert Kentridge, Anthony J. Lambert and Justine Kelly

Department of Psychology, University of Durham, South Road, Durham, DH1 3LE, U.K.

*Department of Computer Science, Huddersfield Polytechnic, Queensgate, Huddersfield, HD1 3DH, U.K.

Developments in technology now allow designers to make use of a wide variety of layouts to present material at an interactive terminal. Our understanding of perceptual and cognitive processes shows that various tradeoffs will need consideration in evaluating such layouts (availability of material *vs* screen clutter; reliance on user memory vs use of reminders etc). We approach these through the framework of attentional switching.

We shall report an experimental study which evaluates these tradeoffs in a frequently encountered text editing situation. Our editor may be set to either 'insert' or 'overtype' mode. This information can be displayed with varying prominence in a peripheral window on the screen,

displayed as a change of cursor, or omitted from the screen display. We have monitored user interaction at a keystroke level during text editing sessions and show that the different forms of presentation of reminder information can result in substantial differences in performance.

Keywords: Visual displays, windows, attention allocation, peripheral vision, reminders

1. Introduction

Interactive computing with visual display units is rapidly progressing from a situation in which the VDU was employed simply to present sequential text to a situation where the full potential of the technology may be exploited so as to distribute information at a variety of different screen locations. In particular, windowing tools are becoming widely used as a design aid in planning interfaces. Our aim in this paper is to suggest ways in which psychological knowledge of the visual, attentional and memory systems can be directed to this application, and to present a pilot study showing how the concepts may be amenable to experimental investigation. The first part of the discussion is rather more general than the specific issue which we finally home in on, which concerns the presentation of visual reminders.

2. Activity with interactive displays

Window based interfaces allow the possibility of presenting a number of separately addressable virtual screens within the confines of a single physical screen. Furthermore, any one of these virtual screens can, in principle, be used to gain access to further displays. One way in which such a potential can be exploited is to allow a user to switch between **different** tasks. A second type of use is to present different sources of information relevant to a **single** task at different locations on the screen. In this paper we concentrate on the latter, but it must be recognised that the distinction between the two is by no means rigid. Most single tasks can be subdivided into components. We are aiming to produce a framework for a task analysis of this type of interaction. It is recognised in the study of task analyses that a variety of different hierarchical levels may be considered. Our analyses consider a low level in the hierarchy, the fine structure of user actions. However we have been struck by the extent to which some of the concepts would seem to be useful for consideration of higher levels also.

The seminal keystroke analysis of Card, Moran and Newell (Card,

Moran & Newell [1983]) showed that certain activities, most notably text editing, could be rigorously analysed into an elementary detailed sequence of operations. A limitation of their approach is the concentration on a single goal-oriented processing stream. A feature of human cognitive activity which becomes of increasing importance when more complex display layouts receive consideration concerns the fact that much processing occurs outside the main conscious processing stream. Work on the psychology of human attention currently offers a model of human operation in which activity (thought or action) in one principal processing stream may be accompanied by activity in several subsidiary processing streams. Attention is seen as a flexible resource with tasks which are overlearned and/or of minimal information content proceeding in an automatized fashion at the same time as an individual engages on a principal task.

This concept can be clearly illustrated from a consideration of the use of vision. Our eyes take in visual information from a wide area of the visual field. At any instant, the gaze is directed to one particular location. Visual resolution is highest at this location and decreases at points away from this location in a very systematic manner. Normally, it is the visual material to which the gaze is directed which receives focal attention. Nonetheless, visual processing outside the active region is still occurring. For example, any substantial change will be capable of eliciting an orienting response wheresoever it may occur in the peripheral visual field.

Intensive investigation of the reading process (Rayner [1983]) has expanded our understanding of how parallel processing is used dynamically. Detailed textual information is taken in from a quite small region (around 7 characters) where the gaze is directed. But less detailed information (word boundaries, initial letters of words etc.) is also being simultaneously assimilated from more distant regions to assist in eye guidance and provide some preliminaries to the detailed analysis. This information is taken in from a wider region, extending in an asymmetric manner further to the right of the fixation point than the left. It appears that certain discriminations in parafoveal and peripheral vision can be made at no cost to the attentional resources required for central processing, whereas other discrimination can be made only if some conscious effort directs attention to the peripheral location (Treisman [1985]). Under normal circumstances, direction of attention to a peripheral visual location would involve direction of an eye movement to that location although the two operations are partly dissociable (Shepherd, Findlay & Hockey [1986])

Miyata and Norman (Miyata & Norman [1986]) have emphasised the need to take account of multiple processing streams when considering the potential of window based systems. Of course, such multiple streams may be occurring both on the human and the machine side of the interface. In general, for the operator, one particular stream will be occupying the current focus of consciousness (although not necessarily exclusively) and a key aspect of activity becomes a consideration of how this focus shifts from one stream to another. Surprisingly little seems to be understood of this aspect of cognitive functioning. A profitable analogy, drawn again by Miyata and Norman (Miyata & Norman [1986]), is with the 'interrupt handling' used in computer function.

Consider as a working hypothesis the idea that conscious human activity can be viewed as consisting of bouts of 'processing' which are ended at an 'interrupt'. Interrupts may obviously be generated **externally** through the senses – a telephone call, the arrival of a visitor. However the interrupt idea seems to have some face validity as a description of **internal** causes of processing terminations as we discuss in the following section. The 'pop-up' occurrence in memory of a task requiring urgent attention is an example.

Situations arise in which interrupts are deliberately preset as **reminders** in order to ensure that a particular task is accomplished. The topic of reminders can link the abstract study of attention and processing streams with practical design considerations since the provision of reminders is rendered feasible by a multi-element display. However, a reminder is also, by its nature, a distractor and its value may vary accordingly. There are times when reminders may be more welcome than others. It is not difficult to point to situations in which human activity is hindered by an overabundance of interrupts. These may be external (the telephone never stops ringing), but lack of concentration seems also characterised by the appearance of too many distracting thoughts from memory. Such situations may be contrasted with the low level of interrupts characteristic of an individual 'lost in thought', perhaps engaging in a search for inspiration.

3. Internal and external memory

The topic of reminders shows the intimate connection between the topics of attention and memory. A reminder is essentially a memory aid and memory aids are widely used in a wide variety of situations. If we need to remember what to buy when we visit a shop we often take a list. External aids to memory are often employed when other, intervening, cognitive events might interfere with the processes of learning and recall, when accuracy is at a premium, and when memory load is to be minimised to facilitate the allocation of attention to other activities. It seems that, in general, individuals prefer to use external aids to memory rather than rely upon their own internal memory (Intons-Peterson & Fournier [1986]). This suggests that the effort occasioned by the use of external memory props is less demanding than the cognitive effort required to encode and retrieve information from internal memory sources.

However external memory aids can, in some situations, become cumbersome and unproductive. In a recent study (Davies, Lambert & Findlay []) we investigated the use of internal and external memory props within the context of learning to use a word processor. It was found that subjects provided with an external memory prop in terms of a window containing a list of available commands performed no better than a group who had spent a short period committing the commands to internal memory. The performance of the former group was considerably disrupted by the removal of the memory prop information. Thus, in this case, use of a simple learning strategy could obviate the need for the memory prop.

In this situation, the command set, once learned, remained unchanged (at least until the user switched to a different system). Memory may also be used in a more dynamic way to follow a changing situation. Human memory, under appropriate circumstances, is very good at such a task. It is generally possible, for example, to 'keep track' of the topic of a dialogue or of the individual's location within the environment. However, it is a familiar experience in interacting with computers that users are liable to become 'lost' during the course of an interactive session. In the remainder of the paper we focus on the problem of keeping track in terms of relatively conventional systems; however the examples given above might also suggest radically different approaches to system design (for example, 'map' type menus (Hitch et al. [1986])).

4. State monitoring

A characteristic of a complex system is that it can manifest a variety of different 'states' and as systems grow in complexity, the number of possible states is also increasing. When interacting with a complex system, the problem of how to 'keep track' of the current state of the system may be termed the '**state monitoring**' problem.

We have concentrated on one rather common situation in which state monitoring is necessary. Many word processors and text editors have available two or more modes that may be used for inserting text. Typically there is an **insert** mode in which new text may be entered without deleting any existing text as an alternative to an **overtype** mode in which new text is typed over existing text. Experience shows that both facilities can be useful at different times and commonly it is possible to switch from one mode to another with a simple command or keypress.

We can use this situation to illustrate the choices that occur at the fine structure level when designing an interactive system. From the user's point of view, we are looking at a place where a processing stream is interrupted: new information must be obtained about the system state before the next task – the text insertion – is carried out. As just discussed above, both psychological theory and evolved design practice suggest that in this particular case external rather than internal memory should be used. How then can this information be presented on the screen ?

We were led to this question through experience with a particular text editor in which such information was presented at the top right edge of the screen in the same font as the remainder of the text. To use the information, it was necessary to look at it. Thus the routine for 'interrupt handling' took the following form: make a saccadic eye movement to the appropriate screen location; retrieve the information; find the text position (flashing cursor); make a saccadic eye movement back to the text position. We have coined the term '**minimum switch**' to describe this sequence, and we can contrast it with both more and less extensive interrupt handling operations as follows:

1. **Normal switch**: Used to obtain information which is not immediately available on the screen. For example, a sequence of mouse operations could be used to open a window to obtain the information.

2. **Mini switch**: (as described above): Used to obtain information that is available on the screen but not at the central viewing location. To obtain the information it is necessary to move the eyes to the screen location.

3. **Micro switch**: Information could be presented in the visual periphery which has sufficient salience for an overt eye movement not to be required to extract it. It is probable that some attentional cost is still involved.

4. **Information at the fixation point**: It would seem that if a state indicator could be made available close to the fixation point, even less attentional capacity might be required for its use.

Analysis of the component activities shows that fewer actions are required as the list is descended. We may expect that the elimination of actions will lead to faster and, perhaps, more easily used, systems. In the subsequent sections we discuss an experimental study we have embarked on to test our intuition that the different ways of presenting reminders discussed above will differ in the attentional demands made on subjects. At the present time, only results from the early stages are available.

5. Method

5.1. Subjects

Twelve University students aged from 20 to 23. All had some experience of the screeneditor used by the University mainframe computer (NUMAC). Records from a further seven subjects were unfortunately lost due to a problem with the monitoring system. The subjects' typing skills ranged from poor to very good. The subjects were divided into two groups with typing abilities roughly balanced between groups.

5.2. Design

Our aim was to compare performance when state monitoring required a 'Minimum switch' (No. 2 above) of a saccadic glance to a peripheral location with that when information was available at the fixation point (No. 4 above). To this end we constructed several modified forms of the screeneditor program which could be run on an IBM PC. All the modified programs allowed the user access to a restricted command set. Forward and backward scroll commands, cursor movement commands, character and line deletion commands were common to each version of the program. Three different versions of the program all used the same pair of control keys for switching between 'character insertion' and 'line insertion' modes (these modes were mutually exclusive). In the former case, characters could be inserted in the middle of the text: in the latter characters entered would overtype existing material unless a new line was entered. The versions differed as follows:

Version P: An indicator was presented in a one-line window on the top left of the screen to indicate which of the two insert modes was current. A solid block line separated this window from the remainder of the text.

Version C: The mode indication was achieved by a change in cursor character. In line insertion the cursor was a solid block (█ This was the customary cursor for the screeneditor. In line insertion mode, the cursor was changed to a pair of bars (⎓). In each case the cursor flashed at the standard rate.

Version E: Both the indicators described above were available.

Version P was similar to the standard version of the screeneditor with which the users were familiar (although on the majority of terminals this displayed the mode information on the top right hand side of the screen and the line delineating the window was thinner).

Both groups of subjects carried out two sessions of text editing as described below. The first session was with editor Version E and was identical for both groups. Group A carried out the second session with editor version P and Group B with editor Version C.

5.3. Stimulus material and procedure

Two texts were prepared in advance. The texts were taken from a book of humourous letters and comprised about three A4 sides. Files containing two degenerate versions of these texts were prepared for the PC, in which a large number of errors were deliberately inserted. These were prepared so that their correction would be most simply achieved by frequently switching between line and character insertion. The number of corrections to be made was the same in both texts. A printout of the correct version of each file was made with the errors requiring correction highlighted in yellow (for character insertion requirements) and orange (erroneous letters where overtype gave the simplest means of correction).

Each subject was tested individually in two sessions. In the first session (Editor Version E), the operation of the text editor was explained to the subject and attention drawn to the two forms of mode information. In addition an instruction sheet giving the operations of the various control keys and the significance of the cursor change information was also available for consultation. Following this instruction period, the subject was given the printout and asked to use the editor to make the necessary corrections in the computer file.

5.4. Monitoring of user interaction

The editing sessions were recorded with the UMIST MMI Monitoring System (Morris et al. [1987]). This is a flexible tool which provides a time stamped record of keypress and mouse activity on (in our case) an IBM PC. The machine consists of a microprocessor with 1MByte of RAM which interfaces via a communications board which has RS232 connections to the user machine. The data record is supplemented by a 'journal' file into which various information can be entered (e.g., indications that some particular activity took place during the session). We made use of the journal record in the preliminary session to indicate the point at which the experimenter handed control over to the subject.

The data record can be subsequently either analysed or used to form a session replay in which the user machine is 'driven' by the recorded data to replicate exactly the original sequence of operations (provided of course that the user machine starts initially in the same state). In this study we used a journal marker to indicate when the subject's activities commenced. The timing data were analysed from this marker. For the data on detailed errors etc. it was necessary to replay and observe the record as the software for automated analysis was unavailable.

6. Results

6.1. User strategies and comments

The initial comments of the subjects when the cursor indicator was explained occasionally expressed doubt about the arbitrary nature of the indicator. However, most of the subjects experienced no difficulty in acquiring the relevant discrimination and one later volunteered the view "it's obvious which one is which". All subjects shifted between modes: one, however (Group B: Subject 4), used the strategy of typing a control character sequence before every correction, even when this was redundant. This strategy avoided the need for state monitoring although would not be useful on a system where a state change is of the toggle switch type.

Subjects in Group A who did not have the cursor information in the second session reported generally that its loss was felt and they had to think more about which mode they were in. Most subjects in Group B who had the peripheral information removed reported that they had learned to use the cursor information in the first session and there was no effect of the change. One exception (Subject 3) needed to refer to the instruction sheet at the beginning of the second session, but very quickly began to use the information.

These comments suggest that even the minimal switch of consulting a peripheral indicator requires appreciable processing effort. The superiority of the cursor information was supported by more objective analyses.

6.2. Time taken for the editing task

Table 1 (below) shows the times in minutes taken by each subject for the two tasks, and also the ratio of the two times.

The difference in editing times largely reflects the differential typing and computing experience of the subjects. However, it is possible to make a comparison which minimises the effect of these differences by using the subject's performance on the first tasks as a baseline measure. The ratio measure uses this baseline and shows that Group A show a much greater improvement in the second task. This result is however not statistically significant ($t = 1.69 : 10 \, df \, p \approx 0.1$) although it seems possible that a larger subject group might well reveal the effect to be a genuine one.

Table 1.

	Group A				Group B		
Subject	Task 1	Task 2	Perc.	Subject	Task 1	Task 2	Perc.
1	46.01	41.09	89.3	7	25.78	21.18	82.1
2	36.52	32.11	87.9	8	53.10	30.92	58.2
3	34.27	48.02	140.1	9	44.14	26.99	61.1
4	48.79	34.08	69.8	10	30.19	25.94	85.9
5	31.89	28.96	90.8	11	23.35	24.10	103.2
6	23.13	22.16	95.8	12	65.97	48.83	74.0
		Mean	95.6			Mean	77.4

6.3. Errors and pauses

The number of mistakes left in the final copy did not differ significantly between the two groups (Group A Session 1: 1.2 mistakes average, Session 2: 1.3 mistakes average, Group B Session 1: 2.6 mistakes average, Session 2: 3.3 mistakes average), nor did the number of typing errors made during the sessions (Group A Session 1: 11 average, Session 2: 10.3 average, Group B Session 1: 17 average, Session 2: 11.8 average). The number of occasions a subject was in the wrong mode (as evidenced by a later correction) was as follows: Group A, Session 1: mean 4.3, s.d. 3.2, Session 2 : mean 4.3, s.d. 2.1, Group B, Session 1: mean 5.7, s.d. 5.0, Session 2 : mean 3.2, s.d. 1.5). Group B shows an improvement in performance which is not shown by Group A, but the difference is not significant statistically ($t = 1.58, 10$ df).

A measure was also taken of pauses occurring before mode changes. A pause was assessed for this purpose as a noticeable delay with no cursor movement during fast replay (equivalent to a pause of about 3 seconds in real time). In Group A the number of pauses increased between sessions (Session 1: mean 8.0, s.d. 1.5, Session 2: mean 10.7, s.d. 6.0). In Group B, on the other hand, the number of such pauses decreased between sessions (Session 1: mean 7.0, s.d. 2.8, Session 2: mean 4.3, s.d. 1.5). The difference between the groups is statistically significant ($t = 3.2, 10$ $df, p < 0.01$). It must be noted that this latter analysis contains an element of subjectivity in the assessment of pauses: we are currently working to replace this measure with an objectively anlaysed equivalent.

7. Discussion

Our results appear to support the contention that the two methods of providing state information were differentially effective. However this result must be interpreted with some caution. Firstly, although all the differences pointed to the greater usefulness of the cursor change indicator, only one difference was significant. We plan to run further subjects in place of those whose data was lost. Another concern is whether our results might be influenced by the demand chracteristics of the experimental situation. We deliberately chose a design which would compare the cursor indicator with the indicator which would have already been familiar from previous use of the screeneditor. However it is possible that the novelty of the cursor manipulation, coupled with an experimental design in which we were obviously emphasizing mode changes, may have resulted in differential motivation between the two groups leading to differences in performance unrelated to the screen changes.

Nevertheless the most plausible interpretation of the results would seem to be along the lines of the attentional differences that we have outlined in the introductory sessions. Russo (Russo [1978]) pointed out that the use of eye movements in scanning is likely to be accompanied by a cognitive cost in terms of both the execution time and the prepration time for the activity. We believe that designers should give more careful consideration to these aspects. If our results are substantiated by further investigation, they indicate that it may pay dividends to explore how extensively cursor information can be developed. Although there are clear limits to the information that can be provided with cursors, there are still many possibilties (colour, patterns, blink rate) which could be explored. Conveying information in this way will certainly be less conventional than current practices; however such possibilities will certainly merit consideration in the course of a technological revolution which may well be of similar significance to the invention of writing.

References

S K Card, T P Moran & A Newell [1983], *The Psychology of Human-Computer Interaction*, Lawrence Erlbaum Associates, Hillsdale, New Jersey.

S P Davies, A J Lambert & J M Findlay, "Availability of Menu Information During the Early Stages of Command Learning in a Word Processing Application," Submitted to Human Factors.

G J Hitch, A G Sutcliffe, J M Bowers & L M Eccles [1986], "Empirical Evaluation of Map Interfaces," in *People and Computers: Designing for Usability (Proceedings of the Second Conference of the BCS HCI SG, York, 23-26 September 1986)*, M D Harrison and A F Monk, ed., Cambridge University Press.

464   *J.M.Findlay, S.P.Davies, R.Kentridge, A.J.Lambert and J.Kelly*

M Intons-Peterson & J Fournier [1986], "External and Internal Memory Aids: When and How Often Do We Use Them?," *J. Exp. Psychol. General* 115, 267–280.

Y Miyata & D A Norman [1986], "Psychological Issues in the Support of Multiple Activities," in *User Centered System Design*, D A Norman and S W Draper, ed., Lawrence Erlbaum Associates, Hillsdale, New Jersey.

D Morris, C J Theaker, S Hope & W Love [1987], "The UMIST Prototype Monitor," UMIST, Technical Report.

K Rayner [1983], *Eye Movements in Reading: Perceptual and Language Processes*, Academic Press.

J E Russo [1978], "Adaptation of Cognitive Processes to the Eye Movement System," in *Eye Movements and the Higher Psychological Functions*, J W Senders D F Fisher and R A Monty, ed., Lawrence Erlbaum Associates, Hillsdale, New Jersey, 89–109.

M Shepherd, J M Findlay & G R J Hockey [1986], "The Relationship between Eye Movements and Spatial Attention," *Quarterly J. Exp. Psychol.* 38A, 475–491.

A Treisman [1985], "Preattentive Processing in Vision," *Computer Vision, Graphics and Image Processing* 31, 156–177.

Flexible Intelligent Interactive-video

T. Webb and D.G. Jameson

Audio-Visual Department, University College London,
Windeyer Building, Cleveland Street,
London W1P 6DB, U.K.

University College and Middlesex School of Medicine are producing two interactive video(IV) discs for use in teaching Clinical and Surgical management. The system is designed to provide three modes of interaction and will have as its core an expert system on the domain covered by the disc. The combination of a knowledge-based system and video is very rich in information. The interface for such a system requires a format familiar enough for the user to assimilate it rapidly, but flexible enough to deal with the range of possible situations and combinations of information formats. Some lessons learnt from a previous IV project are discussed and some problems raised by the new system are aired. The authors have found like many before them, that paper-based information systems provide useful guidelines for effective presentation.

Keywords: Interactive video, expert system, human-computer interface

1. Summary

University College, London already has experience of producing a videodisc for skill training in the medical area (Jameson & Roberts [1987];

Pinnington & Bayard-White []). It was decided to build upon that experience and set up an editorial panel to work with the Audio-Visual Department to produce two video-discs; one on surgical examination and treatment of lumps in the neck, and the other on the diagnosis and treatment of patients with severe and sudden breathlessness. Lessons learnt from the *Back to Basics* project (Jameson [1988]; Jameson [1986]), are discussed and problems raised by the new project are aired. Solutions to some of these problems are offered.

2. Introduction

The School of Medicine in University College, London faces the same problem as many other university medical institutions, namely how the academic staff can meet their clinical commitment and cover the increasing demands of the curriculum. We have responded to this problem by setting up a project to use new technology to design an intelligent tutoring system utilising interactive-video as part of the domain knowledge base.

The system has as its core an expert system based on surgical and clinical experts' view of their tasks, the information is made available through a tutorial, a mixed initiative learning environment and a user-centred browsing facility. Such a system has potential both as an advisory system in the clinic and as a teaching system. The knowledge base represents the experience and logical thinking of a clinician of considerable experience, and can be considered to be a formulation of the information placed before the student in conventional bedside teaching. This can be seen as an example of the apprenticeship style of teaching with the student gaining knowledge by watching, practising and discussing with the 'master'. We are aware that the students' knowledge will be limited and that they may not be satisfied by asking questions purely within the clinical domain. Accordingly it will be possible for students to 'drop down', transparently, to knowledge bases covering pre-clinical material.

3. Back to Basics Video-disc Package

3.1. Objectives

A video-disc training package '*Back to Basics*' was produced by this department to train users in the principles of safe lifting and the prevention of back-pain. Some workers in this field consider it necessary only to make the video-disc as a teaching or utility resource and leave it up to the individual to decide how to use it. We believe it is essential that interactive-video material is produced with associated software as the average teacher/trainer is not likely to be able, or have the time to develop the supporting lesson (Parsloe [1983]).

It is equally important to consider the environment in which the video-disc will operate and how the user can exercise control of the equipment. The software for the interactive-video package *Back to Basics* was written in Pascal and particular attention was given to the users' control of the system, with the aim that they should be able to work unattended. In *Back to Basics* the video and text images are displayed on the same screen, and text can be overlaid on the video image if required.

3.2. Mouse Control

As the video-disc was directed at a wide cross-section of the population, and many people are worried by computer keyboards, it was decided to investigate the use of a mouse to control the system. There were two basic types of control required; firstly to give geographical access to different parts of the disc, and secondly to control the mode of operation of the video-disc play-back system. A simple multiple-choice option was used to locate the different video sequences on the disc. Control of the disc was provided through, the now near standard, medium of a pop-up menu displaying the various possible modes of playing the disc. A 'Help' facility which explained the options was provided as part of the video-control menu.

During the project development a period of time was put aside to test the system on various potential users. We were interested in the ability of the students to use not only the mouse but the system as a whole. Only very few people exhibited difficulties in coordinating the mouse. Many people do however seem to have some difficulty in locating the pointer precisely in a box. As an aid to those people who were unfamiliar with the mouse a small section was included in the introduction of the program to train in its use. Those people who used this routine demonstrated a definite improvement in their ability.

3.3. Structured and Unstructured Teaching Modes

The teaching environment operated in two ways, firstly a highly structured teaching mode in which the student was taken through the subject in a manner analogous to conventional computer based training (CBT). In the second mode an attempt was made to give students control of the manner in which the material was accessed and enable them to browse at their own pace. In this mode the student can have direct control of the video-disc player. Also the student can determine whether or not there should be questions in the tutorial, and is able to choose one of the two available sound tracks which provide voice-over from different viewpoints, e.g., employers and employees responsibilities in health and safety matters. The user determines these parameters by answering a short series of questions at the logging in stage, but cannot move from the browsing to the structured learning phase, or vice-versa during a session.

3.4. Question Types

The software provided multiple choice questions with either single or multiple answers. It was desirable for the user to be able to correct their response if they wished, and so provision had to be made to confirm the final answer. The decision to make the mouse the sole means of interaction restricted the system to multiple-choice questions. Responses were given by clicking on box(es) next to the chosen answer. An incorrect response from the student was followed by an indication of the correct answer, and hence there was no need in the lessons for branching. A problem became apparent with questions on the content of still pictures from the disc. Since a question normally occupied several lines on the screen, it was difficult to overlay on the picture. Hence the student was told that they would have to answer a question about a picture, shown the picture, and then asked the question. The difficulty for the student was that they could not see the question and the picture simultaneously, and so were dependent to some degree upon memorising the contents of the still image. This problem would have been compounded if we had attempted to ask the student specific questions about a video sequence. It could have been avoided by using separate monitors for video and computer-generated material. However, experience has produced a strong conviction that dividing the user's concentration between two screens would seriously impair the student's efficiency.

4. Present Project

4.1. Application of Expert Systems

The aim of the teaching system is to help the user to learn how to develop a working clinical diagnosis to make decisions on patient management. It was decided at the beginning of the project that the best means of achieving this aim is through an expert system. We aim to provide an environment where students can follow the expert system through a diagnosis, and in which the expert system can in turn follow the students' performance in their attempts to resolve diagnostic problems posed by the program. The strength of expert systems most commonly emphasised in relation to their role in education, is their ability to refer back to the rules used in making a decision (Fortescue [1988]; O'Shea &

Self [1984]; Yazdani [1986]). It is this strength which Dr. Robin Brooks has used in Adept (Brooks [1987]) referred to by Sue Fortescue (Fortescue [1988]) as "probably one of the most complex IV programmes to have been developed incorporating an expert system". These rules, though, represent only high level schema which a domain expert has developed over years of experience. In many cases the logic behind such rules is extremely complex. It is essential that students learning such skills understand the reasoning behind the rules they employ. Understanding of this type aids retention, and students should be encouraged to be sure they can fully justify their decisions. Expert systems for education, then, require more than a simple facility for regurgitating high-level rules; they need a backup base of rules or text which explains the reasoning behind the expert's rules.

The different modes for providing information in the *Back to Basics* system have already been discussed. It is intended to repeat the structure of a pre-set tutorial and a facility for browsing in the new system; and to add an environment where the user is free to browse but may be interrupted with guidance from an 'intelligent tutoring program'. We are taking advantage of the multitasking capabilities of the new generation of PC's in designing the intelligent tutor, which will run 'behind' the main system as a second task. This will avoid its interfering with users' interaction with the main system, and will allow it to remain continuously up to date with their actions. As a further improvement, the user will be able to move freely from one mode of presentation to another.

The new system is extremely rich in information, which can be accessed in chunks as small as individual rules. This creates a new problem for us; the *Back to Basics* project is not rule-based and, as with most interactive-videos, information and video are linked in predefined sequences. The increased flexibility brought by representing knowledge in an expert system makes the link between computer-based information, and information on the video far more complicated to organise. An approach to this problem which interests us is the 'video description language' developed as part of the KBET (Rivers & Kriss [1987]) project,though the system is not yet complete and extensive improvements would be difficult to fit into our two-year time-table. Another facility provided in KBET which interests us is the use of a 'notebook' – users can link their own overlays, and text notes with stills and video sequences. Recalling notes and overlays whenever the relevant material is shown helps to build conceptual links between different areas of the domain which refer to the same objects or employ the same techniques.

4.2. Pointing Devices

As a consequence of past experience, and in response to the opinions of collaborating colleagues the present system will make a systematic study of users' preferences for different input devices. The current opinion is that students in higher education should be able to handle a keyboard with ease and it is part of the normal skills they should develop. Further, there is considerable discussion about the relative merits of tracker-balls and mice, so it is intended to incorporate both in the system. Examination of an X-ray or a histology slide often requires that particular features are pointed out, and this makes it desirable that touch screens should also be investigated.

4.3. Constructing a familiar interface

Clearly the system will be very rich in information. This information will cover three levels of knowledge:

1. Clinical (diagnostic rules)
2. Pre-Clinical (explanations of diagnostic rules)
3. Natural science (explanations of Pre-clinical data, where necessary)

All this information must be made available through an interface which requires the minimum of time spent on familiarisation but allows maximum flexibility (Malone [1982]).

One of the most important factors in an efficient human-computer interface is that users should understand implicitly how the program expects them to behave. Students coming to an educational package do not have weeks to learn how to use a system, and even if they did they would not have the incentive. As discussed above, a decision has been taken to test a variety of pointing devices (mouse, trackerball, touch-screen), and it is intended that one device will be the main means of communication with the interactive-video system. Many students are familiar with the pop-down menus provided by WIMPS, and we believe that providing a similar environment will overcome many of the problems of familiarising the user with the system. We have observed some frustrating characteristics of WIMPS: pop-down menus allow the user to establish the full range of facilities without constant reference to a manual, but it becomes frustrating repeatedly to have to locate with a pointing device, those facilities which are used regularly. Since the system we are developing will require only a limited amount of keyboard input, it is intended to make simple key-stroke commands available to call facilities, and importantly, to design the 'intelligent tutor' so that it informs the user of this facility as soon as it judges the student is sufficiently familiar with the system.

In a system designed to develop such complex skills, there will be situations where the user is required to use the keyboard. During browsing students may wish to input the name of a topic they wish to investigate (though all information will be available via an on-screen index). While many questions in the new system will remain multiple choice, there will be some that require single-term responses. Most importantly the keyboard will be required for interacting with the computer during diagnostic exercises. Here single term responses will not be adequate (description of any diagnostic action must include at least one action term and one object term). It may be helpful to build a small natural language subset for communication of this type, though the 2 year time limit on the project makes such an undertaking ambitious, and the practicality of such subsets is still not firmly established (Winograd & Flores [1987]).

4.4. Conveying information to the user with multiple information sources

The new system will be able to provide information in eight ways:

1. moving video
2. still slides
3. still diagrams
4. real-time computer graphics
5. pre-set text
6. computer-generated text (translations of expert system rules)
7. analogue sound
8. digital stored sound

The conventional approach to presentation is to use a single screen, overlaying the video picture with output from a computer. The computer output can be text or graphics, and the video picture can be moving or still (Bayard-White [1985]).

The video aspect of any interactive-video introduces human-factors problems which have not troubled designers of conventional systems. The most basic is familiar to anyone who has watched foreign films: if you are mixing text and video how do you ensure that the text is legible without blocking out part of the video? In commercial video or film, blocking out part of the picture rarely affects the message being conveyed; in an educational interactive-video, on the other hand, particularly with histological slides and other detailed pictures, covering part of the picture may be disastrous. With this problem in mind we are investigating the use of a digital graphics board which we can use as a video-effects framestore and which will allow us to grab and shrink the video image to create room on the screen for text. Clearly if such a board is to form part of the delivery system it is essential that it be fast enough to manipulate images in real time without breaking the flow of user-machine interaction. Speed becomes less of an imperative if the board is used for editing the video before transferring it to the video-disc, but this approach lacks the flexibility of real-time manipulation.

Compressing the video image into a window and putting text into another window along-side it overcomes the problem of losing part of the picture, but opens up a number of new problems. How small can the video image be before it ceases to serve any purpose? It is imperative that the aspect ratio of the video screen is maintained in the dimensioning of any video window: how do you make best use of the remaining L-shaped blank area? How does one reach a compromise between the amount of textual information needed to accompany the video image and the room left on the screen for text? If you need a graphical image to reinforce the information being conveyed do you put it in a separate window, the text window, or overlay it on the video? It became apparent with the *Back to Basics* video-disc that even when users were told what questions they would be asked before viewing a section of video they had difficulty remembering what they should be looking for. If students wish to review a section of video before answering a question, should they have the facility to keep the question on the screen while they do so? If so how is the screen laid out, and where does the user enter a response – in the question window or a third answer window? Some elements of information are best conveyed by dynamic real-time graphics – is it feasible to have more than one dynamic window on the screen at a time? This question arises with text as well, since one means of keeping the users attention is to print text to the screen at reading-pace rather than a page at a time.

The problems of convention in screen layout posed a frustrating problem with the *Back to Basics* disc. Because some questions required more than one selection from the multiple choice provided, a box was placed in the bottom right hand corner of the screen to which a note saying 'click to finish answer' was clearly attached. Many users, coming to their first question would click the mouse on the answer(s) they felt appropriate and wait for the program to continue. Clearly logical design is insufficient to provide efficient use of the system.

There exist plenty of examples of effective visual presentation, at least two of which (text-books and newspapers) specialise in relating pictures and type. Both follow certain general principles, the most important of which is probably simplicity: screen or page should provide not more than one focal point. Headlines are used to draw attention to particular sections, and pictures appear in sections of the page distinct, but not separated, from the text they illustrate. Sticking to these general conventions enables readers of different books or journals to elicit information from a wide range of sources. There is however, a second level of convention: publishers endeavour to develop a distinct house style. The key element from the reader's point of view is the consistency which allows him or her to predict where the most interesting information will be presented. Decisions on the scale and relative positions of windows, then, depend on more than general principles.

Problems caused by having limited space for text become particularly important when we need to show diagrams or other still images. One side of a video-disc contains only 36 minutes of video. It is, therefore extremely wasteful to use continuous shots of still images when a single frame (on which the player can pause without loss of quality) will provide the same amount of visual information. The problem with this is that if the disc is not playing we have no access to the soundtrack. A few seconds of sound are worth screens full of text; spoken commentary is easier to follow and more likely to be noted than reams of text. With this problem in mind we are looking seriously at the (limited) use of digital audio storage for voice-over on the more conceptually complex still images. In other situations where text and video are required at the same time, the best solution seems to be to provide the user with control of the rate at which text is scrolled into the space not employed by the video. Should the graphics board become part of the delivery system it would be possible to allow users control over the size of the video image, thus allowing them to find their own compromise.

On the question of the number of 'windows' of information allowed on the screen at one time, we are guided by the conventions adopted in paper information sources. Areas should only be separated if the information therein refers to different subjects. It seems clear that more than one area of movement on the screen at one time will distract the user and detract from the efficiency of the system. Other questions raised above, e.g., overlays *vs.* separate graphics cannot be given a simple answer, the appropriate option will change according to the situation.

There is a separate set of problems posed by movement on the screen. We can derive some answers from common experience, others we can inherit from layout design. We are all aware that movement attracts attention. It follows, therefore, that if movement is to appear on the screen it should only be in the area most requiring the user's attention.

5. Testing the system

Advances in video-disc production now allow us to produce a glass version of a video-disc before going to final production. While the glass disc is not robust enough for general use, it is cheap to produce and provides the opportunity to test material before moving to the irrevocable stage of mastering a vinyl disc.

This stage of production will provide an opportunity to test the combination of video and software (Steinberg [1984]). We will be particularly interested in how quickly users become competent at manipulating the system and establish what, if any, difficulties they have following the presentation of information. Special attention will be given to the effectiveness of separate windows for text presentation and video material. A final decision will be made on which input devices are most appropriate, and an assessment of the system's suitability for use with small groups , as opposed to individuals will be made (there may be a need to compromise between text and video – if the font-size of text is reduced).

It is planned that the system will be assessed in two ways:

1. Observing the student using the system - how many times does he/she need to call for help? What effect does an introduction to the system from a human tutor have on the rate at which the user gets to know the system?

2. A Questionnaire and interview asking the students for their impressions of the strengths and weaknesses of the system.

Acknowledgements

The authors wish to thank Prof. M. Hobsley, Drs. S. Head and S. Lal, L. Roberts, M. Wallis, D. Kufour, C. Hilton for their influence in shaping the ideas discussed in this paper. Thanks are also due to Sarah Salas for her (almost) infinite patience with interruptions to her work caused by the drafting of the paper. Any errors or failures of judgement are attributable solely to the authors.

References

C Bayard-White [December 1985], in *Interactive Video Case Studies and Directory*, National Interactive Video Centre.

R Brooks [1987], "Interactive Video for Healthcare Training: The ADEPT System," *Interactive Learning International* 4, 30–42.

S Fortescue [1988], "Using Interactive Video and Artificial Intelligence in Training," in *Conference on Culture, Language and Artificial Intelligence*, Stockholm, May 30 – June 3.

D G Jameson [1988], "The Place of Interactive Video in Teaching Systems," in *Artificial Intelligence and Language: Old Questions in a New Key*, H Sinding-Larsen, ed., Tano, Oslo.

D G Jameson [September 1986], "Interactive Video for Training in Manual Lifting Techniques: Some Experiences of Production," in *Proceedings of the First National Conference on the Use of Computers in Healthcare Education and Training*, University of Keele.

D G Jameson & L Roberts [March 1987], "Interactive Video – A New Approach to Training," *Occupational Health*.

T W Malone [March 1982], "Heuristics for Designing Enjoyable User Interfaces: Lessons from Computer Games," in *Proceedings of the Conference on Human Factors in Computing Systems*, Gaithersberg, March 15-17.

T O'Shea & J Self [1984], *Learning and Teaching with Computers*, Harvester Press, Brighton.

E Parsloe [1983], *Interactive Video*, Sigma Technical Press, Wiley, Chichester.

A Pinnington & C Bayard-White, *NIVC Case Study – Middlesex Hospital – Back to Basics*, Interactive Video Case Studies, IV – Box.

R Rivers & B Kriss [February 1987], "Knowledge-Based Engineering Training," *Computer-Aided Engineering Journal*.

E R Steinberg [1984], *Teaching Computers to Teach*, Lawrence Erlbaum Associates, Hillsdale, New Jersey.

T Winograd & F Flores [1987], *Understanding Computers and Cognition: A New Foundation for Design*, Addison-Wesley, Reading MA.

M Yazdani [1986], "Intelligent Tutoring Systems," *Expert Systems: The International Journal of Knowledge Engineering* 3, 154–162.

The Application of Cognitive Psychology to CAD

Andrew Dillon and Marian Sweeney

The HUSAT Research Centre, Elms Grove, Loughborough, Leicestershire LE11 1RG, U.K.

The design of usable human-computer interfaces is one of the primary goals of the HCI specialist. To date however interest has focussed mainly on office or text based systems such as word processors or databases. Computer aided design (CAD) represents a major challenge to the human factors community to provide suitable input and expertise in an area where the users goals and requirements are cognitively distinct from more typical HCI.

The present paper is based on psychological investigations of the engineering domain, involving an experimental comparison of designers using CAD and the more traditional drawing board. By employing protocol analytic techniques it is possible to shed light on the complex problem-solving nature of design and to demonstrate the crucial role of human factors in the development of interfaces which facilitate the designers in their task. A model of the cognition of design is proposed which indicates that available knowledge and guidelines alone are not sufficient to aid CAD developers and the distinct nature of the engineering designer's task merits specific attention.

Keywords: cognitive psychology, CAD, interface design, protocol analysis

1. Introduction

While a large reservoir of empirical evidence has grown up on the value of certain human-computer interface features (see Shneiderman (Shneiderman [1987]) for a detailed review) the concept of usability has become almost inextricably tied-up with the design of text-based office products such as word processors and databases. While these applications represent a significant portion of the IT market for non-specialists, increased technological developments continue to broaden the range of tasks for which computers may offer significant contributions e.g., Computer Aided Design systems (CAD).

Computerisation has aided design in so far as it provides a sophisticated drafting medium, where visualisation of the data is significantly enhanced and where data storage and organisation facilitate analytic procedures such as finite element analysis, weight, stress and mass properties, kinematic analysis and so on.

According to Ullman and Dietterich (Ullman & Dietterich [1987]) future development and integration of CAD technology is dependant on an understanding of the engineering design process at the level of the individual and the organisation. The focus of the present paper is to address the cognitive processes involved in mechanical engineering design. The human factors issue here is to develop a model of how designers work and think, in order to determine how CAD technology must progress so as to facilitate those processes.

2. The design task

The term 'mechanical engineering design' is described by Ullman and Dietterich as a creative decision making process for specifying or creating physical devices to fulfil a stated need. This definition gives no indication of how it is actually achieved. It is useful however, to the extent to which it provides a perspective within which to view and interpret the task, i.e., at the level of cognitive processing underlying decision making. Although the literature on the engineering design process is scant, what exists focuses primarily on a behavioural model of the task (Mostow [1985]). It is the cognitive process involved in design which is of interest to the present research.

3. User psychology: the case of designers

The psychology of the CAD user is relatively uncharted territory. While some research has been carried out which attempts to understand the nature of design as a cognitive activity (Warren & Whitefield [1987]) our understanding of the users of CAD technology is woefully incomplete. Yet the advances afforded by CAD are arguably among the most important of all IT applications.

In discussions of designer psychology, it is possible to identify two trends. The first of these borrows heavily from the literature on cognitive style (e.g., Tovey (Tovey [1986])), while the second discusses how designers think in terms of the problem-solving strategies employed during task completion (e.g., Lawson (Lawson [1980])).

An individual's cognitive style refers to the characteristic manner in which they respond to and process information. According to Messick *et al* (Messick [1976]) 19 different cognitive styles have been proposed and investigated. Of these, a few styles have emerged as the major tools for distinguishing between individuals at a cognitive level e.g., field dependence/independence (Witkin et al. [1977]), holism/serialism (Pask [1976]) and convergence/ divergence (Hudson [1968]). In addition to the more formal cognitive style dimensions outlined, distinction between left and right brain processing are suggested as a meaningful discrimination between individuals (e.g., (Tovey [1986])).

Given the presumed creative nature of the designer's work it has been suggested, though rarely empirically demonstrated, that designers are field independent (capable of clearly seeing patterns in complex displays), holistic (intuitive, suddenly inspired with a solution) and divergent thinkers.

However, the term designer encompasses a variety of individuals who perform widely varying tasks and it is generally agreed that depending on the nature of the task being performed, a designer may need to employ processes characterised by both extremes of any style dichotomy in order to produce solutions. Furthermore, cognitive style considerations have been investigated with respect to interface design for the more typical 'casual user' without any great success (though see Fowler and Murray (Fowler & Murray [1987]) for an alternative view) and are unlikely to offer any tremendous insight on their own for the development of CAD interfaces.

The second trend in the literature on the psychology of design attempts to derive the types of problem solving strategies that are commonly employed by designers in their attempts to produce a solution. Lawson's (Lawson [1979]) empirical work suggests that designers possess a unique strategy which distinguishes them from scientists. That is, designers tend to have a solution focussed perspective, compared to a scientist's logico-deductive problem focussed reasoning.

Current thought emphasises the 'generator-conjecture-analysis' model of design (Darke [1979]) which states that designers structure their problems by exploring aspects of possible solutions in an iterative fashion. This is a particularly high-level analysis of designer cognition and by virtue of its generality is severely limited in prescriptive power for the area of interface design. At a lower level there are numerous strategies and sub-strategies that any individual can adopt to solve a problem (Young [1979]). Rzevski and Evans (Rzevski & Evans [1983]) list 6 situation dependent strategies that designers employ in order to achieve a design solution: imagination, analogy, heuristics, random search, systematic search and transformation. However, how these are employed is not outlined, information which is essential if any translation into interface guidelines is to be made.

4. Overview of the present study

The present research was carried out as part of a larger collaborative project aimed at developing a user modelling tool for CAD interface design. Our contribution was aimed at analysing the users of these systems with a view to classifying interactive styles and predicting the degree to which individual or group variance would need to be incorporated in the modelling tool. Full details of this work can be found elsewhere (Dillon et al. [1987]).

The present paper reports on an empirical investigation of designers *in situ*. The major concern was with increasing the current level of knowledge about the psychology of design beyond speculation around the issues of cognitive style and problem-solving strategy. A secondary concern of the investigation reported here was to shed light on the designers conceptualisation of their task with a view to isolating the relevant human factors issues that need to be addressed for the successful exploitation of CAD technology.

Verbal protocol analysis was selected as the best means of eliciting relevant information for this study. Protocol analytic techniques have been both advocated (Ericsson & Simon [1984]) and criticised (Nisbett & Wilson [1977]) as a means of gaining insight into an individual's thought processes. Verbal protocol analysis been used to good effect in the area of user cognition in HCI studies (e.g., (Lewis & Mack [1983])). Objectivity and reliability are maximised through careful selection of the data that is required (e.g., concurrent verbal descriptions of what is being attended to are more reliable than retrospective descriptions of how a process was performed) and ensuring that data is scored independently by two or more raters (their combined ratings giving an index of reliability).

4.1. Method

In order to gain insight into the psychology of design, a study involving 16 mechanical engineering designers was carried out at the design offices of British Aerospace (BAe) at Filton. The subjects were made up of two groups, one which carried out the task on a CAD system ($n = 9$) and the other on the more traditional board and t-square ($n = 7$). This ensured that the analysis of the cognitive processes involved in design were not overly influenced by the nature of the drawing interface subjects used. It also enabled designers to make comparative judgements on the effect of technology on the process of design.

The selection of the experimental task was based on two fundamental criteria: firstly it must be realistic i.e., the type of task that the subjects would perform in the course of their normal duties; secondly it had to be possible to complete in 3 hours. As a result, a task to design a wing-flap mechanism involving a moving carriage was selected with the help of a BAe supervisor. A pilot study revealed that completion time was within the desired range.

4.2. Procedure

The subjects were briefed about the aim of the study and each was given an identical task and instructions. A senior designer was on hand throughout, to answer technical questions. The subjects were observed independently and two experimenters sat with each subject and prompted verbal protocols as necessary. After 3 hours the session ended. In a post-experimental interview each subject was asked to discuss his reactions to the task and views of technology and design in general. All comments were tape-recorded using discreet tie-pin microphones.

4.3. Analysis

A random selection of half of the tape-recorded verbal protocols were examined in order to determine at a global level how designers structured their task. From this, it emerged that the designers' thought processes seemed to chunk themselves primarily about consecutive and often discrete action points. That is, designers displayed a tendency to structure the problem into perceived manageable units and tackle these independently in a series of action cycles. These cycles were invariably initiated and preceded by a phase of decision making where, for example, the designer considered options and task parameters. It was therefore agreed that the protocols best afforded analysis at the level of these action points and their relevant option considerations.

The action cycle was therefore seen as the obvious parsing unit of the protocols while the associated decision making provided a structured means of examining the processing of information during task performance.

At this level of operationalisation of designer performance, it was decided that insights could be gained into the designers' cognitive activities by focussing attention more closely on the reasoning underlying their decision making and studying the types of knowledge employed by the designers. To supplement this objective examination of the design process, information elicited in the post experimental interview, relating to designers' own conceptualisation of what they were doing, was incorporated in the development of the analysis framework.

5. Results

A classification of the types of knowledge (found to underlie decisions) referenced in the verbal protocols was constructed. The types of knowledge initially identified included:

— domain knowledge;
— task knowledge;
— device knowledge;

Domain knowledge relates to the knowledge which a designer has gained through formal training, reading and experience. It encompasses a structured body of knowledge which the designer accesses in order to solve any design problem. It is likewise expanded by new experiences. No difference was observed between subjects on different mediums. That is, both CAD and board designers employed similar domain knowledge at similar milestones in the development of a problem solution.

Task knowledge relates to information which the designer has about the task or about a class to which the task at hand belongs e.g., computer monitor encasement. A designer may successfully tackle a task for which they possess relatively little task knowledge by applying relevant principles from the domain of design in general. The main difference observed between the subjects here, resulted from the users typical work i.e., designers experienced in process design (moving parts) felt more at home with the experimental task than designers who usually worked on structural design.

Device knowledge relates to knowledge which the designer has about the medium on which the task is executed i.e., CAD system or board and t-square. A designer who may be said to have a high level of device knowledge should display a solving procedure which is more concerned with adding elements to and evolving a workable solution. Low levels of device knowledge would be manifest by the expression of concerns with the means by which goals are executed. This was more commonly characteristic of designers working on CAD systems. In the CAD medium this obviously raises important HF issues in terms of the flexibility and transparency of the interface.

6. Discussion

This view of the knowledge underlying activity, provides a useful insight into the overall psychology of the designer. Firstly it seems that the process of design can be understood at a cognitive level as consisting of a series of decision and action phases, resulting from the designer's perception of the problem. It is important to realise that different designers may perceive the problem in different ways and the level at which they break the problem down into managable units was seen to vary in this study.

Secondly, ordering and completion of these phases are controlled by the decision making routines. These decisions are based on three broad knowledge types which collectively contain a variety of rules, procedures, strategies and experiences.

These knowledge types will interact differently depending on their respective proportionality within the designer's knowledge base at any particular time. For example, an experienced board designer who is transferred to CAD will require support with transfer of relevant knowledge, and the acquisition of new device knowledge in order to utilise their task and domain knowledge to the same effect as before. Designers who find themselves working on a new task will utilise the same device knowledge as before but will rely more heavily on domain knowledge as a resource for supplying information pertinent to the task in hand. It is important to note that in terms of the decision-action cycle not all of these were contingent on a rationalisation of the information at hand. Apart from actions resulting from rationalised decision making, others were found to be the result of trial and error or guesswork and others still were the result of personal preference or habit.

In relation to the more traditional literature on the psychology of design, it is not clear what links can be made with the cognitive style school of thought. It is possible that the initial perception of the problem and the subsequent process of task division may correlate with processing trends such as field dependence/independence or serialism/holism. However as this was not a concern of the present investigation, it would be pointless to speculate further. Links with the 'strategy' literature are somewhat easier to foster. The protocol data suggest that designers do indeed use strategies such as visualisation and imagination as an aid to problem solving. However it is not clear to what extent a general strategy can represent in any detailed and context-independent way how designers think. Some designers obviously do perform the 'conjecture- generator-analysis' routine at certain stages of the design process, but only after they have studied the problem, prioritised their sub-problems and set about the cycle of solution generation.

7. Implications for Interface Design

The most obvious implication of this model for interface design is related to the device knowledge required by a designer to convey a meaningful representation of their ideas to others. The traditional design 'interface' of board and t-square appears rather rudimentary in comparison to CAD, but designers have evolved an array of techniques and supplementary tools to aid their powers of visual representation e.g., geometric drawing aids, adjustable set-squares etc., and the board designers in this study demonstrated an impressive range of (mostly automated) skills in drawing and representing complex shapes and relationships.

With regards to the CAD users it was obvious that the system was capable of reducing much of the complexity of the drawing technique to a few supposedly simple keypresses. However the innate logic of the command sequence seemed to cause some users difficulty and comments to the effect that they often used a local expert as a command dictionary were noted. Similarly, movement of parts of the design was often simulated on the board by using cut-outs of the relevant shape and literally moving it around the drawing by hand. This acted as a powerful visual aid to some designers. No directly comparable facility existed on CAD.

A tendency toward a preoccupation with the means to the solution rather than the end was noted with the CAD users. That is to say they could be described as being method oriented as opposed to the board users who were solution oriented. CAD users expressed concerns with being limited in the way they executed the task rather than using the system as a tool. It was also noted that designers working on CAD systems tended to take more risks hence make more errors and in the final analysis took the same amount of time to complete the task as the board designers.

Here lie the initial usability issues. The board offers its user direct manipulation facilities that are employed on the back of a life-history of visual representation based on physical movements of the arm and fingers to trace an image. CAD systems on the other hand remove the intrinsic physical relationship between drawer and drawing and replace it with command sequences and joystick/mouse movements. This can prove the source of considerable difficulty for designers as there is often no intuitive link between input and drawing/screen display. While the human is capable of adapting to the situation and experienced CAD users seem to interact effectively with the system, a number of CAD users in this study expressed a preference for the tangibility of the board and stated that, in an ideal world, a combination of both the efficiency and speed of the CAD system in drafting and the capacity for physical manipulation on the drawing board would be employed.

Obviously research could fruitfully investigate the types of commands and input devices that designers require in order to minimise processing of device knowledge. Much of this work has been carried out by the human factors community in the domain of office systems and the methodological developments gained in that domain are probably applicable here, even if the results are not. Advocates of CAD systems list the speed and accuracy of these systems as the major advantages of computerised design. This investigation suggests however that such advantages are likely to be eroded on certain interfaces by increased designer concern with device knowledge when they could be more effectively utilising task and domain knowledge.

Usability issues extend beyond device knowledge however. With respect to the task, CAD systems should be designed to support the user who may lack some task knowledge either through unfamiliarity with the task or forgetfulness etc.. For example, Query-In-Depth help facilities offer a chance to embed contextual information into the system, which the designer consults as and when required. Numerous analysis aids could be made available to the designer to facilitate informed decision making on issues such as stress and tolerance. Given the observed tendency of designers in this study to consider variables which appear beyond the immediate task domain, such facilities would seem a useful method of enhancing the designers cognitive tendencies.

Obviously the development of IKBS offers possibilities to provide the designer with even more powerful information sources. Sophisticated error-trapping routines that identify potential weaknesses in proposed designs or automatically tailor a design to the stylistic requirements of company policy may be useful. Mass local storage of previous designs on CD-ROM offer the chance to rapidly access a wealth of design data. Developments of this kind may supplement the domain knowledge of designers. However the human factors issues of such advances have no parallels as yet in other areas and it would be difficult to make recommendations for the CAD domain on the basis of current knowledge.

8. Conclusion

The psychology of designers is poorly understood in comparison with other computer users. For the successful exploitation of CAD technology it is important that this is rectified. The present investigation suggests that designers employ three types of knowledge to guide their action sequences and propose a solution. Human factors issues pertain most immediately at the level of device knowledge, where current guidelines and methods have some relevance. However the results of this study indicate that there are at least two other types of knowledge that are employed in the design process which elevate it above the level of a routine cognitive skill. Therefore the usability issues concern the support of a complex, creative task which requires much further investigation in its own right.

Acknowledgements

This work was carried out at HUSAT under the SERC funded Alvey MMI142 Enabling Technology Project.

We would like to thank the other members of the HUSAT team: Val Herring, Enda Fallon and Phil John.

Thanks are also due to British Aerospace for their time and effort, GEC, The Ergonomics Unit at UCL and City University.

References

J Darke [1979], "The Primary Generator and the Design Process," *Design Studies* 3, 157–162.

A Dillon, E Fallon, V Herring, M Sweeney & P John [1987], "HUSAT Final Report – The Concept of Designer Style," MMI142 HUSAT/12.0.

K A Ericsson & H A Simon [1984], *Protocol Analysis: Verbal Reports as Data*, MIT Press, Cambridge MA.

C Fowler & D Murray [1987], "Gender and Cognitive Style Differences at the Human-Computer Interface," in *INTERACT '87 – The Second IFIP Conference on Human-Computer Interaction*, H J Bullinger and B Shackel, ed., Elsevier Science Publishers B.V., North Holland.

L Hudson [1968], *Frames of Mind*, Penguin, Hammondsworth.

B Lawson [1979], "Cognitive Strategies in Architectural Design," *Ergonomics* 22, 59–68.

B Lawson [1980], *How Designers Think*, Architectural Press, London.

C Lewis & R Mack [1983], "Learning to Use a Text-Processing System: Evidence from 'Thinking Aloud' Protocols," in *CHI '83 – Human Factors in Computing Systems*, ACM, Washington.

S Messick [1976], *Individuality in Learning*, Jossey-Bass, San Fransisco.

J Mostow [1985], "Toward Better Models of the Design Process," *AI Magazine* 6, 44–57.

R E Nisbett & T D Wilson [1977], "Telling More than We Can Know: Verbal Reports on Mental Processes," *Psychological Review* 84, 231–259.

G Pask [1976], "Styles and Strategies of Learning," *Brit. J. Educ. Psy.* 46, 128–148.

G Rzevski & L Evans [1983], "The Impact of AI on the CAD of Machine Systems," in *International Conference of Engineering Design ICED '83*, V Hubka and M Anderasen, ed., Copenhagen.

B Shneiderman [1987], *Designing the User Interface: Strategies for Effective Human-Computer Interaction*, Addison-Wesley, Reading MA.

M Tovey [1986], "Designing with both halves of the brain," *Design Studies* 5, 219–228.

D G Ullman & T A Dietterich [1987], "Mechanical Design Methodology: Implications on Future Development of Computer-Aided Design and Knowledge-Based Systems.

C Warren & A Whitefield [1987], "The Role of Task Characterisation in Transferring Models of Users: The Example of Engineering Design," in *INTERACT '87 - The Second IFIP Conference on Human-Computer Interaction*, H J Bullinger and B Shackel, ed., Elsevier Science Publishers B.V., North Holland.

H A Witkin, C A Moore, D R Goodenough & P W Cox [1977], "Field Dependent and Field Independent Cognitive Styles and their Educational Implications," Review of Educational Research.

R Young [1979], "Strategies and the Structure of a Cognitive Skill," in *Startegies of Information Processing*, G Underwood, ed., Academic Press, London.

Dialogue Design

How Much is Enough? A Study of User Command Repertoires

Paddy Anstey

Computing Centre, University of East Anglia, Norwich NR4 7TJ, U.K.

A critical examination of the VAX/VMS command repertoires of users of a university computing service has been possible following the automatic logging of all operating system commands issued by all users over a period of six months. After preliminary investigation, users selected from a variety of backgrounds and with considerable experience on the system were interviewed to probe the perceived adequacy of their repertoires for their particular tasks, and to determine factors which appear to affect command repertoire development.

A surprisingly restricted command set was revealed amongst user communities in many disciplines, including some with a substantial tradition of computing – and a common core of popular commands across all disciplines was readily identified. Users interviewed were generally satisfied with their command repertoires but it was clear from discussion that many users could be more effective if they had a greater grasp of the system, not least for 'housekeeping' activities. Whatever their attitude to computing as an activity, the users were all applications-driven and mostly gave the learning of the 'extras' a low priority relative to the many other demands on their

time, even though the possible benefits were in some
cases perceived.

The findings from this study are given in detail, and
the implications for organisational and software changes
discussed.

Keywords: User command repertoires, Computing service organisation, Software environments

1. Introduction

An attitude frequently found amongst academic computing service professionals is that the majority of their users know comparatively little
about the systems they use, and should know more (traditionally for
some groups, very much more) in order to be *effective* users. Indeed, the
author's experience of user support in several such computing services,
gained over many years, tends to confirm this notion. However, it can
be argued that not all users need extensive functional knowledge of the
system if their requirements of it are simple, or implemented in a highly
'usable' way. The latter view has been supported recently by Goodwin
(Goodwin [1987]) in a discussion of system functionality and usability,
and by Fowler *et al* (Fowler, Macauley & Siripoksup [1987]) when
considering the appropriate kind of system-user dialogue for different
user requirements and preferences. Whilst such studies make important
contributions towards the longer term goal of 'better systems', in many
situations the requirement is more urgent. In particular, when a large
computing system has already been installed at considerable financial
cost to an organisation, short to medium term user effectiveness also
becomes an important issue.

Consequently, this study set out to establish the facts concerning the user
command repertoires and their development throughout a substantial
and varied research user community, *viz.* that of the central computing
service at the University of East Anglia, and to relate these to the tasks
undertaken in order to see if the repertoires were adequate – and, if not,
to give clues to steps that might be taken to improve the situation.

Useful background to such computing services is given in the work
on computing advisory services by Alty and Coombs (Alty & Coombs
[1981]) and by Anstey (Anstey [1985]), and in a study of the characteristics and behaviour of university computer user communities by Auld,
Lang and Lang (Auld, Lang & Lang [1981]).

1.1. The Computing Centre And The User Community

All members of University staff and research workers (students and post doctoral) are eligible to use the Computing Centre facilities. The main system offered is a large VAX/VMS system with a standard command driven interface. It offers a number of compilers and a wide variety of applications software. Users are consequently drawn from most subject disciplines found in the university, although the university structure is actually based on 'Schools' (akin to Faculties elsewhere), not disciplines. Indeed, some disciplines are found in several Schools. In practice, the Schools operate quite independently of one another in many respects and generally provide the basic social structure of the user community.

Computer users are registered with the Computing Centre as members of their School; they are given allocations of computing resource (cpu and disk space) from their School's allocation as managed by their School's Budget Manager, and given a username reflecting their School affiliation. In this scheme, there are 17 such user groups, being the Schools (e.g., School of Environmental Sciences) together with a small number of separate units (e.g., the Library) and a 'catch all' group for individuals affiliated to academic groupings with no other registered users of the Computing Centre.

The Computing Centre runs courses and produces its own 'Getting Started' documentation. Users are expected to make use of these and then to develop their expertise further according to their own particular requirements, the Computing Centre making available reference manuals, books and on-line HELP, together with a small team of 'Advisers' who offer both a 'Help Desk' and in-depth consultancy. Each user also regularly receives a printed Newsletter which includes articles concerning new and changed features of the service, and periodically offers tips and reminders concerning the use of the system.

2. Method

Data was gathered by command logging and user interview, details of both approaches being given below. The logging was done to determine which commands users actually issued, and how frequently. The results were examined first by user group and then later (selectively) by individual user. The analysis by user group was used, together with knowledge of the number of registered users in each group, to characterise the groups and so facilitate the selection of a representative sample of individual users for interview. The interviews sought to elicit the user's feelings concerning the adequacy of their command repertoires in support of their particular requirements, and reveal something of their actual computational abilities – which could be checked against their logged repertoires. Opportunity was also taken in the interviews to find out both how the users learned to use the system in the first instance and, if they felt their knowledge had continued to grow, the sources of that further information.

2.1. Command Logging

VAX/VMS has an image logging capability such that all images accessed (those associated with operating system commands, applications software and user programs) can be logged with date stamp, associated username (giving user group membership), and a code associated with the outcome – normal completion, failure, interrupted, etc. In computing resource, the system is expensive and not routinely run. However, following a substantial system upgrade which more than compensated for the logging overheads, the logging facility was run for a period of six months to gain a profile of all activity. Images associated with system management and operator activity were afterwards removed , so that only images deliberately executed by users in the course of their work were considered.

In this present investigation, operating system commands are of primary concern. Unfortunately, there is not an exact one-to-one correspondence between these commands and the images they run, and neither do the names of these images necessarily resemble the names of the associated commands. Consequently, an image-command translation table was set up based on information derived from system supplied files. Images logged but not supplied with the operating system are necessarily either associated with software packages or with user programs. The former were readily identified, and remaining images taken to be the consequence of issuing the RUN command to run one's own program.

2.2. User Interviews

The interviews were based on a questionnaire which was presented verbally, and discussion arising was allowed to range quite freely. In order to accurately obtain the desired information some 20 questions were posed, giving rise to an interview duration of about 20 to 30 minutes. Specifically, questions sought details of:

1. The user's computing experience and background.
2. Pattern of working.
3. Attitudes to computing in general and using VAX/VMS in particular.
4. The tasks required of the VAX computer.

5. The user's perceived adequacy of their current command repertoire.

6. How they believed their repertoire had evolved over time.

7. Feelings and knowledge concerning activities related to 'housekeeping' (an activity of necessity common to all users).

8. How much the user discussed use of the VAX with other users of the system.

3. Command Repertoires: The Expectation

All users were expected to need a handful of fundamental commands. They were expected to (at least) create, edit and display files at a terminal, print them at a printer and examine directories. Additional commands would then be necessary to run particular applications, whilst additional operating system commands might be useful to investigate problems arising, and generally assist in the use of the system. However, these should be largely independent of the application and more concerned with 'housekeeping' activities such as file management, and the querying of user budgets and allocations.

Further, a given user's command repertoire and overall expertise was expected to increase gradually with time, depending primarily on:

1. The amount of use made of the system.

2. Social factors – opportunities taken to discuss use of the system with other users and with members of the Computing Centre.

3. User documents read.

... in other words, it was anticipated that computational vocabulary and fluency would extend by need and exposure, in a manner akin to natural language.

It was consequently expected that the long established, larger and more active user groups would use the greatest variety of (operating system) commands, and generate their own very experienced users – probably amongst members of staff rather than the more transient research student population. On the other hand, small groups still relatively new to computing were considered likely to employ a more restricted repertoire.

4. Results And Discussion

The expected 'common core' of popular commands was found. With some variation between groups, the main non-applications oriented activities were (in decreasing order of popularity):

Getting rid of files (DELETE and PURGE)

Defining terminal type, changing default directory (SET)

Editing files (EDIT)

Getting names and details of files (DIRECTORY)

Displaying a file at the terminal (TYPE)

Sending files for execution on a batch queue (SUBMIT)

Sending files to a printer (PRINT)

Getting system wide or own process information (SHOW)

Copying and appending files (COPY and APPEND)

Renaming files (RENAME)

Of these, the first four activities were by far the most popular, each command image being accessed between 80,000 and 90,000 times during the logging period. The last four activities, by contrast, each gave command image counts of less than 20,000 in that same period. Thereafter, 'applications' and 'own' images became increasingly dominant, and the ordering of operating system commands much more variable between groups.

Table 1 indicates the number of different command, applications and 'own' images accessed by each user group over the period, and the total number of times each of the three classes of image was accessed. In view of the expectations, the fact that the Computing Centre (user group A) employs the widest range of operating system commands is no surprise, using 75 out of the 126 possible images. Many of the remaining images are used for privileged systems activities and so not available for 'ordinary' work in any case. For comparison purposes, this level of 75 images could be taken as the level of the 'professional expert' group.

However from Table 1, many groups appear to use a surprisingly small command set, relative to members of the Computing Centre. Further, the group results indicate the maximum possible (demonstrated) repertoire of any *individual* in the group, so that an individual user repertoire within any group could be very much smaller. Examination of the individual repertoires of those later interviewed suggested that this was generally true, with some users relying on (over the logged period) as few as 7 or 8 operating system commands to support their applications work.

Consequently, the belief that many users were not progressing much beyond the 'Getting Started' courses and similarly oriented local documentation was confirmed. This is in spite of encouragement towards wider command repertoires by the Computing Centre, actively through

Table 1.   Images logged for each user group.

User Group	—— O/S —— Images	Accesses	— Applications — Images	Accesses	—— Own —— Images	Accesses	Group Orientation
A	75	100009	28	7592	308	5497	Varied
B	71	296462	20	31378	701	49134	Science
C	60	45023	15	3940	180	6636	Science
D	55	40225	12	4156	76	2860	Science
E	52	54820	16	9689	226	9823	Science
F	52	36868	14	3575	74	2693	Science
G	49	93314	14	8294	313	9669	Science
H	46	7130	13	407	36	214	Varied
I	36	16005	12	1120	14	40	Social Science
J	24	6657	11	481	1	2	Social Science
K	20	1140	3	384	7	136	Varied
L	19	1420	1	25	0	0	Arts
M	17	1836	3	19	1	1	Social Science
N	17	248	3	18	1	2	Arts
O	11	209	5	21	1	1	Arts
P	11	176	4	12	1	2	Arts
Q	8	48	2	10	0	0	Arts

O/S = Operating system commands
Applications = provided applications packages, electronic messaging and compilers/linker
Own = user provided images

demonstration and example to interested users and those seeking assistance through the Advisory Service, and more passively by the provision of extensive online HELP, together with reference manuals available to all in the Centre's Advisory Room.

4.1. Cause For Concern?

Confirmation of lack of repertoire in a group does not necessarily mean that an individual user's repertoire is inadequate for their particular needs. This could only be properly determined from the interviews.

On the basis of Table 1, a sample of users was drawn from *computationally active* members of groups as indicated in Table 2. This particular selection was made primarily to:

1. Compare three groups (B, F and I) which might be thought similar in being numerically large and having a substantial history of computer use, but in fact have quite different sizes of command repertoire. The only superficial difference is that group I has a social sciences orientation, whilst both groups B and F have a physical sciences orientation.

Table 2.   The sample selected for interview.

Group	Group O/S cmd repertoire	Total group size	No. users interviewed	Discipline orientation	Computing history
B	71	63	5	Science	Long
F	52	73	5	Science	Long
I	36	54	5	Social Science	Long
L	19	6	1	Arts	Short
H*	7	1	1	Arts	Short
A	75	30	1	Science	Long
G	49	21	1	Science	Long

* 'Catch all' group: all details relate to the one user, who (computationally) works alone

> 2. Assess the effect of being a member of a group which is relatively new to computing and with very few users (groups L and H).

It also enabled a check for consistency with members of two other groups (A and G).

4.2. Command Repertoires: How Much IS Enough?

Most users considered their command repertoires at least 'just adequate' for their purposes, and the majority of these considered it 'perfectly adequate'. Moreover, as illustrated by Figure 1, nearly all users claimed to be able to immediately correct practically all problems which arose with operating system commands they had issued, by virtue of their existing knowledge, whilst Figure 2 suggests that the majority of users were sufficiently secure in that knowledge (however broad or narrow) to 'type ahead' in anticipation of responses to commands already given. Thus the majority of users seemed to be satisfied with their situation, with some apparent justification.

However, if this satisfaction is truly justified, the users would be expected to deal competently with housekeeping and file management tasks in support of their application, and not be frustrated through lack of knowledge in that fundamental area of computer usage. Users were asked about this, and also asked questions which enabled crude measures of their fundamental knowledge of the system to be determined. These measures were based on their knowledge of the DIRECTORY command and of command procedures (macros). The DIRECTORY command gives details of files owned, and the particular information displayed and the files on which information is given can be controlled by command switches, directory and file specifications. All users could be expected to be familiar with a number of ways of using this command. Command files, on the other hand, can ease the use of the system (e.g., by

In Figures 1 to 5, user group codes are used to represent a response from a member of that group. If more than one member of the same group requires an equivalently placed response, it is indicated as (e.g.) B(2).

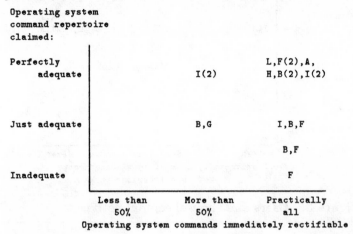

Figure 1.   User's understanding within their repertoire.

defining the working environment through a command file automatically executed at login) and are very widely used.

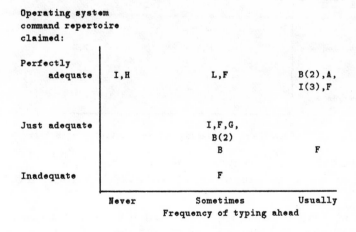

Figure 2.   User's confidence within their repertoire.

Figure 3 suggests that many members of group I (recall that the sample consists of *active, established* users) do find difficulties in housekeeping and file management in spite of claims of adequacy, and the group again

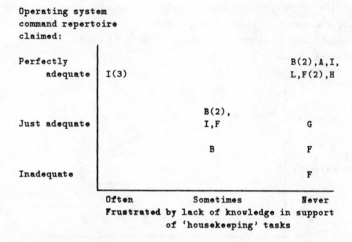

Figure 3.   Users and 'housekeeping' activities.

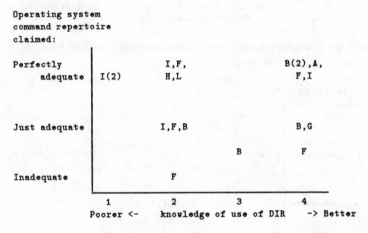

Figure 4.   User's knowledge of system based on
discussion of use of DIRECTORY command.

features primarily towards the low score end of Figure 4 (knowledge of
DIRECTORY) and middle scores in Figure 5 (knowledge of command
procedures). Consequently, members of group I appear not only to select
from a relatively small range of operating system commands but many
also fail to make use of some fairly basic facilities which could be helpful
to them.

In contrast, members of groups B and F (and A and G) appear to have
a more realistic estimate of their abilities. Figures 3 to 5 show that

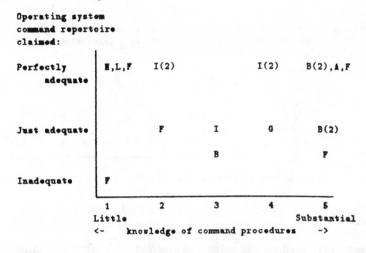

Figure 5.   User's knowledge of system based on use and
discussion of command procedures.

---

these users generally appreciated either that there is more to know that
could be useful (by claiming a 'just adequate' repertoire) whilst actually
having – so far as the present measures could determine – a fair grasp
of the fundamentals, or that they are indeed very competent in these
respects. The general impression given by the interviews supports this
view.

It seems, therefore, that of the three apparently comparable groups,
members of group I do suffer by not using enough of the features
offered by the operating system. However it should be noted from
Figure 3 that the representatives of groups L and H, who might be
thought even more disadvantaged because of the smallness and relative
newness of those working groups, nevertheless appear to be managing
perfectly satisfactorily whilst making little use (Figures 4 and 5) of the
'fundamental' features considered above.

This suggests that the requirements of the system might after all play
a significant role in determining how much knowledge is 'enough'. The
users were each asked what kind of use they made of the computer,
selecting from the broad areas of programming, using supplied applications packages, graphics, electronic mail, and text processing. Figure 6
summarises the results, showing that members of groups B and F (and A
and G) tend to be more diverse in their use of the system than members
of I, L and H. As expected, these individual results reflect the group
results in Table 1.

On this basis, some members of group I might be considered similar to

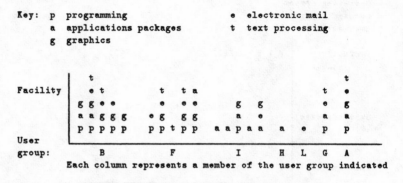

Figure 6. Facilities used by users and groups.

the users in groups L and H, using just one class of facility and employing a low command repertoire. However, the interviews revealed that the computing work done in groups L and H is of a very regular and routine nature, with well established procedures, so it is very unlikely that problems would arise. In contrast, the work within group I – although based primarily on the use of applications packages – is less routine and so requires somewhat greater knowledge of the system on the part of the users.

Overall, these results suggest that those who claimed adequacy were, in fact, able to do their computing tasks more or less to their own satisfaction — whatever their operating system command repertoire or size of user group, and in some cases in spite of only periodic computer access. However, the actual adequacy of the knowledge is questioned in some cases, and particularly amongst users in group I.

4.3. Learning The System

The majority of low-repertoire users said they would like to know more, but time was a major constraint. Volunteered remarks time and again indicated that however much they enjoyed computing, the vast majority of users saw the system as a tool in support of their discipline, and that developing their knowledge above the minimum required to accomplish their tasks is in very strong competition with a wide range of other necessary activities. This is a particular problem for members of staff, who frequently looked to their research students as the computing experts 'because they had the time' [to learn more about the system]. So when and how do users learn about the operating system?

Questions were posed concerning the way in which users believed their command repertoires had developed. The most frequent way in which the system was initially learned was through colleagues within their user group, and by reading documentation. Only three of the nineteen interviewed had been on a formal VAX/VMS course. Timeliness appeared to be a major problem, with users needing to start when there was no scheduled course. Fifteen of the nineteen considered that their repertoires had continued to grow after the initial learning period, and the additional knowledge again came primarily through colleagues – although Computing Centre Advisers and documentation also played their part. Significantly, in view of the above comments made by staff, the research students interviewed learned more 'at every available opportunity' whilst staff were most likely to learn 'when a problem needed to be solved'.

Only those with at least moderate expertise found the online HELP system of much value in learning more about the system. Several of the research student users interviewed said that they browsed the HELP system from time to time, but more generally it was criticised – usually because it did not address matters in the user's own terms. This reflects the more general on-line documentation problems discussed in a bibliographic outline by Girill (Girill [1985]). This applied equally to use of HELP when things went wrong, although in such situations more of those interviewed did try to use it, at least occasionally, because of its convenience in being immediately available without having to move away from the terminal. If HELP did not help, then users generally sought a colleague or Computing Centre Adviser, whichever was more readily to hand. If all else failed, the documentation was consulted. The most important factors to the users were convenience, intelligibility and speed of obtaining a solution, which supports the findings in (Anstey [1985]).

From the above, contact with colleagues is clearly a major means of user learning and growth of expertise. The users were each asked about the frequency of such contacts – with members of their own group, members of other user groups, and with the Computing Centre. Most users indicated a mixture of contacts but members of group I provided a striking exception in that they only 'occasionally' or 'never' discussed their use of the system with anyone outside their user group, as illustrated by Table 3. The considerable insularity of this group may well contribute towards its relatively low command repertoire and general lack of knowledge concerning the operating system.

5. Implications For The Computing Centre

Although the majority of users interviewed were satisfied with their knowledge of the operating system, it is clear that many would benefit from at least a little more expertise. This suggests weaknesses in some of the existing means of promoting computing awareness and competence,

Table 3.   Contacts by individual users with other users.

Contact with	Contact made by group B members* 1 2 3 4 5	Contact made by group I members 1 2 3 4 5
Computing Service	w o o o w	n o o o o
Own group	d d o w w	w w d w d
Other groups	w n n w w	n n o n n

* Group B is typical of most other user groups

Key:
d daily contact
w weekly
o occasional
n never

and the following changes are consequently proposed.

In order to encourage attendance, the introductory courses – which are currently given from time to time by lecture and associated practical – need to be replaced by a 'self-teach' system (CBT or even simple video) so that sound teaching is available, at the user's convenience.

Introductory documentation and short courses need to be supplemented by a self-teach 'progression' session. Separating this from the introductory material would enable the users to better appreciate the usefulness of the features described and consequently give them a better grasp of the system.

Online HELP needs (at least) reorganising to make it more usable. This work has identified the most frequently required commands, so that a basis for this is now to hand. Further possibilities lie in the implementation of a technically straightforward software shell on top of the existing HELP software to overcome some of the present limitations, as proposed elsewhere (Anstey [1987]), although the prospect of a more radical approach using a dialogue manager along the lines of Jerrams Smith's intelligent user-system interface SUSI (Jerrams-Smith [1985]) or the AIM of Fowler *et al* (Fowler, Macauley & Siripoksup [1987]) is very attractive.

Access to the official Advisory Service needs to be more convenient, so that users call on Computing Centre support more readily. The concept of 'Remote Advisory' (Anstey [1986]), whereby human advice is made available interactively via terminals, provides a promising approach.

Whilst each of these features needs attention, the fact remains that at present the most accessible, flexible and user friendly HELP/advisory system is the user's colleague at the next terminal or in the next office.

It is imperative that these existing social structures are used by the Computing Centre – although with some caution. In particular, those regarded as computing experts by their peers should be identified by the Computing Centre, and their expertise carefully nurtured. Otherwise poor advice may limit user horizons and actually hold a user group back. This would be a particular danger where a single local 'expert' is almost invariably consulted in preference to (say) the Computing Centre Advisers, as could be the case with a Departmental Programmer who would be expected by colleagues to be an authority on the system.

Long term progress, however, probably lies in the use of a very different style of interface. For example, the WIMP type of interface is generally accepted as easy to use, particularly for the novice or occasional user.

However, the transition to adequately powerful systems which support such interfaces will be, in many cases, slow. The financial cost of this change is such that the centrally provided multi-user system will remain important to many users for some time, although a continued growth in the use of low cost micros both for standalone work and for access to the multi-user system is also to be expected. This latter point is itself interesting, because some of the operating systems on these microcomputers are actually rather primitive compared with VAX/VMS, and *less* user-friendly. This is often compensated, however, by the self-contained nature of much of the most popular micro based applications software – such that the operating system is often hidden from the user in a totally application-oriented interface.

A further constraint on progress towards 'better' systems is a lack of interface standards. Computing services, and particularly those in communities where sharing of facilities and movement between institutions is common, have need to adhere to international standards where they exist and to *de facto* standards in other cases. Indeed, to depart from a fundamentally standard implementation of the supplied operating system requires a very good reason.

Consequently, the way forward for such services must presently be seen in terms of a supportive interface to assist in the use of the *existing* operating system commands, rather than replacing them with something non-standard but closer to some proposed ideal. When adequately developed, dialogue managers such as those mentioned above will fit this requirement, although for the time being a much simpler (and much poorer) solution would be the addition of an (optional) menu driven interface to the current system, whereby the user is assisted in the choice of commands relevant to the current application.

6. Conclusion

This study has been on one user community. However, there is every reason to believe that the findings will similarly apply to user communities in other large organisations which are served by a central computing service.

In particular it has been shown that user knowledge of the operating system, as reflected primarily in command repertoires, is not always adequate in spite of user satisfaction. With a little more knowledge, many users could use the system far more effectively. Primary causes appear to be lack of willingness to make time to learn more than the minimal command repertoire to achieve the desired goals, and also user (or user group) insularity.

A number of organisational and software changes have been proposed, each of which is intended to help in extending user's ideas and concepts concerning the use of the system. Whilst some of the proposals relate specifically to the organisation at the one site, they are included in the belief that many similar computing services might nevertheless benefit from them.

However, one certain conclusion is the importance to the computing service of social structures amongst users, and their crucial rôle in user support and development. Whatever the claims for 'ease of use' of the operating system to hand, nurturing the expertise of key users in each social group may well be the best way to promote effective use of that system.

Acknowledgement

The author would like to thank John Roper for his constructive criticism and helpful suggestions during the writing of this paper.

References

J L Alty & M J Coombs [1981], "Communicating with University Computer Users: A Case Study," in *Computing Skills and the User Interface*, M J Coombs and J L Alty, ed., Academic Press.

P Anstey [1985], "Computing Advisory Services: A Review," *University Computing* 7, 8–13.

P Anstey [1986], "Computing Advice at a Distance: The 'Remote Advisory' Concept," *Software – Practice and Experience* 16, 1045–1052.

P Anstey [1987], "The Provision of Terminal-Based User Support," *University Computing* 9, 40–44.

R Auld, K Lang & T Lang [1981], "University Computer Users: Characteristics and Behaviour," in *Computing Skills and the User Interface*, M J Coombs and J L Alty, ed., Academic Press.

C J H Fowler, L A Macauley & S Siripoksup [1987], "An Evaluation of the Effectiveness of the Adaptive Interface Module in Matching Dialogues to Users," in *People and Computers III*, D Diaper and R Winder, ed., Cambridge University Press, Cambridge.

T R Girill [1985], "Online Access Aids for Documentation: A Bibliographic Outline," *ACM SIGIR Forum* 18, 24–27.

N C Goodwin [1987], "Functionality and Usability," *Communications of the ACM* 30, 229–233.

J Jerrams-Smith [1985], "SUSI – A Smart User-System Interface," in *People and Computers: Designing the Interface*, P Johnson and S Cook, ed., Cambridge University Press, Cambridge.

Generative Transition Networks: A New Communication Control Abstraction

Gilbert Cockton

Department of Computing Science, The University, 17 Lilybank Gardens, Glasgow, G12 8QQ.

The sequences of operations which are possible in the use of an interactive system can be modelled with different formal structures. Human factors and software engineering both set requirements for the design or selection of these formal structures. This paper surveys the requirements for operation sequence specification techniques for User Interface Management Systems, dialogue specification and early evaluation. To date, most formal structures have been selected from control models developed for other aspects of system specification. These selections have failed to satisfy all requirements equally. A new formal structure, the *Generative Transition Network* is presented which has been designed to satisfy known requirements without bias.

Keywords: UIMS, dialogue specification, generative transition networks, operational sequences, dialogue determination, formal methods.

1. Introduction

Good human-computer dialogues are designed separately from the software logic of the underlying application. A design needs to be explicitly described as some form of formal specification. It should not just evolve as part of a hand-coded implementation. Specifications communicate designs to implementors, who may be humans or software tools. Algebraic formality and rigorous semantics are not essential for human implementors, although efficiency and accuracy may result. Combinations of diagrams and structured text are better than no specification at all. But when the implementor is a program, a software tool, formal rigor is essential. The best known programs which implement user interface designs are called User Interface Management Systems (UIMSs) (Green [1985]).

Description is not the only possible use of a specification. The hope is that descriptions can be evaluated in some way before implementation, or even prototyping. Uses of dialogue specification for early evaluation are still at the research stage. This research is looking for metrics which will predict the relative usability of different designs. Dialogue specifications have been used as device simulations in the modelling of human-computer interaction. These applications of dialogue specification always require high level dialogue structures. The science of human-computer interaction and coherent user interface management thus both require explicit dialogue specifications. Hand-coding of human-computer dialogues is an activity which will isolate the dialogue designer from the potential benefits of a science of the user. Recent run-time developments such as microcomputer toolkits and frameworks have undoubtedly brought major short term benefits, but only the dialogue specification abstractions found in complete UIMSs can provide a bridge between the metrics of cognitive psychology and the implementation of a physical human-computer dialogue.

1.1. Communication Controllers

UIMSs are software tools which manage the end-user interaction for interactive applications. They are configured by descriptions of operation sequences, media-based presentation and linkage to the underlying application. The Communication Controller is the best understood component of a UIMS (Green [1985]). Communication Controllers are better known as *Dialogue Control components* (Seeheim model (Green [1985])). This term is not used here to avoid controversial anthropomorphisms (Cockton [1988a]).

The role of the CC (Communication Controller) is to respond to user and underlying application events in both *active* and *passive* modes. In active mode, the CC controls, usually via prompting, the inputs acceptable from the user and only responds to messages from the underlying application which are the result of a request for computation. At the extreme, the user interface is system-driven, but we still have an external control UIMS (Rosenthal & Yen [1987]). In passive mode, the CC responds to acceptable asynchronous user and underlying application events (for complete separability, a linkage should actually transfer messages and events between the user interface and the underlying application, see (Cockton [1987a]). At the extreme the user interface is user-driven (Miller & Thomas [1977]), to some designers 'modeless', and supports both internal and external modes of UIMS control. Direct Manipulation interfaces usually have passive CCs, essentially *get next event* loops where control is based on a switch on the event type. However, the response may be the initiation of a system-driven sequence, such as a dialogue box hierarchy, so both active and passive control are combined here.

In short, the CC is a *sequencer with synchronous and asynchronous behaviour*. It implements the operational aspects of interaction by or around which user tasks may be structured. Media managers supervise the presentation of these sequences and a linkage can interpret firstly, processed input sequences as requiring computation in the underlying application and secondly, underlying application events/results as abstract 'model' values for presentation ('viewing') at the user interface. The implicit model of an interactive system is as an input and an output pipeline running between media managers and the underlying application. The communication controller and linkage are system components which manage the processing of information between the two endpoints of the pipelines, and also transfer feedback information onto the output pipeline (Cockton [1987b]).

Several CC abstractions have been applied to UIMS design The most common CC abstractions are variants of Transition Networks (Cockton [1985]). Extended context-free grammars have been popular [28]. The sequential limitations of these two CC abstractions has long been recognised (Hopgood & Duce [1980]). Parallel capabilities (i.e. interleaving) are very important in the support of expert users' activity structures (Bannon et al. [1983]). In other situations, such as two-handed input, all users can benefit (Buxton & Myers [1986]). Parallel capabilities have been added to networks, but style-restrictions are imposed on the specified user interface (Jacob [1986]). This is due to the *executive* which distributes events to active networks. It is fixed and its behaviour is unalterable. The direct-manipulation user interface presented by Jacob's UIMS has a fixed style of object-selection.

Production rules have good parallel capabilities and are now dominant in direct-manipulation UIMSs in the form of *event-response* systems. They have long been the basis of run-time support such as application frameworks and notifiers. Formalisations restrict the antecedents and consequents of the production rules, resulting in special dialogue subtypes of production system (Harmelen & Wilson [1987]; Hill [1987]; Hopgood & Duce [1980]). Petri Nets have also been used for their parallel capabilities (Pilote [1983]). Communicating Sequential Processes (CSP) (Hoare [1985]) has also been explored as a CC abstraction (Alexander [1987]; Cardelli & Pike [1985]). Parallel capability CC abstractions are not without undesirable limitations (Cockton [1988b]). Production systems may result in unsupportive dialogues for many novice and casual users, as the detailed sequences which would embody task structure are difficult to specify. Mode management can result in cumbersome specifications (Hill [1986]). CSP is better here. It has sequence as a primitive construct, but compiling CSP may also produce very large run-time modules (Hill [1986]). Petri Nets do not modularise well and rule out the modular benefits of top-down design (Lee & Favrel [1985]).

For UIMSs, it would be valuable to find a single CC abstraction, less complicated and more efficient than CSP, amenable to graphical representation, capable of supporting well-determined dialogue sequences for novice and casual users, but without a restrictiveness that leads to over-determined dialogues for expert users.

1.2. User Views of Communication Control

Dialogue determination is a useful concept for integrating knowledge on control sequence design (Thimbleby [1980]). A good dialogue is *well-determined* for a user and a task. Where the CC is active to the point of constraint, *over-determined* system-driven dialogues result. Operational aspects of the interaction here do not match the user's task model, either by reordering subtask elements, adding spurious non-standard task elements (Thimbleby [1986]) or offering no support for tasks where good computer support is essential (e.g., finding a long-since accessed document in a large archive). In this last case, the interaction is *under-determined* and too user-driven.

1.3. Requirements for Communication Controllers

Avoiding under-determination requires *supportive* sequences. Avoiding over-determination requires *freedom* to interleave inputs and to vary the order in which a task is executed. An example of the latter is the ability to enter data in the order in which a client offers it, rather than to enforce a fixed interview order. The control abstractions which structure CCs are usually biased towards either freedom or supportiveness. Thus grammars and networks are biased towards sequence, but production rules (event-response systems) are biased towards interleaving. However, well-determination requires both in equal balance. Petri nets are less biased, but present difficulties in modularisation. CSP is equally versatile, but is complex and difficult to implement efficiently on single processors. Such *software engineering* requirements must be satisfied for software producers to be able to deliver supportiveness and freedom to end-users. Requirements for communication control are heterogeneous and somewhat complex. Only an overview is being presented here, but the technical points made are supported in other work (Cockton [1987b]; Cockton [1988a]; Cockton [1988b]).

1.4. Psychological Applications of Communication Control Abstractions

In a UIMS, a CC interprets or executes (compiled) dialogue specifications to deliver the run-time behaviour of a user interface. An alternative application of dialogue specifications does not require execution by a UIMS, rather it documents a dialogue design for coding by a programmer and/or presentation by a technical writer for end-user documentation. A related research activity involves the formal evaluation of such 'unexecuted' designs (Reisner [1981]; Sharratt [1987a]; Sharratt [1987b]). The results of such analyses are usability metrics which hopefully reflect the quality of the designed user interface. Certain analyses can be automated.

Cognitive Complexity Theory (Kieras & Polson [1983]; Kieras & Polson [1985]) uses *Generalised Transition Networks* to simulate devices (i.e. interactive systems) and production rules to emulate user cognition. As a transition network, the CC abstraction is biased towards sequence, consequently Direct Manipulation interfaces will be difficult to specify. Where two possible sequences can be interleaved, production rule formalisms support descriptions which are the size of the sum of the descriptions of the two individual sequences. Formalisms based on finite state automata (i.e. transition networks) result in descriptions the size of the product of the two sizes (Hill [1987]).

A simple example of interleaving involves the sequences of a command language and the single string language help. To get help at any point, the user generates a help event by typing or pointing or keying at any point in any command sequence. To represent this using Generalised Transition Networks would involve testing for the help event on an arc from every state in every nested network. The size of such a family of networks could affect the evaluation metrics and suggest that things are harder than they really are. They are not hard, it is Generalised Transition Networks which makes things hard because they are inefficient in their representation of interleavable dialogues. Perversely, an exercise in the psychology of HCI has resulted in the use of a CC abstraction which fails to satisfy known requirements for well-determined dialogues!

There are other considerations when using CC abstractions for both device simulation and as a UIMS specification abstraction. Generalised Transition Networks use the ability to backtrack (Kieras & Polson [1983]). That is, paths through networks are tested, and if one fails, another is tried. Some networks are used as conditions rather than procedures. If the traverser can get across the network named on a transition, then this transition is taken. In a simulation, representations of any output feedback can be stored up until a conditional network traversal succeeds. Accumulated feedback can be discarded when an attempted traversal fails. In a running system, the need for rapid feedback before further input, and the inability to take real output back, rule out unrestricted backtracking in networks and grammar parsing (Cockton [1987b]; Green [1986]). The use of networks to test the input is too weak, and lacks context-sensitivity. Transition conditions should be declarative constraints (Cockton [1985]), not attempts at network traversals. A CC abstraction can be adequate for device simulation, but inadequate for a UIMS implementation.

2. An Advance in Communication Control Abstractions for UIMS Control, Dialogue Specification and Automated Evaluation

The ideal abstraction for CCs would support both sequencing and interleaving without bias. Software engineering requirements for modularisability and executability must also be satisfied. It is now argued that a new CC abstraction, the Generative Transition Network can satisfy the requirements identified here. It is called a *generative* network because it *generates arcs which designers would otherwise have to enumerate.*

2.1. Generative Transition Networks: Fundamentals

The key contribution of Generative Transition Networks (GTNs) is to simplify the specification of responses to globally enabled events within a sequential network formalism. Forms of interleaving are supported without sacrificing ease of sequential and mode specification in structured dialogues. Sequence and mode are difficult to specify in event-response systems (Hill [1986]), The technique used to extend transition networks for interleaving has proved useful for encapsulating regularity rather than enumerating it. The technique *generates* arcs rather than describes them. GTNs are equivalent in power to Augmented Transition Networks (ATNs) (Woods [1970]), but superior in their economy.

They are actually extensions of *Dialogue ATNs* (DATNs) (Cockton [1985]) which are extended ATNs with parameterisation of recursively traversable (sub)networks. A number of scoping strategies are possible for local and global variables. As network traversal can be regarded as procedure execution with input/output and other side effects, networks call other networks as part of a transition action; the initiation of DATN subnet traversal is restricted to arc actions. The registers of ATNs are generalised to a *session data base* of arbitrary user interface support objects, which may be media-independent (e.g., intelligent help object) or media-dependent (e.g., graphical display computation). DATNs and GTNs and their interpreted traversal are now presented formally.

A DATN is a 8-tuple $<l, n_0, N, F, A, i, p, v>$ where

l is the name (label) of the network
$n_0 \in N$ is the start node of the network
N is the set of nodes for the network
$F \subseteq N$ is the set of terminating nodes for the network
$A \subseteq <N \times N \times E \times R>^*$ is the arc list for the network
i is the initialisation vector
p is a vector of session object names used to parameterise the DATN.
v is the vector of names of returned session object values.

$<a, b, c>^*$ is a list of tuples, each with elements of type a, b and c. E and R are the domains of events and responses, they are the name of predicates and procedures defined outside of the DATN. Their definitions reference objects in the session data base. i represents the initialisation of some session objects. It is a vector of pairs, each item being an object name and a value which will be assigned to the named object at the start of a DATN traversal. p is a vector of object names. The named objects will be set to values from a parameter vector passed to the DATN traversal function. Objects named in v are returned together as the value of a DATN on termination.

An arc or edge thus is a 4-tuple $<i, o, e, r>$ where

$i \in N$ is the start of the arc
$o \in N$ is the end of the arc
$e \in E$ is the transition condition of the arc. It is an event name.
$r \in R$ is the transition action of the arc. It is an action name.

DATNs implement user interfaces via arc conditions and actions. These are defined separately in event and response specifications. A DATN traverser begins at node n_0 with the objects in its session data base set from i and the parameter vector. It looks for an arc $<n_0, o, e, r>$ in A where e has occured. When it finds this arc, the actions named by r are executed and the traverser moves to a new node o. If o is not in F, the traverser looks for a new arc $<o, o', e', r'>$ in A and the process continues until a node in F is reached. The values in v are then returned as the value of the traversed network. Traversers thus operate like procedures which return values, but they search their arcs (clauses) in a fixed order and A is thus a list.

The formalisation differs from one as an 9-tuple $<Q, \Sigma, P, \Gamma, \delta, \gamma, q_0, Z_0, f>$ (Green [1986]) in the following ways: the net stack elements Γ and Z_0 are not required – net traversal is an arc action executed by a separate DATN traverser; the input symbols Σ and the transition function δ are implicit in names on the DATN arcs, A, as are the action set P and the action function γ; the DATN elements N, n_0 and F correspond to Green's Q, q_0 and f. These differences are due to the less defined event conditions and response actions, the nested traversal mechanism and its parameterisation, and the representation of the transition function as a set of arcs.

The problem with DATNs is that they can only ever respond to events matched on arcs from the current node. Globally active options must thus be specified using event matching *at every node*. This is tedious. A new CC abstraction, the Generative Transition Network avoids this uneconomical tedium by changing the edge type in networks' defining 9-tuples to create *arc generators* rather than simple arcs.

A GTN is a 9-tuple $<l, n_0, N, F, G, i, p, v, t>$ where l, n_0, N, F, i, p, and v are as for DATNs. The differences are that G replaces A and t is new. The types of these elements are:

$G \subseteq <\mathcal{P}(N) \times seq(N) \mapsto N \times E \times R>^*$ is the list of arc generators.

$t \in seq(N)$ is the GTN traverser's node stack.

$\mathcal{P}(N) = \{S | S \subseteq N\}$ is the *power set* of N. $seq(N)$ is the set of sequences of N. A GTN arc generator is a 4-tuple $<S, f, e, r>$ where

$S \subset \mathcal{P}(N)$ is the set of the starts of the generated arcs
$f \in seq(N) \mapsto N$ computes the ends of the generated arcs
$e \in E$ is the transition condition of the arc. It is an event name.
$r \in R$ is the transition action of the arc. It is an action name.

A GTN traverser behaves almost like a DATN interpreter. One difference is its node stack, which it maintains as it traverses a network. The other is its behaviour when looking for arcs matching events which have occured. At the current node n, it looks for an arc generator $<S, f, e, r>$ with $n \in S$. Event matching and responses are treated as for DATNs. The next node is computed using t. Apart from the constant functions in N (i.e., all nodes are constant functions which return themselves as their value), endpoint functions are applied to the node stack, t. This gives the value of the next node (directly or from the stack). The next node is stacked on t and a transition is made to it. The function $same = top$ (apply top to t) is heavily used. Another useful function, $back = top.tail$, gives the previous node. The use of the concrete tokens such as $same$ and $back$, frees the GTN notation from details of t's provisional domain. Although node stacks seems to be the only values needed for t, only more extensive use of GTNs can increase confidence here.

2.2. A Notation for GTNs

The design of notations requires as much user testing as the design of good interactive user interfaces. This research has only just reached the stage where designing alternative notations for testing is possible. A visual representation is essential. Concepts developed in *Statecharts* (Harel [1987]) may be transferable to representations of GTNs. The use of venn diagrams to surround state subsets in Statecharts transfers easily to the subset initial endpoints of GTN arc generators. However, the visual representation of GTNs is still under study. For the moment, an algebraic notation will have to be used. A provisional notation, which reflects the author's taste and nothing else, is sketched by the grammar below:

                <GTN> ::= <arc_gen> <GTN> | 'ε'
                <arc_gen> ::= <starts> '↦' <endfn> <event> '⇒'
                <response> | <DATN_arc>
                <DATN_arc> ::= '(' <node> ',' <node> ')' <event> '⇒'
                <response>
                <starts> ::= '**all**' | <opd> <setop> <opd> | <name> | '{'
                <node> ',' <rest_starts>
                <rest_starts> ::= '}' | <node> ',' <rest_starts>
                <opd> ::= <starts> | <name> | '(' <starts> ')'
                <setop> ::= '∪' | '∩' | '−'
                <endfn> ::= '**same**'| '**back**' | <node> | ...
                <event> ::= '**none**' | <name>
                <response> ::= '**null**' | <name>
                <node> ::= <name>
                <name> ::= /*letter,then any sequence of letters,numbers etc*/

The notation represents a GTN as a list of arc generators. The starts of an arc generator can be a name, standing for a much used subset of nodes. Set operations can be performed on starts. A special syntax simplifies the description of DATN arcs. The set of end node functions is under development. This grammar is a simplification of an earlier version (Cockton [1988a]). The simplification is due to the replacement of full transition condition expressions and action expressions by event and response names. GTNs expressed in this new grammar are more concise and can be read without knowledge of the algebras for the session database objects and media managers referenced in transition conditions and actions. If events and responses are given sensible names, then non-computer specialists should be able to read (and perhaps write) GTN specifications. This separation of event reference from event definition is used in *Event Response Language* (Hill [1987]) where events are defined as part of objects in a lexical library. A similar separation exists between *eventCSP* and *eventISL* in the SPI formalism (Alexander [1987]).

GTNs expressed in the older fuller notation give a more complete account of user interface behaviour, by revealing the semantics of events and responses. Little is yet known what differences in comprehension for computer specialists, if any, result from replacing event and response names with their definitions.

These examples of arc generators illustrate the use of the grammar:

all $\mapsto$ **same** hit_help $\Rightarrow$
At all nodes, if there's a *hit_help* event, respond with the *do_help* actions. Stay at the same node.

all $\mapsto$ **same** hit_quit $\Rightarrow$ traverse_safe_quit
At all nodes, if there's a *hit_quit* event, respond with the *traverse_safe_quit* actions. Stay at same node.

all $-a, b, c \mapsto$ **same** $\Rightarrow$ hit_quit $\Rightarrow$ traverse_safe_quit
At all nodes except *a*, *b* and *c*, if there's a *hit_quit* event, respond with the *traverse_safe_quit* actions. Stay at the same node.

all $\mapsto$ quit quitflag $\Rightarrow$ **null**
At all nodes, if the *quitflag* event has occured, go to the quit node. This sort of internal event would be defined as a test on a session data base object rather than a media manager query. The traversal of a *safe_quit* network from within the *traverse_safe_quit* response would affect objects referenced in this test.

all $-$(irreversibles $\cup$ no_changes) $\mapsto$ **same** undo_event $\Rightarrow$
undo_last_action
At all nodes except any in subsets *irreversibles* and *no_changes*, if an *undo_event* event has occured, perform *undo_last_action* and stay at the same node.

{layout} $\mapsto$ add_symbol add_symbol_ev $\Rightarrow$ addmode
At the *layout* node, if there's been an *add_symbol_ev* event, execute the *addmode* response and go to *add_symbol* node. DATN arc with alternative syntax: (layout, add_symbol) add_symbol_ev $\Rightarrow$ addmode.

The alternative syntax for DATN arcs in GTNs highlights the main differences between DATNs and GTNs. GTN arc generators have set and function endpoints, whereas DATN arcs have node endpoints. Simple alteration of two elements in arc definition vectors ($<i, o, e, r> \mapsto <S, f, e, r>$), allows economical expression of multi-threaded dialogues without losing the sequential and mode capabilities of transition networks. The simplest arc generators, **all** $\mapsto$ **same** generators, are really production rules which are activated at each node. They bring production system capabilities to a network formalism.

2.3. Example GTN specifications

With no usage data, only the combined power, economy and capabilities of GTNs can be demonstrated by re-expressing three published specifications as GTNs. An example from a user interface developed by the author and others at the Scottish HCI Centre also demonstrates the economy of GTNs over DATNs.

The events consumed by CCs in UIMSs originate from input media managers, interesting states of session data base objects and the underlying application via the linkage. The responses activated by CCs affect all of these originators, as well as the media output managers. As all the affected components have management capabilities, the CC can delegate varying local control to any of them. The CC will either have to compensate for, or benefit, from capabilities in the other interactive system components, such as the media managers which handle basic input and output, and the linkage which translates between the user interface and the underlying application. Varying re-expressions of the third published specification demonstrate this.

2.3.1. Foley and van Dam's room layout program

This user interface is specified as a simple (i.e. unaugmented, not recursive) transition network (Foley & Dam [1982, p.64]). There are 37 arcs in the diagram. Only 24 GTN arc generators are required, a 35% reduction. 20 of these are DATN arcs. The bulk of the reduction is due to the common pattern of time out behaviour, requesting and returning from help and cancelling commands. A subset of nodes **MainCmds** = {**add_symbol, del_symbol, change_symbol**} is defined to simplify specification. The four none-DATN arc generator skeletons are:

> MainCmds $\mapsto$ Layout cancel $\Rightarrow$?
> MainCmds $\cup$ {Title} $\mapsto$ **same** time_out $\Rightarrow$?
> MainCmds $\cup$ {Title, place_symbol} $\mapsto$ do_help help $\Rightarrow$?
> do_help $\cup$ {Title, place_symbol} $\mapsto$ **back** carriage_return $\Rightarrow$?

The published network specification gives no details of the actions, so they cannot be suggested here by response names. These 4 generators

replace 17 arcs in the simple network. They encapsulate all the regularity
about cancels, timeouts and help. A fifth generator is possible, replacing
5 arcs:

$$\text{MainCmds} \cup \{ \text{ zoom\_in, place\_sym} \} \mapsto \textbf{back} \text{ done} \Rightarrow ?$$

However, the response to *done* events would vary with the current node,
whereas responses to *cancel* events are assumed to be uniform resets of
session objects. This sort of collapsing brings limited benefit, but may
still be useful in device simulations which need to highlight regularity.
When used, only 20 arc generators are required, a 46% reduction over
the Foley and van Dam network. An implementation of this very
moded network in ERL (Event Response Language) was reported as
cumbersome (Hill [1986]). This is because the multi-threading economy
of ERL is gained at the expense of sequence and mode economy. This
trade-off does not exist for GTNs, making them a more general purpose
abstraction.

2.3.2. The RAPID restaurant review user interface

The RAPID UIMS tutorial uses a restaurant review information system
as its main example (Wasserman & Shewmake [1984, pages 13 and 22]).
It can be specified as 11 arc generators and 6 nodes. The RAPID
specification requires 11 arc statements and 8 nodes. However, arc
statements represent *all* the arcs from a node, so there are actually 18
arcs in the specification. The GTN specification reduces nodes by 25%
and arcs by 39%. The arc generators are:

    (setup,start) setup ⇒ menu_display
    (setup,finish) **none** ⇒ no_database_error_message
    (start,start) key_A ⇒ traverse_addnew&menu_display
    (start,start) key_M ⇒ traverse_modify&menu_display
    (start,start) key_G ⇒ traverse_giverev&menu_display
    (start,start) key_R ⇒ traverse_readrev&menu_display
    (start,start) key_L ⇒ traverse_listall&menu_display
    (start,finish) key_Q ⇒ quit_message
    (start,help) key_H ⇒ help_display
    (start,error) anyevent ⇒ error_message
    {help,error} ↦ start anykey ⇒ menu_display

Alternative inputs are hidden in event definitions. Response definitions
hide details of actions (mostly node displays in RAPID). If RAPID
allowed events which tested the results of an operation, like the *setup*
event here, and also allowed net traversal as a transition action, only 4
arc statements, rather than 11, would be required. The total avoidance of
conditional side-effects advocated elsewhere (Cockton [1985]) is relaxed
here. Where they are used, there should be only two (generated) arcs

sharing the initial endpoint. The matching event for the second must be **none**. This arc will be traversed if the side-effecting event test fails.

RAPID's idiosyncratic handling of subnetworks is responsible for most superfluous arc statements, and has other more serious drawbacks (Cockton [1985]). But RAPID's use of nodes for display handling does simplify things. Several GTN responses redisplay the menu. The simple solution in GTNs is to introduce a new node between *setup* and *start*, to which all command, help and error arcs connect without redisplay of the menu. A no event arc from the new node to start node could centralise menu display management in a single response.

2.3.3. The ERL command interpreter

The standard small ERL example is a command interpreter which takes the command and single argument in any order (Hill [1987, p.245]). Five ERL rules are required. The three equivalent GTN arc generators are:

> **all** $\mapsto$ **same** arg_event $\Rightarrow$ havearg&set_arg
> **all** $\mapsto$ **same** cmd_event $\Rightarrow$ havecmd&set_cmd
> **all** $\mapsto$ **same** havearg&havecmd $\Rightarrow$ unset_cmd&arg&call_linkage

The *unset_cmd&arg&call_linkage* response passes the command and argument values to a core linkage and waits for the processing to complete before returning control to the GTN traverser. This results in one ERL rule needing no equivalent GTN arc generator. Asychronous communication with a linkage component (Cockton [1987a]), is also possible in responses, and would require an extra generator to respond to an end of processing event, as in the ERL specification. This illustrates how other parts of the user interface architecture can simplify control in the CC. It is not clear how much control should be delegated by the CC, as it can result in distributed control specifications, which will be harder to analyse.

Note that the GTN specification allows the user more freedom than the ERL one, as the first input can be re-entered many times, allowing correction before processing. This is not possible in the ERL example. However, this arbitrary inconsistency between revision of the first and second inputs can be corrected by changing the third generator:

> **all** $\mapsto$ **same** havearg&havecmd&ok_event $\Rightarrow$
> unset_cmd&arg&call_linkage

This generator requires the user to give an explicit 'ok' input, up to which point, both command and argument can be re-entered. Here there is no automatic processing on the second input. An exact specification of the ERL behaviour requires an extra generator and revisions to the first two:

all ↦ **same** not_gotarg&arg_event ⇒ havearg&set_arg
all ↦ **same** not_gotcmd&cmd_event ⇒ havecmd&set_cmd
all ↦ **same** havearg&havecmd ⇒ unset_cmd&arg&call_linkage
all ↦ **same** havearg_or_havecmd ⇒ repeated_input_error

This specification relies on sequential testing of the four arc generators. Note though that the published ERL specification has no error rules, so this GTN specification is 'more than' equivalent with only four generators rather than five rules. However, by changing the sort of events in which the GTN traverser is interested in, we can have complete freedom of revision, until a final *ok_event*, described using only two generators:

all ↦ **same** ok_event_without_cmd_or_arg ⇒
not_all_there_message&dequeue_ok
all ↦ **same** ok_event_with_cmd&arg ⇒
get_events_off_queue_and_pass_to_linkage

The first generator traps early entry of *ok_events* when other inputs are missing, informs the user and removes record of *ok_events*. The second generator matches an event defined as the presence of all three inputs in the queue. In response, the events are removed from the queue and the linkage is called with the values of the last command and argument events. These operations show how sophistication in other interface components reduces the control specification. Here, the ability to search input media event queues and to dequeue arbitrary events transforms the control specification. The generalisation of event queues to event lists will reduce event management in the CC.

Finally, control of closure could be left to the core linkage, with a single generator passing values from a *cmd_event*, *arg_event* or *ok_event* straight to it. However, other generators would be required to respond to the different error tokens which the linkage could pass back. The point is that there is a considerable interaction between a control abstraction, input management abstractions and the core linkage abstraction. Thus crude comparisons of specification size may be misleading. The object types used to define events and responses can greatly (overly?) reduce the size of the control specification. Despite these object-type sleights of hand in this section, GTNs are at least as economical as ERL for multi-threaded dialogues, and considerably more economical for sequential and moded ones.

2.3.4. Reduction in menu hierarchy specification

At the Scottish HCI Centre, the author was involved in the design and implementation of a report processing system which used a hierarchical menu structure. In the most complex case, there were five levels, with two types of objects at the lower two levels. These levels are named level1 etc. in the examples. This created seven nodes in the DATN. Each odd-level node's menu allowed a retreat to the higher levels. Even-level node menus were selections from dynamic lists, and retreat from here was handled differently. The ten resulting arcs, plus one from a higher level to a lower one, can be represented by three arc generators:

$$\{level3,level5a,level5b\} \mapsto level1 \ level1 \Rightarrow to\_level\_1$$
$$\mathbf{all} \ -\{level2,level4a,level4b\} \mapsto level2 \ level2 \Rightarrow to\_level\_2$$
$$\mathbf{all} \ -\{level1,level2,level3\} \mapsto level3 \ level3 \Rightarrow to\_level\_3$$

This is evidence of the practical applicability of GTNs to post-hoc specification of an implemented commercial product. Many other specification reductions over the DATN version are possible, due to the designed regularity of the dialogue. Consistency is expensive in DATNs, due to tedious repetition, but is economically encapsulated in GTNs. The use of set constants such as **level5** = {**level5a,level5b**} would enhance the salience of dialogue consistency – indeed they expose inconsistencies between retreats at different levels.

3. Conclusions

The GTN is the first CC abstraction to combine economy of expressiveness for both unmoded and moded user interfaces. It captures both sequence and interleaving by replacing arc enumeration with arc generation. It can generate arcs from all nodes, and thus bring production system capabilities to a sequential network abstraction. Existing specifications translate readily into GTNs, although variability in event and response semantics due to other UIMS components results in considerable freedom. Control specification cannot be independent of controlled objects, and thus the rigid logical separation of syntax is an ideal which cannot be realised in the multi-party dialogues of human-computer communication.

The work presented here is wholly functional. It is about economy of abstraction, not ease of use. For those who have found the mathematical presentation difficult, it will be clear that a visual representation for GTNs is an urgent priority. If one were available now, the ideas in the paper would have been easier to present. At the moment, understanding GTNs requires a mathematical literacy which is not universal amongst human factors practitioners and user interface designers. However, before we decide *how* to represent something, we need to decide *what* it is that we should be representing. GTNs are hopefully mathematical objects worthy of visual representation and embedding in UIMSs and related tools. Harel's Statecharts (Harel [1987]) are currently being examined for approaches to the visual representation of GTNs.

Although mathematical concepts dominate this paper, the work has been interdisciplinary. Empirical survey skills had to be applied to establish what dialogue specifications were used for and what properties a CC abstraction should possess. HCI research must start with human activities such as design specifications and interactive system operation, and end up with human activities such as UIMS use and the production of specifications. The next goal for research into GTNs is to make the mathematics disappear from view, but not from influence. The combination of freedom and supportiveness in GTN control specifications is a valuable fusion for the design of interactive systems.

Acknowledgements

This work was largely completed while I was at the Heriot-Watt site of the Scottish HCI Centre in Edinburgh. The Scottish HCI Centre was set up as part of Alvey Directorate's MMI programme and is one of three such research and development centres in Britain. I am grateful to members of Glasgow University's Graphics and HCI group who have commented on drafts of this paper, in particular Phil Gray and John Patterson. The development of GTNs was inspired by Zisman's demonstration of the equivalence between labelled production systems and ATNs (Zisman [1977, pp.49ff]), and by Jacob's use of lists of initial nodes and the *same* end node in his network-based specification technique (Jacob [1985, p.232]). Knowledge of the equivalence of ATNs and labelled production systems inspired the idea of extending Jacob's syntactic shortcuts into a generalised automaton.

References

H Alexander [1987], "Formally-based Techniques for Dialogue Description," in *People and Computers III*, D Diaper and R Winder, ed., Cambridge University Press, Cambridge, 201–214.

L Bannon, A Cypher, S Greenspan & M L Monty [1983], "Evaluation and Analysis of User's Activity Structures," in *Proceedings of CHI '83 – Human Factors in Computing Systems*, ACM, New York, 54–57.

W Buxton & B Myers [1986], "A Study in Two-Handed Input," in *Proceedings of CHI '86 – Human Factors in Computing Systems*, ACM, New York, 321–326.

L Cardelli & R Pike [1985], "Squeak: A Language for Communicating with Mice," *ACM Computer Graphics* 19, 199–205.

G Cockton [1985], "Three Transition Network Dialogue Management Systems," in *People and Computers: Designing the Interface*, P Johnson and S Cook, ed., Cambridge University Press, Cambridge, 135–144.

G Cockton [1987a], "A New Model for Separable Interactive Systems," in *INTERACT '87 – The Second IFIP Conference on Human-Computer Interaction*, H J Bullinger and B Shackel, ed., Elsevier Science Publishers B.V., North Holland, 1033–1038.

G Cockton [1987b], "Interaction Ergonomics, Control and Separation: Open Problems in User Interface Management," *Information and Software Technology* 29, 176–191.

G Cockton [1988a], "Generative Transition Networks – A New Communication Control Abstraction," Scottish HCI Centre Report No. AMU8811/01H, Heriot-Watt University, Edinburgh.

G Cockton [1988b], "Interaction Ergonomics Control and Separation: Open Problems in User Interface Management," Scottish HCI Centre Report No. AMU8811/03H, Heriot-Watt University, Edinburgh.

J D Foley & A van Dam [1982], *Fundamentals of Interactive Computer Graphics*, Addison-Wesley, Reading MA, Reprinted with corrections 1984.

M Green [1985], "Report on Dialogue Specification Tools," in *User Interface Management Systems*, G Pfaff, ed., Springer-Verlag, Berlin, 9–20.

M Green [1986], "A Survey of Three Dialogue Control Models," *ACM Trans. on Graphics* 5, 244–275.

D Harel [1987], "Statecharts: A Visual Formalism for Complex Systems," *Science of Computer Programming* 8.

M van Harmelen & S M Wilson [1987], "Viz: A Production System Based User Interface Management System," in *Eurographics '87*, Elsevier Science Publishers B.V., North Holland.

R D Hill [1986], "Supporting Concurrency, Communication and Synchronisation in Human-Computer Interaction – The Sassafras UIMS," *ACM Trans. on Graphics* 5.

R D Hill [1987], "Event-Response Systems – A Technique for Specifying Multi-Threaded Dialogues," in *CHI + GI Conference '87*, ACM, Toronto Canada, 241–248.

C A R Hoare [1985], *Communicating Sequential Processes*, Prentice-Hall.

F R A Hopgood & D A Duce [1980], "A Production System Approach to Interactive Graphic Program Design," in *Methodology of Interaction*, R A Guedj P T W ten Hagen F R A Hopgood H A Tucker and D A Duce, ed., North-Holland, 247–263.

R J K Jacob [1985], "An Executable Specification Technique for Describing Human-Computer Interaction," in *Advances in Human-Computer Interaction 1*, H R Hartson, ed., Ablex, Norwood NJ, 211–242.

R J K Jacob [October 1986], "A Specification Language for Direct-Manipulation User Interfaces," *ACM Trans. on Graphics 5*.

D Kieras & P G Polson [1983], "A Generalised Transition Network Representation for Interactive Systems," in *Proceedings of CHI '83 – Human Factors in Computing Systems*, ACM, New York, 103–106.

D Kieras & P G Polson [1985], "An Approach to the Formal Analysis of User Complexity," *Int. J. Man-Machine Studies 22*, 365–394.

K Lee & J Favrel [1985], "Hierarchical Reduction Method for Analysis and Decomposition of Petri Nets," *Trans. Systems, Man and Cybernetics SMC-15*, 272–281.

L A Miller & J C Thomas [1977], "Behavioral Issues in the Use of Interactive Systems," *Int. J. Man-Machine Studies 9*, 509–536.

M Pilote [1983], "A Programming Language Framework for Designing User Interfaces," *ACM SIGPLAN Notices 18*, 118–136.

P Reisner [1981], "Formal Grammar and the Design of an Interactive System," *IEEE Trans. on Software Engineering 7*, 229–240.

D Rosenthal & A Yen [1987], "User Interface Models Summary," *ACM Computer Graphics 17*, 16–20.

B Sharratt [1987a], "The Incorporation of Early Interface Evaluation into Command Language Grammar Specifications," in *People and Computers III*, D Diaper and R Winder, ed., Cambridge University Press, Cambridge, 11–28.

B Sharratt [1987b], "Top-Down Interactive Systems Design: Some Lessons Learnt from Using Command Language Grammar," in *INTER-ACT '87 – The Second IFIP Conference on Human-Computer Interaction*, H J Bullinger and B Shackel, ed., Elsevier Science Publishers B.V., North Holland.

H Thimbleby [1980], "Dialogue Determination," *Int. J. Man-Machine Studies* 24, 395–304.

H Thimbleby [1986], "Ease of Use – The Ultimate Deception," in *People and Computers: Designing for Usability (Proceedings of the Second Conference of the BCS HCI SG, York, 23-26 September 1986)*, M D Harrison and A F Monk, ed., Cambridge University Press, 78–94.

A I Wasserman & D T Shewmake [April 1984], *A RAPID/USE Tutorial* #Release 1.2, Medical Information Science, University of California, San Fransisco CA.

W A Woods [1970], "Transition Network Grammars for Natural Language Analysis," *Communications of the ACM* 13.

M D Zisman [1977], "Representation, Specification and Automation of Office Procedures," University of Pennsylvania, PhD Thesis.

Text Processing by Speech: Dialogue Design and Usability Issues in the Provision of a System for Disabled Users

Jill Hewitt and Stephen Furner*

School of Information Science, Hatfield Polytechnic, College Lane, Hatfield, Herts. AL10 9AB, U.K.

*Human Factors Division, British Telecom Research Laboratories, Martlesham Heath, Ipswich, Suffolk, U.K.

Commercial speech recognition systems are available as 'add-on' units for popular office micro-computers. A typical office system has been employed to provide a 'transparent' interface to an ordinary text processing package so that it can be used by the disabled. This paper describes the prototyping carried out to develop the dialogue offered by the system as a result of addressing its user performance characteristics.

Keywords: Dialogue design, usability engineering, text processing, speech recognition

1. Introduction

The objectives of the project reported in this paper are:

a) to provide an acceptable and affordable voice operated text processor for the subject, and to investigate the dialogue design and usability issues associated with the use of the commercially available technology.

b) to consider the implications for the wider use of such a system as part of a communications centre for disabled users, and, with improved technology, for the able-bodied worker.

Simple speech recognition systems are now available as 'off-the-shelf' items which can be used as an 'add-on' to a conventional office micro-computer. These system configurations offer the potential of 'hands-free' operation of conventional electronic office products such as word processors or spread sheets. A micro-computer used in this way need not only be employed as a stand alone system, access to a local area network (LAN) and the public telephone network could also be provided as well as the speech recognition capability (Schnabl & Boissinot [1987]). In this situation the processing capacity of machines much larger than the original micro-computer could be made available. With network access it becomes possible to consider authoring and distributing documents entirely in electronic form via existing e-mail systems such as JANET or Telecom Gold. Here, the problems of printing or posting the documents would be removed.

These 'add-on' speech recognition systems do not have the same capacity to understand speech that a human listener would possess. Typically, a recogniser of this type would be speaker dependent, require each word to be spoken in isolation, and be restricted in the size of its recognition vocabulary. The speaker dependence would require that all of the items of the recognition vocabulary be retaught to the system every time a different person used it. The difference between the technical performance of a speech recogniser and the way speech is used in ordinary day to day conversation results in significant Human Factors issues arising in its use as an input device (Simpson et al. [1985]).

A commercial speech recognition system mounted in a typical office micro-computer has been employed to provide a prototype voice controlled text processor for use by the disabled. The prototype was provided to a disabled student to use in the production of written work required for a course he was following at university. This indicated a positive attitude towards the system by the user – an average score of +1.3 was obtained using the questionnaire devised by Poulson (Poulson [1987]) – and areas for improvement in the design of the user interface were identified.

The initial prototype was 'fine-tuned' in accordance with the results of the evaluation and within the limits of the software tool used to construct it. Some simple preliminary laboratory testing indicated that a skilled user could create text with it at approximately 10 words a minute. While some of the usability problems identified in the initial prototype could be dealt with by 'fine-tuning' the design, others could not be addressed due to limitations in the software tool with which it had been constructed. As a result of the information obtained about the usability of the initial prototype a revised design is being produced for construction with a more sophisticated software tool. The revised design will be able to enter into sub-dialogues to deal with doubtful recognitions (Millar, Cameron & Chaplin [1987]) and provide more visual feedback to the user.

2. System components

The prototype consists of a Ferranti PC-860 fitted with a VOTAN VPC2000 Speech Recognition Unit supporting an interface to the public telephone network. The initial prototype was built using the VOTAN VoiceKey software tool. The initial choice of the hardware was determined by the student who was going to use the system, taking into account cost and likely ease of use. The Ferranti PC was recommended by the suppliers of the plug-in VOTAN recognition unit.

The student using the system initially employed a head-set microphone. After the evaluation this was replaced by a desk mounted goose-neck microphone to allow him to access the machine without the need for extra help. The use of the head-set microphone had meant that he had to arrange for somebody to fit the microphone on his head when wanted to use the machine, and come and remove it when he had finished with it.

The text processing package that the speech interface provided 'transparent' (Dabbagh, Damper & Guy [1986]) access to was Perfect Writer. The choice of this package was primarily determined by its availability; it is distributed with the Ferranti machines.

3. Design of the initial prototype

The Voicekey package used to build the prototype provided facilities for alphanumeric characters or recorded messages to be produced when an item was recognised by the system. The concept behind the Voicekey software was that it could be used to replace the keys of the computer keyboard. It provided the tools necessary to train the recognition system and associate the material to be produced when a word was recognised. Voicekey ran in background so that it could be used with an application program to provided a link to the speech recogniser. When a word was recognised an alphanumeric string was passed to the application or a spoken message produced to the user. Some special task words could be trained to carry out special functions such as displaying the list of words in the active recognition vocabulary.

The initial prototype contained five basic vocabularies which were loaded on the machine when the power was switched on (see fig. 1). Every vocabulary was accessible from every other, providing fast switching from one to the other. Subsets of the vocabulary were used to restrict recognition to the vocabulary switching words when a change was required. The special task words were used to activate the following functions from each vocabulary:-

a) Show the names of the items in the active vocabulary.

b) Make the machine dormant so that it would only recognise the 'wake up' command.

c) Train a 'wake up' command.

The 'sleep' and 'wake up' commands produced a spoken prompt when invoked to ensure that the current state of the system (dormant or active) was known by the user.

The initial choice of vocabularies and content was the implementer's. The alphabet was represented by the international phonetic alphabet with some changes made to improve the recognition accuracy. Schnabl and Boissinot (Schnabl & Boissinot [1987]) emphasise the importance of easy addition, deletion and retraining of templates, but the way in which subsets were implemented by embedding actual template numbers in the vocabulary made it difficult for the user to add or delete word entries without destroying the integrity of the system. The student, after an initial training session, was able to refine the vocabularies in use to take into account personalised recognition problems. He also substituted some shorter words in an attempt to speed up the system – in some cases this had the effect of reducing the recognition accuracy.

The number and size of vocabularies in use is limited by the physical capacity of the machine and by the loss of recognition accuracy in large sets. Some simple editing commands and common punctuation were added to each vocabulary to reduce the number of vocabulary switches required when creating text. Early attempts to include even more commands in each vocabulary were counter productive because of the increase in recognition errors.

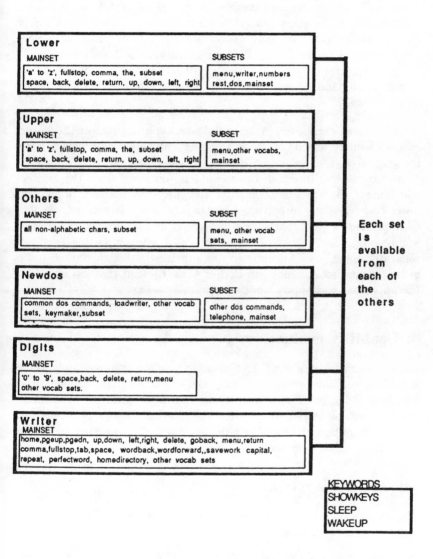

Figure 1. Vocabulary Structure of the initial system

3.1. The text processing vocabulary

Perfect Writer has a hierarchical menu structure which is invoked by the 'menu' voice command. Selections from the menu were made by scrolling up or down (using the voice commands 'up' 'down ' and 'return' to select the chosen option) or by entering the initial letter of the command. Thus, although it was not feasible on the initial prototype to have a voice command for every path through the menu, it was easy to follow through paths with voice commands. Some commonly used paths were given separate entries in the Writer recognition vocabulary (see fig. 1) – e.g., 'capitalise', 'wordforward', 'wordbackward' and 'savework'. A 'repeat' command allowed previously issued Perfect Writer commands to be reissued.

Text input was carried out in the initial prototype mostly from the 'lower' case vocabulary which contained a phonetic alphabet used for character recognition and some simple cursor movement and editing functions. More extensive editing functions could be obtained from the 'writer' vocabulary. On the microcomputer the case shift between upper and lower case was done in hardware on the keyboard. It was not possible to implement a shift character which could be produced as a result of a successful voice recognition to shift cases when inputting text. A separate 'upper' case vocabulary was provided although the existence of the 'capitalise' command in Perfect Writer meant that switches into the uppercase vocabulary were not really necessary.

4. Usability evaluation

After the initial prototype had been in use for approximately three months a usability evaluation was carried out with the student who had been using it. The intention was that a design cycle of iterative development be employed to refine the interface design as a result of knowledge gained about its practical use a text processing tool, and from simple laboratory tests.

4.1. Evaluation methodology

The evaluation consisted of three performance tests and an attitude measurement procedure.

The performance tests were:

    a) Accuracy of the recognition system – the subject repeated the spoken tokens used to represent the letters of the alphabet, and the digits 1 to 0, ten times each.

b) Text correction task – the subject attempted to correct errors in a prepared text file.

c) Speed test – the subject enters text read from a document for a five minute period using the voice input system and any other method used by the subject for text processing.

The attitude measurement procedure was an application of the technique devised by Poulson (Poulson [1987]). The subject completed a questionnaire and was subsequently interviewed about the attitude profile obtained from the questionnaire. The objective of the procedure was to identify the features of the design of the equipment most influential in producing the scores on the attitude scale. By this method the strengths and weaknesses of the equipment design, from a usability viewpoint, were to be exposed.

4.2. Results

4.2.1. Recognition accuracy

a) Alphabet – 92.3%

b) Digits – 97%

These are average scores for all items in the respective vocabularies. There was a large range in the recognition of the items representing the alphabet, the token for w, that was 'whisky', was not accurately recognised on any attempts, whereas others were correctly recognised on all attempts. In 20 cases all 10 recognition attempts for the spoken items were correctly recognised. Thus, for 76.9% of the input alphabet there was not any difficulty of recognition. The letters for which there was a recognition problem in this test with the spoken item used to represent them is shown in table 1.

Recognition errors resulting in a transposition involving a cursor control function, or a recognition vocabulary change, caused difficulty for the subject during this test.

4.2.2. Text correction task

The subject was able only to attempt a few of the errors in the text file, and experienced great difficulty with adjusting the text layout to deal with the changes he had made. The errors in the text were too complex to be effectively dealt with by the voice input system. A double spaced layout had been used in the text file in which the subject was to make changes. When a change had been made it required the subject to

Table 1. Problem Letters

Letter	No. correct recognitions
w	0
i	6
n	8
x	8
a	9
s	9

engage in a large amount of cursor movement, and extensive use of the delete command to remove blank spaces, to reformat the document. This particular type of layout would not be employed in typical documents written with this type of text processor.

4.2.3. Speed test

a) Mouth stick

The subject had a mouth stick and a keyboard adapted for its use. The subject attempted to type with the mouth stick for a five minute period, copying the text from a typed sheet. He was able to input text at approximately 15 words per minute.

b) Text processor

This was abandoned due to recognition errors. Transpositions resulted in cursor repositioning and recognition vocabulary changes. This made text entry very slow due to the time required to recover from these errors. It was far slower than the test with mouth stick.

4.3. Attitude measures

4.3.1. Questionnaire

The average scale value from the questionnaire was +1.3. Three scales resulted in a negative score, these were for 'speed of operation' (−1), 'need for improvement' (−1), and 'discretion of usage' (−0.5).

4.3.2. Interview

The subject had a very positive view of the voice input system and saw it as a useful device. He had it implemented on a microcomputer in the room in which he lived.

The subject had found that the voice system was slow due to recognition errors, and felt that there was room for improvement in this area. Despite the slow entry speed for text the subject used the system for taking notes whilst reading. This was because he could not operate the keyboard with his mouth stick and use it to turn the pages of the book he was reading from.

The subject believed that in its current form the voice input system was useful for situations where large amounts of information was being displayed on the computer screen. The example he gave of this was computer based training packages. The voice input system was useful here because it was difficult to see the display screen and operate the keyboard with a mouth stick.

For text processing the subject suggested that the voice system was useful for dealing with situations where small numbers of commands need to be given to deal with large amounts of displayed information. Typically this would be where page layout was being dealt with. For large amounts of text entry the mouth stick was preferred.

The computer was switched on each morning by staff at the accommodation where the subject lived. However, before the subject could use the system he had to find somebody to place the headset microphone on his head. He suggested that a microphone on a flexible stand would increase ease of access to the system giving him greater discretion in its use. With his motorised wheel chair he would be able to position himself at the microphone and thus use the system without a helper.

The voice input system provided the user with access to a conventional word processing package. The subject found that the instructional material provided by the manufactures of the software was not adequate. They did not clarify and explain, in simple terms, how the package should be set up and used. To support the use of the voice input system, the subject had been given personal instruction and could contact Hatfield Polytechnic to deal with specific problems.

4.4. Discussion of evaluation results

The voice input system was viewed positively by the subject, and was of use in his studies at the University. The recognition errors reduced the speed of text processing to below that which could be achieved by the subject with a mouth stick. For this reason the subject employed the voice input system in situations where it was not possible to use a mouth stick. This was essentially tasks in which the subject wished to view the computer display screen and issue commands at the same time, or where the mouth stick was required for a secondary task. In this capacity it was important for his studies at University, he used the voice input system to take notes whilst reading from a book. Here, the mouth stick is required for the secondary task of turning the pages of the book.

There was a limitation in the software tool used to construct the interface where error handling was concerned. It did not allow for any error checking of the item being recognised. Misrecognitions can be avoided if the information about the quality of the match to the template is used as the basis for requesting confirmation of the recognition from the user (Millar, Cameron & Chaplin [1987]). Confirmation should be requested from the user if there is a close second match to the item being recognised, or if the match were close to the acceptance threshold. If the user does not confirm an item as correct, the next best match can be offered before the user is asked to try entering the item again.

The misrecognition errors which appeared to result in the greatest difficulty for the subject was where the cursor was repositioned a long distance from the point in the text where he was working, or where there was an unexpected change in the recognition vocabulary. One way of dealing with these problems would be to restrict commands producing a large cursor movement to a separate vocabulary to that used to input text, and to provide on screen prompts or audio warnings, to indicate a vocabulary change.

Within the recognition test the keyword used for w, that was 'whisky' was consistently misrecognised for the command word 'sleep' used for switching the system into a standby condition. The command function should be moved to a different recognition vocabulary, or the word used to activate it changed.

5. Fine-tuning the initial prototype

Following the evaluation of the initial prototype, it was decided to implement some of the recommendations for change using the existing software tool, even though it was apparent that this software tool could not provide all of the required functionality. This enabled a further stage in the 'design – prototype – evaluate – redesign' cycle prior to embarking on the reprogramming of the whole of the voice interface.

The revised prototype concentrates on the text editing function and has for the moment been separated from the specialist DOS vocabulary since this was not the subject of the evaluation. It is planned to make this available within the revised structure.

5.1. Improving prototype usability

The general aim was to improve the usability characteristics of the performance of the device and thus reduce the stress and mental workload encountered by the user. The specific factors the revised design attempted to address were:

a) to decrease the cognitive load by providing a simple model of the vocabulary structure (Nusbaum [1986])

b) to provide improved feedback to the user via voice message (Cole [1986]; Nusbaum [1986])

c) to provide enhanced editing functions to speed up the correction process

d) to reduce the potential for large errors

5.2. Design enhancements

The revised vocabulary structure is shown in figure 2. The use of subsets within a vocabulary switching to another vocabulary was abandoned in favour of a separate 'switch' vocabulary. This provides a simple more adaptable model for the user, which is roughly similar to a conventional menu structure, but there is a slight increase in the time taken to move between vocabularies. The use of a spoken prompt on entry to any vocabulary further slows down vocabulary changes, but serves to reassure the user that he or she is in the correct vocabulary. Changing vocabularies is thus a two stage process first the switch vocabulary is selected then the new vocabulary is selected.

The possibility of putting a speech feedback prompt on the 'switch' vocabulary was considered but was found to slow down vocabulary changes to an unacceptable degree. Additional voice feedback was provided in each vocabulary by the 'whereami' option. This does not change the state of the system, it provides a spoken confirmation of the currently active vocabulary. This would be faster to use and less disruptive than the use of the task word to display the currently active vocabulary on the vdt screen. The use of the task word requires two utterances, one to display the vocabulary and another to remove it so that text processing could continue.

All of the cursor movements except 'back' and 'goright' were restricted to the 'writer' vocabulary. This was to avoid problems with misrecognitions repositioning the cursor a long way from the point in the text that the user was working on.

Further editing commands were added to the 'writer' vocabulary to allow an improved editing strategy – Kinkead (Kinkead [1986]) concludes that cursor movement by repeatedly saying 'go back' is neither easy nor popular. Commands to move the cursor forward and backwards one word at a time were included. Larger moves could be carried out using search commands.

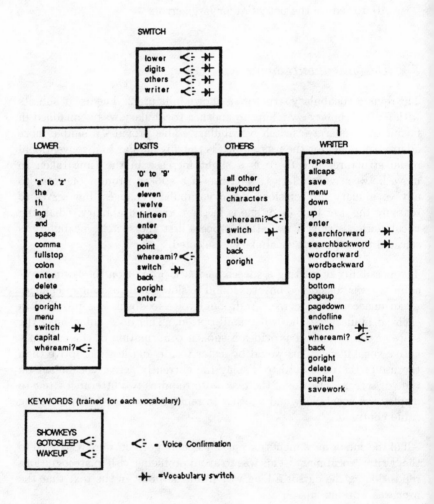

Figure 2.   Vocabulary Structure of the current system

6. Software tools

Although it was felt that the revised prototype represented an improvement on the original, there were limitations in the software tool which was being employed to build the device which could not be overcome. The major problems which were encountered were:

a) The tool did not allow dynamic voice-controlled retraining of a word nor adjustment of the system parameters to deal with sudden changes in levels of background noise. There was a keyboard facility for this however, it may not always be possible for a disabled user to gain access to it – the student using the system could use the keyboard with a mouth pencil, but when using the speech system to take notes whilst reading a book he would not have access to it. The mouth pencil being used in this situation to turn the pages of the book, which was in the position the keyboard would usually occupy.

b) The tool did not make use of information about the second best matched word to improve recognition accuracy, although the information was available within the underlying system. In the case of a recognition failure it was not possible to enter into a short dialogue to elicit the correct item.

c) It was not possible to provide positive feedback that a misrecogntion had occurred, for example a warning tone.

d) There was no last resort mechanism available such as stepping through a whole vocabulary and selecting an item using just 'yes' and 'no'. Thus, in a case of severe misrecognition, where voice is the only input modality, the subject has no method for issuing a specific command.

The major advantage of the software tool was that it provided an excellent means of quickly prototyping a system. In the absence of any guidelines on vocabulary structure it was invaluable to be able to use an iterative design approach and enable the user to be actively involved in the design process.

For further work on the speech system it is planned to use a more sophisticated tool produced by VOTAN which allows the recognition process to be controlled using the C programming language. A further system is currently being designed that will not be limited by the problems of the software tools used in the initial prototype. This, although similar in design philosophy to the initial prototype, will offer a simpler interface to the user.

7. Conclusions

This work has shown that it is feasible to use simple speech recognition for text processing by spelling out the words a letter at a time. While this is too slow for commercial text processing it can provide a viable means of interacting with a micro-computer for users with restricted keyboard access. With the advent advanced telecommunications facilities becoming more widely available through technological developments such as the integrated services digital network (ISDN), and the proposed European integrated broadband communications network (IBCN), the ability to interact effectively through terminal systems is a significant issue if the disabled are to be able to take advantage of the opportunities presented by these developments in information technology. Before facilities such as electronic mail systems, or public bulletin boards, can be used it is first necessary to be able to create text and control the terminal system.

8. Disability and Informatics Design

Disabled users of information technology are not a homogeneous group about which simple generalisations can easily be made. User centred design is thus an important issue if the technology is to be made sufficiently flexible to meet the needs of the disabled.

Independence of operation of the system should be a prime concern for the input and output devices, this is in order to minimise the need for intervention by able bodied assistants. Lack of independence of operation can result in restrictions on access to the facilities being provided and increase the amount of work required to use the device. However, non-standard input and output devices must not only be flexible and easy to use, but also be within a price range which allows them to be a practical proposition given the resources available to pay for them.

Prototyping information technology products in the area of information technology is a viable and easy to use procedure to employ directly with a disabled user since errors, or system failures, will not result in physical harm. For example, this procedure would not be so simple for a voice activated wheelchair, here loss of control could result in physical harm to the passenger if sufficient precautions are not taken when testing the prototype (Schalk [1987]). Once access to an information system has been provided, where the disabled user is sufficently interested in the technology being employed, it becomes possible for him or her to be involved in the technical development of the software.

9. Further work

The interface described within this paper was transparent to a specific text processing package. More work needs to be done to assess the types of application which are suitable for simple speech recognition. Also, more work is required into the problems of authoring documents without access to printed copy for review and editing. The conventional text processor only provides a very limited view of the document under construction. Problems of document organisation and structure may need to be considered in order to reduce the work load in producing written material with restricted access to a text processing system. For the effective use of an input system such as simple voice recognition, a writer's workbench may be more appropriate than a simple text processing package.

References

A Cole [1986], "Experience with a Text Editor for Spoken Input," in *Proceedings of Speech Tech '86*.

H H Dabbagh, R I Damper & D P Guy [1986], "Transparent Interfacing of Speech Recognisers to Microcomputers," *Microprocessors and Microsystems* 10, 371–376.

R Kinkead [1986], "Talking to Typewriters. Human Factors Issues and Findings in the Development of Voice Activated Word Processors," in *Proceedings of Speech Tech '86*.

P C Millar, I R Cameron & D J Chaplin [1987], "A Robust Dialogue Control Strategy to Improve the Performance of Voice Interactive Systems," in *Proceedings of the European Conference on Speech Technology*.

H C Nusbaum [1986], "Human Factors Considerations in the Design of Large Vocabulary Speech Recognition Devices," in *Proceedings of Speech Tech '86*.

D F Poulson [1987], "Towards Simple Indices of the Perceived Quality of Software Interfaces," in *IEE Colloquium – Evaluation Techniques for Interactive System Design*, IEE, Savoy Place, London.

T B Schalk [October/November 1987], "A Voice-Activated Wheelchair," *Speech Technology*.

J Schnabl & R Boissinot [October/November 1987], "A Voice Controlled Integrated Communication Workstation," *Speech Technology*.

C A Simpson, M E McCauley, E F Roland, J C Ruth & B H Williges [1985], "System Design for Speech Recognition and Generation," *Human Factors* 27.

Artificial Intelligence Issues

User Requirements For Expert System Explanation: What, Why and When?

Yvonne Rogers[*]

Department of Computing, Maths Faculty, The Open University, Walton Hall, Milton Keynes MK7 6AA, U.K.

It is generally assumed that one of the important features of an expert system is that it provides relevant and informative explanations regarding different aspects of the system's reasoning. As yet, however, most current systems provide very poor explanation facilities. This paper reports on a study that investigated the extent and types of explanation required by novices to satisfy their needs in understanding deductions made by an expert system. Using the 'Wizard of Oz' technique where, unknown to the subject, a person provides a simulation of the system as an expert an experiment was carried out which looked at the usefulness of various types of explanation. Two types of explanation and their combination were compared. These were 1) rule-based 2) condition-based and 3) rule and condition. The results showed

---

[*]Formerly at the Human Factors Technology Centre, Alcatel ESC, Edinburgh Way, Harlow, Essex (now located at SEL, Dillweisenstein, Hirsaurerstrasse 210, D-7530, W. Germany).

that all users accessed the explanation facility and that
the level of user satisfaction was found to depend on the
type of explanation provided. In general, the rule and
condition group found the explanations to be the most
satisfying and useful. A further experiment was carried
out to evaluate the type of questions users ask when the
dialogue was not initiated by the system. The findings
from both studies are discussed in relation to the task
demands and the level of user understanding.

Keywords: Expert Systems, Explanation

1. Introduction

The advent of second generation expert systems has seen a growing
concern among the HCI community regarding the need for these systems
to be tailored more towards the user's requirements. In particular, it is
now generally accepted by both researchers and system designers that if
the new generation of expert systems are to be any more successful than
the first they must provide better explanation facilities (Steels [1987]).

If explanation is to be of any value at the interface, however, it should be
helpful at various levels catering for different user needs. At the very least
it should help knowledge engineers and programmers develop a system.
For actual applications it should also be able to inform the naive user
about the knowledge in the system and its underlying reasoning while
providing a level of transparency for the advanced user, assuring them
that the system's reasoning processes are appropriate. Moreover, at all
levels it should be able to answer a range of questions. These may fall
into a number of categories, including 'how and why' questions where
the user wants to know why a particular decision was selected or system
question asked; questions concerning the causality and relation between
knowledge structures within the expert domain and 'what would happen'
type questions where the user wants to know the effects of hypothetical
alternative situations or the implications for future states. Within these
categories more specific types of questions should be answerable, such
as those regarding methods, events, terminology, etc. (see Swartout
(Swartout [1986]), for an extensive review of types).

The need for such extensive explanation facilities, however, has not
convinced everyone. There are those who believe that explanation
facilities currently available with commercial systems are under used
and tend to become redundant. Johnson (Johnson [1984]), for example,
in a survey of expert systems in the UK and USA found that, while
explanation facilities were valuable during the system's development,

there appeared to be little interest shown in them by the end users. Similarly, Caristi (Caristi [1985]) noted that once users have become experienced with a system they don't want to know how it performs its actions.

But as pointed out by Morris (Morris [1987]) the reason why commercial system explanation facilities have not proved to be particularly helpful is because they have been grossly inadequate in terms of being too basic or unitelligible. For example, in a review of current UK developments Berry and Broadbent (Berry & Broadbent [1987a]) found that current explanation facilities rarely match any of what is usually considered to be the most fundamental of user requirements.

How can explanation facilities be improved, therefore to match users' needs without making unacceptable demands on computing resources? Specifically, what are the important features which will make an explanation facilitiy truly useful while at the same time not be too costly or daunting to implement? To answer this question it is necessary to consider a number of psychological and contextual factors. In particular, the type of application domain e.g., whether it is procedural or declarative, and the users prior knowledge of if should be taken into account (see Carroll and McKendree for discussion (Carroll & McKendree [1987]),). On another level the role of individual differences needs to be considered – such as the different levels of the users' experience and knowledge.

The key issue underlying the acceptance of any explanation, however, is the communication process between the user and the expert system. This in turn is a function of the level of user understanding. The easier it is for the user to assimilate any advice given the more likely they are to accept it. Its usefulness, however, also depends on the form of mental model the user has of the application domain and their task goals. At one level a user may require a great deal of detail to help them with their task whilst at another level other users may require only general information. Take for example, the analogy of how people differ in their understanding of TV sets. Someone who needs only to operate a TV is likely to have a mental model which contains only the idea of a box that displays moving pictures with accompanying sound. On the other hand a person who repairs TV sets is likely to have a much more comprehensive model of them which may embody the notion of a cathode-ray tube firing electrons at a screen, with the beam scanning across in a raster controlled fashion etc.

The point that needs to be emphasised is that the role of explanation should be viewed as a function of a person's understanding of the application domain and their task requirements (Johnson-Laird [1983]). Hence increasing the level of explanation will not necessarily increase the usefulness of an expert system. Alternatively, a more useful strategy would be to provide appropriate types of explanation when most suitable.

The effectiveness of any form of explanation, however, will ultimately depend on the language and concepts used. In most cases the types of explanation provided by commercial expert systems consist simply of a trace of rules based on syllogistic reasoning patterns. These fall mainly into the 'if-then' type rule format, echoing the trace of rules fired by the system. While this type of approach may be useful for a knowledge engineer, in debugging a program, it is generally considered unsuitable for other types of end users – the reason being that most people find it difficult to follow this type of reasoning. Furthermore, rule traces are rarely able to give an overview of what is happening or to be able to provide adequate justifications of the system's actions (Morris [1987]).

Another approach has been the insertion of 'canned' text in the system, used separately or in combination with rule traces. While this technique has the potential of providing more meaningful explanations, it requires the knowledge engineer to anticipate all the questions the users are likely to ask and then storing all the answers in english text in the system. Clearly this is an unsatisfactory situation. What is required is for a systematic framework to be developed in which the various levels and types of explanation in relation to users needs are structured. Furthermore, it would be of great benefit to the knowledge engineer and the system designers if constructive guidelines could be produced on the types of questions that users are likely to ask together with the form the answers should take.

At present there appears to be very little 'technology transfer' taking place in this domain. Furthermore, there is currently very few controlled experiments that examine the role of explanation in any systematic way. Most existing reports simply consist of informal accounts of users' experience with just one type of explanation. Moreover, while there are numerous reports stating what are considered to be the user's needs there is a paucity of empirical or theoretical support to back these claims.

One exception, however, is a recent study by Berry and Broadbent (Berry & Broadbent [1987b]), who compared the effects of different types of explanation and verbalisation in a problem-solving task. They carried out a series of experiments, investigating the effects of presenting explanation either as a single block at the beginning of a task or intermittently during the task. The task involved determining which of a set of factories was responsible for polluting a river by testing for the presence or absence of various pollutants. Interestingly, they found that subjects receiving multiple explanations performed significantly better than those who received just a single block of explanation. The significance of this finding is that it suggests that the amount and timing of an explanation are critical to its success.

The purpose of our study was primarily to investigate the helpfulness of different types of explanation when provided intermittently throughout an information-seeking task. Specifically, the aim of the study was to compare rule-based and condition-based explanations. This was to determine whether it was more useful to provide explanations based on the underlying causes behind the system's reasoning or just to present specific information focussing on the condition causing the event. A third condition was also included, in which the two forms of explanation were combined. A further aim was to evaluate the types of questions users ask and to determine the extent to which users seek explanation underlying the system's reasoning in a context-free setting.

2. Task 1. System-Initiated Dialogue

This experiment looked at the effects of two different types of explanation – rule-based and condition-based – on an investigative task in which subjects were required with the assistance of a simulated advisory expert system to deduce the culprit of a fictitious murder. Using the 'Wizard of Oz' technique (c.f., (Diaper [1986])), where unknown to the subject the experimenter provides a simulation of the system as an expert, subjects were required to provide information to the system on the murder. Based on this evidence, the system then provided deductions as to who the most likely suspect was together with explanations underlying them.

2.1. Method

A between subjects design was employed meaning that each subject received only one type of explanation. The extent to which users requested an explanation and how satisfied they were with it was measured throughout the task. In addition, a global measure of the subject's overall satisfaction with the explanation was assessed through the use of rating scales on a post task questionnaire.

2.1.1. Subjects

24 subjects (8 for each explanation condition) aged between 18-40 from a range of vocational professions participated in the experiment. None had any experience with expert systems but all were familiar with a computer keyboard and could at least 'finger-type'.

2.1.2. The Task

To prevent any individual bias in expertise affecting performance a task domain was selected which was context-free in the sense that subjects had no prior knowledge of it. The task was based on a criminal investigation in which subjects had to imagine that they were investigative reporters working for a newspaper and were required to report on a crime. The crime that has been commited was a murder in an old peoples' home. As part of their assignment they were required to write a report on the crime, giving a full account and adequate reasons of how the culprit was identified from a list of 5 suspects. They were told that the police had provided them with information on the suspects. The scenario continues by saying that the newspaper has just bought a new computer system which has been designed specifically to investigate various crimes. In particular, it has been programmed to work out who is the most likely suspect of a crime. All that is required for them to do is to answer the questions asked by the system.

The system initiates the dialogue by asking for a list of suspects. It then asks for a piece of evidence on each of the suspects regarding their relationship to the victim. Following this the system offers its latest deduction on who is the most likely culprit at that stage of the investigation and an explanation behind its reasoning. Subjects are subsequently asked if they would like to ask any further questions or proceed with the investigation. The sequence of dialogue continues between the subject and the system until all the necessary information has been input to the system where upon the system provides its final verdict.

2.1.3. The Knowledge-Base

There are 5 suspects and 5 pieces of evidence against each one. These are the nature of the relationship each suspect had with the victim, their character, forensic evidence, the whereabouts of each suspect at the time of the murder and a possible weapon in their possession. To enable 'the expert' to make deductions weightings of 1-5 were assigned to each piece of evidence, where a 5 is given to the most incriminating piece of evidence and a 1 to the least incriminating. For subsequent pieces of evidence, both individual and cumulative weightings were calculated so that deductions were made on individual pieces of evidence and their combination. This meant that different suspects were deduced as being the most likely suspect at different stages of the investigation. At the end of the investigation the suspect with the highest cumulative weighting is suggested as the most likely culprit. Table 1 provides a summary of the evidence and their respective weightings.

The expert system was also provided with a list of facts about the scene of the murder e.g., where the body was found, the time of the murder, etc.

Table 1. **Individual and cumulative weightings assigned to the evidence against each suspect**

Suspect evidence	suspect	weighting	cumulative weighting
1. Relationship with victim			
family feud	smith	5	5
former lover	jones	4	4
jealous lover	green	3	3
business partner	magee	2	2
no known connection	rogers	1	1
2. Character			
mental case	rogers	5	6
criminal record	jones	4	8
alcoholic	green	3	6
bad tempered	smith	2	7
senile	magee	1	3
3. Forensic evidence			
blood stains	smith	5	12
teeth marks on stick	magee	4	7
victims hair on knitting	green	3	9
none	rogers	2	7.5
none	jones	1	9.5
4. Whereabouts			
landing	magee	5	12
sitting room	green	4	13
bedroom	jones	3	12.5
cellar	rogers	2	9.5
kitchen	smith	1	13
5. Weapon			
walking stick	magee*	5	17
tie	jones	4	16.5
knife	smith	3	16
knitting needles	green	2	15
poison	rogers	1	10

* most likely suspect

Explanation Two types of explanation underlying the system's reasoning based on judgements associated with the weightings were provided. These were rule-based and condition-based. The rule-based explanations were based on an 'if-then' rule structure while the condition-based explanations consisted of a statement of the information relevant to each deduction. A third condition was included whereby the two formats were combined into one. Table 2 provides examples of each of the three conditions. Based on previous assumptions it was predicted that the rule-based type explanations would be the least helpful while the combination condition would be the most useful.

2.1.4. The Expert System

Two personal computers were connected together and positioned in different rooms. They were programmed so that the subject's input was displayed in the top half of their monitor and bottom half of the experimenter's monitor. Conversely, the experimenter's input appeared in the top half of their monitor and the bottom half of the subject's monitor. The subject's input was displayed immediately on both screens, while the experimenter's output was displayed only on the subject's screen after the experimeter had pressed the return key. This allowed the experimeter to delete any errors, e.g., typo's, before sending a message. To make the system appear even more authentic all the system questions and explanations were stored as canned text and activated by the experimenter when required through the use of a control key.

1)	Rule-based	if x is equivalent to y then x is most likely
		e.g. someone who is closest to the murdered body is the most likely suspect
2)	Condition-based	x meets the requirements of y
		e.g. Green was in the living room nearest the murdered body
3)	Rule and condition	x is equivalent to y, therefore x is most likely because x meets the requirements of y
		e.g. Green was in the living room and, therefore, was the nearest to the murdered body which makes her the most likely suspect

Table 2.   Types of explanation

2.1.5. The Questionnaire

A post task questionnaire was designed to evaluate the subject's satisfaction with the different types of explanation. Four 7-point rating scales were used. These were:

1. satisfaction with the explanation
2. the helpfulness of the explanation
3. the ease of understanding the system's reasoning
4. the ease of performing the task

2.1.6. Procedure

Subjects were run individually. They were briefed of the scenario and told that the aim of the experiment was to investigate how effective the computer system was at providing advice and information. A list of suspects and the various pieces of evidence against each of them was provided. The subjects were told to answer the questions as requested by the system but also to feel free to ask it questions themselves. On completion of the dialogue session, the subjects were asked to write their report and then fill in the questionnaire. They were then debriefed about the experiment.

2.2. Results

The number of times a deduction and subsequent explanation was requested was recorded from the protocols for each subject. It was found that subjects always asked for a deduction when offered throughout the investigation and that in the majority of cases subjects requested the underlying explanation. Group means as a percentage of the total possible number of requests are shown in Table 3. The mean number of times subjects were satisfied with the explanation was then calculated as a percentage of the total number of times each subject requested it. The group means for these are also presented in Table 3. As can be seen the rule-based (R) group and the condition-based group (C) only found 25% of the explanations satisfying whereas the R & C group found them satisfying 40% of the time. The low level of satisfaction across all groups, however, suggests that there were certain inadequacies with all the explanations at various stages of the task.

The protocols were further analysed for the number of times each subject requested further explanation if they were not satisfied with the first explanation they had received. These explanations referred to judgements based on each piece of evidence alone. From Table 3 it can be seen that 75% of the R group requested further explanation, 55% of the C group

Table 3.   Mean number of requests for explanation as a
            percentage of the total possible and
            subsequent satisfaction with it

| | Explanation Group | | |
	Rule	Condition	R&C
request for explanation	78%	97%	90%
satisfaction with explanation	24%	23%	41%
request for further explanation	75%	55%	44%
satisfaction with further explanation	31%	16%	50%

while only 44% of the R & C group. The mean percentage satisfaction
with these explanations was also calculated and are shown in the table.
As can be seen the R & C and R groups were slightly more satisfied with
the extra explanation. On the other hand the C group tended to be less
satisfied than when just receiving the first explanations.

The median scores on the rating scales were taken as a global measure
of the subjects' satisfaction with the explanation facility. As shown in
Figure 1 the C group found the explanation the least helpful, the least
satisfying and the most difficult to understand the system's reasons. In
contrast with the protocol scores the R group rated the explanation as
being the most satisfying and the most helpful. No significant difference
was found between the R & C and R groups, however, implying that the
two were equally as helpful.

Interestingly, the R & C group found the computer's reasoning the
easiest to understand. This result is consistent with the finding from
the protocols in so far as the R & C group were more satisfied with each
explanation and requested less further explanations.

The types of questions subjects asked intermittently throughout the task
when not satisfied with the explanation were also analysed. A number of
questions were asked, ranging from requests for factual information, e.g.,
where was the body found, was it clubbed to death, etc., to questions
concerning the plausibility and validity of the rules and judgements
underlying the explanations. For example, subjects in the rule-based
group who were not satisfied with the explanations tended to make their
own judgements, e.g., asking why it is that someone with a criminal
record is more suspect than someone with a bad temper. Other questions
concerning the validity of the system's deductions were about the basis
on which the judgements were made, e.g., where did the system gets its
information from and how was it possible that the system could make a
deduction based on so little evidence.

A number of why questions were also asked, suggesting that the subjects
found it necessary to understand the justification behind the explana-

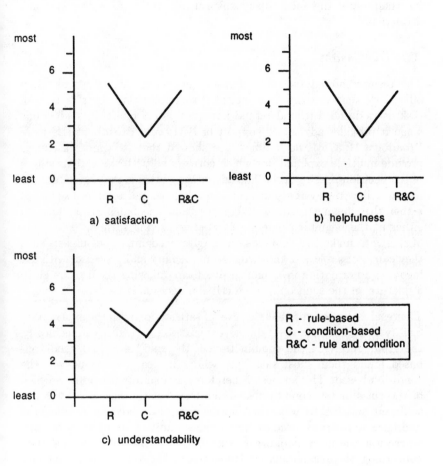

Figure 1. Median scores of each explanation group
($n = 8$) from rating scales

tions in relation to the task. In addition it was often the case that subjects conceptualised the solution of the task from various possibilities even though the system had recommended just one solution. For example, hypothetical questions were frequently asked such as "why is Magee the most likely suspect when he had no motive and was not strong enough". Other questions simply asked "why not any of the other suspects". Sometimes they included qualifying clauses such as "... , given that Smith was covered in blood and Magee was not". These types of questions suggest that the subjects were not satisfied with the justifications behind the explanations and were trying to infer for themselves the most likely suspect, irrespective of the system's deductions.

2.3. Discussion

The results showed that all groups requested the explanations when offered by the system. This suggests, therefore, that for this type of task users do need to understand how the system makes its deductions when it provides advice. In support of Berry and Broadbent (Berry & Broadbent [1987b]) the findings also showed that it is more useful to provide multiple explanations which correspond with the various stages of the decision-making task. The advantage of this is that it enables the user to follow the system's decisions in a logicial and temporal sequence rather than having to make inferences from one block of explanation either at the beginning or end of an advice-giving session. The effect of this is to make less demands on the user's cognitive resources. Thus they can access relevant knowledge from memory and process it with the incoming information in a manageable form, allowing them to build up a 'picture' of the solution as each criticial decision is made.

The results also showed that the level of satisfaction with the explanation facility depended on the type of explanation provided. Specifically, the group receiving the combination of the rule-based and condition-based found them most satisfying while the least satisfying was the condition-based. This suggests, therefore, that simply providing an echo of the rules or the condition in which the decision was made was not sufficient and that it was more beneficial to have both. Moreover, the finding that the rule-based group and the condition-based group tended to request significantly more further explanations when not satisfied with the first explanation indicates that they did not find the first explanations particularly helpful in relation to the deduction made at that stage and hence were hoping that the further explanation would be more elucidating. On the other hand it appears that the subjects in the combination group were able to use the first explanations in inferring the reasoning behind the system's deductions.

The most surprising finding, however, was that over half the subjects in all groups did not find the explanations particularly useful. The implications from this is that in general all three types of explanations offered were unable to meet the subjects' needs in understanding the systems deductions. It may be, therefore, that just having one type of explanation is not sufficient and that a range of explanations may be necessary within any one task domain. In particular, it may be that different forms of information are required at the various stages of a decision-making task. For example, justification-type explanations may be useful at an early stage to help the user in making initial inferences, whereas condition-based explanations may be more helpful at a later stage when the user has a reasonable understanding of the decision task but might need some form of clarification.

In order to assess further the types of explanation which are required at the various stages of a decision making task a second experiment was designed which specifically looked at the types of questions subjects ask and, reciprocally, to see what level of understanding they require to accept the advice given.

3. Task 2. User-Initiated Dialogue

The aim of this task was to assess the types of questions users ask when obtaining information and advice from an expert system. It differs from the previous experiment insofar as the system takes a passive role in the dialogue with the user, only providing information and explanations when requested. This situation was considered analogous to an advice-giving system whereby the user has an overall goal to obtain information and advice on a particular subject but must construct a plan of action as to what to ask the system to achieve this. A further aim of the experiment, therefore, was to evaluate the pattern of user questioning in relation to the system's response and to see how the various forms of information satisfied their needs and affected their subsequent questioning strategy.

3.1. Method

Six subjects (3 male, 3 female), who all had some experience with computing, but not with using expert systems, individually took part in the experiment. Using the same 'Wizard of Oz' technique, the subjects were required to interact with the 'expert' system to obtain advice. The same scenario was presented to the subjects with the exception that this time they were not given any information on the list of suspects but were told that information regarding the crime and the suspects had already been fed into the system. They were told that with this information the 'expert' system had been able to make deductions regarding the culprit. The subjects were also told that the system could explain its reasoning. Their task was to access this information by typing in questions at the keyboard.

Table 4. **Range and frequency of types of questions asked**

Types of questions

subjects	who	what	why	where	is/was were	when	how/ does	had/ list	give	total
1	1	6	2	3	2	0	1	2	0	17
2	1	15	1	3	15	1	2	2	0	40
3	1	5	10	1	9	0	2	3	0	31
4	1	2	2	2	13	0	0	7	4	31
5	1	4	1	2	4	0	1	2	7	22
6	1	9	1	4	7	1	3	2	1	29
total	6	41	17	15	50	2	9	18	12	170
mean	1.0	6.8	2.8	2.5	8.3	0.3	1.5	3.0	2.0	
s.d.	0	4.6	3.5	1.1	5.0	0.5	2.0	2.0	2.9	
% relative to total	3.5	24.1	10.0	8.8	29.4	1.2	5.3	10.6	7.1	100

3.2. Results and Discussion

The subject's protocols were initially analysed for the types of questions asked and their frequency. Table 4 shows the mean number of each type of question asked as a proportion relative to the total number of questions asked. As can be seen from the table the types of questions asked covered a wide range, including the 5 wh- questions (i.e., what, where, when, why and who). By far the most frequent types of questions were the 'what' and 'is/was/were' types of questions. These constituted just over half of the total questions asked. This is as expected, however, considering the investigative nature of the task and the subjects's initial state of have no information. Other types of questions included those asking for location and temporal information. In addition, all the subjects asked one 'who' question refering to the system's judgement as to who was the most likely culprit. Interestingly, with the exception of Subject 3, relatively few 'why' and 'how' questions were asked. This indicates, therefore, that subjects rarely requested explanations about the system's reasoning. Indeed, nearly all the subjects appeared to just accept the information and recommendations provided by the system.

This general acceptance of the system's deductions without explanation is in contrast to the findings from the first experiment where, in general, most subjects requested explanations whenever offered by the system. This suggests, therefore, that when subjects have to initiate the dialogue themselves in this type of task their primary goal is to get the facts and then make the inferences themselves rather than get the system to explain everything.

The one exception to this strategy, however, was Subject 3 who persistently asked 'why' questions. For example, after initially asking who the murderer was, his following four questions were all directed towards finding out what the murderer's motives were and how the system had come to this conclusion. Later on in the dialogue it appeared that this subject was still not satisfied with the system's deduction as to who the most likely culprit was and instead began to believe that one of the other suspects was more likely. Moreover, the subject then continued by trying to prove that the system had made a wrong deduction by pointing out that the evidence on Magee (the culprit) was less convincing than for Smith. This suggests, therefore, that the types of questions subjects ask is indicative of their willingness to accept the system's advice and reasoning behind it. A very high rating in the subsequent questionnaire on how difficult this subject found it to follow the system's reasoning also reflects this (in contrast to the other subjects who gave a relatively low rating on this scale).

The protocols were also analysed for the sequencing of questioning and their content. In general, all the subjects started off by being very direct in their questioning asking who the murdeerer was, how many other suspects were involved and what were the various pieces of evidence. At various stages most subjects then attempted to determine the motive of the culprit (having accepted that he was the murderer even though the system had explicitly stated that he was the most likely suspect). Instead of asking the system directly, however, they changed tact and began to test their own hypotheses about the motive. Typically, these included theories about Magee's job, his relationships with the victim, his previous record. Having obtained information on Magee most of the subjects then tended to ask questions concerning the other suspects. The most frequent types of questions were those regarding the other suspect's relationship to the victim and whether they were in possession of a weapon.

4. General Discussion and Conclusions

The findings from the two experiments showed that the need for explanation and subsequent satisfaction with the types offered by the system depend on the nature of the task. In the system-initiated dialogue task, subjects always asked for explanation when offered while in the user-initiated dialogue task, subjects rarely asked the system to explain the reasoning behind its deduction but preferred instead to make the inferences themselves. This implies, therefore, that the more active a role the user of an expert system is required to play in reaching a decision the less likely they are to expect the system to justify itself, whereas the less involved they are in the decision-making process the greater the need to understand the system's reasoning. Hence it would seem preferable for expert systems to be designed which encourage the user to actively participate in the resolution and definition of the problem. This view has also been advocated by Pollack (Pollack [1985]), who found that in naturally occuring seeker-expert dialogues the seeker tends to resolve the problem in hand through a negotiation process with the expert. The implications for expert system design, therefore, is that by involving the user more in the decision-making process it allows the user to pitch the dialogue at their required level of understanding for the task in hand, together with reducing the need for extensive explanation resources.

It follows, too, that the efficacy of any type of explanation will depend on the nature of the dialogue between the user and the expert. In the first experiment where the system solved the problem and controlled the flow of dialogue it was found that the subjects always requested explanation but that in general were not satisfied with the explanations provided. On the other hand, in the second experiment where the subjects were actively involved in finding the solution to the problem and had control over the dialogue it was shown that their needs for explanation were quite different. In particular, it appeared that they preferred to make the deductions themselves using the system more as an aid.

When considering which type of explanation is necessary for an expert system for it to be acceptable to its users, therefore, it is important initially to determine the nature of the dialogue process which is intended between the user and the expert system. An expert system that simply provides advice without the user taking an active role in the decision-making process will need to provide a much more comprehensive explanation facility. On the other hand it is argued that an expert system that allows the user to participate in a negotiative dialogue will not need to have such extensive facilities since it is presumed that the user will make more use of their own inferencing skills in understanding the decision making process.

These two preliminary experiments have shown that the amount, type and timing of an explanation are all critical to its usefulness. No doubt other factors will play an important role in determining the extent to which explanation will be beneficial – most notably the task domain and prior knowledge of the user. Primarily, however, it is argued that the success of any explanation facility will depend essentially on the nature of the dialogue between the user and the expert system. It is proposed that the more the dialogue is constructed along the lines of mutual negotiation the easier it will be in the long run for the user to understand the expert system advice and the less need there will be for a comprehensive explanation facility.

Acknowledgements

This work was carried out whilst working for Alcatel ESC. Thanks are due to Patricia Henry (University of Ulster) and Robert Leiser (Yard Limited) for their contribution to the project.

References

D C Berry & D E Broadbent [1987a], "The User Interface: Expert Systems," *The International Journal of Knowledge Engineering* 4, 18–27.

D C Berry & D E Broadbent [1987b], "Explanation and Verbalisation in a Computer-Assisted Search Task," *The Quarterly Journal of Experimental Psychology* 39A, 589–609.

J A Caristi [1985], "A Micro-Computer Based Expert System for Predicting Crop Disease Epidemics," in *Proceedings of the First International Expert Systems Conference*, Learned Information, Oxford.

J M Carroll & J McKendree [1987], "Interface Design Issues for Advice-Giving Expert Systems," *Communications of the ACM* 30, 14–31.

D Diaper [1986], "Identifying the Knowledge Requirements of an Expert System's Natural Language Processing Interface," in *People and Computers: Design for Usability*, M D Harrison and A F Monk, ed., Cambridge University Press, Cambridge.

T Johnson [1984], *The Commercial Application of Expert Systems Technology*, Ovum, London.

P Johnson-Laird [1983], *Mental Models*, Cambridge University Press, Cambridge.

A Morris [1987], "Expert Systems-Interface Insight," in *People and Computers III*, D Diaper and R Winder, ed., Cambridge University Press, Cambridge.

M E Pollack [1985], "Information Sought and Information Provided. An Empirical Study of User/Expert Dialogues," in *Proceedings of CHI '85 – Human Factors in Computing Systems*, ACM, New York.

L Steels [1987], "The Deepening of Expert Systems," *AICOM* 1, 9–16.

W Swartout [1986], "Knowledge Needed for Expert Systems Explanation," *Future Computing Systems* 1, 91–114.

Knowledge Elicitation: Dissociating Conscious Reflections from Automatic Processes

R.J. Stevenson, K.I. Manktelow*, M.J. Howard

Department of Psychology, University of Durham, Durham DH1 3LE, U.K.

*Department of Social Sciences, Sunderland Polytechnic, Sunderland SR1 7EE, U.K.

One major difficulty with standard techniques of knowledge elicitation is that they require an expert to give a verbal report of his or her knowledge. This assumes that people have conscious access to all of their cognitive processes. 'Thinking aloud' techniques explicitly make this assumption. However, recent developments in cognitive psychology suggest that this assumption is not appropriate. When solving a problem, people may use fast, automatic processes which are not available to conscious reflection. These fast automatic processes can be distinguished from conscious reflection.

Two computer programming experts were videoed while each taught a class of students some basic programming concepts. Four 'novice' students from each class were also videoed while explaining the taught material to another person. These videos recorded the fast, automatic actions of people describing concepts. A week later, each person's video was played back to them and key questions were asked about the subject's intentions at different points in the video. These interviews recorded the conscious evaluations and interpretations of the original performance. The reports given at these interviews were classified into production rules. A standard knowledge elicitation technique was also used on the same subjects and the same material. Subjects were presented with ten concept names from the lectures and carried out paired comparisons of the ten concept names. The outcome of the paired comparisons was then subjected to multidimensional scaling. The type and extent of the knowledge elicited in the two situations is compared for both experts and novices.

Keywords: Knowledge Elicitation, Experts, Novices, Thinking

1. Introduction

It has long been appreciated that a major problem in the development of expert systems is the 'bottleneck' caused by the difficulty of externalising the knowledge of a human expert so that it can be transformed into a usable computer database (see Hayes-Roth, Waterman, and Lenat, 1983 for a review (Hayes-Roth, Waterman & Lenat [1983])). Some of the reasons for this are obvious and practical; for instance, a leading expert may simply be too 'high up' in an organisation to be able to devote the large amount of time necessary for the knowledge elicitation process (McGraw & Searle [1988]).

However there are also significant psychological questions associated with the very idea of eliciting someone's knowledge. They have to do with the cognitive nature of expertise and also with the ability of people to give reliable self-reports. We shall deal with these two issues in turn. Expertise is synonymous with skill: to say that someone is an expert is to say that they are highly skilled in some domain. Skill has been studied by psychologists for many years, and it appears that many of the basic principles described in classical skill acquisition research may generalise from simple motor tasks to the more complex cognitive skills which interest the expert system builder (Hammond [1987]). For instance, Fitts and Posner (Fitts & Posner [1967]) observed that skill acquisition seems to proceed in three discrete stages:

i. A cognitive stage, where the learner tries to use existing modes of behaviour under conscious control.

ii. An associative stage, where aspects of the new skill become chunked into patterns, and redundant behaviours decrease.

iii. An autonomous stage, where the new skill is more automatised, less likely to suffer from interference, more rapid and accurate.

Such distinctions are echoed in more recent approaches to skill which emphasise the cognitive processes underlying it.

One well-known approach is that of Anderson (Anderson [1982]). He appeals to the familiar distinction in computer science between declarative and procedural knowledge, broadly, knowing what and knowing how. In Anderson's scheme, declarative knowledge is represented as connected propositions, whereas procedural knowledge is represented in production systems. Production systems consist of condition-action rules which specify a given action on establishment of a given condition. Skill acquisition thus centres on the transition between declarative knowledge and procedural knowledge. Anderson calls this knowledge compilation. It has a lot in common with Fitts and Posner's associative stage; knowledge first coalesces into larger units and then, as the conditions under which a skilled unit is produced becomes reliable, these larger units can be allowed to flow without continuous feedback monitoring. Anderson calls this proceduralisation and it seems to correspond to Fitts and Posner's autonomous stage. All of this is a laborious process: hundreds and perhaps thousands of hours of practice are involved.

These properties of skill acquisition lead to the second major factor introduced above: the ability to introspect and hence report on the knowledge embodied in expertise. There is a straightforward consequence of the progression from the declarative knowledge of the novice to the procedural knowledge of the expert, which arises from the unit size of knowledge and the role of feedback. In the novice stage, unit size is small and the performance is under conscious control and continuous monitoring. This is because there are relatively few regularities in the situation, so the learner needs to keep track of both successes and failures. People can report on their declarative knowledge, and may even do so for their own benefit, as when talking aloud when experiencing difficulty. However, once knowledge is compiled it becomes unavailable to conscious inspection: it becomes automatic. In fact, it *must* become unconscious since the amount of knowledge in an expert production would, if it became conscious, overwhelm the capacity of working memory.

Automatisation therefore confers benefits in the shape of a great increase in the size of performance unit which can be run off without feedback monitoring and hence it allows smooth and efficient total performance.

But there is a price, in that the components of the performance are covert and irretrievable. It may therefore be impossible to recall compiled knowledge, and attempts to do so may even disrupt the performance in question (Ericsson & Simon [1984]).

The problem is compounded because people are often quite unaware of their unawareness, both of their own skill and of other covert aspects of their experience (see Nisbett and Wilson (Nisbett & Wilson [1977]) for a classic account). It is not that people refuse to attempt to account for their own behaviour. On the contrary they do attempt to do so. However, this is done on the basis of what is available to conscious inspection, and this excludes compiled expertise.

For these reasons some of the standard techniques for eliciting knowledge from experts may not succeed. For example, the use of verbal protocols has been widely used not only for the development of expert systems but also for simulating human problem solving (Newell & Simon [1972]). Verbal protocols are the results of 'thinking aloud' techniques: people give verbal reports of their thought processes while solving a problem. But the analysis that we have given above indicates that this technique may fail to reveal an expert's knowledge.

An alternative class of techniques makes use of statistical scaling procedures to infer the cognitive organisation of a set of concepts. For example, Schvanaveldt, Durso, Goldsmith, Breen, Cooke, Tucker and De Maio (Schvanaveldt et al. [1985]) used a paired comparison task to investigate the cognitive organisation of domain specific concepts in advanced and novice pilots. They took 30 concepts important in air-to-air combat and presented these 30 concepts to the subjects in all possible pairwise combinations. The subjects were required to rate the concepts in each pair according to their similarity. These ratings gave a measure of psychological distance between the concepts and multidimensional scaling techniques were then used on the resulting distance matrices to uncover latent structure in the data. This structure is represented in multidimensional space which can then be used to infer the cognitive structures of the subjects.

The differences among scaling procedures usually lie in the outcomes they produce. Thus, there are procedures for generating hierarchical clusters, additive clusters, multi-dimensional spaces and link-weighted networks. Schvanaveldt et al used the latter 2 procedures and multidimensional scaling is the one described in the previous paragraph.

It might seem that tasks like this which make use of scaling techniques can provide a better estimate of an expert's knowledge than can verbal protocols, since the subject is not required to carry out an automatic action and give a conscious report of that action at the same time.

However, there are still a number of problems with using this class of techniques for knowledge elicitation. Two most notable ones have been pointed out by Palmer, Duffy, Gomoll, Palmquist-Richards and Trumble (Palmer et al. [1987]). They comment first on the problems posed by relying on statistical techniques to infer cognitive structure. The ordering imposed by, say, hierarchical clustering or a mapping in multidimensional space does not necessarily exist in the original data. In addition, the resulting structures can be very difficult to interpret, partly because of the complexity of the data and partly because of anomolies in the structure that is derived by the scaling technique. In particular, different techniques will produce different anomolies, so the choice of a specific scaling method will differentially affect the resulting structure.

Palmer *et al* also comment on the tasks that provide the data for scaling techniques. They used a card sorting task to measure the organisation of menu information of an EMACS help system in novices and experts. But as they point out, the sorting task does not mirror the task of using a help facility. The relationship between the processes involved in the real world sorting task and the use of a help facility on a computer is very indirect. Indeed there is no guarantee that the cognitive processes of the two tasks have much in common. The same is true of the paired comparison task that was used by Schvanaveldt *et al.* Thus we cannot be sure that the structures elicited by these tasks have any bearing on the kinds of cognitive structures that are routinely used by experts of a domain or the users of a particular computer system.

In this paper, we investigate an alternative technique which both allows us to dissociate automatic actions from conscious reflections (unlike verbal protocols) and also to mirror the task of the expert more exactly than do tasks which are used for scaling procedures. We call this alternative technique an evaluation technique and it has two phases. In the first phase the subject carries out the skilled behaviour in a routine fashion, but this behaviour is video-taped. In the second phase, the subject is shown portions of his or her video and asked to comment on the behaviour depicted. (See Clark and Peterson (Clark & Peterson [1986]) for a review of methods based on this technique.) The critical features of the technique are that subjects act automatically, unlike verbal protocols; the automatic actions can be the precise actions that are carried out by the expert, unlike tasks used for scaling procedures; and the subjects provide commentaries on their behaviour after rather than during the activities themselves. We also compare this technique with a paired comparison task and multidimensional scaling of the kind used by Schvanaveldt *et al.*

2. Method

2.1. Subjects

Ten subjects were used. Two were 'experts' (lecturers in Computer Science) and eight were 'novices' (lst year undergraduate students in Computer Science, four from each lecturer's class).

2.2. Design and procedure

For the evaluation task, each lecturer was videoed giving a lecture in an introductory course on PASCAL programming. Both lectures were on the same topic, which was the introduction of the idea of procedures in PASCAL. On the same day as the lecture, four students from each class were videoed while they described the contents of the lecture to one of the authors.

One week later, each subject was shown four sections of his or her own video. Each section contained one of four common themes and the subjects were asked a question about each theme. The four common themes were identified by the investigators viewing the films of the two lecturers. They were: 1) procedures, 2) declaring and calling, 3) local variables, and 4) compile and execute. Each lecture lasted one hour. The time taken to describe the lecture by the students was, on average, ten minutes. The questions asked while the students viewed the relevant sections of their videos a week later were as follows: Theme 1 (procedures) "What did the lecturer assume you already knew about PASCAL programs when he introduced the concept of *procedures*?" Theme 2 (declaring and calling) "What do you already know about the concepts *declaring* and *calling*?" Theme 3 (local variables) a) "What did the lecturer assume you already knew when he brought up the concept local variables?" b) "What do you understand about the term local variables now?" Theme 4 (compile and execute) "What do you know about the concepts compile and execute"? The questions asked of the lecturers when viewing their videos a week later were similar, except that they were asked what they thought the students knew. The students took approximately 30 minutes to view the video sections and answer the questions. The lecturers took approximately 40 minutes.

The answers were transcribed and coded into a series of production rules for each subjct. These production rules were of the form *If you know about x, then you know about y.* E.g., *If you know about procedures then you know about variable declarations.* Production rules can be very complex in both the left hand context (x) and the right hand context (y). In the present study, the right hand context could consist of more than one fact. E.g., *If you know about procedures then you know about*

variable declarations and constant declarations and program sequencing.
The left hand context always consisted of a single fact.

The subjects were given a paired comparison task 2 to 3 days after
viewing their videos and answering the questions. For this task, the
films of the two lecturers were examined by two of the authors. Ten
concepts that were referred to by both of the lecturers were used in
the task. The ten concepts were: procedure, declaration, parameter,
variables, definition, calling, compile, execute, identifier, and constants.
Each word was paired with every other word making a total of 45 pairs.
Each pair was presented separately on white card.

All subjects were presented with the 45 word pairs and asked to rate
the similarity of each pair on a scale from 1 to 7, where 1 indicated very
similar and 7 indicated dissimilar. All subjects took approximately 15
minutes to complete these similarity ratings. The resulting similarity
matrix for each subject was analysed using a multidimensional scaling
technique developed by Carroll and Chang (Carroll & Chang [1970]) and
implemented on MDS(X) by Coxon, Jones and Tagg (Coxon, Jones &
Tagg []).

3. Results

3.1. Evaluation Task

The production rules that were derived from the answers to the 4
questions about the videos were of the form: *if you know about x then
you know about y*. For all the rules, x had a single value, e.g., procedures.
The values for y, however, consisted of one or more facts. The number of
values for y that were produced, yielded a 'surface' complexity measure
for each production rule.

Two major points emerge from an examination of the production rules.
One is that a large number of facts are produced for the y values of the
rules. The second is that the facts produced by the experts seem to
express larger units of knowledge than those produced by the novices.
This latter observation is compatible with the view that, to a large
extent, the experts have proceduralised their knowledge of programming.
We will consider a portion of the results derived from these production
rules.

First, the average number of production rules that were produced by
each subject was 7.9. Second, the average 'surface' complexity was 2.02.
There were no clear differences between novices and experts on these 2
measures.

**Table 1.   Complete set of production rules produced by
the subjects when the x value was** *procedures.*

Set 1 was produced by both experts and novices, set 2 was produ
only by the novices, set 3 was produced only by the experts.

Set 1

variable declarations
constant declarations
local variables
calling
program sequencing

Set 2 (novices)	**Set 3 (experts)**
variables	global variables
program substage	problem breakdown
programming	PASCAL program lay
repetition	temporary storage
program simplification	self containment
naming	scope of names
simple declarations in program	defining
writing of a simple program	structure of contents
program lay-out	structure of variables
program division	complete units/blocks
program running	procedure definition
loops	
names	

Third, and more crucially, we examined the nature of the information
that was represented by y. We found that there was very little overlap
between the facts in the production rules produced by experts and the
facts produced by novices. Two examples are given in Tables 1 and 2.

Table 1 shows all the production rules that were produced when the
value of x was procedures. Set 1 shows the y values that were produced
by both experts and novices; set 2 shows the values that were produced
only by the experts. In Table 1 the complete set of y values that were
produced when x stood for procedures is shown. The average number of
y values produced by each subject was much smaller than this: subjects
produced, on average, 4.6 facts for y. However, experts produced an
average of 9.5 facts while novices produced an average of 3.4 facts. In
addition, inspection of Table 1 suggests that experts are producing higher
order concepts than are the novices.

Table 2 seems to confirm this suggestion. When x stood for *local
variables*, no facts were produced that were common to both groups.
But here too the experts appear to have used higher order concepts
compared to the novices. This is the case even thouggh the experts only

Table 2.   Complete set of production rules of the form:
If you know about x then you know about y **where** *x*
stands for local variables.
In each case, set 1 contains rules only produced by the novices and set 2 contains rules only produced by the experts. (No rules were produced by both novices and experts.)

Set 1	Set 2
temporary storage	procedure boundary
variable	parameters
internal variables	local declarations
declaring	
types of variable (global and local)	
procedure specificity	
procedure	
declaration in procedure	
program division	

produced an average of 1.5 facts for *y* while the novices produced an average of 2.25.

3.2. Paired Comparison Task

A two dimensional scaling solution was produced for the ten concept names in the comparison task. This yielded a similarity matrix of three concepts in two dimensional space. Figure 1 shows the grouping of the concepts in this space when the ratings for all the subjects are considered. Observation of Figure 2 suggests that the most informative dimension is dimension 2. Dimension 2 seems to distinguish between what we might call static features of programming, and active features. Static features can be viewed as those that are defined rather than used. These features appear on the right hand side of the space. By contrast, the active features are all aspects of a program that are used rather than defined. These appear on the left hand side of the space. Dimension 1 seems to have captured a difference between program use and language translation, but it only applies to the active (left hand) part of the space.

Carroll and Chang's (Carroll & Chang [1970]) INDSCAL program can be used to locate individuals along the same dimensions in which the concepts are placed. Thus, it is possible to determine how closely each individual's similarity matrix is reflected by the group space. Figure 2 shows the location of the subjects in relation to this space. The closer the individuals are to a line which passes from the origin to the point of maximal weighting on both dimensions (the top right hand corner) the more similar are the cognitive structures of the individuals to the cognitive structure revealed by the group space. Observation of Figure 2

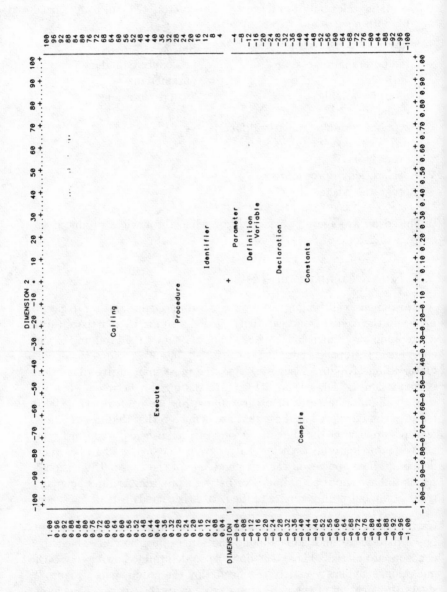

Figure 1. The location of the ten concepts used in the paired comparison task in two dimensional space.

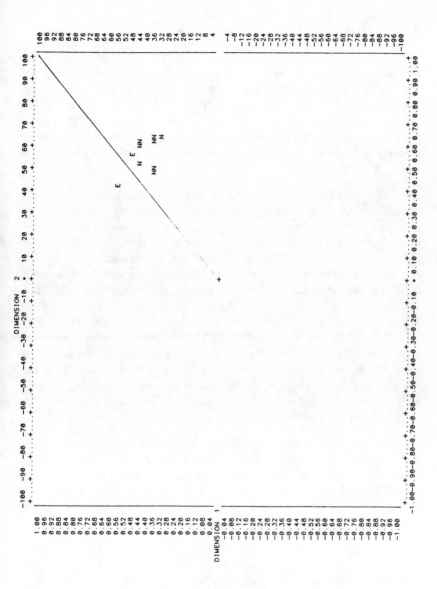

Figure 2.   The distribution of the subjects in relation to
            their weightings on the two dimensions in the
            concept space.

indicates that all subjects are reasonably represented by the concept space. In addition, on average the novices tend to be further away from the line than the experts.

4. Discussion

Overall, we have found that the evaluation task not only yielded a rich but manageable set of data; it also revealed quite marked differences in the type of knowledge displayed by novices and experts. Inspection of Tables 1 and 2 suggest that novices produce facts that reflect surface details while experts produce facts that reflect a deeper organisation of the knowledge into higher order 'chunks'. This was true despite the fact that the novices were reporting on lectures that they had just received from the experts.

By contrast, the paired comparison task yielded a much more predictable set of results. The cognitive organisation that was inferred by the program seemed to reflect the cognitive organisation of the concepts of both the experts and the novices, although the novices were more likely to have lower weightings on the two dimensions than were the experts. However, it is also the case that the number of subjects was small for this kind of analysis. In particular, we did not compute a separate concept space for the experts and evaluate how heavily the novices weighted on that concept space. This kind of analysis is possible with INDSCAL, but the distortions in the concept space that would arise from using only two experts would have yielded very unreliable data. Thus, we were unable to get an accurate measure of how well the paired comparison task discriminated between the novices and the experts. Such a measure of discriminability would be a good indicator of the validity of the technique.

However, despite the small number of experts, the evaluation technique did discriminate between the novices and experts. Thus the technique appears to be a valid one, even when a small number of subjects is used. For this reason, therefore, as well as for the reasons stated in the Introduction, we suggest that the evaluation task is the most appropriate technique to use when eliciting knowledge from experts.

The evaluation task also gave an indication of the degree of proceduralisation of programming skills on the part of the experts. They produced higher order facts or 'chunks' than the novices. This is in agreement with the proposals made in the Introduction and suggests that the task does allow people to give a coherent account of their knowledge and hence may be useful for developing expert systems.

This ability for people to make a commmentary on their own performmance has been investigated in the field of deductive thinking. It has become apparent that when solving deductive problems people do not naturally access the formal structure of the tasks, but appeal to their prior knowledge if applicable (see Griggs (Griggs [1983]), Cheng and Holyoak (Cheng & Holyoak [1985]),) or use other situation-specific heuristics (Evans [1984]). However, when asked to explain their decisions, people do not describe these heuristics, but appear to believe they were actually solving the problems logically (Wason & Evans [1975]). This is just what we would expect if the processes were well-practised and automatic, and hence unavailable to conscious inspection, but the task was ostensibly about logical reasoning.

This natural ability which people seem to have to give logically sound evaluations of their own behaviour is reflected in the evaluation task used here and offers a way round the elicitation bottleneck.

What this work on reasoning suggests, therefore, is that it is possible to make use of people's ability to give formal accounts of their actions even though they may not be aware of the processes that really underly their actions. However, for the development of an expert system this former ability may well be sufficient. The use of this ability by means of the evaluation task also seems to yield information that is easily coded into production rules, distinguishes between novices and experts, is less time consuming for the expert than the use of verbal protocols, and mirrors more exactly the way knowledge is used by an expert than do either verbal protocols or paired comparisons.

Acknowledgement

We thank David MacNamara, Malcolm Munro, Dave Robson and Bob Williams for help and advice.

References

J R Anderson [1982], "The Acquisition of Cognitive Skill," *Psychological Review* 18, 396–406.

J D Carroll & J J Chang [1970], "Analysis of Individual Differences in Multidimensional Scaling via an N-Way Generalisation of 'Eckart-Young' Decomposition," *Psychometrika* 35, 283–319.

P W Cheng & K J Holyoak [1985], "Pragmatic Reasoning Schemas," *Cognitive Psychology* 17, 391–416.

C M Clark & P L Peterson [1986], "Teacher's Thought Processes," in *Handbook on the Research of Teaching*, M C Wittrock, ed., Macmillan, 3rd Edition.

A P M Coxon, C L Jones & S K Tagg, "MDS (X) Series of Multidimensional Scaling Programs.

K A Ericsson & H A Simon [1984], *Protocol Analysis: Verbal Reports as Data*, MIT Press, Cambridge MA.

J StB T Evans [1984], "Heuristic and Analytic Processes in Reasoning," *Brit. J. Psychology* 75, 457–458.

P M Fitts & M I Posner [1967], *Human Performance*, Brooks/Cole, Belmont CA.

R A Griggs [1983], "The Role of Problem Content in the Selection Task and THOG Problem," in *Thinking and Reasoning: Psychological Approaches*, J StB T Evans, ed., Routledge and Kegan Paul, London.

N V Hammond [1987], "Principles from the Psychology of Skill Acquisition," in *Applying Cognitive Psychology to User Interface Design*, M M Gardiner and B Christie, ed., Wiley, Chichester.

F Hayes-Roth, D Waterman & D Lenat [1983], *Building Expert Systems*, Addison-Wesley, Reading MA.

K L McGraw & M R Searle [1988], "Knowledge Elicitation with Multiple Experts: Considerations and Techniques," *Artificial Intelligence Review* 2, 31–44.

A Newell & H A Simon [1972], *Human Problem Solving*, Prentice-Hall, Englewood Cliffs NJ.

R E Nisbett & T D Wilson [1977], "Telling More than We Can Know: Verbal Reports on Mental Processes," *Psychological Review* 84, 231–259.

J E Palmer, T M Duffy, K Gomoll, J Palmquist-Richards & J A Trumble [1987], "The Design and Evaluation of Online Help for UNIX EMACS," in *INTERACT '87 – The Second IFIP Conference on Human-Computer Interaction*, H J Bullinger and B Shackel, ed., Elsevier Science Publishers B.V., North Holland.

R W Schvanaveldt, F T Durso, T E Goldsmith, T J Green, N M Cooke, R G Tucker & J C De Maio [1985], "Measuring the Structure of Expertise," *Int. J. Man-Machine Studies* 23, 699–728.

P C Wason & J StB T Evans [1975], "Dual Processes in Reasoning?," *Cognition* 3, 141–154.

GOMS meets STRIPS: The Integration of Planning with Skilled Procedure Execution in Human-Computer Interaction

Tony Simon & Richard M. Young

MRC Applied Psychology Unit, 15 Chaucer Road, Cambridge CB2 2EF. U.K.

In the context of modelling user behaviour in HCI, deliberate planning based on problem solving and the fluent execution of skilled procedures are usually treated as different kinds of behaviour and modelled by different kinds of model. In this paper we draw on previous work which argues that user modelling requires a different notion of planning from that commonly discussed in the Artificial Intelligence literature, and show that problem solving and routine cognitive skill can be regarded as opposite ends of the same continuum. A simple planner, making use of a flexible hierarchical representation for plans and operators, can provide a single mechanism able to generate behaviour spanning the entire spectrum. This integration of planning with routine cognitive skill offers a basis for unifying existing models of HCI and for extending their scope.

Keywords: User Models, Planning, Problem Solving, Routine Skill

1. Introduction

One of the tools that scientists are now employing in the effort to improve the design of human-computer interfaces is the predictive model. Such models generally employ some representation of (certain aspects of) the cognitive system of the user and also of the task at hand. By the inclusion of a control regime, such models are able to predict the transformations of 'task data' by the cognitive system that are assumed to underly the behaviours produced by a user when attempting a task.

Due to the complexity of human cognitive behaviour such models must necessarily limit their scope in order to be able to provide predictions. Accordingly, a contrast is usually drawn between two classes of behaviour, referred to as routine cognitive skill and problem solving. Many of the models of how users in HCI contexts decide what actions to take to accomplish a task fall correspondingly into these two classes, depending on which kind of behaviour they try to explain. Within HCI, models of routine cognitive skill are dominated by the GOMS model of Card, Moran and Newell (Card, Moran & Newell [1983]), which accounts for performance in terms of a set of Goals, Operators, Methods, and Selection rules. The GOMS model applies only to users who are task experts able to call upon fully proceduralised Methods (i.e., pre-packaged sequences of Goals and Operators) to execute the subtasks of the job being tackled. All such users have to do is to manipulate the goals and subgoals relevant to the task and choose between alternative Methods when necessary.

In contrast, accounts of more deliberative problem solving behaviour draw primarily upon the analysis of planning made in Artificial Intelligence, as embodied in programs such as STRIPS (Fikes & Nilsson [1971]) and NOAH (Sacerdoti [1977]). Such planning models decide on their actions by searching for a sequence of operators whose preconditions and effects form a chain reaching from the starting conditions to the given goal.

The different nature of these types of models leads to a weak area of predictive power where one wishes to examine aspects of computer usage such as how someone with 'a little' knowledge of a system is able to use it. There is a great paucity of models that are able to predict user behaviour in the intermediate area where the users have *some* experience of the system and are neither novices nor experts.

Some steps towards integrating the two kinds of model were taken by

Young and Simon (Young & Simon [1987]), who discuss some of the special characteristics of HCI as an environment for planning. In contrast to the traditional use of AI planners to produce complex, complete plans before execution is attempted, Young and Simon stress the kind of 'partial provisional planning' (c.f., (Schmidt [1985])) manifested by people. As in more recent AI work on planning (e.g., (Ambrose-Ingerson [1986]; Wilkins [1985])) which interleaves planning with execution, people produce plans which are hierarchical but partial and shallow, extending or expanding them as the situation demands.

An important role in Young and Simon's (Young & Simon [1987]) argument is played by the way that plan steps are represented. Following Wilkins (Wilkins [1984]), they recognise that each step has two aspects: the Action, or what it actually does, and the Purpose, or what it is meant to achieve. (The distinction is important for clarification, since many descriptions of decomposition into 'goal trees' in the literature slip into talking about actions rather than goals.) At the same time, it has to be recognised that the Purpose may be a description of either a state to be attained or a performance to be carried out. Often only the end-state is specified and suitable means can be found for achieving it, but sometimes the focus is on a specified performance. In dancing a waltz, for example, alternative ways of moving from the starting location to the finishing point are *not* necessarily acceptable (Steel [1987])!

In this paper, we show that by using such a representation it is possible to integrate deliberative planning and GOMS-like procedure execution in a single model. GOMS and planning are shown to be the end points of a whole spectrum of HCI behaviours, all generated by the same mechanism. In this way we are able to situate the model in the general context of accounts that hold that the basic means by which novices become experts in a great many domains is by increased acquisition and organisation of knowledge.

2. An Integrated Spectrum

In the representation used by Young and Simon (Young & Simon [1987]), each step of a hierarchical plan has potentially three components. The first is the Action which the step implements. In the case of a plan to enter a room this component of one of the steps might be 'turn-handle(Door)'. The second is the Purpose that the step achieves, here 'latch(Door)=free'. The third is the Body, which is the hierarchical expansion indicating how the step is realised, in this case a description of how one actually turns a door handle.

Great flexibility results from the fact that various combinations of these components may be left unspecified. If the Action component is left blank, this indicates that all that is known is that the step is being taken in order to achieve the state specified by the Purpose. Conversely, if the Purpose component is blank, which would be less usual, all that is known is that the step is being taken in order to realise the Action. The Body component is filled (i.e., with a subplan) or left empty depending on whether or not this step has been expanded into its lower level realisation.

Correspondingly, individual operators have a 'body' which may or may not be filled with a subplan. Where filled, this indicates that it is known how to carry out the operator (at one further level of expansion). Where empty, the planner must be called in order to find a subplan to implement the operator. These possibilities imply that it is also possible for an operator to have a body that effectively provides just a partial specification, or some hints, about how the operator should be implemented.

A major consequence of this flexible representation is that it allows a simple planning mechanism to generate behaviour that spans the entire spectrum from, at one extreme, pure problem-solving requiring deliberate planning to construct each step at each level of the plan, to, at the other extreme, the fluent production of behaviour characteristic of routine cognitive skill. For if none of the operators has its body specified, then the planner will behave like a hierarchical version of a simple STRIPS-like planner where each step is decided by problem-solving based on backwards chaining (or some other method) through the goals and preconditions. However, if all the operators have their bodies fully specified, then the planner acts like an interpreter for a GOMS procedure, where the body serves as the 'Method' for the operator, and results in a straightforward hierarchical generation of behaviour. Intermediate cases, where the bodies of some of the operators are partially or fully specified, lead to correspondingly intermediate kinds of behaviour.

3. An Example

We now illustrate the argument with a small example drawn from one of the most popular domains of HCI, that of text editing. It employs a simple planner which conforms to the principles described above. However, it should be clear that this is not intended as a commitment to any one implementation of a planner, but simply as a demonstration that, by employing such a system, the properties discussed above will emerge.

3.1. The Editor

The editor is assumed to be an EMACS-like command-driven document editor which operates on 'blocks' or 'ranges' of text. Such a block can be as small as a character or as large, say, as a paragraph. Any text that is deleted is placed on a 'shelf', and copying text to another position is accomplished by first deleting and replacing it at its original location, and then placing it again at the new position. The text remains on the shelf until the next deletion overwrites it.

The four basic operators relevant to our task are **LocateAt**(L) which places the cursor at location L, **MarkText**(L,T) which causes the text T at location L to become marked, **Wipe**(L,T) which removes the marked text T from location L and places it on the shelf, and **Yank**(L,T) which places at location L a copy of the text T from the shelf.

For simplicity, we represent locations not by the text which occupies them, but (say) by being bounded by the neighbouring pieces of text. This allows us, for example, to delete the text at a specified location, but still have the location itself remain unproblematically in existence. It also has the consequence that two distinct pieces of text are allowed to be 'at' the same location, which is convenient for present purposes.

3.2. The Task

The task requires the user to replace a piece of text at location B by a copy of an existing piece of text at location A. The most efficient solution involves **locating** at location A, **marking** the text and doing **wipe**. This puts a copy of the text at location A on the shelf but deletes the text from A. The **yank** action is done next in order to replace the text at A. Then after **locating** at B, the **yank** command is re-issued in order to place the text from the shelf next to that at B. Finally, the original text at B is **marked** and the **wipe** command used to delete it, leaving a copy of the text from A at location B as well as at its original location A.

There are, of course, other orderings of the the actions that can be used to produce the desired result such as deleting the text at B before copying the text from A, though this requires a slightly longer sequence of actions. There are also sequences of actions which do not achieve the desired result, some of them subtly so. If the text at A were **marked** and **wiped** and then the text at B were **marked** and **wiped**, there would remain no copy of the text originally at A to be replaced at A and copied to B, either in the text or on the shelf.

4. The GOMS Model

Figure 1 shows a GOMS model for expert performance on the task, presented in the same style as the models in Card, Moran and Newell

Goal: Replace-B-by-Copy-of-A
◇   Goal: Copy-Text-A-to-Shelf
◇   ◇   Locate-at-A
◇   ◇   Mark-Text-A
◇   ◇   Wipe
◇   ◇   Yank
◇   Goal: Copy-Shelf-to-B
◇   ◇   Locate-at-B
◇   ◇   Yank
◇   Goal: Delete-Text-B
◇   ◇   Mark-Text-B
◇   ◇   Wipe

Figure 1. A GOMS model for the task

(Card, Moran & Newell [1983]). The overall task is subdivided into three main subgoals: firstly, to copy the text at A onto the shelf; secondly, to copy the text now on the shelf to location B; and lastly, to delete the text originally at B. Each of these subgoals is in turn expanded into a sequence of (in this case) basic operations. The first subgoal, for example, to copy the text at A onto the shelf, is implemented by the sequence of **locating** the cursor at the desired text, **marking** the text, **wiping**, and then **yanking**, as described above.

Note that according to this model, the whole procedure is a known, pre-existing unit. There is no uncertainty or problem-solving. At each point in the procedure, the user knows precisely what to do next.

4.1. A Terminological Warning

We need at this point to forestall a possible confusion over terminology. The GOMS analysis makes use of the terms *Goal* and *Operator*, both of which occur also in the domain of planning – but with different meanings. In the GOMS world, Goals and Operators are not really different sorts of things. They both refer to actions taken by the user, of greater or lesser scope. Operators are simply Goals which are treated as primitive at a particular grain of analysis. If, for example, we chose to spell out the implementation of Mark-Text-At-A, in terms of lower-level actions, then it would have to be treated as a Goal instead of an Operator. In the planning world, goals and operators are different sorts of things. Goals are, roughly speaking, states or performances to be attained by the planner, as discussed earlier. Operators specify the repertoire of possible actions that can be taken in order to attain a goal. Thus operators (in the planning sense) correspond quite well to Goals and Operators (in the GOMS sense). Goals (in the planning sense) are not represented at

Figure 2. Planning operators for the task

OPERATOR	PRECONDITIONS	EFFECTS or ADD(+)/DELETE(-)
LocateAt (L)		LocatedAt = L
MarkText (L,T)	LocatedAt = L	MarkedText = (L,T)
	TextAt (L,T)	
Wipe (L,T)	TextAt (L,T)	ShelfContents = T
	MarkedText (L,T)	MarkedText = nil
		- TextAt (L,T)
Yank (L,T)	LocatedAt (L)	+ TextAt (L,T)
	ShelfContents (T)	
CopyToShelf (L,T)	TextAt (L,T)	ShelfContents = T
CopyFromShelf (L,T)	ShelfContents = T	+ TextAt (L,T)
DeleteText (L,T)	TextAt (L,T)	- TextAt (L,T)
	ShelfContents = T	

all in the GOMS analysis, something that is consistent with the totally *proceduralised* nature of the GOMS model.

5. The Planning Model

For the kind of planner being considered, the task environment is described in terms of a set of planning operators that specify the possible actions the user can take. A section of this data base is shown in Figure 2. Operators are characterised by their *preconditions*, i.e., what has to be true for an operator to be applicable, and their *effects*, i.e., what changes they make when applied to the current state.

The upper half of the Figure shows the four basic operators: LocateAt, MarkText, Wipe, and Yank. The next three operators are the higher-level ones: CopyToShelf, CopyFromShelf, and DeleteText. These correspond, of course, to the main Goals in the GOMS model. For total correspondence one could imagine an even higher-level operator, ReplaceTextByAnother, which would be able to do the whole task by itself. We do not include such an operator, but referring to it as an analogue to the topmost GOMS Goal will simplify the later discussion.

6. A Spectrum of Behaviour

6.1. Pure planning

A representation such as that shown in Figure 2 can be used by a simple hierarchical planner to devise a sequence of actions that accomplishes the given task. For example, one of the task requirements is that we should finish with a copy of text A at location B, i.e., that TextAt(locB,textA) should be true at the end, although it is not true at the beginning. Focussing on this aspect of the goal, the planner might decide to use the operator CopyFromShelf, which has an effect of the desired kind. But that operator in turn requires that there already be a copy of text A on the shelf, so the planner has to precede the CopyFromShelf operator by a CopyToShelf, in order to supply it. And so on. In this manner, the planner is able to construct the three-step high level plan

         CopyToShelf(locA,textA) --> CopyFromShelf(locB,textA)
              --> DeleteText(locB,textB)

(corresponding to the main Goals of the GOMS model) to accomplish the task.

Whether or not the planner then needs to do any further work depends on how much information is given with the operators. If none of the three high-level operators has its body specified, then the planner has to do all the work, and it discovers that it can complete a successful plan by expanding each of the operators in turn. For instance, the operator CopyToShelf can be realised by the sequence of basic operators

         LocateAt --> MarkText --> Wipe --> Yank

(again corresponding to the expansion of the first subgoal in the GOMS model).

This behaviour is shown schematically in Figure 3a. In Figure 3, the shaded triangles represent places where the planner has to engage in search-based problem solving in order to find a sequence of actions to accomplish its goal. By contrast, the tree-like, branching parts of the diagrams represent places where the system can directly find out what to do, by being given a sequence of steps as the body of an operator. Within the shaded triangles, the exact pattern of behaviour is of little relevance to the present discussion. What is important is the contrast shown in Figure 3, namely the distinction between (i) knowing directly how to realise a step of the procedure, because it is given as the body of an operator, and (ii) not knowing, and so having to search. In the latter case, this corresponds to the behaviour of a user who has to figure out the optimum next action to perform at each step (and at each level) of the sequence.

6.2. Pure procedure

The behaviour shown in Figure 3a is only one point, an extreme one, on a whole spectrum of possible behaviours. The opposite extreme occurs

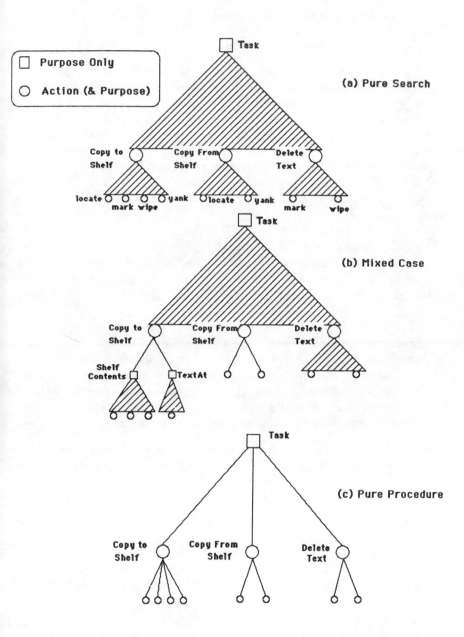

Figure 3.   A spectrum of behaviour

in the case where all operators have their bodies fully specified, in other words, where our imaginary very-high-level operator, ReplaceTextByAnother, exists with a body specified as the sequence of operators

$$\texttt{CopyToShelf} \texttt{ --> } \texttt{CopyFromShelf} \texttt{ --> } \texttt{DeleteText,}$$

and each of those operators in turn has a body specified in a similar way.

The behaviour in this case is as sketched in Figure 3c. Once it has found the topmost operator, the system has to do no planning at all. The activity of the planner reduces in this case to that of a GOMS-structure interpreter. The resultant behaviour, of a fluent procedure without problem solving, models the behaviour of an expert user who, when faced with a task, can immediately identify the sub-tasks involved and can more or less effortlessly execute the necessary steps.

6.3. A mixed case

Figure 3b shows one of the many possible intermediate cases, where some of the operators have fully or partially specified bodies. For this particular case, we assume firstly that the planner has no access to an entity such as our imaginary topmost operator (or else that its body is unspecified), so that it has to construct the three-step high level plan. We assume that the body of the first operator, CopyToShelf, is partially specified, in the form of two subgoals (but not actions), telling the planner first to achieve 'ShelfContents=textA', and then to re-establish 'TextAt(locA,textA)'. So the planner has to construct subplans to achieve each of these subgoals. We assume that the second operator, CopyFromShelf, has a body specified as a sequence of two basic operators. And we assume that the third operator, DeleteText, has no body, so that the system has to plan how to realise it.

The resulting behaviour in this case, an intimate mixture of planning and fluent execution, models a user who is well practised at some aspects of the task in question, and so executes those parts easily, while being unfamiliar with, and so having to figure out, how to accomplish other aspects.

7. Discussion

In this paper we offer an integrated view of what are usually regarded as two different kinds of cognitive behaviour occurring in human-computer interaction. The first is usually described as deliberate problem solving, requiring backtracking and local search. The second is characterised as the relatively effortless invocation of ready-built procedures to carry out each sub-task of the problem being attempted. We suggest that one factor tending to maintain the view of these behaviours as being independent is that separate models have been developed to explain them.

We have shown that additional knowledge, stored in the form of sub-plans within operators, is sufficient to generate characteristically different behaviour from similar operators within the same framework. Thus we argue that routine skill and problem solving behaviour lie at opposite extremes of a single continuum. By making use of a flexible hierarchical representation for plans and operators, we have shown that a simple hierarchical planner enables the entire spectrum from problem solving to routine procedure execution to be modelled with a single mechanism. Depending on how much, and what, information such a system is given, it can generate either kind of behaviour, as well as the range of intermediate cases.

The first implication, and the one most directly relevant to HCI, is that such a scheme offers the possibility of extending the scope of the GOMS model. Users engage in an intimate mixture of problem solving and routine cognitive skill, and we have shown how the same kind of analysis as characterises experts can be applied also to the partly proceduralised 'middle ground' of behaviour, where some GOMS Methods are fully specified but are freely intermingled with others having partially specified and unspecified operator bodies.

In this way one can model the intermediate problem solver who is skilled at certain aspects of a task but who also needs to search for information or actions on other, less familiar, territory. If, as seems likely (Young & Simon [1987]), users engage in only simple forms of planning, then we can predict certain errors in user behaviour due to the characteristics of a particular interface design. In our text editor, for example, users may well plan for the primary first subgoal of getting onto the shelf a copy of the text at location A, while overlooking the secondary, 'maintainance' goal of keeping a copy of the text at A. This would lead to their omitting the final **Yank** from the implementation of CopyToShelf, which would leave them with the text originally at A having been deleted. Similarly, as we have already seen, a less than perfect ordering of the main subgoals can lead to particular inefficiencies or irrecoverable errors.

A more theoretical point is that our argument is consonant with the growing body of opinion that there exists a great continuity between novice and expert behaviour. This view holds that, in general, more intelligent or expert behaviour stems from larger and more highly organised knowledge bases. This phenomenon has been demonstrated to be instrumental within a great diversity of fields in modern cognitive science.

Various aspects of the growth and organisation of knowledge have been shown to play a role in cognitive development by the likes of Chi and Koeske (Chi & Koeske [1983]), Klahr (Klahr [1984]) and Siegler (Siegler [1984]). Sternberg (Sternberg [1984]) has also argued its function within his information processing theory of intelligence. Most consistently, the phenomenon has been at the core of certain analyses of learning and problem solving (Anderson [1981]; Chase & Simon [1973]; Laird, Newell & Rosenbloom [1987]).

With particular reference to these last approaches, one might speculate that the concepts of knowledge compilation (Anderson [1983]; Anderson [1987]) and chunking (Rosenbloom & Newell [1986]) would tell a similar, though more comprehensive, story about the progression from deliberate, planning-like problem solving to fluent, search-free procedure execution. Those accounts attempt to supply the transformational mechanisms that we have not addressed here, but at a more abstract level there is considerable compatability between those schemes and the one presented here.

Acknowledgements

This work was carried out in the context of an Alvey-funded project on Programmable User models (project MMI/112) which is a collaboration between the MRC Applied Psychology Unit, Logica Cambridge Ltd and STC Technology Ltd.

References

J A Ambrose-Ingerson [1986], "Relationships between Planning and Execution," *AISB Quarterly* 57, 11–14.

J R Anderson [1981], *Cognitive Skills and Their Acquisition*, Lawrence Erlbaum Associates, Hillsdale, New Jersey.

J R Anderson [1983], *The Architecture of Cognition*, Harvard University Press.

J R Anderson [1987], "Skill Acquisition: Compiling of Weak Method Problems," *Psychological Review* 94, 192–210.

S K Card, T P Moran & A Newell [1983], *The Psychology of Human-Computer Interaction*, Lawrence Erlbaum Associates, Hillsdale, New Jersey.

W G Chase & H A Simon [1973], "Perception in Chess," *Cognitive Psychology* 4, 55–81.

M T H Chi & R D Koeske [1983], "Network Representation of a Child's Dinosaur Knowledge," *Developmental Psychology* 19, 29–39.

R E Fikes & N J Nilsson [1971], "STRIPS: A New Approach to the Application of Problem Solving," *Artificial Intelligence* 2, 189–208.

D Klahr [1984], "Transition Processes in Quantitative Development," in *Mechanisms of Cognitive Development*, R J Sternberg, ed., Freeman, New York.

J E Laird, A Newell & P Rosenbloom [1987], "SOAR: An Architecture for General Intelligence," *Artificial Intelligence* 33, 1–64.

P S Rosenbloom & A Newell [1986], "The Chunking of Goal Hierarchies: A Generalised Model of Practice," in *Machine Learning Vol II*, R S Michalski J G Carbonell and T M Mitchell, ed., Morgan Kaufmann, Los Altos CA.

E D Sacerdoti [1977], *The Structure of Plans and Behaviour*, Elsevier.

C F Schmidt [1985], "Partial Provisional Planning: Some Aspects of Commonsense Planning," in *Formal Theories of the Commonsense World*, J R Hobbs and R C Moore, ed., Ablex, Norwood NJ.

R S Siegler [1984], "Mechanisms of Cognitive Growth: Variation and Selection," in *Mechanisms of Cognitive Development*, R J Sternberg, ed., Freeman, New York.

S Steel [1987], "The Bread and Butter of Planning," *Artificial Intelligence Review* 1, 159–181.

R J Sternberg [1984], "Mechanisms of Cognitive Development: A Componential Approach," in *Mechanisms of Cognitive Development*, R J Sternberg, ed., Freeman, New York.

D E Wilkins [1984], "Domain-Independent Planning: Representation and Plan Generation," *Artificial Intelligence* 22, 269–301.

D E Wilkins [1985], "Recovering from Errors in SIPE," Technical Note 346, SRI International.

R M Young & T Simon [1987], "Planning in the Context of Human-Computer Interaction," in *People and Computers III*, D Diaper and R Winder, ed., Cambridge University Press, Cambridge.